REFUGEE COUNCIL

Refugees: We left because we had to

A citizenship teaching resource for 11–18 year olds

Third edition

Jill Rutter

The Refugee Council is the largest refugee charitable organisation working with asylum seekers and refugees in the UK by providing practical assistance and working to influence policy and public opinion.

Refugees: We left because we had to
Jill Rutter

First published by the Refugee Council in 1991.
Second edition 1996. Third edition 2004.

The Refugee Council is registered as the British Refugee Council under the Charities Act 1960, No. 1014576. Registered address: 3 Bondway, London SW8 1SJ.

ISBN: 0 946787 59 X

Written by Jill Rutter
Edited by Iris Teichmann
Designed by David Summers
Picture research by David Summers and Iris Teichmann
Map illustrations by Elanor McBay, Department of Geography, University of London
Printed by CPL Associates Ltd

The author would like to thank the Royal Literary Fund for funding this publication.

Other organisations and individuals contributed ideas and teaching material. They include: Channel 4 Learning, the Jewish Council for Racial Equality, Medicins Sans Frontiers, the Ethnic Communities Oral History Project, Pier 21 Canada, the Minority Rights Group, Replay Productions, Amnesty International (UK), TAPOL, Oxfam, the Danish Refugee Council, Penguin Books, the English Speaking Union, UNHCR, Evans Brothers, Save the Children, the Institute for Citizenship, the Children's Society (East London), the London Borough of Newham, Diane Taylor, Bill Bolloten, Tim Spafford, Nora McKenna, Mike Kaye and Howard Davies. A particular thanks to Iris Teichmann for editing the book and to the 2002-03 PGCE Citizenship students at London Metropolitan University whose comments and feedback improved many of the teaching activities. Finally, the author would like to thank all those refugees, named and anonymous, who told their stories, making their extraordinary experiences available to the world's future citizens.

Contents

Teachers' notes

Why teach about refugees?

About 14 million people are refugees in today's world and another 25 million people are internally displaced within their own country. They have escaped conflict and human rights abuses. The last 15 years have also seen an increased number of refugees fleeing to Western Europe. In the UK, like in other European countries, the number of refugees has increased substantially since the mid-1980s. Almost every London school, and many other schools outside of London now have refugee students - something that could not have been predicted ten years ago.

Television and newspapers have brought the experiences of refugees into everybody's sitting rooms. Sadly, the media portrayal of refugees, particularly in the British tabloid and local press, has contributed towards increasing popular misconceptions about and prejudices against refugees. Even young children may pick up on these popular misconceptions, and the racist bullying of refugee children is an all too common occurrence in European schools. One of the aims in writing this book is to challenge children's misconceptions and prejudices about refugees, and to therefore help make refugee children feel more welcome in their new environment.

Refugees: We left because we had to has been written to meet the needs of students of citizenship in schools. Most students are interested in, and often knowledgeable about the events that cause people to become refugees.

Work about refugees enables school students to find out more about these current events. It also gives young people the opportunity to explore concepts such as human rights, justice, leaving home and being a newcomer. Such work should encourage students to develop empathy towards refugees and a commitment to justice. It should also encourage children to act responsibly and take action themselves to support refugees. Both an understanding of concepts such as human rights, as well as developing the skills to enable students to take responsible action comprise citizenship education, a new subject in many schools across the UK.

More specifically, this book aims

- to explore themes demanded in the Citizenship Education Programme of Study in England and in citizenship teaching in Scotland, Wales and Northern Ireland. Such themes include human rights, justice, identity and how the UK treats newcomers;
- to help students gain greater understanding of the flight of refugees and their needs in a new society;
- to help children see that they are linked to other nations through migration;
- to develop greater empathy towards refugees within the local, national and international context, and to help young people understand that refugees are ordinary people, but had to go through extraordinary experiences;
- to encourage positive attitudes towards cultural diversity and to help children challenge prejudice and racist behaviour in their own environments;
- to help children act responsibly to support refugees locally, nationally and internationally.

The book is aimed at students aged between 11 and 18 years, although some of the written information may require amendment for some ages and ability levels. The activities are suitable for use in schools and youth groups. All activities featured in this book have been tested in schools prior to publication.

Refugees: We left because we had to contains background information, testimonies and activities. The background information and testimonies are all written for children themselves to read. All activities featured include instructions for teachers and group leaders.

Chapter One and Chapter Eight incorporate text from *Refugee Voices*, a video made by Channel 4 Learning showing five young refugees telling their stories. The use of this video or similar is highly recommended when introducing work on refugees to young people. Refugee Voices can be purchased from the Refugee Council.

Challenging racism and promoting equality and diversity

Refugees: We left because we had to has been written at a time of growing hostility towards asylum seekers and refugees. The book aims to challenge some of this hostility and develop greater respect for cultural diversity. While writing the book, the author conducted research about how schools can effectively use curriculum resources including this one to challenge racism and promote diversity. The research findings indicate the following:

- Schools cannot challenge racism in isolation. They need to work with other service providers and organisations. Many local authorities have multi-agency working groups on race equality. Schools need to be part of local initiatives to challenge racism and promote diversity and equality.

- Locally, anti-racist initiatives need to run alongside practices that address other oppressions such as poverty.

- Students' misconceptions about refugees vary according to locality and time.

- Curricular initiatives to challenge racism and promote diversity and equality must go hand in hand with other practices such as effective sanctions against pupils who perpetrate racial harassment, for example.

- Schools with a welcoming ethos were found to be most successful in challenging racism and promoting diversity.

- Schools involving all parents in their work about diversity and equality were more successful in challenging racism.

- Time needs to be allocated to teaching about issues such as diversity, racism and migration. One hour of teaching about refugee issues is not enough to change pupils' thinking and misconceptions, nor to change behaviour towards refugees at school and in their neighbourhood. A minimum of 15 hours of work on refugees appears to be needed in order to start tackling students' attitudes and behaviour.

- Effective teaching about refugees and migration MUST start with the personal experiences of refugees. This approach mirrors that used in Holocaust education - people first, then the event. This way, students see refugees as human beings and not as statistics or the dehumanised victims of war or persecution. Schools need to use video testimony of refugees' experiences, but should also explore getting refugee speakers confident enough to talk about their experiences to students.

- Students with a non-refugee background should be given the opportunity to debate controversial issues such as the reception of refugees in the UK. They need to feel that their opinions are heard.

Teaching controversial issues

Teachers are sometimes wary of tackling refugee issues as they are controversial and may require a lot of knowledge to understand them. Teachers may assume that they must solve or at least confront the problems in advance of presenting them to children. This is not easy when issues are contestable and when different opinions can be put forward by different sides. Because of these difficulties, some teachers may ignore controversial issues such as refugees completely.

This book has been written from the perspective that children should be helped to understand how different opinions are formed. Many of the activities give students the opportunity to explore different opinions. They also have a chance to explore the complex feelings generated by examining how we receive newcomers in our society.

Teachers need to consider how they should position themselves when working with students on refugee issues. The teacher is legally obliged to ensure that teaching does not promote a biased or one-sided coverage of a controversial issue. Presenting information as if it is not open to alternative interpretation is biased teaching. So is failure to challenge a consensus that emerges too readily.

But teachers can still present personal views. When approaching the teaching of a controversial issue such as the reception of refugees, teachers might wish to adopt different roles in different circumstances. They might adopt

- an objective or academic role by transmitting an explanation of all available views and also ensuring that written sources and pupils' contributions are balanced;
- the devil's advocate role by adopting provocative and oppositional views, irrespective of the teachers' own viewpoints;
- the declared self-interest role by explaining their own views and reasons for holding them so pupils can better judge bias and by then trying to present all available viewpoints as objectively as possible.

Schools with refugee students

More and more schools in the UK have refugee students, especially schools in the Greater London area. Teachers will obviously have to be sensitive to the needs of refugee children, particularly when initiating class projects on refugees.

Refugee children may have experienced traumatic events in their home countries or during their escape. They may have seen members of their family injured, killed or arrested. Such horrific events cannot easily be discussed in classrooms.

Refugee children may also not want to talk about their home country or family circumstances because they are worried about family members left behind, or because they feel that it might jeopardise their chances of staying in the UK or of eventually being able to return home. Refugee children may not want to discuss their circumstances because they do not want to feel different from their peers. And they may feel embarrassed about the popular images of their home country. For example, some Somali children in British schools have felt unable to admit they were from Somalia because the only image their teachers and fellow pupils have of Somalia is that of famine and war.

- Teachers' notes -

But there are many ways of making refugee students feel secure, while at the same time increasing knowledge about their home countries. Displays about life in students' countries of origin are one way. Schools can also invite parents and members of refugee communities to talk to students. All school work on refugees must seek to humanise those who flee, and to enable non-refugee students to feel empathy towards refugee students.

The curriculum

Refugees: We left because we had to has been written to meet the teaching needs of the Citizenship Programme of Study in England and citizenship teaching in Scotland, Wales and Northern Ireland. The following components of the English Citizenship Programme of Study are covered in the book:

1A The legal and human rights responsibilities underpinning society

- Chapter One: Links and responsibilities
- Chapter Two: Refugees in today's world
- Chapter Five: Protecting the human rights of refugees

1B The diversity of national, regional, religious and ethnic identities in the United Kingdom and the need for mutual respect and understanding

- Chapter Three: Refugees in history
- Chapter Four: Refugees 1930-1980
- Chapter Ten: Refugees in Europe
- Chapter Eleven: New to school
- Chapter Fourteen: Welcome or unwelcome?

1C Central and local government, the public services they offer

- Chapter Twelve: Immigration law and refugees

1F The work of community-based, national and international voluntary groups

- Chapter Two: Refugees in today's world
- Chapter Five: Protecting the human rights of refugees
- Chapter Nine: Refugees and displaced people in poor countries
- Chapter Ten: Refugees in Europe

1G The importance of resolving conflict fairly

- Chapter Seven: Fleeing from war
- Chapter Fifteen: Hopes and solutions

1H The significance of the media in society

- Chapter Seven: Fleeing from war
- Chapter Thirteen: Refugees and the media

1I The world as a global community, and the political, economic, environmental and social implications of this, and the role of the European Union and the United Nations

- All chapters in this book

Refugees: We left because we had to also encourages students to

- think about topical political, moral, social and cultural issues, problems and events by analysing information and its sources, including internet-based sources;
- justify orally and in writing a personal opinion about such issues, problems or events;
- contribute to group and exploratory class discussions and take an active part in debates;
- use their imagination to consider other people's experiences and be able to think about, express and explain views that are not their own;
- negotiate, decide and take part responsibly in both school and community-based activities;
- reflect on the process of participating.

English: *Refugees: We left because we had to* can be used in other curricular areas. In the secondary English curriculum students can, for example, develop their speaking and listening skills by role-play and debate about refugee issues, presenting information and negotiation. Students can be given non-fictional texts to read such as newspaper articles about refugees, autobiographies, diaries, letters and leaflets. Students can develop writing skills by setting out to inform others about refugees, or by presenting written arguments, stories and narratives about refugees.

History: *Refugees: We left because we had to* also covers important topics in history:

- Jewish migration in Victorian Britain
- The growth of multi-ethnic Britain
- The era of the Second World War and the Holocaust
- The development of the United Nations and international humanitarian law
- The Arab-Israeli conflict
- The Viet Nam War
- Oral history as a method of historical research

Geography: The secondary geography curriculum can examine similar issues and explore the impact of refugee migration on the host society.

Religious education: Religious education can concern itself with religious festivals of many faiths, or with some of the many cases of persecution because of religious beliefs. Stories in religious texts can be used as a basis for looking at the way society treats the outsider, as, for example, Jesus' flight to Egypt or the Hegira, Mohammed's journey from Mecca to Media. Religious education also involves the study of contemporary moral issues, such as poverty, war, the arms trade, social justice, race, immigration and responsibility to others.

Social studies: The social studies curriculum examines race and immigration issues as well as pressure groups within a democratic society. Schools who take integrated humanities may examine refugee issues through work that considers equality and inequality, conflict and cooperation, freedom and constraint, pressure groups and political movements.

1 Links and responsibilities

A refugee camp classroom in Pakistan. © UNHCR / S. Errington

Using testimonies and activities, this chapter outlines key definitions of who refugees are. It then gets students to think about their own links with and responsibilities towards refugees.

Links and responsibilities

Giang's story

Giang was very young when she had to leave South Viet Nam in 1979 with her family.

"We knew we could not stay in South Viet Nam. I was going to school and learning all these things my father felt were propaganda. We therefore decided to leave Viet Nam. The only way to leave was to escape by boat. In April 1979 we escaped. We just chugged along out there into international waters. We passed huge tankers from Russia. We passed cruise ships. At night we saw beautiful lights, floating lights across the water. We saw American boats going past. It was a busy shipping lane. Finally, we saw this British shell tanker. The tanker ended up towing us. In the end, the captain's wife said, 'this is ridiculous, you have got to rescue them'. The captain said, 'OK, we have got to figure a way round this'."

"When I came to England, I got a bit of name-calling, a bit of racism, a bit of stick. It was really unpleasant, it was lonely, it was a bit uncomfortable, it was the first time I ever realised that I was different and people saw me differently from other people."

"It's no easy thing to be a refugee and I feel angry when some people say we are here to live off the state's benefits. We don't want to be refugees, we want to be in our own country but we can't do that."

Adil's story

Adil was brought up in Mogadishu, the capital city of Somalia. He came to the UK as an unaccompanied child.

"I remember the sounds of the bombs and the guns. I had never heard guns shooting before. It was like an earthquake; everything was shaking. The whole house was shaking. You could hear what was happening next door. Sometimes they would do raping. You could hear people crying; you could hear people screaming. And that just made me more scared. Then about 20 guys came into our house. They were armed with guns. They took all the food and everything we had."

"Some neighbours were leaving. My mother agreed and she took me to the family's house. She gave them money to take care of me and take me to Kenya. Then we went to Kismayo. I eventually got a boat going to Kenya. It was a very long journey. The family did not like the idea of me going for free. I had to sit in the worst place in the boat. They had this big box where they had everything. I had to sit between the boxes. I had a big towel, this big white towel. I covered myself with the white towel. They had some water; they had some food, but I did not ask for it. I just covered myself up; I did not care."

"When I came off from the plane [in London], security guards knew there was something wrong with me. They followed me and they asked if they could see my passport. I didn't know you had rules here and that you couldn't just hit people. I thought they were like the Kenyan police; they were going to hit me or do something. I was very scared. That's when I passed out. I just fainted."

Jasmine's and Saliha's story

Jasmine and Saliha are sisters. They escaped from their village in Bosnia and eventually arrived in Liverpool.

"Serbs came to our village and they took all the men and left the women. Men had to put their hands at the back of their heads. They had to sing this Serb song. Then they took the men with them. They took my father straight away. They took the men who were best for work. They took him to a camp - Omarska. They beat him. They beat his legs so that he couldn't run away."

"Then after a few days, the Serbs came and told us, 'if you don't leave this village we are going to burn you', and they burnt out mosques and they started burning houses. So we took a few things and we left."

"We went to another village, our first camp. There were a lot of people there, old people, women and children. There were people dying in that camp because of the food; they got diseases. It took two hours just to get dinner because the queue was so long. There were about 300 people in that camp. All of them had to get food, so half of them didn't get any. We asked other people for food. Some people were very thirsty too."

"I want to go back, even if it is not safe yet, even if I know my house is burned and the village has dead bodies in it. I still want to go back."

"Most of all I miss my dad. I miss my family. They are all over Europe; they are everywhere. I miss my village and my friends. It's where I belong; it's where I was born and where my family are. It is the only place I will see my family together again."

Filiz's story

Filiz was 9 when her family had to flee to the UK because of the arrest and torture of her father, a Kurdish trade unionist.

"It was six o'clock at night. Someone knocked on the door and my mum, she came to open it. It was the police - non-uniformed police. My dad went to the door and said, 'what do you want to do?' The police said that they wanted to search the house. They didn't say the reason properly because it was Turkey. It was not like here where the police have to say the reason for searching, but they just came and searched. They took out all the books that my dad was reading. They wrote down all the books' names and all the magazines. They took him to prison. They tortured him as well."

"When my dad came out of prison he had lost a lot of weight. There were physical differences before and after prison because of the torture. In Turkey, he wanted me to say I am a Kurd; I can speak my language; I can do whatever I want. But I could not do that because of the pressure around me, because of the students, because of the head teacher. Everyone is scared to talk Kurdish in schools; they think their families will get into trouble. After a few months in my new school I was having friends, but not English friends. It wasn't the English people I was communicating with, it was people from other countries."

(All four testimonies reproduced with kind permission by Channel 4 Learning and taken from the recordings of the Channel 4 Schools Video "Off Limits: Refugee Voices")

Activity ☝

Discussing refugee children's stories

Learning objectives: At the end of the activity, pupils should understand that fear and flight are experiences common to most refugees.

Time needed: 25 minutes

Instructions: The students will need to watch the video and have copies of Giang's, Adil's Jasmine's and Saliha's, and Filiz's testimonies. Each student should have copies of the questions below and answer them either by working individually or in small groups:

1. What do Giang, Adil, Jasmine, Saliha and Filiz have in common?
2. Where are the countries Giang, Adil, Jasmine, Saliha and Filiz used to live? Use an atlas or a globe to find them. Write them down.
3. What made them leave their homes?
4. Were they living in a safe place?
5. What similarities were there between their lives and yours?
6. What differences were there between their lives and yours?

Activity ☝

Understanding how young refugees may feel

Learning objectives: The activity aims to develop empathy towards refugees. It also helps students understand that refugees may feel loss, sadness, anger and other emotions as a result of persecution and exile.

Time needed: 1 hour

Instructions: Students should watch the *Refugee Voices* video. They should also have copies of the testimonies of Giang, Adil, Jasmine and Saliha, and Filiz. The students will need paper, paint or other art materials.

Students should consider how Giang, Adil, Jasmine, Saliha and Filiz might be feeling as a result of their experiences. Students should draw or paint a picture that portrays the feelings expressed in the testimonies.

Activity ☝

Brainstorming the word 'refugee'

Learning objectives: To get students to think about who refugees are and how refugees are perceived. The activity can be an introduction to most schemes of work about refugees.

Time needed: 20 minutes

Instructions: Thick colour marker pens and some large sheets of paper are needed.

Divide the students into groups of four or five. Each group should write down on a sheet any ideas that come into their minds when they hear the word 'refugee'.

When the papers are filled, pin them up. Are there any similarities between the sheets? The group should keep the sheets until they have found out more about refugees. The teacher or group leader can refer to the United Nations (UN) definition of refugees on page 13.

Students can return to their definitions at a later date and see if their views have changed.

Information: Who is a refugee?

The word 'refugee' is used in everyday speech to describe people who have fled their home and country because of danger. But under international law, the word 'refugee' has a precise meaning and describes people who have fled because of fear of persecution, are unable to be protected by their own government, have fled to another country and been given refugee status by the government of the new country.

To be given refugee status, the government of the new country has to decide whether the person meets the definition of a refugee as set out in the *1951 UN Convention Relating to the Status of Refugees*. The definition says that the person must have left his or her own country, or not be able to return to it "owing to a well-founded fear of being persecuted for reasons of race, religion, nationality, membership of a particular social group or political opinion".

Asylum seekers are people who have formally applied for asylum and therefore want to be recognised as refugees, and are still waiting for a government to decide on their application.

The definition of who is a refugee, and how countries are meant to treat asylum seekers and refugees, is outlined in international law in the *1951 Refugee Convention* and the *1967 UN Protocol Relating to the Status of Refugees*. The *1967 Protocol* was added to ensure that not just European refugees could seek protection but refugees from other parts of the world as well. Today, at least 145 of the world's countries have signed these laws. It is the task of the United Nations High Commissioner for Refugees (UNHCR) to ensure that countries respect these laws.

Other groups of people have fled from their homes in fear but are not recognised as refugees.

Internally displaced persons are people who may have left their homes because of war or human rights abuses, but have not crossed an international border. There are about 25 million internally displaced people in the world.

Sometimes people leave their country in fear, but do not apply for refugee status in their new country. Sometimes people may flee from their homes and then move to another country where they live without permission as undocumented immigrants. Other people may flee from their home country but are given permission to stay legally in another country, perhaps because they have relatives or work in that country. For example, all Sudanese people can stay legally in Egypt and many endangered Sudanese have chosen to live in Egypt in this way instead of applying to be recognised as refugees.

> **People flee their home and country and become refugees for many different reasons. Refugee movements are caused by the following:**
>
> - War between countries
> - Civil war
> - Persecution of minority ethnic groups
> - Persecution of religious groups
> - Persecution of members of political organisations
> - Persecution of people because they belong to a distinct social group. For example, gay men and lesbians are persecuted in some countries. There are also countries where women who refuse to wear veils are risking persecution.

Information: Refugees - an issue for the 21st century

There are nearly 14 million refugees in today's world. Another 25 million people are internally displaced within their own countries. There are more refugees now than at any other time in history. Most refugees live in poor countries in Africa and Asia, where many of them lack the basics of life such as clean water, food and shelter.

Refugees living in camps in Africa and Asia may seem distant from our own lives. But we are linked to them in ways we normally don't think about. For example, coltan, an essential mineral used to manufacture mobile phones is mined in the Democratic Republic of Congo. This country has suffered civil war fought between the government and two main guerrilla groups. Soldiers from these guerrilla groups have stolen coltan and sold it in order to pay for weapons. The fighting has resulted in the deaths of 2.5 million people and has left 2.3 million people internally displaced. Another 400,000 people have become refugees.

Today, Western European countries are receiving refugees. But in the recent past, refugees and displaced people have fled their homes in Europe. In 1945, at the end of the Second World War, there were at least 14 million refugees and internally displaced people in Europe alone. In 1971, at the start of the more recent troubles causing refugee movements, thousands of people were forced to flee their homes in Northern Ireland.

In Europe, we have again seen a rise in racism and nationalism. One aspect of this has been a change in the way that governments treat refugees. Since the mid-1980s, immigration laws have been changed to make it more difficult for refugees to reach safety in Europe. At the same time, refugees have also been scapegoated by some politicians and the media. They have been blamed for causing social problems, such as unemployment and homelessness. Throughout Europe, the general public has become more hostile to refugees.

The movement of refugees and their reception in new countries is a major political and moral issue facing today's world. The Refugee Council believes that it is important for young people to understand why people become refugees, and the support refugees need when they are forced to move to a new country. With this knowledge, young people can make informed decisions about how our society should treat refugees. We may also want to take action to support them.

Even small things can make a difference to the lives of refugees:

- We can inform our friends about refugees and challenge some of the current misconceptions and prejudices about refugees.
- We can campaign for refugees, for example, against the sale of weapons to countries in conflict.
- We can raise funds to help organisations that work with refugees.
- We can also give direct support to refugees themselves, making our schools and local communities more welcoming to refugees.
- We can also volunteer to help refugees.

Above all, we need to remember that refugees are ordinary people like ourselves - it's just that their recent experiences have been extraordinary.

Rabbi Hugo Gryn's story

Rabbi Hugo Gryn (1930-1996) was born in Poland and is a survivor of the Nazi Holocaust. After the Second World War, he came to the UK and later trained as a rabbi. He also played a prominent role in public life. The following is taken from his last public speech.

Poland

"It seems to me that true religion begins with the law about protecting and shielding the stranger. It's there in practically every religious tradition and it is there that men and women discover the idea of humanity. As I was coming here today, I was thinking of an episode, which was in a movie under the heading of the Voyage of the Damned."

"It was about a ship, the SS St Louis. It was a German passenger ship which set out from Germany in 1939 and had on board 1,128 German Jewish asylum seekers, each of whom by the way, had a Cuban visa. Some of them paid an extraordinarily large amount of money for the journey. When the ship gets to Cuba, the Cuban authorities look at the visas and say that only 22 of the visas are authentic - the rest must go back."

"The only decent person in this whole story was the German captain of the ship. He tries whatever he can. He negotiates with the United States, with Colombia, with Chile, with Paraguay, with Argentina, but nothing comes of it. So the ship recrosses the Atlantic and comes back to Europe. Here 228 of them are allowed to disembark in Britain. Some 619 of them were admitted to what they thought was the safety of Holland, Belgium and France. But other than those that came to Britain and the 22 who were allowed to land in Cuba, none of the others survived. None of them. It is a very painful and unacceptable fact, that half a century later, we act as if nothing happened. It is unacceptable."

"Voltaire said if we believe in absurdities we shall commit atrocities. And if we believe in the absurdity that people who are fleeing their home, their families, their jobs, are doing it for a whim, we shall be on the way to committing atrocities. Nobody does it unless they have to."

"I have a definition of lawlessness that when the force and power over life and death issues - asylum is a life and death issue - can be at the disposal of whoever is at the controls, that is a kind of lawlessness. I am also desperately concerned over the fact that asylum-seeking and the authorities' mean-spirited response to it are part of the process which is the hardening of the caring arteries. There is such a process going on. I see here in civilised Europe that it is an abomination, but it is happening."

"A civilised society has a responsibility for shielding and protecting life. In biblical times such places of refuge were a guard against the miscarriage of justice and the arbitrary use of power. I think that any society that wants to call itself a civilised society must have in it these areas of refuge."

"I believe that future historians will call the 20th century not only the century of great wars, but also the century of the refugee. It has been an extraordinary period of movement and upheavals. There are so many scars that need mending. It is imperative that we proclaim that asylum issues are an index of our spiritual and moral civilisation. How you are with the one to whom you owe nothing. That is a grave test. I believe that the line our society will take in this matter on how you are to people to whom you owe nothing is a signal. It is a critical signal we give to our young, and I hope and pray that it is a test we shall not fail."

(Source: 'A moral and spiritual index', leaflet published by the Refugee Council in 1996)

"We are birds of the same nest
We may wear different skins,
We may speak in different tongues,
We may believe in different religions,
We may belong to different cultures,
Yet we all share the same home –
Our Earth."

– from the Athava Veda

"Let brotherly love continue
Be not forgetful to entertain
strangers; for thereby some have
entertained angels unawares.
Remember them that are in bonds,
as bound with them; and those
who suffer in adversity, as being
yourselves."

– Hebrews 13: 1–3

What do these two pieces of religious text say about how we should treat refugees?

Can you find any other religious writings about how we should treat refugees?

Activity

What responsibility means

Learning objectives: This activity helps students reflect on what responsibility means.

Time needed: Students will need about 30 minutes to complete this task. It can be done as a homework task and brought to a lesson for discussion.

Instructions: Students will need a copy of the responsibility diagram below. They should then be given three tasks:

1. Students should find out what responsibility means. They can

- ask family members;
- ask their teacher;
- look it up in a dictionary;
- see what their friends think.

2. Students should find examples of people of their age who have acted responsibly.

A blank version of this diagram can be found on page 339.

3. Students should complete the **responsibility diagram** below.

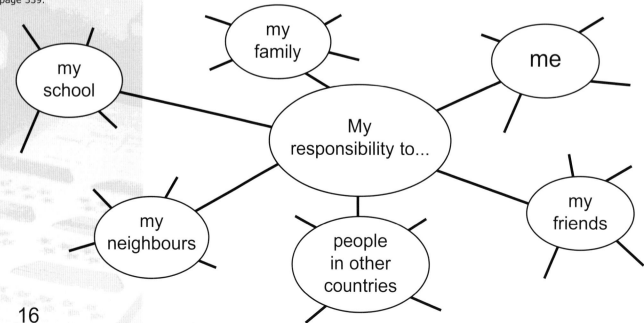

Learning objectives: This is to get students to think about their links with refugee issues and to start to examine their responsibilities towards refugees.

Time needed: 20-30 minutes

Instructions: Below are cross-sections of opinions about refugees. They were collected from students in two British secondary schools. In pairs or in groups, students should look at each statement and decide what they think about each opinion. Do they agree or disagree with it? Why?

Different opinions about refugees

"There are no refugees living near us or going to my school. It is not our problem."

"We should all be welcoming to newcomers. It is not just refugees who move homes. You could be new in a school. If it was you, you would want to be welcomed."

"It is up to politicians to sort out refugees."

"Refugees are ordinary people just like us. It could be me that had to become a refugee. So it is important that we find out about refugees and help them."

"Newspapers often give wrong information about refugees. So it is important to find out the truth."

"My grandma came to live here from Scotland. Most of us have relatives who have moved. Refugees are just another group of people who have moved here. We should welcome them."

"Our country has sold weapons to countries at war. Often these weapons have caused people to become refugees. So we do have a link with refugees in other countries."

"It isn't my fault that there are wars in other countries. So why should i bother about refugees?"

"We should try and help people who are in difficulty or are less fortunate than ourselves."

"Refugees live far away. I can't really do very much to help them."

"Einstein was a refugee. Refugees often contribute things to their new country. It is important that we know things like that."

Activity 👆

Making a difference

Learning objectives: To get students to think about how they can support refugees.

Time needed: At least 1 hour

Instructions: The activity starts by getting the class to think about the needs of refugees. Divide the class into pairs and present them with the scenario below. Each pair should make a list of all the difficulties that the newly arrived Somali refugees might face after arriving in the UK. Such a list might include not knowing how to ask for advice, not knowing how to get your children a place at school and so on.

It should take about ten minutes to make a list. Then ask one or two pairs to feed back their ideas in order to make a class list of some of the difficulties and challenges refugees encounter when they come to the UK. Then introduce the idea that all of us can make a difference to the lives of refugees. Divide the class into six groups. Present each group with one of the *Making a Difference* cards. Each group should answer the question posed on the card and make a difference to the lives of refugees.

The activity should end with feedback.

This activity can be used to start community projects and further action to support refugees.

Making a difference

Scenario
You have fled from your home in Somalia and have arrived in the UK with your three children aged five, nine and ten years. You have some summer clothes for yourself and your children, but nothing else. You have no money and you only speak a few words of English.

New children arrive in your school. They have fled from Somalia. The children speak very little English and are finding it difficult to make friends.

How can you make a difference?

Some people in your school say that refugees have come here to take advantage of our benefits. Other pupils go further and say refugees should be sent home. You disagree with them.

How can you make a difference?

A local drop-in centre for refugees is in need of money to stay open. The centre offers advice, English language training and has a café.

How can you make a difference?

Some of the refugee children in your class say that they want an opportunity to share their stories with the rest of the school. They want to mark Refugee Week.

How can you work with them to make a difference?

Two unaccompanied refugee children aged 13 and 15 attend your school. A brother who is 19 looks after them. It is Christmas time. You don't know if they are Christian or not, but you would like to include them in the celebrations.

How can you make a difference?

You see from the TV news that fighting in southern Somalia has got worse. Refugees have fled from their homes and are crossing the border into Kenya. You would like to help them.

How can you make a difference?

Information: Children making a difference

In different parts of the UK, refugee children and their classmates have worked together to improve the lives of refugees and to make a difference. Here are some examples of the big and small things they have done.

- Secondary school students studying art and citizenship worked with two local primary schools to design Christmas cards. These were printed and sold in local shops. The proceeds went to refugee charities. One charity worked locally with young refugees. The other charity provided medical assistance to refugees in war zones.

- Over 400 schools put on pupil-led assemblies for Refugee Week in 2003.

- After finding Albanian and Somali newspapers on the internet, a group of students decided to organise an after-school computer club for newly arrived refugee families in their neighbourhood. The students provided refreshments and helped the adults learn how to find and download information.

- As a result of the bullying experienced by a refugee student, a GCSE drama class wrote and produced a play about being a newcomer in the UK. The play was performed in the school and then toured neighbouring schools.

- A school in central England received their first refugee pupil. He was 15 years old and had come from Kosovo all on his own. His new tutor group made him a poster, which said 'welcome' in Albanian and English. Two weeks later, on his birthday, they bought him a cake with candles. Now more refugees have come to the school and the first arrival is helping them settle.

- School students in Glasgow, including many refugees, produced a video and teaching pack called *Going Global*. The teaching material was to inform their peers about why people become refugees.

- Year Seven pupils in a school in East London successfully campaigned to stop one of their friends being removed. Natasha Matambele had come to the UK from Angola after her father had been imprisoned and beaten by the government. One morning she came in and told her teachers that the family were going to be sent back to Angola the next day. Students and teachers then began a campaign against the removal and Natasha's story was covered in the local media. The UK government delayed Natasha's removal. Eventually, the family was allowed to stay. As a result of the campaign run by the students, the school thought about other things they could do to support refugees. An early morning homework club was started for children living in hostels or overcrowded housing. This helped lots of children, not just refugees.

Discussion point:

⇨ Can you find examples from your own area of young people supporting refugees?

Refugee Week celebrations help raise awareness about asylum seekers and refugees.
© **Refugee Council**

NOTE

You can read more about Natasha's story on the Schools Against Deportation website at: www.irr.org.uk/sad.

2 Refugees in today's world

Kosovar refugees whose villages were burned down. © UNHCR / A. Harper

Refugees are people who have fled from their homes in fear. They are some of the many people who migrate every year from their homes. This chapter also gives refugee statistics and describes some of the organisations that work with refugees.

Refugees in today's world

"I moved from Morocco to France in 1995. I had just left school and there was very little work in the area. I decided to join my dad who lived in Paris. I am now working as a security guard."	"I am Nepali and lived in a small village in eastern Nepal. During heavy rains in 1994, there was a landslide near our house. The landslide was caused because the trees in the area had been cut and could no longer protect the soil. Our house and most of our land were destroyed. I've had to move to Katmandhu, the capital city, to find work. I am now a porter for tourists."
"I was born in Bangladesh, but I now live in a block of flats in London. Throughout 1999, a group of teenagers harassed my family. My children were spat on when they came home from school and rubbish was put through the letter box. We decided to move to an area where there were more Bangladeshi families."	"I am from Northern Ireland. I'm Roman Catholic but in 1982 I married a Protestant and went to live with my new husband's parents in a part of Belfast where the population is Protestant. We were sent threatening letters saying that Protestants and Catholics should not marry. We were continually harassed and decided to move to London."
"I lived in a small village in Cornwall until recently, but now I have moved to study at university in Leeds."	"I was born in a village in southern India. My family were not wealthy and our house had no electricity or running water. But I did well at school and won a place at university in Delhi, the capital of India. After studying I decided to stay in Delhi as there are more job opportunities in the city."
"I am a doctor and I used to work at a hospital in Turkey. I was active in politics and also campaigned for better health facilities for Kurdish people. In 1999, I was arrested and tortured, but later released. Fearing that this may happen again, I decided to come to the UK where my brother was living."	"I am 14 years old and was born in Sierra Leone. My mother and father were both killed in the civil war. I walked with other orphans to a nearby town. Here we found a children's home where we are still living."

The majority of Bosnian children have lost family members and experienced nearby shooting and shelling.
© UNHCR / A. Hollmann

Learning objectives: To help students understand the range of reasons that cause people to migrate.

Time needed: 30 minutes

Instructions: Students will need scissors, glue and copies of the testimonies on page 22. The students should be divided into groups of three. They need to be told that the aim of the activity is to examine the different reasons that cause people to migrate. The students should read through the testimonies and sort them into different groups according to the reasons that the people have had to move home. You might want to sort the case studies on the cards into forced and voluntary migrants.

The teacher or group leader can use the cards and the different methods of sorting them to prompt a discussion about forced and voluntary migration.

Activity ☝

Migration

Learning objectives: To make students aware that people move or migrate for different reasons. Refugees are one group of people who migrate every year. They move involuntarily because of fear.

Time needed: 40 minutes

Instructions: You will need some pens, a large sheet of paper and some 'post-its'. You will also need to copy the four refugee stories featured at the start of Chapter One on pages 10 and 11.

Divide the students up into groups of three or four. Each group should write on 'post its' the reasons why people move their homes. Write down one reason on each 'post-it'. The group should all think about reasons why they and their family might have moved house. The group can also use their own general knowledge and ideas taken from the refugee stories in Chapter One.

Everyone should then come together and use all the 'post-its' to make a single list of why people might leave home. Sort the 'post its' into two columns:

* Reasons why people move voluntarily
* Reasons why people move involuntarily (against their will)

Activity ☝

Why do people move?

> **Discussion points**
>
> ⇨ Why do people move involuntarily?
>
> ⇨ Do refugees move voluntarily or against their will?
>
> ⇨ Are there any other groups of people in the world who might move home involuntarily?
>
> ⇨ Participants can read the information sheet on migration on page 24 after taking part in this activity. The group may want to discuss some of the points raised in the information sheet.

Information: Migration

Migration means people moving from one place to another. Migration can be temporary or permanent. Commuting for a job is a form of temporary migration, as is moving to work in a seaside town during the summer. The movement of some refugees is a form of permanent migration.

People move for many different reasons. These can be divided into:

- **Push factors** - things that push or force people to move from their homes to live in another place.
- **Pull factors** - things which attract people to a new place.

Economic migrants are pushed from their homes because of poverty. They may be pulled towards a new area by the promise of higher wages, work and better opportunities. In many cases, economic migrants have left their homes voluntarily, although famine victims are forced to leave their homes against their will. In 2003, an estimated 175 million people moved home for economic reasons. Most of them are poor people living in poor countries who move from the countryside to towns to look for work.

Refugees and internally displaced people have been pushed from their homes because their lives or freedom are threatened. They are pulled to a new home by the promise of safety. They are involuntary or forced migrants because they left their homes against their will. In today's world, there are about 14 million refugees and 25 million internally displaced people.

Migration involves individuals and families making the decision to move. For migration to happen, there needs to be differences in wealth and safety between countries and regions. If there was no war, no human rights abuses, no poverty and no unemployment, there would probably be very little migration.

The last 30 years have seen an increase in global migration. The numbers of economic migrants and refugees have increased. One of the reasons is that more people have been affected by civil war, particularly in Africa.

Migration may also have increased as a result of globalisation. **Globalisation** is mostly about the activities of transnational companies and the movement of capital, goods and services in the international markets. Globalisation means that transnational companies can close factories in one country and move to another country where labour is cheaper. This creates unemployment and often increases migration.

Globalisation also means we have more information about different parts of the world, through the internet and through emails, telephone calls and letters from friends and relatives in other countries. We know more than ever before about life in other countries. This information may act as a pull factor making people want to migrate.

Push factors include:

- No work
- War
- Threats to freedom
- Threats to life
- No educational opportunities
- Poverty
- Hunger
- Drought

Pull factors include:

- Work
- Safety
- Good housing
- Good schools
- Food

Learning objectives: At the end of the activity students will understand that almost every student has a history of migration. The activity also develops students' map-reading and geographical skills.

Time needed: 1 hour

Instructions: The teacher or group leader will need to collect local, national and world maps, drawing pins and small pieces of card. Using the maps, pin the name of each child in the class on the places where they have lived. The activity can be used to prompt discussion on who has moved the furthest or stayed in the same place the longest.

The activity can be extended, and students can make displays from where their class has come. The display or map of the world can be placed in the school foyer.

Learning objective: The activity enables students to reflect on migration within their own family history.

Time needed: Two lessons with homework time for research.

Instructions: The teacher or group leader should show the class how to construct a family tree, recording names, births, marriages and deaths of children's parents and grandparents. Students should then prepare a family tree on a large piece of paper. For homework, children should research where each family member was born and to where they moved during their lives.

The family trees can be used to prompt class discussion on migration and the different reasons why people move.

Example of a family tree.

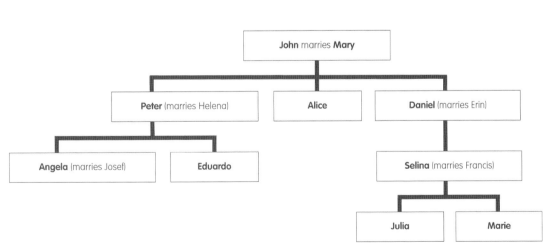

Suada's story

Suada is 13 years old. She is living in a reception centre run by the Refugee Council.

"It was a nice morning in May. I was in my house in my home village, Cejreci, near Prijedor, Bosnia. I was about to have breakfast. I often heard people talking about the war going on around us, but I could not imagine it happening to me. That morning it did, and it turned my life upside down. First I heard the sounds of shooting."

"Then I heard our neighbour crying. 'They are taking the men away', she said. My father came out to see what was happening. I came out as well. I saw a lot of soldiers coming towards us, screaming and using indecent words. Soldiers, tanks, the smell of shooting everywhere."

"I was afraid as I had never been in my life. The soldiers made us children and our mothers gather under a tree. They were shooting over our heads and threatening that they were going to slaughter us. I saw them take my daddy away together with the other men. They were beating them all the time. I was crying. Then a dirty soldier took my first cousin Nermin and killed him in front of my eyes. I was too afraid even to cry."

"Many houses in the village were burned down - ours as well. We were taken to Trnoplje camp. We stayed there for two weeks. We thought that we would never get out."

"Two weeks later they let us go to our home village. Most of the houses were burned down so we stayed in those that were less damaged. Two or three families stayed in a house. My mummy and I lived with my aunt and her daughter."

A school in Bosnia is used to accommodate displaced people.
© UNHCR / A. Hollmann

"Soldiers would come every night bumping the door. They had socks over their faces and guns. They were so scary. One night they broke into the house. They demanded money and gold. One of them grabbed me and put a dagger under my chin. The other one shot his gun around us threatening he was going to kill us all. I thought I would never see my dad again. My cousin Naida stood up and said 'Shoot'. I admired her for being so brave. Luckily they just took money and gold from my mum and my aunt and left. They told us not to go out when they left, or they would shoot us. We kept still for a while and then my cousin and I went out to our neighbour. He was a Croat and helped us go to Croatia the next day."

Suada, her mother and aunt made the dangerous journey through battlefields to reach Croatia. Life in the camp was very hard, but for the children, after all the horrors they had seen, it seemed like heaven. Suada was eventually reunited with her father. Her family was then told they were going to Britain.

"I am very happy now being in London with my parents and my cousin and her parents. But I often think of my friends and my toys I left in Bosnia. Sometimes I have nightmares and I think that the soldiers with socks over their faces are coming to get me again. I wish that they could never frighten and kill children and their parents again."

Matthew's story

"My life has been in danger many, many times. People are very, very homophobic in Jamaica. You can be sent to prison if you are behind closed doors with a man, even if you are not having a sexual experience. And if people see a young man without a girlfriend they assume he's gay even if he is not."

"I've always known I was gay. In Jamaica I had a long-standing relationship with my boyfriend and we tried to be very discreet. But news started to fly around and we were kicked out of our house and had to flee. When my family found out my own brother beat me up."

"It was torment for me in Jamaica as I always had to be running from one place to another. Jamaica is so small and news travels so easily. I feared for my life all the time, every day."

"Once I went to a different town and I was attacked at the bus stop. A group of guys started beating me up and calling me AIDS-man. In Jamaica people think that once you are homosexual you have AIDS. Someone called the police, but they just asked me what I was doing there and told me I should go back home before I got killed. The police do nothing if it is a gay issue. You can't go to them as it'll just turn into a scandal."

"A lot of gay people try to suppress their sexuality, but it's not easy because if you are gay you are gay."

"I got refugee status, but I don't know if I am just lucky. I have a friend who has been through a really terrible experience, with articles in the newspaper and everything, but he was turned down."

"My mother always stood by me, and it was her who told me to leave. She's very happy that I'm here, although she misses me so much. And I'm really relieved. I can remember walking through Leicester Square with my boyfriend, holding hands. Some people here look and stare - but in Jamaica you can't even think of holding hands. You can't give someone a brotherly hug as people will throw stones at you."

"Jamaica is very beautiful compared to here, but being gay there is a hell-house. It's horrible, a nightmare. I'm very happy and glad to be alive. I would be dead now in Jamaica."

Mathew's name has been changed.

Discussion point

⇨ How do you think Suada and Matthew feel now they have reached safety?

New Kingston is a very developed area.
© H. J. Davies / Exile Images

Learning objectives: To draw students' attention to the varied experiences of refugees and to develop empathy with refugees.

Time needed: 30 minutes

Instructions: Each group or pair needs a copy of the case studies so these will need to be prepared in advance. The participants will need to know who are refugees and be familiar with the UN definition of who is a refugee.

The students should be divided into groups of three. Everyone should receive a copy of the case studies. Explain to the participants that they have to decide whether each of the case studies fits the UN refugee definition.

The groups should examine the case studies and make a group decision on who fits the definition. The groups can then come together and compare their answers. Information is included on what happened to the people in real life.

Abdi is from a town in southern Somalia. His father owned several shops in the town. Since 1991 the town has been a very dangerous place in which to live. There has been continued fighting between the supporters of two rival warlords. The family thought that they would stay and defend their business, but last year, armed men broke into the family home. They took almost everything of value and beat Abdi's mother. After this, the family fled to Kenya. Here they were sent enough money to buy forged passports and air-tickets to come to the UK.

Ramon is from Colombia. He is 28 years old and worked as a lawyer in Colombia. During the day he worked for a firm of lawyers. In his spare time he gave his services to a human rights organisation which worked to monitor conditions in Colombia. Ramon started to receive threatening telephone calls telling him to stop his work with the human rights organisation. He then received a letter saying that he would be killed. As many people who have worked for human rights organisations in Colombia have been killed, Ramon decided that he must leave the country. He flew to the UK.

Ibrahim is an Albanian Muslim from Prishtina, Kosovo. In 1989 he married a Serbian woman. In 1997 Ibrahim and his family fled to London, as he and his wife had been threatened by Serbian extremists. But now Kosovo is separate from Serbia and its government is run by the European Union. Ibrahim wants to remain in the UK, as he believes that Albanians who have married Serbs are targets of harassment.

NOTE

A refugee is a person who has left his or her own country, or is unable to return to it "owing to a well-founded fear of being persecuted for reasons of race, religion, nationality, membership of a particular social group or political opinion". *(Taken from the 1951 UN Convention Relating to the Status of Refugees)*

Ayden is a Kurd from Turkey. Her son fled to the UK in 1991 after he was detained by the Turkish police and then beaten in detention. He was allowed to stay in the UK. Ayden's husband died in 1998 and now she has severe arthritis. She has no other close relatives living near her and she wanted to come to London to join her son and grandchildren. Last year she paid £4,000 to a smuggler to arrange her travel to London. She made a journey by boat, then lorry to London. When she arrived she was so ill she was taken to hospital.

James is Zimbabwean. He owned a garage in a town in Matabeleland in Zimbabwe. In 1999 he became involved in opposition politics. After this he and his family were harassed. Then in 2001 James was kidnapped and severely beaten by supporters of President Robert Mugabe. Fearing for his life James flew to London and applied for asylum.

All five case studies are real. Their stories were collected by the Refugee Council, but their names have been changed.

Discussion points

⇨ Was there anyone that all the groups believed to be a refugee? Why?

⇨ Was there anyone that all the groups believed was definitely not a refugee? Why?

⇨ Which people did the groups disagree about whether they should be given refugee status or not?

⇨ Were the groups surprised about what happened to them in real life?

⇨ Why might they wish their names to be changed for use in this book?

What happened?

Abdi was told he had humanitarian leave to remain. He and his family are allowed to stay in the UK, initially for one year.

Ramon was refused refugee status. His lawyer made an appeal but it was not successful. Ramon is thinking about leaving the UK and may go to Venezuela.

Ibrahim was not given refugee status. Instead he was given permission to remain in the UK for four years. Now his time has expired, but when he went to extend his permission to remain he was told he must go back to Kosovo. He was told that Kosovo was now safe for people in mixed marriages.

Ayden's son first tried to apply for permission for his mother to join them. This is called family reunion. But family reunion is usually given just to children. It is much harder for older people to get family reunion. Ayden's request for family reunion was refused. When she got to the UK she applied for asylum. This request was also refused and now it looks like she might have to go back to Turkey.

James applied for asylum in the UK, but this was refused. He was returned to Zimbabwe by plane. He has now fled to Zambia.

Activity ✍

Quiz on myths and facts about refugees

Learning objectives: To highlight some of the popular misconceptions about refugees.

Time needed: 45 minutes

Instructions: The group should be divided into pairs. Each pair should be given a copy of the quiz sheet and write down the answers to the quiz. The class should come together for a discussion. The quiz could also be used as a basis for a fundraising activity. Participants could be charged a small amount to answer the quiz and there could be a prize for the first set of correct answers.

Discussion point

⇨ Did any of the answers surprise the group? Why?

The refugee quiz

In the UK, there are a wide range of views about refugees. Some people have ideas and prejudices about refugees which are not based on facts. See how much you know about refugees!

1. Who are refugees? Give your own definition.

2. How many refugees are there in today's world? Is it
☐ 3 million ☐ 14 million? ☐ 39 million? ☐ 155 million? ☐ 272 million?

3. Most of the world's refugees flee to rich European countries.
☐ True or ☐ false?

4. Name three countries from which refugees are presently fleeing.

5. Refugees from Iraq are the largest refugee group in today's world.
☐ True or ☐ false?

6. Wars cause people to flee as refugees. How many wars are being fought in today's world? Is it
☐ 9 ☐ 14 ☐ 32 ☐ 52 ☐ 74

7. Over 300,000 asylum seekers came to the UK in 2002.
☐ True or ☐ false?

8. Asylum seekers who come to the UK get paid more benefits than British citizens.
☐ True or ☐ false?

9. Name one member of the Royal Family who was a refugee.

10. What links a roll of Andrex toilet paper and the paintings of Lucian Freud with Albert Einstein's theory of relativity?

Quiz answers

1. A refugee is someone who has "a well-founded fear of being persecuted for reasons of race, religion, nationality, membership of a particular social group or political opinion." This definition is taken from the 1951 UN Convention Relating to the Status of Refugees. The right answer should include words such as escaping from danger and persecution.

2. There are approximately 14 million refugees in today's world.

3. False. In 2002, some 383,800 refugees entered European Union countries. This compares with 815,000 Rwandan, Burundi and Congolese refugees living in central Africa - just one region. Most of the world's refugees live in poor countries in Africa, Asia and the Middle East.

4. Your answer could include the Ivory Coast, Burundi, the Democratic Republic of Congo and Somalia.

5. There are more Palestinian refugees than any other group of refugees. They number over 4.1 million people. While most fled in 1948-49 and 1967, Palestinian refugees have also fled more recent violence.

6. There are 32 conflicts that are currently causing people to become refugees.

7. False. Some 85,865 asylum applications were made in 2002. If the dependants of the main asylum applicants are taken into account, this represents about 103,030 people.

8. False. Asylum seekers are no longer allowed to claim benefits. Instead they get support from the National Asylum Support Service. The amount of cash given to asylum-seeking adults is 30 per cent lower than income support given to British citizens.

9. In 1922, Prince Philip fled from Greece hidden in a crate of oranges. King Constantine, his uncle, had just been overthrown in a military coup.

10. All three are contributions made by refugees. Andrex was founded by German Jewish refugees. They manufactured the first soft toilet paper in Britain in the 1930s. Lucian Freud and Albert Einstein were also refugees.

Countries producing refugees

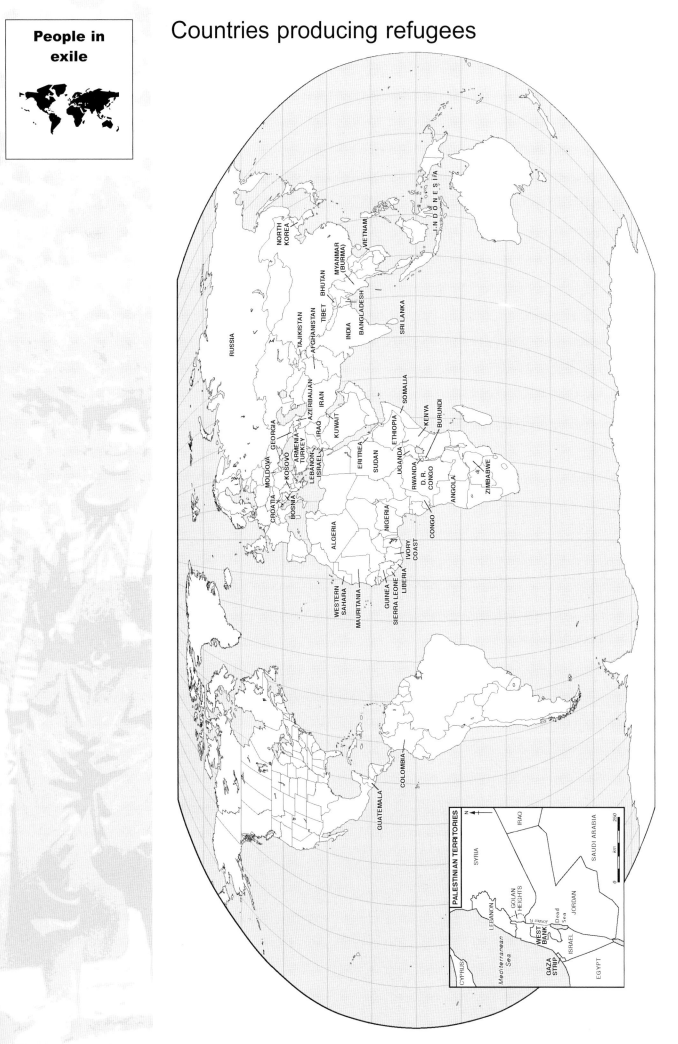

People in exile

AFRICA

Algeria
Nearly 100,000 people have been internally displaced as a result of violence. Refugees have also fled to Europe.

Angola
Fighting in Angola started in 1961. In 2002, there was a peace agreement. However, 300,000 Angolans are still refugees and another 800,000 Angolans are internally displaced.

Burundi
There are 440,000 Burundi refugees in Rwanda, the Democratic Republic of Congo and Tanzania. Another 500,000 people are internally displaced having fled extreme violence perpetrated by armed guerrillas and the army.

Congo-Brazzaville
Fighting between government forces and armed opposition groups has destroyed Brazzaville, the capital city. Some 30,000 refugees have fled and another 150,000 people are internally displaced.

Democratic Republic of Congo
The civil war has caused 440,000 to flee as refugees. Another 3.2 million Congolese are internally displaced.

Eritrea
Some 50,000 people are still internally displaced after the recent war with Ethiopia. There are 300,000 Eritrean refugees living in Sudan. The poverty of Eritrea prevents them from returning.

Ethiopia
About 20,000 people are refugees. Another 70,000 have been internally displaced by the recent war with Eritrea.

Guinea
In 2002, rebel groups from Liberia and the Ivory Coast, and the Guinean army started fighting each other. The fighting has displaced 80,000 Guineans.

Ivory Coast
Fighting between armed opposition groups and government forces has caused 100,000 Ivorians to flee as refugees. Another 700,000 people are internally displaced.

Kenya
There are 100,000 internally displaced people in Kenya. They have fled ethnic conflict.

Liberia
Civil war started in 1989 causing almost all Liberians to flee at one time or another. Although there is now a peace agreement, over 200,000 Liberians are still refugees and another 200,000 people are internally displaced.

Mauritania
There are 23,000 Mauritanian refugees living in Senegal and Mali. They are mostly of black African origin who have been expelled from their home country on the basis of their ethnic group.

Nigeria
Some 30,000 people have been displaced by inter-religious and inter-ethnic violence.

Rwanda
There are 60,000 Rwandan refugees, most of them living in neighbouring countries. Another 150,000 Rwandans are internally displaced, some as a result of fighting in western Rwanda.

Sahrawis

There are 200,000 Sahrawi refugees in Algeria. The refugees fled after the Moroccan occupation of Western Sahara.

Sierra Leone

There are 68,000 Sierra Leoneans still living as refugees. Another 100,000 people are internally displaced, although the war has ended in Sierra Leone.

Somalia

There are over 1 million Somali refugees living in Kenya, Ethiopia, Djibouti, Yemen, the Gulf of Arabia and Europe. Another 400,000 people are internally displaced. Most recent refugees and displaced people have fled fighting in southern and eastern Somalia.

Sudan

There are 700,000 Sudanese refugees living in Chad, Kenya, Uganda, Ethiopia and in European countries. Additionally, many Sudanese live in Egypt where they can stay without needing to register as refugees. Another 4.8 million Sudanese are internally displaced. They have fled civil war and human rights abuses.

Uganda

Some 1.4 million people have been internally displaced by fighting in northern and western Uganda.

Zimbabwe

Nearly 600,000 people have been internally displaced by violence and land seizures and about 15,000 people have fled as refugees.

ASIA, AUSTRALASIA AND MIDDLE EAST

Afghanistan

There are about 2 million refugees, mostly in Pakistan, Iran and other parts of Asia. Another 300,000 people are internally displaced.

Bhutan

There are 130,000 Bhutanese refugees living in Nepal and India. The refugees are ethnic Nepalis who have fled persecution.

Bidoons

The Bidoons are stateless Arab people who lived in Kuwait. The Gulf War made them homeless. Some 120,000 Bidoons are now refugees in Iraq and another 120,000 Bidoons are stateless in Kuwait.

Burma

There are over 450,000 Burmese refugees living in Bangladesh and Thailand. Up to 1 million internally displaced people may be living in Burma. The refugees have fled human rights violations and civil war.

Indonesia

Over 700,000 Indonesians have been internally displaced by religious and ethnic conflict.

India

Some 500,000 people are internally displaced, most of them in Kashmir and Gujarat. Another 40,000 people, mostly Kashmiri and Gujerati Muslims, have fled as refugees.

Iraq

There are 295,000 Iraqi refugees living in Iran, Syria, Europe and North America. The refugees include Arabs, Kurds, Turkmen, Armenians and Assyrians. Up to one million people may be internally displaced.

Iran

Some 300,000 Iranians have been forced to flee their country because of human rights abuses. The majority are living in India, Iraq, Europe and North America.

Lebanon

As well as Palestinian refugees, some 200,000 Lebanese people are internally displaced.

North Korea

At least 100,000 people have fled as refugees, mostly to China. Another 100,000 people are internally displaced in North Korea.

Palestinians

There are 4.1 million Palestinian refugees living in Syria, Lebanon, Jordan, Egypt, Iraq, the Palestinian Territories, the Israeli Occupied Territories and other countries. They became refugees in 1948-49, 1967 and since 2002. Other Palestinians fled Kuwait after the Gulf War.

Sri Lanka

There are 800,000 refugees and 400,000 internally displaced people. The refugees have fled human rights abuse and civil war between Tamil guerrillas and the Sri Lankan army. Most of the refugees live in India, North America or Europe.

Stateless Biharis in Bangladesh

There are over 238,000 stateless Muslims who fled India in 1947 and now live in Bangladesh.

Tibet

There are 133,000 Tibetan refugees living in India and Nepal. They have been living in exile since China invaded Tibet in 1959.

Vietnam

International organisations still count 350,000 Vietnamese people as refugees as they still need protection and help. Over 1 million refugees have left Vietnam since 1975.

EUROPE AND FORMER SOVIET UNION

Armenia

Some 50,000 Armenians are still internally displaced as a result of conflict with Azerbaijan.

Azerbaijan

Some 760,000 Azeri people are still displaced as a result of the conflict in Nagorno-Karabakh.

Bosnia-Herzegovina

Some 140,000 Bosnians remain as refugees and another 375,000 are internally displaced. Most of the refugees and displaced are people who have been unable to return to their homes after the war ended.

Croatia

There are still over 250,000 Croatian refugees, mostly ethnic Serbs, who fled from eastern Croatia and are now living in Serbia.

Georgia

There are 20,000 Georgian refugees, mostly living in Russia. Another 260,000 Georgians are internally displaced. The refugees and displaced are Abkhazians, Georgians and Ossetians who have fled fighting and human rights abuses.

Kosovo

Over 200,000 Kosovars remain as refugees and another 54,000 people are internally displaced in Kosovo.

Moldova

Nearly 20,000 people have been displaced by violence in the Transdniestr region.

Russia

Some 370,000 people are internally displaced, the majority having fled the conflict in Chechnya. Over 60,000 Russians have also fled as refugees, mostly from Chechnya.

Tajikistan

There are 53,000 Tajik refugees living in Afghanistan, Russia and other parts of central Asia.

Turkey

Some 220,000 Turkish Kurds live as refugees in western Europe. At least 1 million people have been displaced in eastern Turkey.

NORTH AND SOUTH AMERICA

Colombia

Over 2.8 million Colombians are internally displaced because of armed conflict and human rights abuses. Another 230,000 Colombians have fled as refugees.

Guatemala

There are 240,000 Guatemalan refugees living in Mexico and the USA.

Note

The figures on refugee numbers include asylum seekers, people granted refugee status and people living in refugee-like situations outside their home country. The figures only include refugees who need legal protection, or are in other ways vulnerable. They do not include people who fled their home country and are now permanently settled in a new country.

Statistics on internally displaced people are estimates, mostly taken from the Internal Displacement Project (www.idpproject.org). Such statistics are hard to collect as humanitarian aid workers do not always have access to populations of displaced people in war zones.

(Sources: UNHCR and the US Committee for Refugees. Refugee numbers are in relation to total population of selected receiving country.)

Somalian refugees at a camp in Ethiopia.
© UNHCR / M. Benamar

Calculate the following:

- The total number of refugees in 2004
- The total number of internally displaced people in 2004

The above statistical data can be used in project work on refugees. Students can present the data in accessible forms to illustrate arguments. For example, students can draw pie-charts or graphs to show the proportions of the world's refugees who are living in each continent.

Activity ☝

Calculate refugee numbers

Learning objectives: This activity develops research skills and knowledge about particular refugee-producing countries.

Time needed: It depends on how much detail goes into the students' presentations.

Instructions: Using the internet, students have to find out additional information about the refugee-producing countries listed below. When the students have completed their research, they should present it as a piece of written work. They could use the suggested headings, or present it in another way.

Activity ☝

Finding out more

Countries to research:

- Algeria
- Bhutan
- Bosnia
- Burma
- Congo-Brazzaville
- Haiti
- India
- Mauritania
- Nigeria
- Tajikistan
- Tibet
- Uganda

You can use the following headings to present your research:

Map and country name

Population

Capital city

Languages

Ethnic groups

Why people have become refugees

Economy

Information: Organisations working with refugees

There are many different organisations working to help and support refugees around the world. Some are large but most are small. Some work in many different countries, others in just one country. Here are some examples of organisations that work with refugees.

International organisations

Two United Nations organisations work with refugees: the United Nations High Commissioner for Refugees (UNHCR) and the United Nations Relief and Works Agency for Palestine Refugees in the Near East (UNRWA).

⇨ *United Nations High Commissioner for Refugees (UNHCR)*

UNHCR was set up by the United Nations in 1951. Its headquarters are in Geneva, Switzerland, and it has offices in more than 70 countries. UNHCR has three areas of responsibility:

* It works to make sure that the governments of countries that have signed the 1951 UN Refugee Convention and 1967 Protocol Relating to the Status of Refugees treat asylum seekers and refugees in a way that meets the requirements of international law.
* It works with other organisations to make sure that aid reaches refugees.
* It works on long-term solutions for refugees. UNHCR tries to help people return home if it becomes safe for them to do so. If this is impossible, UNHCR helps people settle in a new country.

⇨ *United Nations Relief and Works Agency for Palestine Refugees in the Near East (UNRWA)*

The 1948 Arab-Israeli War and the 1967 Six-Day War left many Palestinians as refugees. They are living in the Israeli-occupied West Bank, the Gaza Strip, Lebanon, Syria and Jordan. UNRWA began its work in 1950. It currently has its headquarters in Gaza. UNRWA provides education, training and healthcare to Palestinian refugees who live in the West Bank, Gaza, Lebanon, Syria and Jordan.

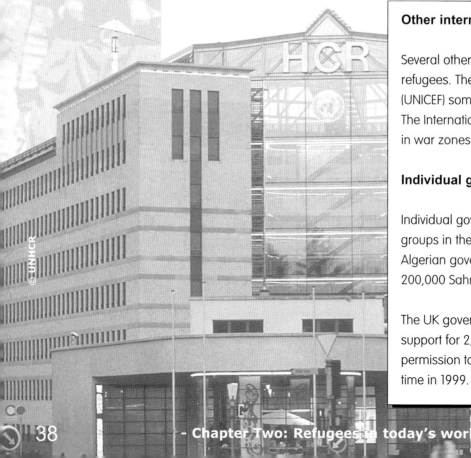

Other international organisations

Several other international organisations work with refugees. The United Nations Children's Fund (UNICEF) sometimes works with refugee children. The International Committee for the Red Cross works in war zones with refugees and displaced people.

Individual governments

Individual governments may work with refugee groups in their own countries. For example, the Algerian government pays for food aid for the 200,000 Sahrawi refugees living in Algeria.

The UK government paid for reception centres and support for 2,500 Kosovar refugees who were given permission to stay in the UK for a limited period of time in 1999.

Non-governmental organisations

Non-governmental organisations are not run by governments and are usually much smaller than international and government organisations. They usually obtain their money from various sources including donations from members of the public.

There are over 700 non-governmental organisations working with refugees in the UK. They include overseas aid agencies, organisations that solely work with refugees in the UK, pressure groups and self-help groups.

Overseas aid agencies

Oxfam, Save the Children and Medicins Sans Frontieres are examples of overseas aid agencies. They are working with all the major refugee groups in the world. Overseas agencies do receive small amounts of money from governments but for most of their work they rely on donations from members of the public.

Here is an example of Medicins Sans Frontieres' work with Sudanese refugees in Chad:

The refugees had fled fighting in western Sudan and are living in towns and villages just inside Chad. The refugees lack access to food, clean water and shelter. Until now, the refugees have had no medical care. Then Medicins Sans Frontieres opened a health centre in the border town of Tiné, and built four tents on the outskirts of a camp where thousands of refugees - most of them women and children - were living. The tents house a consultation room, a paediatric unit, a pharmacy, and male and female in-patient areas.

During the first days of the clinic the main health problem was diarrhoea. This was caused by drinking dirty water. Other common complaints were chest infections and malnutrition.

Medicins Sans Frontieres then brought more supplies to Tiné, including vaccines against measles, therapeutic milk powder, food for the malnourished, pumps, pipes and tanks to help supply clean water.

British refugee organisations

© Refugee Council

These are usually charity organisations and independent from government. The Refugee Council is currently the largest charity in the UK working with and helping asylum seekers and refugees of all nationalities. Here is some information about its work:

The Refugee Council helps asylum seekers and refugees from many different countries. Its offices are in London, Birmingham, Ipswich and Leeds.

The Refugee Council gives advice to asylum seekers and refugees on a wide range of issues such as support, the asylum process, accommodation, health, education and work.

The Refugee Council has a special team of advisers who help refugee children under the age of 18 who have come to the UK on their own.

The Refugee Council trains refugees to help them find work.

The Refugee Council writes leaflets for asylum seekers and refugees so they learn more about their situation in the UK. The Refugee Council also writes books and other information to help people in Britain understand why refugees have left their countries.

Pressure groups

Pressure groups are an important part of a democratic society. A pressure group is an organisation that campaigns to defend the interests of its members or it can campaign for a certain cause. Most pressure groups concentrate on one issue. Pressure groups work by

- building support with the public;
- organising protest demonstrations and public meetings;
- getting their interests covered in the media;
- lobbying government and others in power.

Some pressure groups concentrate on lobbying government, parliamentarians and other people who hold power. These groups are sometimes called 'insider pressure groups' because they try to influence government from inside. Other pressure groups may organise demonstrations or be involved in other types of protest. These pressure groups are called 'outsider pressure groups', because they try and build support for their cause from outside.

Some refugee organisations provide direct help to refugees but also act as a pressure group. For example, the Refugee Council employs parliamentary lobbyists and press officers to do such work. Other examples of pressure groups that campaign for refugees are Amnesty International and Asylum Aid.

Self-help groups

A self-help group is an organisation founded by a certain group of people, and works for its own members. Refugee community organisations are self-help groups that work with refugees. The Uganda Community Relief Association is one example of a self-help group.

There are over 14,000 recently arrived Ugandan refugees in the UK. They have fled the human rights abuses of successive Ugandan governments. Most Ugandan refugees who have come to the UK are highly qualified people who held good jobs in their home country. As English is the language used in Ugandan schools and universities, almost all Ugandan refugees arrive speaking very good English. Unlike many other groups of refugees, Ugandans don't need extra help to learn English.

The Uganda Community Relief Association was founded by a small group of Ugandan refugees in 1984. Today, it has offices in north London and employs seven full-time staff. The organisation also uses volunteers in its work.

The Uganda Community Relief Association offers a wide range of services to Ugandan refugees living in London. These include:

- Immigration advice
- Help in finding housing
- Advice on finding work, training and education and help in getting welfare benefits
- Language classes in Luganda, Luo and Swahili for Ugandan children
- Cultural activities such as music and art workshops
- Advice on keeping healthy

Learning objectives: To improve internet research skills and oral presentation skills. The activity also familiarises students with a range of organisations that work with refugees.

Time needed: About 1 hour

Instructions: Students will need access to the internet and copies of the table on page 42. The activity can be done as a group activity, individually or in pairs. Each pair or individual should be allocated a particular organisation. Using a search engine, they should find the websites of their organisation and then research its work, filling in the table on the next page. The class should then come together. Selected students should then give a one-minute presentation to the class about their particular organisation.

- ⇨ **Amnesty International (UK)**
- ⇨ **Asylum Aid**
- ⇨ **Medical Foundation for the Care of Victims of Torture**
- ⇨ **Medicins Sans Frontieres**
- ⇨ **National Coalition of Anti-Deportation Campaigns**
- ⇨ **North of England Refugee Service**
- ⇨ **Oxfam**
- ⇨ **Refugee Action**
- ⇨ **Refugee Arrivals Project**
- ⇨ **Refugee Buddies Australia**
- ⇨ **Refugee Council**
- ⇨ **Save the Children**
- ⇨ **Save the Children Scotland**
- ⇨ **Scottish Refugee Council**
- ⇨ **Student Action for Refugees**
- ⇨ **UNHCR**
- ⇨ **US Committee for Refugees**
- ⇨ **Welsh Refugee Council**

Other organisations to research include:

- A local race equality council
- Refugee community organisations in the UK such as the Ethiopian Community in Britain, the Kurdish Cultural Centre, the Iranian Community Centre, the Iraqi Community Association, the Uganda Community Relief Association
- Smaller refugee support groups in your local area

The Refugee Council and Amnesty International share a stall at a Labour Party conference.
© Refugee Council / David Carroll

Finding out about different refugee organisations

Name of organisation						
How many people work there?						
What type of things does the organisation do?						
Does the organisation just work with refugees, or does it work with other groups of people?						
Does the organisation work with refugees from a certain country or with refugees from different countries?						
Is the organisation a non-governmental organisation?						
Is the organisation a self-help group?						
Does the organisation act as a pressure group?						
Does the organisation give practical support to refugees? If so what kind of practical support?						

3 Refugees in history

Resettlement of German refugees in 1951. © UNHCR

Throughout history people have been forced to flee as refugees. In the last 500 years, more than 1 million people have arrived in the UK and Ireland as refugees. They have made enormous contributions to life in their new countries. Many British people, both black and white, have refugee ancestors and the UK has always been a multi-ethnic society. This chapter looks at the growth of multi-ethnic Britain, focussing on the Huguenots, Eastern European Jewish and Belgian refugees.

Information: Refugees in ancient history

Throughout history, the idea of giving hospitality to people who are in danger has been seen as something good. Many religious books or works of literature describe stories of refugees who were forced to seek asylum. Here are some examples:

Ancient Greece

Oedipus, a hero of Greek mythology, freed the city of Thebes from the oppression of a monster called the Sphinx. As a reward, Oedipus was given the throne of Thebes and married Jocasta, the widow of the previous king. Oedipus and Jocasta rule Thebes wisely, but Oedipus does not know that Jocasta is really his mother. Disaster soon strikes, and Oedipus's life is threatened by his relatives, who wish to rule Thebes.

Oedipus flees to Athens and asks King Theseus for protection. Theseus, too, was a refugee in his youth. He was forced to hide from his enemies. Theseus was full of sympathy for Oedipus, and allowed him and his daughters to stay in Athens for the rest of their lives. Oedipus's story is told by Sophocles in his book *Oedipus at Colon*.

The Jewish tradition

The early history of the Jewish people contains many stories of refugees and exiles. The *Book of Exodus* describes the escape of Jewish people from Egypt. The Egyptians so hated the Jews that the Pharoah ordered all Jewish baby boys to be killed. One child escaped because his mother hid him in a basket by the river. An Egyptian princess found him and took care of him. The child's name was Moses who later led the Jews out of exile in Egypt into the Land of Israel (then known as Canaan) about 3,250 years ago. Every year at Passover, Jewish people remember their journey from slavery and danger to freedom.

In 722 BC, the Assyrian army attacked the Land of Israel driving the Jewish people into exile. In 586 BC, the armies of Babylon (now in Iraq) attacked the area around Jerusalem and destroyed the temple. Some 10,000 Jewish families went into exile in Babylon. Babylon became a centre of Jewish learning. Today's Iranian, Iraqi, Kurdish and Georgian Jews are the descendants of Jewish people who stayed in Babylon.

The Christian tradition

Soon after the birth of the infant Jesus, Mary and Joseph were forced to flee with him to Egypt to escape the persecution of King Herod. And in the famous scene from the Final Judgment, God blesses good people, saying, "I was a stranger and you took me into your homes." (Matthew, 25 v. 35)

The Muslim tradition

The Prophet Mohammed was also forced to flee from his home in Mecca. Mohammed started life as a poor shepherd in Mecca. It was at Mount Hira, near Mecca, that Mohammed received his prophecies from Allah. But Mohammed's beliefs were considered so dangerous and subversive that he and his followers were forced to flee from Mecca. They took refuge first in Abyssinia (Ethiopia) and then, in 622 AD, in the city of Medina. Mohammed's journey from Mecca to Medina is known as the Hegira.

Because of Mohammed's journey, the Koran contains many references to the importance of welcoming strangers.

Activity

Students can carry out further research into how refugees were treated in the ancient world. They might want to find out more about the stories mentioned here. Alternatively, they might want to research other religious stories such as the Hindu story of Rama and Sita who had to flee from danger, for example.

Information: Britain's first refugees

Throughout history, many different people have had to flee to escape political and religious persecution. In the 16th century, the rift between the Roman Catholic Church and the Protestant movement caused many Protestants to flee Continental Europe. In the 1680s, over 100,000 French Protestants, known as Huguenots, settled in Britain.

⇨ 'Arbour', 'Bygott', 'Delahunt', 'Courtauld', 'Lefevre' are Huguenot names. The Huguenots gave the word 'refugee' to the English language.

During the 18th and 19th century, many wars were fought in Europe. In France, Poland, and other countries, there were changes of government. For many people, life had become too dangerous and they had to leave their homeland.

⇨ Political exiles left France, Germany, Austria, Italy, Poland and Russia. Many of them came to Britain. The British government did not formally welcome these refugees, but the police did not bother them. They were allowed to travel and live where they pleased.

⇨ London became known as a place where refugees could find safety. In the 1850s, about 4,000 refugees were living in London.

⇨ Between 1880 and 1914, about 120,000 Eastern European Jews settled in Britain. They had left their homes in the Russian empire because after the death of Tsar Alexander II, a wave of 'pogroms' was organised against the Jewish people there who suffered systematic killings, persecutions and violence. 'Pogrom' is the Russian word for riot.

⇨ The Jewish people were also subject to other forms of religious persecution in Russia. They faced discrimination in education, forced conscription into the Russian army and discriminatory laws which excluded them from certain jobs and forced them to live in particular places.

Refugees in the UK 1560-1970

Countries of origin	Main dates of entry	Numbers
Protestant refugees from the Spanish Netherlands and France	1560-1700	150,000
Jews from Poland, Russia, Austria and Romania	1880-1914	200,000
Belgians	1914-1918	250,000
Germany, Austria and Czechoslovakia	1933-1939	56,000
Basque refugee children	1937	4,000
Poland	1939-1950	250,000
Other refugees from the Nazis	1940-45	100,000
Czechoslovakia, Hungary and Romania	1945-1950	50,000
Hungary	1956	17,000
Czechoslovakia	1968	5,000

NOTE

These famous people were refugees living in London:

Karl Marx
philosopher and historian (1818-1883)

Giuseppe Mazzini
Italian nationalist (1805-1872)

Information: The Huguenots

The Huguenots were a refugee group who made enormous contributions to life in England and Northern Ireland. Today Huguenot industries still survive in the UK.

There was a great deal of religious persecution in Europe in the 16th century. One such persecuted group were the Huguenots - French Protestants - who found themselves a minority in a Roman Catholic country. An earlier group of French Protestant refugees fled in 1572 after the St Bartholemew's Day Massacre. But in 1598 King Henry of France passed a law that was meant to guarantee religious minorities safety and freedom of worship. This law was called the *Edict of Nantes*. This helped the Huguenots feel safer.

By the mid 17th century the safety of the Huguenots was again under threat. Some of their churches were destroyed. In 1685 King Louis XIII repealed the *Edict of Nantes*. After this most Huguenots felt that they had no future in France. Between 200,000 and 250,000 refugees fled the country, mostly to the Netherlands and England.

Huguenot communities grew up in many parts of England and also in some towns in Ireland. The largest Huguenot community was to be found in Whitechapel, East London. Other towns with large Huguenot communities included Canterbury, Norwich, Ipswich, Dover, Rye, Southampton, Exeter, Dartmouth, Plymouth, Barnstaple, Bristol, Dublin and Derry.

The Huguenot refugees transformed the British and Irish clothing industry. They brought new skills, new dyes and new fabrics. In London many Huguenot refugees were employed in the silk weaving industry. By 1700 there may have been as many as 10,000 silk looms in the Whitechapel area. Courtauld's Textiles, a company which has survived to the present, was founded by Huguenot refugees. Other industries that employed Huguenots included fishing, market gardening, gun-making, silversmithing and papermaking. Huguenot refugees were also successful soldiers, lawyers and actors.

But like other groups of refugees, not everyone welcomed Huguenot refugees. There was a great deal of anti-French feeling in 17th century England, and the Huguenots were French. Workers in the textile and clothing industry also felt that their livelihoods were threatened by the refugees. Throughout the reign of James I, the Company of Silkweavers protested about the 'multitude of aliens' engaged in their trade in England. In 1675 and 1681, there were anti-refugee riots. Huguenot refugees also saw themselves stereotyped in books and drawings of the time. Other people were more sympathetic to refugees. Many bishops urged their congregations to support the refugees.

The Huguenots' contributions to life in the UK can still be seen over 300 years later, and many people in the UK and Ireland have Huguenot ancestors.

NOTE

Some family names that may indicate Huguenot ancestors

- Batchelor
- Burgess
- Delamere
- Devine
- Gascoingne
- Mercer
- Mitchell
- Oliver
- Parmenter
- Reynolds

Activity ☝

Tracing the Huguenots

Students may wish to carry out research about the Huguenots. They could start by finding out who has Huguenot family names. A local museum may have examples of Huguenot silver or other antiques. There may be Huguenot buildings such as houses or Huguenot churches in the neighbourhood that students could visit. A local history library may be a good source of information about the Huguenots.

Information: Eastern European Jews in Britain

Between 1870 and 1914 over 200,000 Jewish refugees from Eastern Europe settled in Britain. They fled from Russia, Russian Poland, Austro-Hungary and Romania. At this time half of the Jewish population of these countries migrated. Nearly three million Jews moved to the US, Canada, Britain, Germany and France.

The reasons why people fled were complex. In Austro-Hungarian Galicia, Romania and Russia, extreme poverty forced some Jewish people to leave their homes. In Romania, Russia and Russian Poland, Jewish people were also persecuted.

Life for Russian Jews was hardest of all. By 1870 about 5.4 million Jews lived in the Russian Empire. The Tsar ruled Russia. There were no elections. Most Russian people lived in the countryside in great poverty. They were serfs, working on farms owned by a few rich families. Life for the serfs had not really changed in hundreds of years. Most Jewish people lived in small towns and villages called shtetlach. In the shtetlach, Jewish people worked as potters, blacksmiths, rent collectors and farm workers.

Given the impoverished conditions, many Russian people were unhappy with the Tsar and the landowners. In order to divert attention from the real causes of poverty, the Russian government needed a scapegoat to blame for rural poverty. The scapegoat was the Jewish people. Jewish rent collectors were accused of extorting money from Russian peasants. The Russian Orthodox Church encouraged Russian peasants to think that Jewish people sacrificed Christian children so that their blood could be used to make Passover bread.

The governments of Catherine the Great (1762-1796) and Nicolas I (1825-1855) attempted to gain popularity by expelling Jews from certain parts of Russia. By 1835 almost all Jews were confined to an area of Russia called the Pale of Settlement. Nicolas I introduced new military laws, after which thousands of Jewish boys were forcibly conscripted into the Russian army. If a young conscript survived, he often served for thirty or more years.

In 1881 Tsar Alexander II was assassinated by a political movement called Narodnaya Volya. Among the assassins was a young Jewish woman. To divert Russian people from this difficult situation, officials of the Tsar's government encouraged peasants to riot in many towns in the Pale of Settlement. Hundreds of Jewish people were killed in riots (usually called pogroms). After this, large numbers of Jewish refugees left Russia.

In May 1882 Tsar Alexander III passed the May laws. Jewish people were not allowed to work on Sundays. They could not travel and they could not own land, work or live in large parts of the Pale of Settlement. Further repression continued. In 1896 Jews were prevented from selling alcohol (previously an important occupation). There were more pogroms. Many Russian Jews were active in political groups that opposed the Tsar's government. Others fled as refugees. They made their way to the ports, and then bought boat tickets to Britain and North America.

> Almost all Russian Jews spoke Yiddish as their first language. A Yiddish folksong of the 19th century laments conscription:
>
> Trern gissen zikh in die gassn
> In kinderishe blut ken men zikh vashn...
> Kleine oifelekh resist men fun kheyder
> M'tut zey on yevonishe kleider.
> Unzere parneyssim, unzere rabbonim
> Helfen noch zu optzugeben zey far yevonim.
> Bei Zushe Rakover zeynen do zeibn bonim,
> Un fun zey nit einer in yevonim.
> Nor Leye die almones eintsike kind
> Iz a kapore far keholishe zind.
>
> Tears flow in the streets
> One can wash oneself in children's blood...
> Little doves are torn from school
> And dressed up in non-Jewish clothes.
> Our leaders and our rabbis
> Even help disguise them as Gentiles.
> Rich Zushe Rakover has seven sons,
> But not one puts on the uniform.
> But Leah the widow's only child
> Becomes a scapegoat for communal sin.

Deciding what to take wasn't much of a problem because we had so little. We took some of the boxes and some linen - we didn't know what we were coming to.

A Jewish woman describes preparing to go to Britain in 1890.

A VOICE FROM THE ALIENS

About the Anti-Alien Resolution of the Cardiff Trade Union Congress.

—✕—

WE, the organised Jewish workers of England, taking into consideration the Anti-Alien Resolution, and the uncomplimentary remarks of certain delegates about the Jewish workers specially, issue this leaflet, wherewith we hope to convince our English fellow workers of the untruthfulness, unreasonableness, and want of logic contained in the cry against the foreign worker in general, and against the Jewish worker in particular.

It is, and always has been, the policy of the ruling classes to attribute the sufferings and miseries of the masses (which are natural consequences of class rule and class exploitation) to all sorts of causes except the real ones. The cry against the foreigner is not merely peculiar to England ; it is international. Everywhere he is the scapegoat for other's sins. Every class finds in him an enemy. So long as the Anti-Alien sentiment in this country was confined to politicians, wire-pullers, and to individual working men, we, the organised aliens, took no heed ; but when this ill-founded sentiment has been officially expressed by the organised working men of England, then we believe that it is time to lift our voices and argue the matter out.

It has been proved by great political economists that a working man in a country where machinery is greatly developed produces in a day twice as many commodities as his daily wage enables him to consume.

Information: Jewish refugees in Whitechapel, East London

Most Jewish refugees settled in the East End of London, in an area where previously Huguenot refugees had settled, and where it was easy to find work in the clothing industry, or making shoes, furniture or cigars. But housing conditions were poor. Many Jewish refugees lived in overcrowded, insanitary conditions.

Whitechapel was a very lively place. Some Jewish people spent their time at the synagogue. Others were active in trade unions and political organisations. There were anarchists, socialists, communists and Zionists among the Jews of Whitechapel. Between 1880 and 1905 many Jewish political organisations worked to oppose new laws that would limit the entry of Jewish refugees into Britain.

Information: Anti-immigration legislation

There was much opposition to the entry of Eastern European Jewish refugees, just as there is opposition to the entry of refugees today. Newspapers started blaming Jewish refugees for causing housing shortages and unemployment. Jewish workers in the clothing industry were accused of undercutting wage rates. After 1888 the anti-immigration movement began to get more organised. Some Conservative MPs tried to introduce laws to limit immigration. In 1900 Major-General Evans Gordon, MP for Stepney in East London, formed the British Brothers League, which successfully mobilised popular support against Jewish immigrants by organising petitions and meetings, and called for a stop to all Jewish immigration.

By 1904, the British government decided it must act. It tried to pass anti-immigration legislation in 1904, but this was rejected after pressure from shipping companies. In 1905 the Aliens Bill was passed by Parliament. Newly arrived immigrants were subject to more complicated checks when they entered Britain. The immigration officer had powers to reject people he considered to be undesirable. In 1906 some 38,527 'alien' boat passengers entered the UK. Of these, 931 were rejected immediately, 489 were rejected after appeal, and 360 were rejected due to poverty or disease.

Discussion points

⇨ Read 'A Voice from the Aliens'. This was a political leaflet written in 1904 by Jewish trade unionists in Britain. What were the main points made in the leaflet?

⇨ What similarities are there in the treatment of Eastern European Jewish refugees in Britain and the treatment of refugees today?

Information: Belgian Refugees

In 1914 and 1915, over 250,000 Belgian refugees fled to Britain escaping the fighting of the First World War (1914-1918). The arrival of the Belgians is one of the biggest migratory movements in British history. Yet most accounts of the First World War today hardly mention the Belgian refugees.

The refugees were mostly from cities. When they first came to Britain, a charity called the War Refugees Committee was set up to help them. But soon, this organisation could not cope. In late 1914, Government decided to take responsibility for Belgian refugees. The Local Government Board was put in charge of supporting the refugees. This was the first time in British history that the Government had taken direct responsibility for looking after refugees. When the refugees arrived, many went straight to reception camps where they stayed until permanent housing could be found anywhere in the UK.

Unlike the Jewish refugees, who came between 1880 and 1914, the popular press portrayed the Belgian refugees as heroes. Resentment and hostility towards Belgian refugees was rare. Ordinary people set up small organisations to help the refugees, mainly to find housing. In 1915 there were at least 2,500 groups helping the Belgian refugees. There has never been an involvement of the public on this scale in supporting refugees.

Most Belgian refugee children attended local schools where the teachers and other children welcomed them. Helping the Belgian refugee schoolchildren was seen as a way of supporting the war effort. With such a warm welcome, many Belgian children felt very happy in their new schools.

By 1916 some Belgian refugees had begun to return home. In 1921, there were less than 10,000 Belgian refugees remaining in Britain.

> **❝** *Our inspectors say that all over the country these children are finding their way into the public elementary schools in a very normal and easy manner ... The Belgian children seem very happy at school, though sometimes they do not like leaving their compatriots. I mean that sometimes a single child will not like to go into a class of only English children.* **❞**
>
> (School Inspectors' Report to the Departmental Committee on Belgian Refugees, 1916)

Activity ☝

All about me

Learning objectives: The activity aims to help students think about aspects of their own identity.

Time needed: This activity can be carried out in one lesson, or the class may wish to spend more time on it.

Instructions: Students will need paper, pens and art materials. They are to produce an autobiographical booklet about themselves. The title of the booklet is *All About Me*.
The writing that the children produce can be made into a booklet by mounting and stapling the pages. The activity should be introduced by the teacher. The children should be given the titles of sections to guide them, but the child should decide what goes into the booklet. Possible titles for each section might include:

- **Me**
- **My family**
- **My friends**
- **My house**
- **School**
- **What I do in my spare time**
- **Future hopes and plans**

After students have produced their booklet, the teacher should give feedback about what we mean by identity and how our identity is influenced by the world around us.

Activity 👉

Ways we are the same and ways we are different

Learning objectives: The activity aims to highlight diversity as something positive.

Time needed: 30 minutes

Instructions: Students will need paper and pens. They should be divided into groups of four. Each group should make a list of ways in which people are the same. For example, they can list physical characteristics, activities, needs and future hopes. Then the students should make a list of ways in which people are different. They should include their physical characteristics, as well as hobbies, needs, future hopes, religion and so on.

This activity can be followed up with a classroom discussion about diversity and similarity.

Activity 👉

British identity

Learning objectives: The activity aims to help students think about their own identity in multi-ethnic Britain.

Time needed: About 45 minutes and homework time.

Instructions: Students need marker pens and large sheets of paper, and should work in pairs.

The teacher should introduce the activity by explaining that students are going to be thinking about British identity. The students are going to imagine that they are living in China. They have been asked by teachers at their new school to give a five-minute talk about life in the UK. Each pair should choose seven things that they think are typical of life in the UK. They should make a list of their choices on a large sheet of paper. The group should come together. Each pair should pin up the list. The class should discuss the points below. For homework, the students should take away their lists, and find out more about the origins of the items on their lists.

The teacher might wish to point out that fish and chips were brought to the UK by Portuguese Jews who settled in London in the 17th century.

Discussion points:

⇨ What items were common to most of the lists?

⇨ Were their any major differences between the lists made by different groups?

Newly arrived Jewish immigrants in the late 1880s.
© **Jewish Museum**

Learning objective: This activity helps children understand how the food we eat is produced through contact with different cultures, including migrant cultures.

Time needed: 20 minutes plus homework time for research.

Instructions: The teacher or group leader will need to bring in a selection of foods such as potatoes, pasta, rice, tinned food, spices and so on. The information about foods from around the world on page 52 needs to be copied. The activity should be introduced by explaining that many everyday foods have their origins overseas and were brought to the UK through trade and migration. Students are going to keep a diary, listing what they have eaten during a three-day period.

Then for each item of food stuff, students should list where it has its origins. For example, potatoes are native of South America and were brought to Europe in the 16th century. There are many way in which this activity can be developed. Students can make a display of food stuffs from different countries. Children studying history could compare their diet with that of a medieval English peasant and see how much their diet has been enriched by trade and immigration.

© H.J. Davies /
Exile Images

Information: Food from around the world

Fish and chips were brought to the UK in the 17th century by Jewish refugees from the Spanish Netherlands.

Potatoes, tomatoes and chillis were brought to Europe in the 15th century by explorers who sailed to South America.

Oxtail soup, many biscuit recipes and blancmange were brought to the UK by Huguenot refugees.

Bagels and potato latkes are among the many Jewish foods now eaten by many people. These foods were brought to the UK at the end of the 19th century.

When did you last eat pizza? Do you know what country pizza is from? Do you know what country spaghetti comes from? Did you know that pasta was originally a Chinese recipe, brought to Europe by the explorer Marco Polo in the 13th century?

Indian food is very much part of the British diet. But did you know that most Indian restaurants are run by people whose families originally came from Bangladesh?

Chinese food is widely eaten in the UK, with Chinese speaking people from many different countries running restaurants. Chinese people from Hong Kong, Vietnam, Malaysia and Singapore are all involved in catering.

Food from Cyprus and Turkey can also be bought in supermarkets and restaurants. People from Cyprus and Turkey have introduced food such as hummus, taramasalata, kebabs, pitta bread and halva to our national diet.

Information: Refugees' contributions

The UK has been receiving refugees for hundreds of years. Most refugees are ordinary people living ordinary lives. They may be longing to return home to their own country, but in the meantime, they get on with life in the place they have settled. A refugee may work hard, as a teacher, an office worker, in a shop or a factory. Refugees contribute to community life, as much as anyone else and, like most people, they contribute quietly.

But some refugees or groups of refugees are famous for particular achievements.

- During the 17th century over 100,000 Huguenot refugees settled in Britain. They regenerated economic life in southern England, draining the fens and building houses. Does your home town or city have any links with the Huguenots?

- Some 18 Nobel Prizes have been won by refugees living in Britain, most of them in science and medicine. Famous refugee scientists include Albert Einstein, Sir Hans Krebs, Sir Ernst Chain, Charlotte Auerbach, Sir Walter Bodmer and Sir Rudolf Peierls. Can you find out about their scientific achievements?

- The psychoanalyst Sigmund Freud was a refugee. He fled Vienna in 1938 and settled in London.

- There have been many famous refugee painters. Lucian Freud is probably the best known British painter who was a refugee. See how many other artists you can find who were refugees.

- Playwrights and novelists such as Bertold Brecht, Thomas Mann, Sousa Jamba and Franz Kafka were refugees. Many publishing companies such as Gollancz, Heinemann, Andre Deutsch, Thames and Hudson and Paul Hamlyn were founded by refugees.

- Refugees have brought recipes to enrich our diet. The Huguenots brought oxtail soup to Britain. More recently refugees such as the Vietnamese and Turkish Kurds have set up restaurants.

- Refugees have contributed to many of Britain's industries. Some 30,000 Polish refugees were employed as coal miners by 1950. There have been many refugee industrialists such as Calouste Gulbenkian (Armenia), Minh To (Viet Nam), Sieng Van Tran (Viet Nam) and Siegmund Warburg (Germany). Andrex, the first soft toilet paper in Britain, was manufactured by a firm founded by German Jewish refugees.

- Refugees have particularly contributed to the fashion and textile industries. Courtaulds, the textile firm, was founded by Huguenot refugees. Many clothing firms in London are still owned by the descendants of Eastern European Jewish refugees.

- Refugees are involved in all types of music, as composers and performers, for example Hugh Masakela from South Africa.

Musicians performing at Refugee Week in London.
© **Refugee Council**

Activity 👆

Refugee Week display

Learning objective: The activity enables students to understand the contribution refugees have made to their new countries. It also helps develop students' organisational skills.

Time needed: At least 2 hours. The activity can be carried out in a sequence of lessons.

Instructions: The information about refugees' contributions should be copied for each student. They will need access to the internet and library to carry out the research. In order to make the display, students will need display boards, paper and art materials.

The activity should be introduced with an explanation about Refugee Week. This is an annual event that takes place in June. It aims to raise awareness about refugees. It marks and celebrates the contributions that refugees have made.

Many schools participate in Refugee Week. Some school students organise assemblies. Another favourite Refugee Week activity is creating student displays.

Students should be given the task of researching and producing a display about refugees' contributions to the UK. They can use the information about refugees' contributions as a starting point. They can research the list of famous refugees, but may also want to research the life of someone less well known, perhaps someone living in their neighbourhood. Refugee community groups might be able to provide the class with a person to interview.

Refugee Week events.
© **Refugee Council /
David Levene**

4 Refugees 1930 - 1980

A Vietnamese family resettled in the UK. © Bournemouth News and Picture Service

This chapter examines the growth of multi-ethnic Britain and the settlement of four major refugee groups in the UK: Refugees from Nazi Germany, the Poles, Hungarians and Vietnamese. The chapter also examines the cases of British and Irish people who have been displaced.

Information: Refugees from Nazi-occupied Europe

Over 60 million people became refugees during the Second World War. But one group of people, the Jews of Nazi-occupied Europe, were largely prevented from seeking asylum in safe countries.

During the Middle Ages, Jews were persecuted by some Christians. They were accused of killing Christ and of practising black magic. And in many countries only Jews were allowed to lend money for interest, so soon Jews were blamed for causing misery, by profiting from poor peasants who owed them money.

Anti-semitism was revived in the 19th century, at the end of the Russian Empire. This was a time of great poverty and dissatisfaction. Rather than blame Russian landlords who charged high rents, the Tsar's government blamed Jewish rent-collectors. The Jews were made a scapegoat - a group who could easily be blamed for society's problems.

The Jews were also a convenient scapegoat for the Nazis. After the First World War, the German government had to pay large amounts of money to Britain and France as compensation. By the mid-1920s inflation was out of control. Bank savings became worthless overnight and many small businesses were ruined. Millions of workers lost their jobs. As there was no social security, people without work starved.

In these conditions, discontent spread. The Nazi Party offered simple solutions to Germany's problems. They built on old prejudices and blamed Jewish bankers for ruining the German economy.

The Nazis also believed that the Germans were a superior race; most other races were either destined to become slaves of the Germans, or to be exterminated. Jews, as well as Roma (Gypsies), were destined to be killed. **Adolf Hitler's** ideas about the German 'master race' restored national pride for a demoralised nation.

Anti-semitic parties received support in other countries during the 1920s and 1930s, but not to the same extent as in Germany.

Anti-semitism

Anti-semitism means discrimination against Jews. It is a form of racism. The Nazis did not invent anti-semitism, but they revived something that had existed for centuries.

Information: Events in Nazi-occupied Europe causing flight of refugees

1918: The end of the First World War. Germany was forced to pay compensation to the UK and France.

1920: The National Socialist (Nazi) Party was formed in Germany.

1923: The failure of the Munich Putsch. This was an attempt by Adolf Hitler and his supporters to take over the government in the German state of Bavaria. The Nazis failed and Hitler was given a prison sentence. It was during his time in prison that Hitler wrote *Mein Kampf*. This book outlined Hitler's racial theories and his plans for Germany. Hitler believed certain races to be superior to others. Blonde-haired, blue-eyed 'Aryan' Germans were the 'master race' who would one day rule Europe. Other people, such as Poles and Russians, were 'sub-human'. Hitler planned to take their land and property and make them slaves to the Germans. Jews and Gypsies were 'non-human' and he planned to kill them.

1928: Nazi party membership reached 109,000 and the party got 2.6 per cent of the votes in elections to the Reichstag, the German parliament.

1930: The Nazis won 18.3 per cent of the votes in elections to the Reichstag.

July 1932: The Nazis got 37 per cent of the vote in elections to the Reichstag. The combined vote of the Communist Party and the Social Democratic Party was greater, but these two parties could not agree to form a united opposition to the Nazis. A further election in November 1932 did not produce a conclusive result.

January 1933: The political parties of the centre and right agreed to accept Adolf Hitler as Chancellor (the head of government). Chancellor Hindenburg resigned and Adolf Hitler became Chancellor on 30 January 1933.

April 1933: The first official boycott of Jewish shops. All Jewish enterprises had to be marked with signs. Laws were passed to define who was 'Aryan' and to enable 'undesirables' (Jews, Communists and trade unionists) to be sacked from the civil service. Universities and secondary schools were only allowed to accept 1.5 per cent Jewish students.

1933: Random street violence was carried out by Nazi supporters. This was directed against Jews and political opponents of the Nazis.

1934: More Jews were dismissed from the civil service, medical and legal professions, as it became necessary to be of 'Aryan' origin.

1935: The Nuremburg Laws were passed forbidding marriage and sexual relations between Jews and Germans.

1936: The more violent aspects of Nazi anti-semitism were halted as Germany hosted the 1936 Olympic Games. Some refugees returned to Germany.

Inmates at Auschwitz I Camp in 1945.
© United States Holocaust Memorial Museum

1937: Throughout 1937 the Nazis seized all remaining Jewish businesses.

1938: All passports for Jews were stamped with the letter 'J'.

March 1938: Anschluss. Germany and Austria were unified. Some 183,000 Austrian Jews came under Nazi rule.

October 1938: Over 15,000 Jews of Polish nationality were expelled from Germany. They waited in camps on the Polish-German border.

9-10 November 1938: Kristallnacht (the Night of Broken Glass). Hirsch Grynzpan, a young Jew, assassinated Ernst vom Rath, a German diplomat, in Paris. The Nazis organised street riots in response. Jewish homes, synagogues and shops were destroyed. 91 people were killed and over 20,000 arrested.

15 November 1938: All remaining German Jewish children were expelled from school.

March 1939: The Nazis occupied Czechoslovakia.

1 September 1939: Germany invaded Poland. The UK and France declared war on Germany on 3 September 1939.

1940: Much of Europe was under German occupation. Some 7 million Jews were living under German rule, mostly in Poland, Hungary and Czechoslovakia. About 250,000 Polish Jews managed to escape to the Soviet Union, but for most Jews and Roma (gypsies), escape routes were sealed.

1941: Germany invaded the Soviet Union. Special killing squads called Einsatzgruppen murdered thousands of Soviet citizens after the German army advances.

Autumn 1941: Mobile gas vans were put into operation at Chelmno in Poland. From 1941-45 over 360,000 people, mostly Jews, were gassed. Only two people survived Chelmno.

20 January 1942: The Wannsee Conference was held in Berlin for top Nazi officials. The plans for the 'final solution to the Jewish problem' were revealed. They were to be deported eastwards, to ghettos, and to be used as slave labourers. The ghettos would be systematically emptied as Jewish people were murdered in extermination camps.

1942: In Nazi-occupied Poland extermination camps were opened at Auschwitz, Belzec, Majdanek, Sorbibor and Treblinka.

26 March 1942: The first deportation to Auschwitz. During the next 32 months over 4 million Jews, Roma, Poles and Russians were gassed at Auschwitz. Gays, lesbians and the disabled were also murdered. The victims came from all over Nazi-occupied Europe.

1943: There were Jewish uprisings in the Warsaw and Vilna ghettos. Several thousand Jews secretly joined partisans who were fighting in the forests. There were also revolts in the labour and extermination camps in 1943 and 1944.

View of the execution wall nest to Block 11 in Auschwitz I Camp after liberation.
© United States Holocaust Memorial Museum

Late 1944: The Red Army pushed the Germans out of the Soviet Union and advanced into Eastern Poland.

October 1944: The last gassings at Auschwitz. The inmates of the slave labour and extermination camps were marched back towards Germany in the winter of 1944-45. Very few survived these death marches.

27 January 1945: Auschwitz was liberated by the Red Army. As the Allied armies advanced across Europe, the full extent of the Nazi horror became obvious. Nearly 6 million Jewish people had been murdered in camps and by Einsatzgruppen.

Information: The fate of refugees escaping from the Nazis

February - April 1933: Over 1,000 refugees left Nazi Germany, most of them teachers at colleges and universities. The leaders of Britain's Jewish community told the British government that the Jewish community would meet all the expenses of incoming Jewish refugees. They hoped that such a promise would result in the British government allowing in more refugees.

Late 1933: Over 65,000 refugees left Nazi Germany. As well as Jews, the refugees included political opponents of the Nazis. Most of them settled in France, but a small number fled to the UK and the US. At that time most refugees found it fairly easy to come to the UK. Many organisations were set up to help them.

1934: Refugees leaving Germany had to pay a very high 'emigration' tax. This meant that most refugees arriving in the UK had very little money.

1935: The British government introduced visas for German citizens who wanted to enter the UK, her colonies or British-administered Palestine. It was almost impossible to get a visa unless the person concerned had a job offer. Refugee organisations helped German doctors, university lecturers and teachers find jobs as domestic servants.

1935-37: Some 165,000 refugees left Germany. About 43,000 fled to Palestine and 30,000 to the UK. Others escaped to France, the US or the Netherlands.

In the UK public sympathy for the refugees decreased. Some politicians and newspapers were openly hostile to refugees.

By 1935: The British Union of Fascists, a political party with views very similar to the Nazis, had 80,000 supporters. It had anti-semitic policies and blamed refugees, who were mostly Jewish, for taking away the jobs of 'British' workers.

1937: Jewish emigration to Palestine became a problem for the British government. The numbers of refugees settling in Palestine doubled in two years. Worried about their future, Palestinian Arabs protested. The British government decided to act. It needed to keep friendly relations with Arab governments in the Middle East, and to keep the Suez Canal open. The UK decided to limit the number of Jewish refugees allowed to travel to Palestine. No more than 10,000 refugees would be allowed in over a five-year period.

British ships patrolled the Mediterranean Sea to stop refugee ships entering Palestine. Diplomatic pressure was put on the Greek and Yugoslav governments to stop refugees passing through these countries.

July 1938: An international conference about refugees from Germany and Austria was held at Evian in France. The conference could not agree on a solution to the settlement of refugees from these countries. The British government continued to prevent most refugees entering Britain or Palestine. Some sympathetic officials in the Foreign Office gave a few refugees travel documents to enter Mauritius, British Honduras or British Guyana. Small numbers of refugees also travelled to South American countries and Shanghai.

" Once it was known that Britain offered sanctuary to all who cared to come, the floodgates would be opened, and we would be inundated by thousands seeking a home. "

(Daily Mail, 1935)

November 1938: After the Kristallnacht more Jewish refugees queued to get visas to leave Germany. In the UK there was an emergency debate in the House of Commons on the Kristallnacht. The British Government decided to allow 10,000 unaccompanied refugee children to enter. This was the Kindertransporte (the children's transports). Altogether 9,732 children from Germany, Austria and Czechoslovakia came to Britain. Most never saw their parents again.

September 1939: The UK declared war on Germany. Some 50,000 citizens of an enemy country were living in the UK as refugees. Some newspapers and politicians believed that the refugees were not loyal to the UK, and that it would be easy for German spies to live among the refugee community. A small number of refugees were interned in camps to protect 'national security.'

May 1940: After the Nazi invasion of the Netherlands, there was a public outcry about the dangers of 'enemy aliens' living in the UK. Some 27,000 refugees were interned in camps. Refugees were also deported to Canada and Australia.

Conditions in the camps were harsh. One particularly bad camp was Warth Mill in Lancashire. It was dirty and there was not enough bedding. The refugees went on hunger strike to try and improve conditions.

By May 1940: The numbers of refugees reaching Britain was very small. During the next five years less than 6,000 refugees from Nazi-occupied Europe managed to come to Britain.

Refugees from Eastern Europe at a camp in Germany at the end of the war.
© UNHCR

August 1942: Evidence reached the UK of the deportation of Jewish people to ghettos in Nazi-occupied Poland, and of the extermination of Jews at Chelmno and Auschwitz. On 17th December 1942 Anthony Eden, the Foreign Secretary, made a public statement on behalf of the War Cabinet. He described conditions in the ghettos and how they were being emptied. But on 30 December 1942 Anthony Eden secretly told the War Cabinet that the UK could only admit another 1,000 to 2,000 refugees.

Spring 1943: There was enormous public sympathy towards European Jews. Protest meetings were held. Many refugees were released from internment camps at this time. Public pressure also persuaded the British government to organise an international conference about refugees. This was held in Bermuda in April 1943. It was unsuccessful because no country would agree to accept large numbers of refugees.

Autumn 1943: Public interest in refugees and the fate of European Jewry began to fade.

Discussion points:

⇨ What is a scapegoat?

⇨ Have you ever had a scapegoat in your school? What were they blamed for? Why do you think they were made a scapegoat?

⇨ Can you think of individuals and groups of people in history who have been made scapegoats?

Refugee Blues by W. H. Auden, 1939

Say this city has ten million souls,
Some are living in mansions, some are living in holes:
Yet there's no place for us, my dear, yet there's no place for us.

Once we had a country and we thought it fair,
Look in the atlas and you'll find it there:
We cannot go there now, my dear, we cannot go there now.

In the village churchyard there grows an old yew,
Every spring it blossoms anew:
Old passports can't do that my dear, old passports can't do that.

The consul banged on the table and said,
'If you've got no passport you're officially dead':
But we are still alive, my dear, but we are still alive.

Went to a committee; they offered me a chair;
Asked me politely to return next year:
But where shall we go today, my dear, but where shall we go today?

Came to a public meeting: the speaker got up and said:
'If we let them in, they will steal our daily bread':
He was talking of you and me, my dear, he was talking of you and me.

Discussion point:

⇨ What do you think W. H. Auden felt about the treatment of refugees?

Learning objectives: The activity aims to help students decide why refugees were not allowed to escape to the UK, her colonies and British-administered Palestine between 1933 and 1945.

Time needed: 1 hour

Instructions: Make copies of the cards on page 62, student instructions and the chronology about refugees in Nazi-occupied Europe. Cut up the cards. Divide the class up into groups of three or four and give each group their instructions, a set of cards and the chronology.

Each group should decide the reasons why refugees were not allowed into Britain between 1933 and 1945. The students should read out the cards in turns and then rank the cards in order of importance, starting with the most important reason for not allowing refugees to come to the UK, to the least important reason. The groups should come together, compare their answers and examine the discussion points.

It is worth noting that this period of history is very controversial, and there are no right answers to the questions posed by the activity.

Activity

Why were Britain's doors closed to refugees?

Discussion points:

⇨ What could ordinary British people have done to improve the situation for refugees stranded in Nazi-occupied Europe?

⇨ What can we learn today from the way that refugees were treated in the period 1933-45?

Why were Britain's doors closed to refugees?

The organisations that were formed to help refugees in Britain did not speak out against human rights abuses in Nazi-occupied Europe.	The British government believed that all efforts had to be directed towards fighting the Germans. Helping refugees was a distraction from this aim.
Civil servants and diplomats who wanted to help refugees found it very complicated to get visas for them.	The British government feared that if it was seen to be too generous to refugees, there would be a flood of millions of Jews, Czechs, Poles and other refugees who would want to come to Britain.
There was no international organisation to protect human rights.	Britain believed that the persecution of Jews was a purely German affair, and that the British government should not interfere.
The British government did not want refugees to come to Britain, as it would be easy for enemy spies to come with a group of refugees.	The British government only responded to public pressure. There was not enough sympathy and pressure from the British public to help refugees.
If Jewish refugees were allowed to leave Europe, they might eventually go to Palestine. This would cause unrest in Palestine and damage Britain's interests there. Use of the Suez Canal might be threatened.	Powerful members of the British government were anti-semitic and anti-communist. They did not care what happened to the Jewish people and communists.
The British government believed that people did not want a large number of refugees to settle in Britain or her colonies. There would be race riots.	The British government did not think that the Nazis were murdering people. The accounts of the concentration camps were too horrific to believe.
The British government believed that refugees would be a financial burden. They would need housing and food.	The British government believed that refugees would take 'British' people's jobs at a time when unemployment was high.

Learning objectives: This activity helps students develop their research skills. At the end of the activity students should also understand how Marc Chagall represented persecution and exile in his paintings.

Time needed: 1 hour

Instructions: Students will need access to the internet or a library with art books. The activity should be introduced by explaining that Europe in the 1930s was a time of great artistic achievement. Students are going to research some of the artists who fled the Nazis.

Each student or group of students should be assigned an artist from the list below. They should research and produce a 400-word biography of the artist. It should describe key events in each of the artists' lives and how they influenced their art.

The class should then focus on Marc Chagall. His biography should be shared with the whole class. Students should then look at copies of his paintings and discuss how the themes of persecution and exile are represented in his paintings.

Some artists who were refugees

- Max Beckman
- Marc Chagall
- Max Ernst
- Lucian Freud
- Wassily Kandinsky
- Ernst Ludwig Kirchner
- Paul Klee
- Kaethe Kollwitz

Marc Chagall

Lucien Freud

Max Beckman

Max Ernst

Ron Baker's story

Ron Baker was born Rudi Aschheim in Berlin in 1932. At the age of six his family sent him to Holland to escape the Nazis. He came to the UK in May 1940, on the last Kindertransporte (children's transports). He was fostered by the Bakers, a Jewish family from Salford, near Manchester. Ron Baker has worked as a psychiatric nurse, social worker and university teacher.

Jewish refugee children, members of the first Kindertransporte from Germany, on arrival in Harwich, England.
© **United States Holocaust Memorial Museum**

"I was born in Berlin in 1932, the year before Hitler came to power. Because I was so young I don't have many memories of life in Berlin. I can remember the Nazi rallies. As a child I stood on the balcony of our house. For such a young child, the rallies seemed exciting."

"I can remember Kristallnacht. I went with my father, on the Saturday, to the synagogue. The damage was as bad as portrayed. Pews were overturned and chandeliers smashed."

"My parents were born in Poland, although they had lived in Germany for a long time. At first it was Nazi policy to deport Polish Jews. When I was about five years old my father was deported to Tarnow in Poland. My mother, brother and I continued to live in Berlin. My father returned illegally one Friday to spend the Sabbath with us. The atmosphere at home was one of apprehension bordering on fear that my father would be discovered. I remember my mother very gravely telling me that if anyone asked for my father I was to say that I had not seen him for a long time."

"In the middle of the evening there was a knock on the door and my mother told me to open it. A smiling Gestapo officer stood there, impeccably dressed in his uniform. He quietly asked if my father was at home. I was terrified, but said 'no'. He then asked quietly, almost gently, when I had last seen my father. I replied that I had not seen him for a long time. His smile remained constant. Surprisingly he neither asked for my mother, nor insisted on searching the house. He turned round and left."

"Not long after, my mother sent my brother and me to Holland. My brother and I were separated when we got there and fostered by different families. We had very little contact over the next two years. I went to school in Holland and learnt to speak fluent Dutch."

"When Hitler invaded Holland I was put on the last boat that left for England. That was in May 1940. As the Nazis invaded Holland, Jewish children were herded together. We were escorted through the German firing line in the docks. We were put on a Chinese cargo boat. The memories of the boat were quite awful."

"It was a boat full of children, very few adults. There was a lot of fighting and bombing and we soon moved away from the quay. As the boat steamed out, we passed through bombing for two or three hours. Why the boat did not sink I do not know. It took a week for the boat to get to Liverpool. We must have been a pathetic sight when we reached Liverpool."

"On arrival in Liverpool we walked through the crowded streets to a reception hostel. Suddenly a woman darted out of the crowd and grabbed the first child she got hold of who happened to be me. She held me tightly, tears were streaming down her face, yet she was warm and smiling through them. Putting me down she pushed six pennies into my hand and went back into the crowd. Experience had taught me not to trust smiling people anymore and I was filled with confused feelings and intense anxiety."

"We were housed in a church hall in Wigan for six months. We were looked after by volunteers. Although people were very kind we couldn't actually communicate, as language was a problem. Gradually the appeal went out to foster refugee children and one by one the hall emptied. I remember being bundled into a car. I was picked up by this family called Baker. Overnight my name changed from Aschheim to Baker."

"The next twelve months were difficult. I suffered nightmares and later the Bakers told me I sobbed myself to sleep for months. I was with the Bakers until 1947, when suddenly the International Red Cross tracing service linked me with my mother who had survived."

"My mother escaped from Germany in 1941 and by a roundabout route got to Uruguay. She lived in dire poverty in Montevideo for five years. In 1947 she came to Israel via England."

"The Bakers became very upset when they realised I had a mother. She stayed for three weeks. It was an odd time. To me she was a stranger. I was totally English. She went off to Israel. I did not see her until 1954. By that time I was playing a lot of table tennis and had been selected for the England team. I went to Israel for the 'Maccabi', an international Jewish sports competition. By that time my mother was married again. After seeing her again we began to write to each other. My mother died in March 1988. She was 86."

"When I was at university I happened to be in Manchester. At the time there was an exhibition on concentration camps. We decided to go and have a look at the exhibition. It was good and they had copies of some of the Auschwitz documents. I began to leaf through them. I was looking for the name Aschheim of course. I found the name of my father, Michael Aschheim, and my brother's name, Bernard Aschheim. I felt very sick, but I did not talk about this to anyone. It was not until about 1978 that I could talk about my refugee experience."

"Very recently something incredible happened. When my mother died in Israel we had to go though her possessions. We found a letter from a lady in Holland saying a book had been written in which Bernard Aschheim had been featured. This woman gave a telephone number in Holland. When we got back to England my wife spoke to her and she said she would send the book. We got the book and it was translated. It mentioned my brother. He was seven years older than me."

"My father and brother perished. At the end of the war I knew they had died and I was told they perished in Auschwitz, although I had no evidence of this."

"My brother and a group of children were being trained as farmers to go to Palestine. When the Nazis invaded Holland seven of them tried to escape. They were caught by the Gestapo on the Belgian border, and were eventually sent to Auschwitz. A monument was put up to the children in the village in Holland where they had lived. I hope to visit this monument soon."

> *My father and brother perished. At the end of the war I knew they had died and I was told they perished in Auschwitz, although I had no evidence of this.*

Information: Unaccompanied refugee children

The children who arrived on the Kindertransporte were unaccompanied refugee children. The UNHCR defines an unaccompanied child as "a person under 18 years old who is separated from both parents and is not being cared for by an adult who, by law or custom has responsibility to do so". In the past other groups of unaccompanied refugee children have settled in the UK, including Basque children who arrived in 1937, Polish children in 1946 and Hungarian children who came in January 1957. Some of these unaccompanied refugee children had an unhappy childhood and received little care. Today unaccompanied children still come to the UK. How has the care of unaccompanied refugee children changed?

Basque children playing after being evacuated to Britain.
© **La Columna**

The Basque Children

In 1937 some 3,889 Basque children were brought to Britain, having been evacuated from war-torn Spain. Other unaccompanied Basque children were evacuated to France, Belgium, the USSR, Denmark, Switzerland, the US and Mexico. Altogether about 20,000 Basque children were evacuated.

In 1936, the Spanish people had elected a left-wing government that was committed to improving the lives of poor people. The Government was opposed by a very conservative catholic church and the aristocracy. Soon, those opposing the Spanish government were joined by the army. On 17 July 1936 General Franco led an army revolt against the Spanish Republican government and the Spanish Civil War had begun. By August 1936 the Basque cities of Irun and San Sebastian were under siege. German planes were then used to bomb the Basque region including the town of Guernica (portrayed in a painting by Pablo Picasso). Refuges began to flee from Bilbao. Over 10,000 people left in a few days in April 1937.

After the bombing of Guernica, many people in the UK wanted to bring Basque children to safety. On 30 April 1937 the Home Office agreed to evacuate Basque children and bring them to the UK, providing certain conditions were met. There should be no cost to the British government. The children should be housed in children's homes, rather than in foster homes. The Basque refugee children were not to be allowed to attend state schools. Private funds should pay for their education and care.

An organisation called the Basque Children's Committee was set up by those who wanted to help. Leah Manning, a former MP, travelled to the Basque region to arrange to bring the children. Within two weeks of her arrival some 20,000 children had been signed up for 4,000 places. After a medical examination the children were evacuated on ships. Some 3,889 children, 219 women teachers and aides and 15 Basque priests sailed into Southampton on 23 May 1937.

In Southampton, thousands of people came to welcome the 'Basque babies'. Indeed there was more sympathy to this group of refugees than almost any other group. A reception camp had been set up at Stonham, near Southampton, in a three-week period. Accommodation was in tents and there were guards on the gates. Eight children slept in each tent. The children were allocated tents according to their parents' political beliefs. There was little by way of an organised educational programme and later this was judged to be a major mistake.

Other problems encountered were that Spanish-speaking staff were rare, and those that did speak Spanish were often very religious and had difficulty in dealing with Basque children who had been brought up in communist or socialist homes.

Soon after the arrival of the children, the Basque Children's Committee began to form local groups, which started to move the children to more permanent children's homes. The main organisations that ran these 'colonies' were the Salvation Army, the Roman Catholic Church, the Quakers and the trade unions.

Conditions in the Salvation Army hostels were grim, and noted for the strong discipline, lack of love and terrible food. In Clapton, London, one boy describes the food:

"When we arrived at Clapton they served us a stew of sorts, nothing identifiable. We all sat there unable to eat it. Reproaches like 'we'll see if you eat it or not' and 'how many British children would love to eat this food' followed. The same food reappeared at lunch and dinner; again no-one ate. A hunger strike!"

Soon the children rebelled at the Clapton hostel and the police were called to quieten them. Children were treated better in other homes. One particularly commended children's colony was the Leah Manning colony in Theydon Bois, Essex. This was funded by the London Teachers' Association. Thirty children were housed there and allowed to attend local schools. At the end of the Spanish Civil war many of the Basque children returned to their parents. In September 1939, of the 3,889 children brought to the UK, some 8 had died, 2,726 had been repatriated and 1,155 remained in the UK.

Eduardo Martinez's story

Eduardo was one of the Basque children to be brought to Britain. Here, he recalls arriving in Southampton.

"In Southampton there were many people when we first came over, about 5,000, which was too big and too impersonal. I came with my elder sister, she was 15. My sister and me, we were separated because she was a girl and I was a boy. I hardly saw her at all, I don't recall that I ever saw her in Southampton. I don't know how long we were there, but I have a feeling it must have been something like two months."

"I remember queuing for food, and I remember the music that they used to play to wake us up in the morning over the tannoy. That kind of thing is very vivid indeed. We lived in tents, it was about eight or so to a tent. From there we went to what I think was a transition camp. We were there only for about two weeks and it was in army sheds. Afterwards we were taken to Bray Court. We were in a house that was a hotel at one time, with very imposing grounds. It was a mixed colony and I was there with my sister."

Information: Unaccompanied refugee children today

Children are still arriving in the UK by themselves. At present most unaccompanied refugee children are arriving from Somalia, Afghanistan, Sri Lanka, Turkey and Iraq. The majority of unaccompanied refugee children who arrive in the UK are between 13 and 18 years old. At the moment more boys than girls arrive as unaccompanied refugee children.

The United Nations defines unaccompanied children as "children and young people under 18 years who are separated from both parents and are not being cared for by an adult who, by law or custom has responsibility to do so". Unaccompanied refugee children therefore include:

• Children who have become separated from their parents and have arrived in the UK by themselves;

• Children who are being cared for by older siblings, distant relatives and family friends - people who would not by custom be their usual carers.

Some children who come to the UK by themselves have seen their family killed or disappear. Other unaccompanied refugee children have become separated from their parents in the chaos of war. Yet others have been sent away by their parents when the situation in their home countries became very dangerous. In this group are boys and young men who have been sent away to avoid conscription into the army or a guerrilla organisation.

Unaccompanied refugee children need care and support just like any other children. Local authority social services departments are responsible for looking after unaccompanied refugee children, just as they are responsible for any other needy or vulnerable child or young person. Unaccompanied refugee children can be cared for in different ways.

Social services departments will often place unaccompanied refugee children with older brothers and sisters or aunts and uncles. Other children may live with foster parents. Some unaccompanied refugee children live in children's homes. There are a number of children's homes that are specifically for refugee children, where they have a great deal of contact with members of their own community and the support of trained staff. Some older unaccompanied refugee children are provided with their own housing but supported by a social worker. But most 16 and 17 year old unaccompanied refugee children end up living by themselves in a hostel or rented room. They get a cash allowance but rarely have a social worker to help them.

It is very important that unaccompanied refugee children receive the right kind of help. Some unaccompanied children find it difficult to get over distressing events in their past - they may have seen their parents killed or witnessed other terrifying events. Those who still have parents will naturally miss them or may be very worried about them. The children will have left friends and familiar things behind.

© H. J. Davies / Exile Images

- Chapter Four: Refugees 1930-80 -

The Refugee Council's work with unaccompanied young refugees

The quality of care offered to unaccompanied refugee children varies a lot. The Refugee Council is worried that some unaccompanied children are not being supported. It has campaigned about the quality of care offered to 16 and 17 year old unaccompanied young people. The Refugee Council also offers practical help to unaccompanied refugee children. It runs a children's home for young people aged 16-18. Here unaccompanied young people are prepared for independent life.

© **Refugee Council**

The Refugee Council employs a team of adults who help unaccompanied children and young people get the help they need. This team is called the Panel of Advisers for Unaccompanied Refugee Children. The advisers speak a wide range of languages. Children are paired with these trained advisers according to factors such as their language and gender. The advisers befriend the young person, give advice and help find an immigration lawyer. The adviser will also ensure that the young person gets health care and education.

Learning objectives: This activity helps students develop their skills in historical research. When completed, students will also understand changes in the ways that unaccompanied children have been treated in the UK.

Time needed: 1 hour

Instructions: The teacher or group leader will need to collect and reproduce primary and secondary source material on unaccompanied refugee children. The material should include the information sheet on unaccompanied children, and primary and secondary sources relating to the Basque children, the Kindertransporte and unaccompanied children today.

The testimony of Ron Baker can be given to students. Other resources on the Kindertransporte are listed at the end of the book. The Refugee Council website has material about unaccompanied children today (www.refugeecouncil.org.uk). Save the Children's website includes *Cold Comfort*, a report about the treatment of unaccompanied children in the UK (www.scfuk.org.uk).

The teacher should explain who unaccompanied refugee children are and divide the class into pairs. The students should imagine they are unaccompanied refugee children arriving in the UK. Each pair should make a list of unaccompanied children's needs.

After the list has been completed, each pair should be given the copies of the primary and secondary sources about the Basque children, the Kindertransporte and unaccompanied children today. Students should then examine the following questions:

- How were unaccompanied refugee children looked after in the 1930s?
- Do you think unaccompanied children who arrived in the 1930s had all their needs met?
- How did the treatment of unaccompanied children in the 1930s differ from today?

Activity ☝

Making a difference

Additional activity

Caring for unaccompanied asylum-seeking and refugee children is one of the important things that local authorities (local government) do to help refugees. See if you can list some of the other things that local government does to help refugee communities.

Information: The Poles

Between 1945 and 1970 most of the world's refugees were from Eastern Europe. Two of the largest groups were Poles and Hungarians. Many of them came to the UK.

Some 250,000 Polish refugees settled permanently in the UK. They arrived at different times. The first group to arrive were Polish refugees who fled their homeland in September 1939 after the German invasion. About 440,000 people fled Poland at this time, of whom 60 per cent were Jewish. Of these refugees, about 2,000 entered the UK. Others made their way to France where a Polish government in exile was formed.

After Nazi Germany invaded France in 1940, over 30,000 Polish refugees fled to the UK. The Polish government in exile, led by General Sikorski, moved to London. Many of these Polish refugees became soldiers and airmen alongside British forces.

When Nazi Germany invaded, Poland was divided between Germany and the Soviet Union. Some 1.8 million Polish citizens found themselves living in the Soviet Union where they were treated very badly. Nearly 1 million Poles were deported eastwards to labour camps in Siberia. But in 1941, after the Nazis invaded the Soviet Union, the latter entered the Second World War. An agreement was signed between the Soviet Union and the Polish government in exile. The Polish government was allowed to organise an army made up of Poles who were living in the Soviet Union. That army was led by General Anders. The army of 220,000 people left the Soviet Union in March 1942 and started on an incredible journey across many countries. They travelled through Iran, Iraq, Jordan, Palestine and Egypt. In Egypt the army was organised into the Polish Second Corps who fought with the British in Italy. In 1945, at the end of the Second World War, many of the soldiers who had fought in the Polish Second Corps came to the UK as refugees.

At the end of the Second World War, many other Poles were living in refugee camps in Europe. Some of them were opponents of the new communist government in Poland and did not want to return home. Others were from the Polish Ukraine, which became part of the Soviet Union in 1945. Between 1946 and 1950, some 101,000 Polish refugees from refugee camps in Europe came as refugees to the UK. Later another 14,000 Polish refugees entered Britain as part of the European Volunteer Worker Scheme. This group of refugees was sent to work in key industries where labour was in short supply.

Most Polish refugees soon found work in all parts of the UK. They helped rebuild the British economy. Industries which particularly benefited from the efforts of the Polish refugees included building, agriculture, coal mining, the hotel trade, the brick industry, iron and steel manufacture and the textile industry.

Polish children in a Warsaw ghetto. © **Wiener Library**

Rita's story

Rita was 26 years old when she joined General Anders' army in the Soviet Union. With the army she travelled through Iran, Iraq, Palestine, Egypt and finally to Italy where she was a nurse. She arrived in Britain in 1946. Her story was collected by the Ethnic Communities Oral History Project.

Poland

"When the Russians invaded Lithuania, my father and I were arrested besides hundreds of others. I was taken to Altaj in the middle of the Steppe region. We were told that this is where we were going to live and work. They directed me to a house where a young couple lived with a small son. I had a very small room, one table and a chair. There was no light there. There was no sanitation at all. Fuel was unobtainable so animal dung was mixed with straw and dried in the sun at the brick farm. It was called kiziaki, when burned it gave little heat but plenty of smoke. I worked in a workshop where we made uniforms for the army. Then I was transported to a barber shop. Men called to serve in the army had to have their hair cut."

"When General Sikorski signed an agreement with Stalin we were freed, an amnesty was announced on the radio. Then the winter came, each day it was colder and colder, we knew we would never survive the winter. There was one remedy, to go south where the Polish army was forming into units."

"London (the Polish government in exile) decided to send us to Persia. We crossed the Caspian Sea in a very old ship. We met other Polish soldiers in tropical kit, how different we looked in our woolly dresses. We felt we were newly born, we were free after so many months of being suppressed, starved and living without hope."

"The next stop was Egypt, then Italy where the fighting was in full swing. We all tried to do impossible tasks as we expected that this would be the last stage before we reached our homeland. But it wasn't to be, our country was sold down the river."

"When we came to England we were disillusioned and knew we were destined to further wanderings. Some people returned to Poland to be arrested and imprisoned. Others went to Canada, Argentina or Australia. My husband and I toyed with the idea of going to Ecuador, we even started learning Spanish. I started work in a hairdressing business. Then we opened a delicatessen shop where we both worked together. The time came to retire and I hope to be in good health to see what other changes the future will bring."

> **❝** *I was taken to Altaj in the middle of the Steppe region. We were told that this is where we were going to live and work. They directed me to a house where a young couple lived with a small son. I had a very small room, one table and a chair. There was no light there. There was no sanitation at all.* **❞**

Members of General Anders' army attend an outdoor class at their military bse in the Iraqi desert where they are stationed from the summer of 1942 until the summer of 1943.
© **United States Holocaust Memorial Museum**

Information: The Hungarians

Hungary was an ally of Nazi Germany in the Second World War, although in 1944 the German Nazis invaded Hungary and murdered 300,000 Hungarian Jews. The Soviet Union freed Hungary from German rule in 1945. Communists became the largest single political party in elections held in 1947 and by 1949 controlled the country. Small numbers of refugees left Hungary between 1946 and 1956.

In 1956 there were many demonstrations. These were caused by a split in the Communist Party between hardline communists and more liberal party members. For a while it looked possible that Hungary might return to democracy. But on 4 November 1956 a Soviet-led army invaded Hungary and 3,000 people were killed. Over 200,000 people fled as refugees mostly to Austria and Yugoslavia.

Between November 1956 and January 1957, over 21,000 Hungarians entered Britain as refugees, including 400 unaccompanied refugee children. Some 4,000 refugees only stayed a few months, but most remained in Britain. Two organisations supported the newly arrived refugees: the National Coal Board and the British Council for Aid to Refugees. The National Coal Board housed Hungarian men and their families and found them work in coal mines. The British Council for Aid to Refugees set up temporary hostels before finding the Hungarian refugees work and a permanent home.

An aged Hungarian refugee at an emergency station in Austria, followed by her dog. She has lost all trace of her family.
© **Associated Press**

Yolan's story

Yolan was born in Hungary. He was eight years old when his family fled in 1956 and ended up in Canada. His full story, photographs and papers can be viewed at: www.pier21.ca.

"We huddled each night around our radios giving us the news from Budapest. I saw five pointed stars in our town square tumble to the ground. Political prisoners were freed from jails. But as the army troops moved in, the fighting escalated. Each night we had our clothes by our bed ready to flee if they were to bomb our part of the town. The borders opened in October. My father wasted no time to plan our escape. He was tired of the constant pressure to join the communist party and not having any money for the necessities of life."

"My sister Eva who was six years old and I, who was eight at the time, were told that we were going to visit our relatives. None of our relatives knew about our plan to leave Hungary because my father thought that if they knew they would somehow detain us. As the hours passed we walked some, took a ride with a truck load of soldiers, a truck that carried pigs, the driver of which turned out to be the husband of a relative. My inner instincts told me as we hitch-hiked that this was definitely not the way to either one of my grandparents' homes."

"As we walked we got wearier and wearier. My dad had to carry my sister and me alternately. From time to time we would inquire when we would be reaching our destination. My dad replied 'see that light in the distance, that's where it is'. We were definitely not going to visit grandma, this I knew. It was now October 30, 1956. The escape itself was not unpleasant. I remember the green grass, it was a sunny day, it all seemed very easy."

"The Red Cross was there to aid us as we crossed the border into Austria. They helped to direct us to hostels. As a child of eight this was a strange and different place, but to my dad this was freedom, freedom to think, freedom to plan for the future, freedom to dream. He was 34, mother was 26."

1957, Timmins, Ontario. 'Brand New Canadians', Yolan and his family.
© **Pier 21**

Information: Refugees from Viet Nam

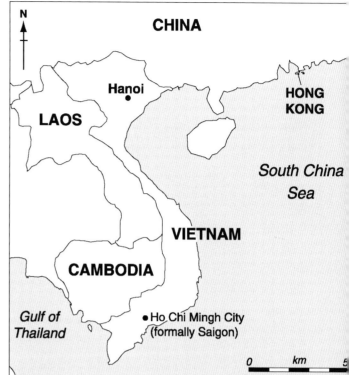

Over 26,000 Vietnamese live in the UK. They include those who fled from Viet Nam after 1979 as well as their descendants.

Population: 78.4 million
Capital: Hanoi
Ethnic groups: Some 96 per cent of the population are ethnic Vietnamese; the rest are ethnic Chinese, Cambodian, Hmong or Montagnards.
Languages: Vietnamese, Chinese, Khmer and Hmong.

Events:

1887: Colonial power France controls all of present day Viet Nam, Laos and Cambodia.

1940: Japan invades French Indo-China. Communist leader Ho Chi Minh forms the Viet Minh, a broad-based independence movement, and fights a guerrilla war against the Japanese from a cave in northern Viet Nam.

1945: The Viet Mingh control most of northern Viet Nam. The Allies agree for Britain to administer the south and for China to administer the north.

September 1945: The Viet Mingh march into Hanoi before the Chinese and proclaim the Democratic Republic of Viet Nam. The British and French ruthlessly suppressed the Viet Minh, reconquering southern Viet Nam.

March 1946: The French - backed by the US who fear a communist takeover in South East Asia - install a colonial government in the south and guerrilla fighting continues with the Viet Mingh until 1954. Over 172,000 French soldiers are killed.

1954: The Viet Minh defeat the French. Viet Nam is divided in two along the 17th parallel with the Viet Mingh to govern the north, and the nationalist leader Ngo Dinh Diem to govern the south. Not all Vietnamese in the south support Diem's government which tortures and kills thousands of its opponents including Buddhist monks.

1961: The US help the south, send troops to Viet Nam and bomb the country including Cambodia and Laos. By 1973, nearly two million people are killed. Opposition in the US against the war in Viet Nam grows. US President Nixon is forced to hold peace talks.

1973: The US sign the Paris Agreement and withdraw from Viet Nam. But the North and South Vietnamese armies continue fighting.

1975: The North Vietnamese reach Saigon. The South Vietnamese government collapses. Viet Nam is united under a communist government. Many refugees flee the new communist government in Viet Nam. The first refugees to leave are mostly ethnic Vietnamese from the south who were officials in the former South Vietnamese government or have had close contact with the US during the war. Most flee to the US.

1977: 880,000 people flee, many by boat. Between 1977 and 1990 over 155,000 Vietnamese refugees from both north and south Viet Nam die at sea from dehydration, drowning or murder by pirates. Some were opponents of the new regime, who had been imprisoned in re-education camps. Others were north Vietnamese who did not want to be moved to farm the new economic zones.

1978: Relations between Viet Nam and China grow tense. Chinese people living in Viet Nam are subject to attacks in the press. Many ethnic Chinese flee Viet Nam to China, Hong Kong, Malaysia, Singapore, Indonesia, the Philippines and Hong Kong.

By **1979:** The exodus of people from Viet Nam is so great that the UN convenes in Geneva. Here the British Government agrees to accept 10,000 refugees from the camps in Hong Kong.

Vietnamese boat people.
© UNHCR

Information: Vietnamese refugees in the UK

About 65 per cent of Britain's Vietnamese community is from northern Viet Nam. Until 1979 Britain received very few Vietnamese refugees, mainly those rescued at sea by British registered ships. The 10,000 refugees from Hong Kong accepted as part of the First Vietnamese Settlement Programme came between 1979 and 1984. Three organisations ran reception centres. Save the Children, the Ockenden Venture, and the British Council for Aid to Refugees ran reception centres, where the refugees stayed for three to six months. They were then sent to local authority accommodation throughout Britain, where they received some initial support, but were soon left in isolation.

In 1984 the Government agreed to take another quota of refugees as part of the Second Vietnamese Programme. About 4,500 people arrived and they spent time in reception centres, then were sent to areas where there were existing Vietnamese communities. Between 1988 and 1992, another 2,000 Vietnamese people were allowed to settle in the UK. This group of people had all escaped Viet Nam and fled to Hong Kong.

The Vietnamese refugees were settled mainly in rural areas causing secondary migration. About 50 per cent of all Vietnamese refugees had already moved away from their first housing in the UK by 1989. Most of them have moved to major cities, particularly London, Birmingham and Manchester.

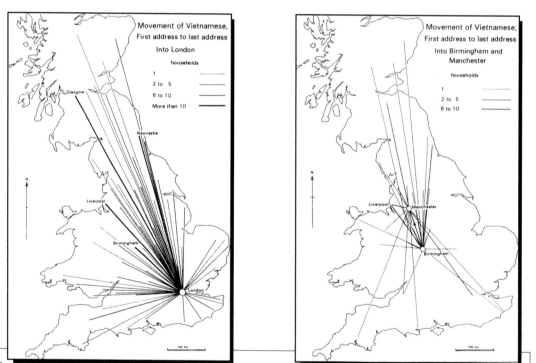

Discussion points:

⇨ What does secondary migration mean?

⇨ What do the maps show us about the secondary migration of Vietnamese?

⇨ Imagine you are a newly-arrived refugee. Make a list of the advantages of living in London. Then make a list of the advantages of living in a small town at least 100 miles from a large city.

⇨ The UK government still disperses newly-arrived asylum seekers. Asylum seekers who need housing are usually not allowed to live in Greater London. Instead they are given housing outside London, most often in towns and cities in the Midlands, northern England and Scotland. Do you think this is a good idea or not?

Nghi Luu's story

Nghi Luu is from Viet Nam. His family are ethnic Chinese. He came to the UK in 1979 and this is his story.

"Due to the conflict between the Vietnamese and Chinese governments, all the Chinese living in Viet Nam were deprived of their jobs and were driven to the new economic zones where the land had been poisoned by chemical bombs. Rice was the Vietnamese main food and was rationed by the government, as were other foods. Hunger was threatening most families because they could not afford to depend on the black market. No one could endure living like that, but the government neglected its people, they spent most of their money building up more modern weapons."

"Our problems forced us to think of a way out, and the idea of running away came into our mind. We sold most of our furniture and kept saving money for our secret journey. It cost a few thousand Vietnamese dongs for a place on the boat. I was in one of those boats together with my family and dozens of other families."

"When we first got into the open sea everyone was healthy and energetic, anxious to get going. After a few hours in the open sea, most of us seemed to be worn out or were seasick because we could no longer stand the rocking, jerking or shaking of the boat. But we were not demoralised by that."

"It wasn't long before the water ran out. Survival was hanging in the balance, because the possibility of bad weather or lack of food worsened the already serious lack of water. Some of us prayed for help and good luck from God. Imagine the sadness of all the people on the boat who were approaching death, yet still wanted desperately to live. I did not fear the physical act of dying, but I did not want to be dead."

"What a relief it was when we saw some fishing boats pass by. They came to us as soon as they saw us. Some of them were Chinese so we could communicate with them. We got their fish, lobsters and water in exchange for clothes."

"We kept going steadily for quite a few more days. But once again, water was the first to run out. On top of that there was hardly any wind at all. Food, too, soon ran out. 'Is this the end of us?' we thought. But no, in the far distance appeared a ship. But in vain, they were too far from us."

"Frankly, I can't remember exactly what happened the second time we saw another ship. But somehow we managed to attract their attention. It was a Chinese fishing ship. We appealed to them for a tow. They agreed, but we had to pay them with gold rings and chains. They gave us fresh water and food and left us just outside the Hong Kong water. Tall buildings appeared. By then the atmosphere on the boat was electric, some smiled and delighted expressions appeared in everyone's faces. We had been so lucky. Then we had help from the Hong Kong Authority patrol ship and were towed close to the dockyard where we were observed by apprehensive residents. We were supplied with food and water but were not allowed to go ashore until the next day."

Imagine the sadness of all the people on the boat who were approaching death, yet still wanted desperately to live. I did not fear the physical act of dying, but I did not want to be dead.

[Continued over page]

> ***I would like to say we are very grateful to the British government and British people for their kindness towards us.*** "

"We were overjoyed to be in the land of freedom but to our disappointment we were locked up there like in prison camps. Even the camp's officers were strict and furious. Everything in the camp had to be done under strict order. There were no beds in the camps so we all had to sleep on the floor. Food was brought in from the main kitchen outside. After a short spell in the Dockyard camp we moved on to less crowded conditions - an open-centre camp where we were free to go out. People were encouraged to get jobs and build up the things they needed while waiting for resettlement."

"When Britain offered a number of places to refugees, my family decided to take that opportunity. So we had interviews with consular officials and were accepted. By the time my family actually left the departure camp more than a year had passed since our arrival. It was a hard-working year, a year that gave us the opportunity to earn money. But it wasn't a good year for young people like me because we wasted a year of school."

"At the end of 1979 we were on a big jumbo jet flying towards our new homeland, the United Kingdom. At the airport the first thing we felt when we put our foot on the ground was the cold British weather. From the airport we were driven to a reception centre which was near an ex-RAF base at Thornley Island near Portsmouth. As soon as we arrived at the reception centre we were offered rooms and some of the basic things we needed in everyday life. There were about 50 rooms for families in this two storey old building."

"We all hoped to resettle not far away from each other so that when we left the centre we would not feel completely isolated. We left the centre at the beginning of 1980 and headed towards Milton Keynes, our new home. After about four hours' journey we finally approached our new home."

"A few days after settling down we all started school. At school I found myself completely lost in the middle of this huge school of about 1,500 students, because everything was so different, so strange at first. Living in a different world like this without knowing the language is really miserable, therefore we all worked hard to learn English."

"After only two years we swapped houses with an English family who lived in Tottenham, London and wished to move to a peaceful place like Milton Keynes. In London I joined the Gladesmore School Sixth Form, but I was the only Vietnamese student in the sixth form. I felt lonely and sorry for myself after leaving my teachers and all my friends."

"At Gladesmore it didn't take me long to settle down again. To end this story I would like to say we are very grateful to the British government and British people for their kindness towards us."

Vietnamese refugee family on a shopping trip to Soho, London.
© H. J. Davies / Exile Images

Information: Oral history

Nghi Luu's story was collected for an oral history project. Refugee pupils in one school wrote about important memories and events in their lives. The oral history project increased Nghi Luu's confidence as a young writer. His story was shared with other refugee children, who could understand that there were others who were in their position. Nghi Luu's story also helped all young people become more aware about the experiences of refugees. The boy's story also keeps the memory of the flight of Vietnamese refugees alive for future generations.

Nghi Luu's story is oral history. Oral history is history with a difference. Instead of relying on text books and experts, it draws on the experiences of ordinary people, giving them a chance to record their lives for themselves.

Oral history can

- shed new light on well-known events;
- build a more complete picture of a time, subject or area;
- fill in gaps left by other historians;
- give a voice to ordinary people who are seldom heard.

Every person has a history and can take part in oral history projects.

An oral history project is often centred around a topic or event, such as childhood, journeys, moving home, the Second World War and so on. Oral history involves

- collecting taped interviews from ordinary people;
- collecting written accounts written by ordinary people;
- collecting photographs, maps and other ordinary objects;
- collecting information about a family's history.

Activities: Oral history

There are many ways that students can be involved in oral history projects about migration and refugees.

Interviewing refugees in their community: Local refugee centres may be able to put a school in touch with a refugee speaker who is willing to be interviewed by a class. In the lesson preceding the visit, students should be given some background about that particular country. The class should then decide on the questions that they would like to ask the refugee speaker. The visit can be recorded; later students can write up the questions and answers.

Class oral history on the theme of 'journeys' or 'moving': Students can collect their own testimonies. They might work in pairs and formulate a list of questions. The paired students can then use a tape recorder to interview each other. After the interviews, each student can write up their interview and produce the material for a display. Alternatively students may want to produce their own written accounts of a journey or about moving. Some schools have published such oral history in booklets.

Activity ☞

All about our neighbourhood

Learning objectives: This activity helps students understand historical changes in their neighbourhood. It teaches students about the growth of multi-ethnic Britain.

Time needed: A series of lessons

Instructions: A local history project offers many opportunities to look at historical changes brought about by migration. The teacher will need to collect some primary and secondary sources about different migrant groups that have moved into the neighbourhood:

- Census data
- Old newspaper articles
- Photographs from a library or local history society
- Oral and written accounts of ordinary people
- Artefacts from a local museum

The information can be collected from the local history section in the local library, a local history society, a local museum, older members of the community and community bookshops. Other sources of evidence can be used to research historical change brought about by migration. Such sources can include:

⇨ **Place names:** These can indicate what groups of people have lived in the area. The class may be able to find examples of Celtic, Roman, Anglo-Saxon, Viking and Norman place names. A few street names indicate the nationality of a group of people that settled there, for example 'the Little Sanctuary' (London) is a small street near Westminster Abbey, where previously refugees sought safety. Jew Lane (Sheffield) was a street where Jewish people lived and worked. Petty France (London) was a place where Huguenot refugees settled.

⇨ **Buildings:** These can give clues about groups of people who have moved into a neighbourhood. The Huguenots built their own churches and their homes had a distinct architectural style. Children can find out if there are any Huguenot buildings in their locality. Places of worship are also worth researching. When were Roman Catholic churches built in the neighbourhood? What groups formed the congregation? Are there any synagogues in the locality? When were they built? Are there mosques, temples or gurudwaras? When were they built? A class visit to local places of worship may provide useful information.

⇨ **Businesses and shops:** These can give clues about recent local history. Children can research the restaurants and cafes of their neighbourhood. They can see if shops cater for the needs of certain communities. The travel agents and shops that offer cheap international telephone calls can also give clues about groups of people that live in the neighbourhood.

⇨ **Famous inhabitants:** People from different parts of the world may have stayed or lived in the neighbourhood. A library, local history society or local museum is often a good place to find out about the neighbourhood's well-known past residents.

⇨ **Oral history:** Children can interview older members of their family about changes to their neighbourhood. The school may also wish to contact local community groups and invite members to the school to be interviewed by children.

Children may wish to examine the reasons that each group has moved into the neighbourhood.

Once students have completed their research, they should then write up their project. They can make their own book about migration and change in their neighbourhood. Alternatively they can make a collage or displays about refugees and migrants in their neighbourhood.

Learning objectives: The activity develops students' research skills and enables them to understand changes brought about by migration.

Time needed: 45 minutes. A greater length of time can be spent on this activity if desired.

Instructions: Students will need access to local telephone directories, recent census data and, if available, a school language survey. Summaries of census data can be obtained from local libraries.

The activity should be introduced by explaining that many people living in the UK were born abroad or have ancestors who came from other nations. Three ways of studying this are to examine census data and to study people's family names.

The census: The teacher should explain about the census. Students should then be given local data from the 2001 census. They should compete the following tasks:

- Using your local census data find out what percentage of the population in your local authority was born outside the UK.
- List the five countries where most of the residents in your local authority were born.
- Using the census data can you find the names of countries from where people might have fled as refugees?

Family names: These can also give an approximate guide to the ethnic origins of people in a given area. However, some people change their names when they arrive in a new country or have new names given to them by officials.

Using a telephone directory, the teacher selects two pages where there are a reasonable number of different names. With a highlighting pen, students should mark all the names of people that they think may have families that have come from outside the UK.

- What percentage of names may originate from outside the UK?

School language survey: If this is available, students should be given a summary of its findings. They should be asked to represent and analyse the data.

> **NOTE**
>
> A **census** is a government survey which is carried out to count the population and find out other facts. In the UK, a census is carried out every ten years. The census usually records a person's country of birth.

Information: Refugees and displaced people who have fled Britain and Ireland

Refugees have been arriving and settling in the UK since the 13th century, but refugees and internally displaced people have also fled from the UK and Ireland. From 1100-1290 Jews were persecuted in England. Many were deliberately killed, as in York, Norwich and London. Others fled as refugees. All remaining Jews were expelled from England in 1290.

Many thousands of internally displaced people fled from their homes during the Middle Ages escaping violence. During the Reformation and English Civil War refugees fled from all parts of the British isles mostly because of their religious beliefs. John Calvin and John Knox, both Protestants, are just two well-known religious refugees who fled Scotland during the Reformation. Hundreds of Catholics also fled Scotland during the Reformation and settled in Poland.

In the Second World War, German bombing forced thousands of people to flee their homes. In Plymouth, the bombing was so heavy that almost everyone took a few belongings and fled. Some of these displaced people stayed with relatives, others walked and sought shelter in the countryside. The Second World War also saw the evacuation of children from cities to the countryside. Many of these evacuees were very unhappy in their foster homes in the countryside - they missed their parents greatly.

From 1968 to 1973, some 25,000 people from Northern Ireland fled to the Republic of Ireland to escape the violence of the Troubles. Although they did not have to apply for refugee status, their experiences are very similar to refugees.

August 12, 1943 - Blitz on Plymouth, bombing started at midnight.
© Denis Samuel Posten, taken from the website of the Canadian Firefighters in England during WW2.

- Chapter Four: Refugees 1930-80 -

Theresa's story

"It was 1971, just after internment I happened to live at the top of the Springfield Road, in Springfield Park … It was a lovely street, lovely neighbours. But there were Protestant estates either side and across the Springfield Road it was all Catholic estates, so when the Troubles began we were right bang in the middle."

"After 9th August 1971 things got really bad. There were streets burning. British soldiers, the IRA and Loyalist gunmen were shooting. At nights we took the mattress off the bed and lay on the floor. In between times there were bombs going off in Belfast. I went to my mother's but things were really bad there too. My Daddy had to put a mattress up against the back window."

"The following day a committee was set up - the Citizens' Defence Committee. They were sending round lorries for people who wanted to get away from the area. I had no notion of going away until I was making my way down the Springfield Road to see how my house was. Injured people were being ferried away in ambulances and I saw two lorries of furniture going up the road. I didn't get far when my Daddy stopped me and said not to go any further. My house was being wrecked. The furniture I'd seen on the lorries was mine. I decided to go away with the refugees the next day."

"By this stage nobody was thinking straight. My Mummy, my young sisters, myself and my children ended up getting in one of the lorries and going to the railway station. The train was packed with women and children. We got as far as Dundalk (in the Republic of Ireland) and a priest led us through the streets in a crocodile line … We were taken to Gormanstown where all the refugees had to register. The Irish Army had taken planes out of hangars and put rows and rows of mattresses in. Each family had a wee square each. Hundreds and hundreds of refugees were arriving each day. I remember going to the canteen. There were thousands queuing for everything."

British Army patrol in Sandy Row. Tensions were particularly high because of the marching season.
© **Panos Pictures / David Rose**

Ireland

Beth's story

"It all happened in 1972 when I was eight years old. My family lived off the Cliftonville Road in North Belfast at the time. It was an area known to be a flashpoint as Protestant and Catholic people lived in close proximity to each other. My father was a church minister. At the time he was regularly summoned to the streets to tend to many emergencies. When he came home he was always agitated, but would never tell us what he had been up to. He and Mum would talk in code about what he had been doing. The worst thing he must have witnessed must have been the day when he came upon a young policeman who had just been shot. He was the first on the scene and he cradled what was left of the man's head in his hands while he died."

"There was an intense period of street fighting during this time. There was an unofficial curfew and only the foolhardy would breach it. We used to lie in bed listening to the gunfire outside. My Mum used to get us all in one room and we'd lie on the floor or on the beds. My sister who was a year older than me used to cry with fear. I couldn't understand this and I found it somewhat exciting."

"We knew things were not right at school those days as there were bomb scares when we all trooped outside with our pac-a-macs on and our teachers would count us in a panic. One day part of the school was burnt down so we were sent home."

"I recall the strange day when my Mum and Dad collected us from school. The car was filled with sleeping bags and cases, and my parents were very nervous. They told us we were going on our holidays to see our Auntie who lived in Cork. We were delighted - an unexpected holiday on a farm. We had to get through a number of roadblocks and checkpoints to get to the station. We couldn't understand why our parents were not pleased about this surprise. We arrived at the railway station just in time and were bundled on a train. Once he saw that we were installed my Dad hugged my Mum and said goodbye as he hurried off the train. We wanted Dad to come with us. He kissed Mum through the train window as it pulled away from the platform. We waved at him as he got smaller in the distance. It was the first time I ever saw my Mum cry."

"We were refugees for a number of months before we were able to return. We were the lucky ones who had somewhere to go. My main memory is of the confusion between my perceptions of what was happening and that of my parents. It was the first time I had spent any time away from my Dad and that I'll never forget."

Discussion point

⇨ See if you can collect other testimonies of British people who became internally displaced or have had to become refugees.

5 Protecting the human rights of refugees

Burundian refugees at a camp in Rwanda. © UNHCR / B. Press

This chapter examines the development of international human rights law including international human rights laws to protect refugees. It also looks at organisations and people who have worked to protect the human rights of refugees.

Information: The development of international human rights law

People leave their homes and become refugees for a variety of reasons. What refugees have in common is that their human rights are not being respected in their home country. But what do we mean by human rights?

A right is something to which everyone is entitled. Rights that are laid down in law are called legal rights. Legal rights change as the laws of a country change. But not all laws are fair. People also have moral rights. Such rights reflect what is believed to be fair and just.

Human rights are universal moral rights. They apply to all people at all times and in all situations. Throughout history, there have been both governments and individual people who have worked for human rights. The French Revolution of 1789 resulted in the passage of a constitution which included the *Declaration of the Rights of Man* setting out the rights of French citizens. This included the right to personal freedom, property, security and freedom of speech. Soon after, philosophers began to think about what we mean by human rights. Among them were utilitarian philosophers such as **Jeremy Bentham** who thought that a test of human rights was to create the greatest good for the greatest number of people.

Political leaders became involved in developing human rights laws in the 20th century. After the horrors of the Second World War, representatives of 48 nations met and wrote the *Universal Declaration of Human Rights*, which the United Nations General Assembly passed in 1948. It aimed to create just societies in all countries of the world. There have been other international declarations about human rights such as the *1950 European Convention on Human Rights* and more recently the *1989 Declaration on the Rights of the Child*. The *1951 United Nations Convention Relating to the Status of Refugees* is the most important international human rights law to protect refugees.

Politicians, philosophers and ordinary people continue to discuss human rights. In 1998, the UK government passed the *Human Rights Act*. There was much debate about what comprised human rights at that time. Recently, across Europe, politicians and newspapers have been debating what rights asylum seekers should be given. These are difficult questions.

To help answer such questions and decide what are human rights, we can use a philosophical test called the 'veil of ignorance', developed by the American political philosopher **John Rawls** (1921-2002). His most important book was *A Theory of Justice*. Rawls believed that democratic governments must act to protect the human rights of individuals. In order to help people think about human rights, he developed the idea of the 'veil of ignorance'.

Rawls asked us to imagine a situation where a group of people are brought together to agree the principles and human rights of a future society. To ensure that they act impartially and not as a result of self-interest, they are placed behind 'the veil of ignorance'. The 'veil of ignorance' denies them any knowledge of their race, gender, social class, religion, talents and wealth. Not knowing what will be in their best interests as individuals or members of a group, their task is to devise human rights that are best for everyone.

The United Nations

The United Nations (UN) was founded on 24 October 1945. It replaced the League of Nations. It aims were

- to save the next generation from war;
- to protect human rights;
- to establish the conditions under which justice and respect for international law be met;
- to promote social progress.

The UN's headquarters are in New York. The head of the organisation is the UN Secretary-General, currently Kofi Annan. Power is shared by the UN General Assembly and the Security Council. The UN General Assembly is made up of representatives of all the UN's member countries. It meets for three months every year, and it can only pass resolutions. Firmer action must come from the UN Security Council. The Security Council has 15 members who are representatives from member countries. China, France, Russia, the UK and the US are the five permanent members of the Security Council. The remaining ten members of the Security Council are non-permanent members. They are chosen from the remaining countries of the world and serve a two-year term of office.

The UN also manages the work of a number of UN specialised agencies. These include:

The UN High Commissioner for Refugees
The UN High Commissioner for Human Rights
UNICEF (UN Children's Fund)
The World Health Organization
The World Food Programme
The World Bank
The International Monetary Fund

Find out about the work of the UN on the internet at: www.un.org

Activity

Wants and needs

Learning objectives: To enable students to link rights to real needs. The activity also helps students understand that 'needs' are different to 'wants'.

Time needed: 20 minutes

Instructions: The students should work in pairs. Each pair needs paper. The pairs should make a common list of 40 things that they think that they need for a happy life.

When students have produced their lists, bring the class together and explain the difference between things we want and things we really need. Explain that our real needs as children should be our rights.

The students should then go back into their pairs. The students should then cross off the items that are 'wants' from their list leaving only 'needs'. This list can then be used in the activity below, to help students draw up a charter of children's rights.

Activity

Drawing up a charter for children's rights

Learning objectives: At the end of the activity students will have considered the rights that all children should have.

Time needed: 45 minutes

Instructions: Pens and large sheets of paper are needed. Divide the class into groups of two or three. Explain about the *Universal Declaration of Human Rights* and the *Convention on the Rights of the Child*.

Each group should then work to produce a charter for children's rights. Each group should decide on ten things that children around the world should have. The charters should then be pinned up and compared. Obviously, each charter will be different.

The teacher or group leader can discuss similarities and differences in the charters and then use the charters to produce one common charter. The charters can also be illustrated.

Discussion points:

⇨ Do you have all the things you listed in your charter?

⇨ Do you think young refugees have all the things listed in your charter?

⇨ Can you think of other groups of children who do not have the rights that you listed?

Information:

The Universal Declaration of Human Rights in simple language

Article 1: All people are born free and equal and should behave with respect to each other.

Article 2: Everyone should have the rights outlined in the *Universal Declaration* regardless of their race, colour, sex, nationality, religion, political opinion or social origin.

Article 3: Everyone has a right to live in freedom and safety.

Article 4: No one has a right to make people slaves.

Article 5: No one should be tortured or punished in a cruel way.

Article 6: The law must treat everyone as people not objects.

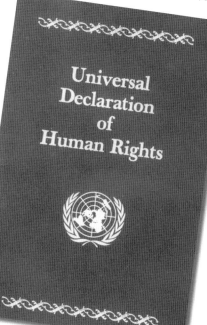

Article 7: Laws must not treat people differently because of their race, sex or way of life.

Article 8: Everyone has a right to legal protection if their rights are ignored.

Article 9: Nobody should be arrested, kept in prison or sent away from their country without a just reason.

Article 10: Everyone is entitled to a fair and public trial if charged with an offence.

Article 11: If charged with an offence, a person should be considered innocent until it is proven that he or she is guilty.

Article 12: A person has a right to privacy. No one has a right to say untrue and damaging things against another person.

Article 13: Everyone has a right to travel and live anywhere in their home country. A person also has the right to leave any country, including his or her own, and to return to it.

Article 14: People have the right to ask for asylum in another country if they fear persecution. A person loses the right to ask for asylum if he or she has committed a serious non-political crime and has not respected the *Universal Declaration of Human Rights*.

Article 15: Everyone has a right to a nationality.

Article 16: Every adult person has the right to marry and have children. Men and women have equal rights in marriage and if they divorce. No one should be forced to marry against his or her will.

Article 17: Everyone has the right to own property. No one can take other people's possessions without a fair reason.

Article 18: Everyone has the right to think and believe in what they want including the right to practise a religion.

Article 19: Everyone has the right to express their thoughts whether by speaking or in writing.

Universal Declaration of Human Rights

Article 20: Everyone has the right to organise peaceful meetings and to form groups. But no one can be forced to join an organisation.

Article 21: Everyone has the right to take part in the government of his or her country, whether by voting or being an elected member of parliament. Fair elections should be held regularly and everyone's vote is equal.

Article 22: Everyone has the right to social security. This includes shelter, health care and enough money on which to live.

Article 23: Everyone has the right to work. Wages should be fair and enable a family to live decently. Men and women should receive the same pay for doing the same work. A person has the right to join a trade union.

Article 24: Everyone has the right to reasonable working hours, rest and paid holidays.

Article 25: Everyone has the right to a decent standard of living. Those who cannot work should receive special help. All children, whether born outside marriage or not, have the same rights.

Article 26: Everyone has the right to education. Primary education should be free and compulsory. A person should be able to continue his or her studies as far as he or she is able. Education should help people live with and respect other people. Parents have the right to choose the kind of education that will be given to their child.

Article 27: Everyone has the right to join in cultural activities and enjoy the arts. Anything that a person writes or invents should be protected and the person should be able to benefit from its creation.

Article 28: For human rights to be protected, there must be order and justice in the world.

Article 29: A person has responsibilities to other people. A person's rights and freedoms should be limited only so far as to protect the rights of other people.

Article 30: No government, group or person may ignore the rights set out in the *Universal Declaration of Human Rights*.

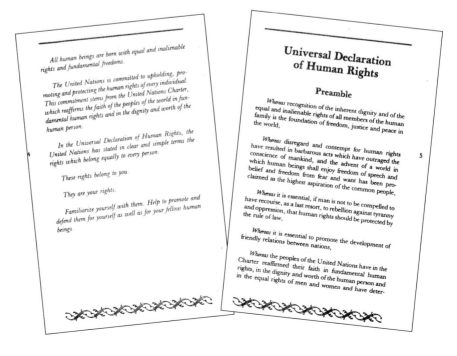

Learning objectives: In this activity students will familiarise themselves with the *Universal Declaration of Human Rights*.

Time needed: 30 minutes preparation time and about 60 minutes in the group.

Instructions: Students will need copies of the simplified version of the *Universal Declaration of Human Rights*. (The group leader may should prepare sets of articles for distribution.) Each set should be place in an envelope.

The class should be divided into pairs with each pair receiving a set of articles.

The groups are going to examine the *Universal Declaration of Human Rights*. Each pair should read through each article, taking turns to do this. After each student has read an article, the pair should decide whether they agree with it or not. Do they think what each article states is a human right?

Make a group decision on this. Divide the articles into two piles:

- Human rights with which we agree
- Statements which we don't think are human rights

The class should then come together for a discussion.

Additional activity

Using newspapers, students can find examples of people losing their human rights.

Discussion points:

⇨ What did everyone think was a human right?

⇨ Were there any statements with which everyone disagreed?

⇨ Can our rights as individuals conflict with the rights of other groups of people?

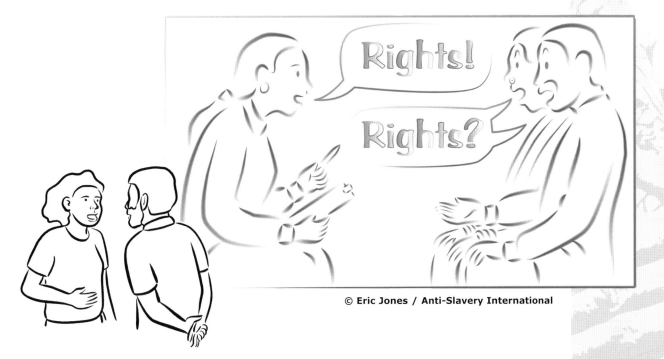

© Eric Jones / Anti-Slavery International

Activity ☝

Using the 'veil of ignorance' to help us think about refugees' rights

Learning objectives: To familiarise students with John Rawls' concept of the 'veil of ignorance' as a way to decide about rights. The activity examines asylum seekers' rights.

Time needed: At least 1 hour

Instructions: All students should receive a copy of the information on the development of international human rights law. Each student will need paper, pen and a role card (see page 93), which will need to be copied beforehand. About one third of the cards should be those of asylum seekers. The role cards should be folded and stapled, so that students cannot see the characters they will play.

The activity is best run in a hall and the optimum number of participants is 20 to 30. Students should have completed some preparatory work on human rights. The teacher or group leader should give students an explanation about John Rawls' idea of the 'veil of ignorance' with us being ignorant of our interests. The group leader may also need to remind students of the definition of an asylum seeker. The class should then be divided into groups of five. Each group represents a country. The students should be told that the year is now 2020. There is peace throughout the world and very few human rights violations. The nations of the world have decided to revise their laws on the rights of asylum seekers.

Students should spend 10 to 15 minutes in their country groups deciding on the rights of asylum seekers. These rights could include the right to enter a country and seek asylum, quotas for asylum seekers, where asylum seekers might live, the rights to benefit payments, schooling or medical care. Each country group should then write a charter of five to ten points outlining the rights of asylum seekers. The groups may be generous or very restrictive towards asylum seekers. The charters will then form the basis of asylum law in that particular country.

Students should remain in their country groups. Each student should then be given a stapled role card. The class should then be told that it is 2030 and the world is a different place. Students should open their role cards. Some will have to leave their 'country' and try to enter another country as an asylum seeker. They should move from country to country stating their situation. The country groups should refer to their charters and decide what to do with each new asylum seeker.

All asylum seekers must try and find new countries, or have tried to gain admission to all countries and failed. At the end of the simulation the group should be brought together for a discussion.

Discussion points:

⇨ What did you learn from this activity?

⇨ How did you feel after you found out your role?

⇨ How did the 'asylum seekers' feel when they were refused entry to a country?

⇨ How did the 'citizens' feel at the end of the activity?

⇨ Were any of the 'asylum seekers' in 2030 from countries that were harsh to asylum seekers in 2020? How did they feel?

⇨ Who do you think should write international human rights laws?

⇨ Treat others as you wish to be treated yourself. Do you agree or disagree with this statement?

Role cards

You own a business making clothing. Recently you have found it hard to recruit workers.	You are a school student in a secondary school in the capital city of your country.
You work in a bank. You got that job because you speak four languages. You got your language skills from your parents who came to your country as refugees over 40 years ago.	You used to work as a farm labourer but you are currently unemployed. There are no benefits in your country.
You are a politician representing a very poor city in your country.	You are a farmer producing milk, meat, wheat, potatoes and onions. You own enough land to have a good standard of living.
You work as a manager in a factory making computer parts. You have a nice house, a car and enjoy eating out with your family.	You are a pensioner. You live in your own home and get a pension from the government and from your former employer. You have a long memory and enjoy telling people about what we can learn from the past.
You sell fruit and vegetables on a market stall in a very poor country.	You are a doctor in a government clinic.
You were a doctor. But your ethnic group has been discriminated against for many years. Now things have got worse. You have lost the right to work and to vote in your home country. You have decided to leave and seek asylum in another country.	You are a farm labourer working in fields near the border. Life was good until the civil war started. Now the fighting has got near. You fear being killed by the guerrillas or the army. You have decided to run and to seek asylum in another country.
You are a school student. Your parents have been detained by the government because of their occupation. Your parents both worked for an organisation that tried to stop damage to the environment. Your grandmother gives you some money and tells you to leave the country. You leave and seek asylum in another country.	You were a factory worker and a member of a religious minority. Now people who openly practice your religion face arrest. You have decided to leave and seek asylum in another country.
You are a famous footballer. But there is civil war in your home country. Life has become dangerous and uncomfortable. You have decided to leave and seek asylum in another country.	

Information: Human rights and refugees

Refugees are people who have been forced to flee because they have lost their human rights in their home country. But refugees also need their rights to be protected in their new countries.

One of the human rights that was being discussed during the early part of the 20th century was the right of people who had been forced to flee from their homes. These people - refugees - needed to be protected from danger. As international human rights law began to develop, so did international law to protect refugees.

Between 1912 and 1921 there were huge movements of people in Europe. During the Balkan Wars of 1912-1913, Greeks, Bulgarians and Turks fled from their homes. Soon afterwards, thousands of Armenians and Assyrians living in the Ottoman Empire were uprooted and became refugees. The chaos of the First World War (1914-1918) caused over six million people to become refugees.

Between 1917 and 1921, over 1.5 million people became refugees in the Soviet Union. The fighting with Germany during the First World War caused Russians, Ukrainians, Germans and others to flee their homes. In 1917 the Tsar was overthrown by the Bolsheviks. The Bolshevik-led Russian Revolution was opposed by some Russians who joined the White Russian army. Fighting between the Bolshevik Red Army and the White Russian army caused thousands of other people to flee.

As a result of the Russian Revolution, the League of Nations - an international organisation which worked like the United Nations does today - became concerned about the plight of refugees. In January 1946, the United Nations was formed and the League of Nations ceased to exist.

The League of Nations defined refugees as people who were in danger if they returned to their home countries. In 1921, it appointed the Norwegian explorer, **Fridjof Nansen**, as the High Commissioner for Russian refugees. Within a few years, Nansen was asked to help other groups of refugees such as the Greeks and Turks.

Nansen died in 1930, and the League of Nations underwent many changes in the 1930s. Some of these changes were necessary to meet the needs of refugees escaping from the Spanish Civil War and Nazi Germany. By 1938 Nansen's organisation was called 'The Office of the High Commissioner for Refugees under the Protection of the League of Nations'.

But the upheavals of the Second World War stopped this organisation from working effectively. It was replaced by a short-lived organisation called the United Nations Relief and Rehabilitation Organisation which helped refugees between 1943 and 1946. This organisation helped some of the 30 million refugees who were homeless at the end of the Second World War.

When the United Nations replaced the League of Nations in 1946, it set up a new body called the International Refugee Organisation, which handed over its responsibilities to a new body, the United Nations High Commissioner for Refugees (UNHCR), in 1951. At the same time, the United Nations General Assembly passed the *1951 UN Convention Relating to the Status of Refugees*. This

- defined a refugee as someone who has "a well-founded fear of persecution for reasons of race, religion, nationality, membership of a particular social group or political opinion";
- protects asylum seekers by requiring governments who have signed the Convention to allow them to present their case to stay in a way that is fair;
- prevents refugees being returned to places where they would be endangered.

The *1951 UN Convention Relating to the Status of Refugees* only protected people who had been displaced by conflict in Europe. In 1967, the UN added an extra piece of human rights law to the *1951 UN Convention Relating to the Status of Refugees* - the *1967 UN Protocol Relating to the Status of Refgees*. This allowed UNHCR to work with all groups of refugees not just those in Europe. Today, the 1951 Convention and the 1967 Protocol are still the most important human rights law protecting refugees. By 2004, 142 countries had signed the *1951 UN Convention Relating to the Status of Refugees*.

There are other international human rights laws about refugees. In 1969, African countries drafted the *Organisations of African Unity (OAU) Convention* which governs the specific aspects of refugee problems in Africa. This broadened the definition of who is a refugee to include people who had fled in the chaos of war. As well as people fleeing their home countries as a result of persecution, the OAU definition of a refugee includes people who have fled due to "external aggression, occupation, foreign domination or events seriously disturbing public order."

Fridtjof Nansen, High Commissioner for Refugees, League of Nations 1921-1930 (Norway). © **UNHCR/1908**

Information: Refugees from Indonesia

1960s: Many poor Indonesians support the Indonesian Communist Party during the height of the Cold War. The US and the UK help political leaders opposing the Indonesian Communist Party financially.

Population: 232 million
Capital: Jakarta
Ethnic groups: Javanese (45 per cent), Sundanese (14 per cent); Madurese (7.5 per cent), coastal Malays (7.5 per cent)
Religion: Islam (88 per cent), Christianity (8 per cent), Hinduism (2 per cent).

Events:

1670-1900: Dutch colonists bring the whole of Indonesia under their control naming the country the Dutch East Indies. By the 20th century Indonesia people begin to want their independence from the Dutch.

1942: The Japanese invade the Dutch East Indies helping the Indonesian independence leader, Sukarno, to return and declare independence. A four-year guerrilla warfare with the Dutch begins.

1949: The Dutch finally give Indonesia independence (not including West Papua and East Timor).

1950s: The Molucca Islands declare independence from Indonesia and wage an unsuccessful guerrilla war against Indonesian rule.

1965: President Sukarno is overthrown by Mohammed Suharto. The Indonesian army kills at least 500,000 suspected Communists.

1969: West Papua becomes part of Indonesia and is called Irian Jaya Province. Some West Papuans take up arms to fight for independence.

1976: Indonesia invades newly independent East Timor. There are many concerns about human rights violations in Indonesia. Opposition politicians, human rights activists and trade unionists are at risk. People supporting independence for West Papua and East Timor also risk arrest or worse.

Late 1990s: There is growing dissatisfaction with President Suharto's rule. There is also an economic crisis. Widespread protests and riots - of which Chinese people are targets - lead to Suharto resigning. Some Chinese flee as refugees.

1999: Ethnic violence increases. In Ambon and Halmahera in the Molucca Islands, armed Christian and Muslim groups force thousands of people to flee.

2001: There is more ethnic violence in Kalimantan as indigenous Dayaks forced out Madurese settlers.

2002: Indonesia sets up a human rights court which is expected to try military leaders for atrocities in East Timor in 1999. It also signs a peace agreement with the Free Aceh Movement (Gam) to try and end 26 years of violence.

2003: Peace talks between the Indonesian Government and Gam separatists break down. The army launches a military offensive against Gam guerrillas in Aceh.

By 2004: Indonesia is a very unstable country, and over 700,000 Indonesian people have become internally displaced by six conflicts:

- There is continued violence in the Maluku province between armed Muslims and Christians.

- In Aceh, the struggle for independence between Gam guerrillas and the Indonesian army has forced over 200,000 people to flee.

- An armed group is fighting for independence in Irian Jaya in West Papua.

- There is continued violence between Muslims and Christians in central Sulawesi.

- Conflict between indigenous Dayak people and Madurese settlers has forced thousands of people to flee in west and central Kalimantan.

- Armed Christians and Muslims have fought each other in Lombok in Bali.

There are also many concerns about human rights in Indonesia. Here is what Amnesty International said about human rights in Indonesia in 2002:

"In Aceh and Irian Jaya the human rights situation remained grave, with hundreds of reported cases of extrajudicial execution, 'disappearance', torture and unlawful arrest. The government's failure to take decisive action to end human rights violations undermined efforts to resolve the conflicts resulting from long-standing demands for independence. Impunity was reinforced by the failure of trials of the ad-hoc Human Rights Court on East Timor to satisfactorily resolve serious crimes, including crimes against humanity, committed in 1999 in East Timor."

Indonesia

(Taken from the Amnesty International Report 2003. This is available on the internet at www.amnesty.org)

East Timor

East Timor, a Portuguese colony in the 17th century, was part of Indonesia between 1976 and 2002.

In 1974 the new Portuguese government overthrew the facist regime promising freedom for East Timor. In 1975 Fretilin (Revolutionary Front for an Independent East Timor) declared East Timor to be independent. But the Indonesian army invaded it using its fight against communism as a pretext. Many East Timorese joined Fretilin to fight for independence. Over 250,000 East Timorese people probably died between 1975 and 2002. The Indonesian government encouraged Javanese people to settle in East Timor to secure greater control.

In the UN-organised referendum in 1999, 78 per cent of East Timorese voted for independence. But many Javanese settlers opposed independence. Some organised themselves into armed militia groups. After the referendum, these militia went on a killing spree helped by the Indonesian army. Over 1,000 East Timorese were killed and 250,000 people fled from their homes, mostly to West Timor. Soon an Australian-led peace-keeping force arrived and restored some order. Many of the anti-independence militia members fled to West Timor to avoid arrest. Finally, the Indonesian parliament agreed to grant independence to East Timor. Xanana Gusmao, the Timorese independence leader, was released from house arrest. In May 2002 East Timor became an independent country.

Carmel Budiardjo's story

Carmel Budiardjo is a British citizen who was forced to flee Indonesia in 1971 and returned to London. Throughout her life she has worked to help endangered people.

Carmel Budiardjo originally went to Indonesia in 1951 after marrying an Indonesian government official. Her husband was imprisoned for 'political offences' after President Suharto seized power. In 1965 he was sent to prison without trial for 12 years. Carmel herself was detained for three years without trial or charge, before being forced to leave Indonesia in 1971.

In 1973 there was a small demonstration of human rights activists outside the Indonesian Embassy in London. Many of the demonstrators went on to found TAPOL, a campaign for human rights in Indonesia. The organisation's name comes from 'tapol', a contraction of two Indonesian words meaning 'political prisoner'. In the 1970s much of TAPOL's work was to campaign for the release of hundreds of thousands of political prisoners who had been held as being suspected of sympathising with the communist party. Many of the political prisoners had been jailed without trial. But TAPOL's work soon broadened as human rights violations in Indonesia and East Timor worsened.

Carmel Budiardjo has now run TAPOL for 30 years. It has a small staff base who work in her house but many volunteer supporters. Part of the work has been to publish the TAPOL bulletin documenting human rights abuses in Indonesia and East Timor. Under Carmel's leadership, TAPOL has also campaigned against the UK selling arms to Indonesia.

In 1995 Carmel Budiardjo won Right Livelihood, an international award given to individuals and groups who have worked to promote human rights or to facilitate conflict resolution and environmental sustainability.

Indonesians crossing the West-East Timor border on foot in 1999.
© **UNHCR / M. Kobayashi**

Learning objectives: At the end of the activity, students will know more about some of the individuals who have worked to protect the human rights of refugees.

Time needed: About 1 hour for the first part of the activity.

Instructions: Students will need access to the internet, A4 card, pens and coloured crayons. The activity should be introduced by explaining that many people have worked to defend the human rights of refugees. Some people working to defend refugee rights are refugees and others are not. The class is going to research the background of some of these defenders of refugee rights.

Each student should be allocated one of the names listed below. They should write down their brief life story. The students should describe how they have worked for refugee rights. If possible, a picture of the person should be found.

Students should then produce a biography card of their allocated person. These can be illustrated. They should be used to make a collage about defenders of refugees' rights.

The activity can be extended. Students could also be asked to give short class presentations about each person. Students can also research local people who support refugees' rights including students in local schools.

Defenders of refugees' rights

- Chinua Achebe
- The Dalai Lama
- Jose Ramos Horta
- Leah Manning
- Rigoberta Menchu
- Fridjof Nansen
- Sadako Ogata
- Alicia Partnoy
- Abune Paulos
- Arne Rinnan
- Edward Said
- Jelena Silajdzic
- Nicholas Winton

Information: Protecting human rights - Amnesty International and Young Amnesty

Amnesty International is a pressure group that campaigns for human rights. Using information supplied by Amnesty International's headquarters in London, ordinary people in many countries write protest letters to governments and other groups which abuse human rights. Young Amnesty brings together young people to work for human rights.

How Amnesty began

In November 1960, **Peter Beneson**, a 40 year old lawyer who lived in London, read a newspaper article about two Portuguese students. In Portugal, their home country, the government was a fascist dictatorship. The two students had been arrested and sentenced to seven years' imprisonment for raising their glasses in a public toast to political freedom.

Angered by this injustice, Peter Beneson thought about ways that the Portuguese government - and other repressive governments - could be persuaded to release such victims. His idea was to send thousands of letters of protest to the Portuguese government.

Together with **Eric Baker**, a Quaker, and lawyer Louis Blom-Cooper and others, Peter Beneson launched a one-year campaign. It was called 'Appeal for Amnesty, 1961' and highlighted the fate of prisoners of conscience. The campaign was launched with an article in the Observer newspaper. It focussed on eight prisoners of conscience. The article received a tremendous response. Many people sent letters of support and money. Other people volunteered to work for the campaign. And, importantly, more information about other prisoners of conscience was collected. Amnesty International had begun.

In the next 12 months Amnesty International sent delegations to four countries to lobby on behalf of prisoners of conscience. They took up another 210 cases of prisoners of conscience. In its first year, Amnesty International set up national bodies in seven different countries.

AMNESTY INTERNATIONAL
UNITED KINGDOM

Today, Amnesty International has over one million members in 150 different countries. There are national sections of Amnesty International in 55 countries. Amnesty International's headquarters, known as the International Secretariat, are in London. Here staff collect and analyse information about human rights violations. Individual members and national sections are then mailed with 'actions'. The 'actions' contain information about human rights abuses to help individuals and groups write protest letters to authorities that are not respecting human rights.

Amnesty International 2003
National Conference in Belfast.
© Marie-Anne Ventoura/AIUK

- Chapter Five: Protecting the human rights of refugees -

The work of Amnesty International

Amnesty International works to uphold international human rights laws such as the *Universal Declaration of Human Rights*. Its mandate outlines the type of work that the organisations should do. Amnesty International seeks

- The release of all prisoners of conscience - Prisoners of conscience are people detained for their beliefs, colour, sex, ethnic origin, language or religion. Prisoners of conscience must not have used or supported violence.
- Fair and prompt trials for all political prisoners.
- Abolition of the death penalty and an end to extrajudicial execution - Amnesty International opposes all executions. It campaigns against killings ordered by legal systems - the death penalty. Amnesty International also opposes killings outside the legal system. These are called extrajudicial executions.
- An end to torture and other cruel, inhuman or degrading treatment of prisoners
- An end to 'disappearances' - Amnesty International opposes such practices. Disappearances are where individuals are detained by governments or security forces, but their detention is never admitted. People who have 'disappeared' may be prisoners of conscience, or be facing torture or death.
- An end to human rights violations by opposition groups - Amnesty International opposes practices such as killings, torture and hostage-taking by opposition groups. However, it believes the responsibility to uphold human rights to be a matter primarily for governments. This is because only governments are bound by international law.
- An end to the forcible return of refugees - Amnesty International opposes the return of refugees to situations where they would face imprisonment for their beliefs, or torture, execution or cruel, inhuman and degrading treatment.

It is very important that Amnesty International is seen as an independent and impartial organisation. Therefore Amnesty International does not accept funds from governments.

Young Amnesty

Young Amnesty is for people under 18 years. It was started in 1988 and now has over 10,000 members in the UK. Young Amnesty members are active as individuals, or in Young Amnesty groups in schools and colleges. Every year, Young Amnesty holds a conference for its members.

Young Amnesty members are involved in

- Letter-writing
- Fundraising
- Information campaigns
- Contacting MPs and MEPs
- Writing press releases

For more information, contact Young Amnesty, Amnesty International (UK), 99-119 Rosebery Avenue, London EC1R 4RE.

Information: Collecting evidence of human rights abuses

Accurate, reliable evidence about human rights abuses in different countries is essential for organisations working to support refugees or to promote human rights.

Lawyers working with asylum seekers in the UK need to know how they were persecuted and why they fled in order to present evidence to the Home Office of the UK government. In order to be given refugee status in the UK, asylum seekers have to present evidence of persecution in their home countries. Often, lawyers who represent asylum seekers obtain evidence from Amnesty International.

The Refugee Council also needs to know why refugees flee and the human rights conditions in their home countries. It needs this information to ensure that asylum seekers are treated justly in this country. For example, in 2003 many Afghan asylum seekers were refused refugee status, as the UK government did not believe that they would be in danger in Afghanistan. The Refugee Council gathered its own human rights information on Afghanistan and was able to challenge the policy of the UK government.

Evidence about human rights violations has to be accurate. How do organisations like Amnesty International collect their evidence?

Amnesty International

Amnesty International has a large research department based at its international headquarters in London. Each researcher is responsible for an individual country or a small number of countries, and uses a wide range of information sources to monitor events there. Information sources include:

- The statements of people who have suffered or witnessed human rights abuses
- The statements of lawyers acting for people who have suffered human rights abuses
- Newspapers, radio and television reports
- Evidence from journalists who have fled a particular country
- Academics
- Human rights groups within a particular country
- The statements of prisoners
- The statements of relatives and friends of prisoners, or people who have disappeared or been killed
- Evidence from religious organisations, community groups and trade unions
- Evidence from refugees who have fled a particular country
- Diplomats
- Human rights research missions to a particular country

All the information that Amnesty International receives has to be checked very carefully. Where Amnesty International is dealing with allegations rather than established facts, it will say so. If Amnesty International makes a mistake, it issues a correction immediately. Many other organisations, including the Refugee Council, rely on the accuracy of Amnesty International information. And if Amnesty International is to lobby governments, its information has to be seen as independent and accurate.

Learning objectives: The activity helps students determine the objectivity of different types of evidence.

Time needed: 30 minutes

Instructions: Each student needs a copy of the student instructions and statements (page 104). They also need marker pens in three different colours. The activity should be introduced with an explanation about collecting evidence. The students should then be divided into pairs. Each pair should examine the statements and answer the questions.

Student instructions

British and Irish human rights researchers visited Indonesia after 11 villagers were shot and killed by the Indonesian army. Three other villagers have disappeared. The human rights researchers talked to many people. To be able to take further action, the researchers need clear evidence of human rights abuses. Read the statements below and decide:

- Which statements provide clear evidence of human rights abuse? Why? Underline these in one colour.
- Which statements need further investigation? Why? Underline these statements in a different colour.
- Which statements are not reliable as evidence of human rights abuse? Why? Underline these in a different colour.

The homes of many East Timorese were devastated during the militia rampage following a ballot on self-determination.
© UNHCR / M. Kobayashi

Statements

A priest living in the next village says that the day after the shooting, a visitor to his church said that three villagers had disappeared.

A villager gives an account of being dragged out of his bed by soldiers and taken to the army camp. He is held in the camp for three days before being released.

A villager alleges she was forced out of her house by soldiers and taken to an army camp. Here she was beaten. She has severe bruising on her back which she says is from the beating.

A farmer finds a body buried on his land just outside the village. The body has a gunshot wound.

An Indonesian soldier deserts from the army. He goes into hiding but contacts a human rights organisation. He gives them an account of how soldiers were ordered to shoot villagers and to cause terror.

A villager reports that on the night of the shooting, she heard much shouting coming from a neighbour's house.

A villager reports that he heard shots being fired.

There has been a long history of conflict in this area. Separatist guerrillas want independence for this province. The Indonesian army has responded by terrorising villagers who it suspects of supporting the guerrillas.

A school teacher, now a refugee in Australia, reports that he saw the body of one of his students taken away by soldiers.

A newsletter from an opposition political group that supports the separatist guerrillas, reports that a number of villagers were shot and killed by the Indonesian army.

The Indonesian government denies to journalists that villagers were shot or arrested. It has stated that the villagers have made up the reports of the shooting because they support the separatist guerrillas and want to gain publicity for their cause.

 # Persecution

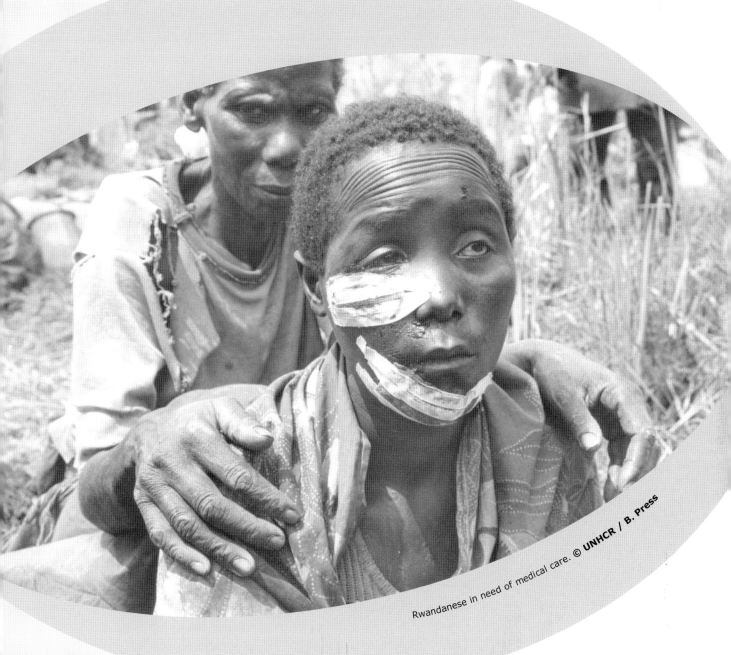

Rwandanese in need of medical care. © UNHCR / B. Press

Many refugees have fled persecution. This chapter examines what persecution means and how it impacts on people's lives. Torture and genocide are forms of persecution examined in this chapter. Sri Lanka, Rwanda and Burundi are used as case studies.

Learning objectives: At the end of the activity participants will have some understanding of what is meant by persecution.

Time needed: 30 minutes

Instructions: The quotations below should be copied for each student. There should then be a whole class discussion about persecution. The teacher or group leader should explain

- that 'persecution' is a common experience for many of the world's refugees;

- that to be granted refugee status in the UK and be allowed to stay, asylum seekers have to prove that they have fled their own countries or are unable to return to them "owing to a well-founded fear of being persecuted for reasons of race, religion, nationality, membership of a particular social group or political opinion" - this definition is taken from the *1951 UN Convention Relating to the Status of Refugees*;

- that the word persecution can be difficult to define as different governments have their own definitions of what makes persecution. This difficulty leads to asylum seekers being treated differently in different countries. For example, the Canadian government accepts that Eastern European Roma asylum seekers have been persecuted. It grants them refugee status and allows them to remain in Canada. The UK government does not accept that Eastern European Roma asylum seekers are persecuted in their country. They are not granted refugee status and are usually forced to return to their country.

The students should be divided into pairs. They should use the ideas in the quotations and write a paragraph about what they believe makes persecution.

The students should then mark the quotations in the box below where they believe the speaker is being persecuted. When the students have finished, some of the definitions should be read out and compared.

"I want to leave my country and it is illegal for me to do this."

"Military service is compulsory in my country and I do not want to serve in the army. I believe what the army is doing is wrong."

"I want to buy more land and expand my farm, but it is illegal for me to own a lot of land."

"My parents are going to force me to marry someone I do not want to marry."

"It is illegal for me to practise my religion and I wish to do so."

"I want to divorce my husband. But if I do that I may never be allowed to see my children again."

"I have already spent four years in prison for criticising the government in a public meeting. I am worried that I may be arrested again."

"I have been attacked because I am gay."

"I am in danger of being arrested because of my political beliefs. Those who are arrested are often tortured in my country."

"I cannot get a better job because my name and my papers show I belong to a certain religious group."

"It is illegal to speak my home language in schools in my country."

"My political party has been made illegal."

Information: Sri Lanka

There are over 71,000 Tamil refugees living in the UK. Sri Lanka was known as Ceylon until 1972.

Population: 17 million
Capital: Colombo
Ethnic groups: Some 74 per cent of the population are Sinhalese. They speak Sinhala as a first language and are mostly Buddhist. Another 18 per cent of people are Tamils. Some of the Tamils are descendants of people brought from south India in the 19th century. They speak Tamil as a first language. Most Tamils are Hindu although a small number are Christian. Muslims make up 7 per cent of the population and speak Tamil as their first language.

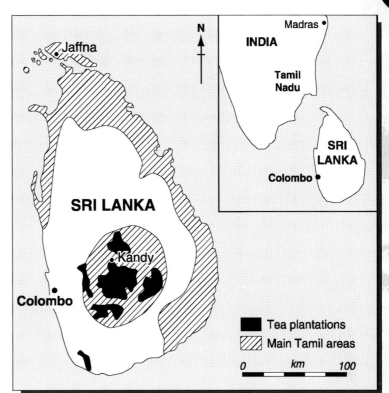

Events:

1505: The Portuguese colonists arrive trading in spices.

1656: The Dutch colonise Portuguese Ceylon and introduce plantation crops such as coffee, sugar cane, spices and tobacco.

1796: Parts of northern Ceylon are handed over to the British East India Company to expand plantation agriculture and the spice trade.

1802: Ceylon becomes a British colony.

1840: The British pass the 'Waste Land Ordinance' which allows them to claim any land of which ownership cannot be proven. As few farmers hold title deeds, the British colonists claim much land and sell it cheaply to plantation owners. Over 200,000 Tamils are brought from southern India as indentured labour to work on the plantations.

1944: The Soulbury Commission arrives from London to prepare Ceylon for independence. Tamil politicians request legal safeguards to protect their rights.

1949: Ceylon gains independence but the new government promptly passes the Citizenship Act making all Plantation Tamils stateless.

1956: Sinhala replaces English to become Ceylon's official language and the language of government. Many Tamils protest, fearing the loss of government jobs. Twelve Tamil MPs and their supporters stage a peaceful protest outside Parliament. A Sinhalese crowd stones the protestors while the police take no action. Rioting spreads to many parts of Colombo. Over 150 Tamils die.

1958: Sinhalese crowds attack Tamils. Over 1,000 are killed. British and French ships rescue some of the Tamils stranded by the riots.

Sri Lanka

1964: India and Ceylon sign an agreement allowing 525,000 Plantation Tamils Indian citizenship and return to India. Another 300,000 Plantation Tamils are given Ceylonese citizenship and allowed to stay.

1972: Ceylon becomes Sri Lanka. Buddhism is declared state religion. There are no more legal safeguards to protect minorities' rights.

1976: Tamil leaders meet and call for a separate state for Tamils, which is widely supported by the Tamil people. Tamil Eelam, the proposed state, would be located in northern and eastern Sri Lanka. Young Tamils form a group that later becomes the Liberation Tigers of Tamil Eelam (LTTE). They soon resort to armed struggle to try and gain independence.

1983: A week of riots leaves 2,500 Tamils dead, 150,000 people in refugee camps, and 23,000 homes and businesses destroyed. Many Tamils leave Colombo for good, fleeing to northern and eastern Sri Lanka where they are not in a minority. Others flee to India, North America and Europe.

By 1987: At least 85,000 Tamils have fled to southern India where today many of them still live in poverty. Fighting between the LTTE and the Sri Lankan armed forces grows worse. India arranges peace talks and sends the Indian Peace Keeping Force (IPKF) to northern Sri Lanka. But the LTTE and the IPKF are fighting each other.

1989: The LTTE and the Sri Lankan government begin peace talks. The IPKF agrees to leave. But the peace talks are not successful.

1990: The LTTE attack 17 police stations and execute 110 police officers. The Sri Lankan army retaliates. The war enters a new stage. Within two weeks, over 1,000 people are killed and 200,000 left homeless. The Sri Lankan government besieges Jaffna, a city held by the LTTE. Food, medicines and many other essential goods are banned from sale in northern Sri Lanka. Electricity is cut off. The siege lasts four years.

1994: Government troops capture Jaffna. But fighting continues.

February 2002: The Sri Lankan government and LTTE declare a ceasefire, but peace talks later break down. Over 400,000 Tamils are still internally displaced in Sri Lanka and about 800,000 remain as refugees, mostly in India, Europe and North America.

Large numbers of Sri Lankan civilians have been repeatedly displaced by the ongoing conflict.
© UNHCR / M. Kobayashi

Markandu Gnanapandithan's story

I went to school and then was admitted to the University of Jaffna. I won a scholarship and then entered the University of Peradeniya in 1983. I was politically active at school and university. The rights of Tamil people were being eroded by successive Sinhala governments. The Tamil workers on tea and rubber plantations had been made stateless and denied their basic rights. Tamils also suffer discrimination in education."

"I joined a Tamil youth organisation in 1976 when I was at school. I also did voluntary work with an organisation helping Tamil refugees who had fled from southern Sri Lanka during the riots of 1977. This organisation was given funds by Oxfam in the UK. But as it was working with Tamil refugees, it was a target. Its offices were eventually destroyed by Sinhalese racists, and the workers and volunteers arrested and tortured."

"In 1983 I was at the University of Peradeniya. We had student elections and the Tamil undergraduates supported and worked for progressive Sinhalese candidates and they won. After this the Sinhalese candidates who had lost began to make life difficult for the Tamil students. They were stripped naked, dragged out of their rooms and paraded on the streets. As a result of this the university had to close."

"In the riots of July 1983 the house where I was living was burnt down. My books and other belongings were destroyed. I was forced to abandon my studies and return home."

"On 8 January 1994, about 30 police officers came to my house to arrest me. I was kept in Vavuniya police station on 8 and 9 January 1994. On 9 January 1994, I was taken to Kandy. On the way to Kandy the police stopped the jeep opposite a Sinhalese Buddhist temple. The crowd outside the temple shouted abuse at me."

"I was kept in another police station from 9 to 11 January. Here I was locked up with Sinhalese remand prisoners who also attacked and abused me. On 11 January 1984, I was taken to Norwood police station and kept there for 15 days. During the time I was detained, I was removed to another police station and tortured. I was forced to lie down on a bench. My hands and feet were tied up and the soles of my feet were hit with clubs. I was burned with lighted cigarette ends. I was beaten on the head and also hung upside down from a bar and assaulted."

"On 26 January 1984, I was taken to Iratperiyakulum army camp and questioned by Ronny Wikramsinghe, an Assistant Superintendent of Police. He got the soldiers to torture me. They inserted a wire into my penis and drove pins under my fingernails."

"On 1 February 1984, I was taken to another army camp and kept alone in a dark cell for 15 days. I was then taken back to Iratperiyakulum army camp with 12 other young men. Here we were tortured and sexually assaulted."

"On 22nd March 1984 I was taken to Wellikade prison in Colombo. It was in this prison that Tamil political prisoners were murdered by Sinhalese prisoners during the riots of 1983. The prison officers did nothing to stop the riots."

"On 9 April 1984, I was taken to Tagalle prison with 90 other Tamils. We were denied medical treatment and water for washing. Here we went on hunger strike, demanding that we should either be put before a court of law or released."

> *I joined a Tamil youth organisation in 1976 when I was at school. I also did voluntary work with an organisation helping Tamil refugees who had fled from southern Sri Lanka during the riots of 1977.*

"In December 1984, I was taken to an army camp in southern Sri Lanka. I was given very little food here and when I asked for more I was beaten. In January 1985, I was taken back to Tagalle prison. In September 1985, I became ill. In all my time in Tagalle we were abused and beaten by prison officers. A Tamil prisoner was murdered by one of the prison guards."

"In October 1985, with the help of friends, I managed to pay a bribe of about £75 to police officers and I was released. I returned home to my village near Jaffna. But soon after my return I was summoned to Mankulum army camp. I did not answer the summons but went into hiding. I had no alternative other than to flee the country as I feared for my life. I paid an agent to help me leave Sri Lanka and left by boat to India on 3 October 1986."

"I travelled on my own passport without knowing the visa stamp on it was forged. When I arrived at Heathrow airport on 19 October 1986, I was told that the visa stamp was false. I asked for asylum and was granted temporary admission to Britain and was told to report to the immigration office when they called me for an interview."

"My asylum application was refused on 7 March 1987. The Home Office's immigration department told me that even though my life was in danger in Sri Lanka, it was not the only country in which I could live. I think they wanted to send me to India."

Markandu Gnanapandithan was eventually given leave to remain in the UK. The interview is reproduced with thanks to the Tamil Refugee Action Group.

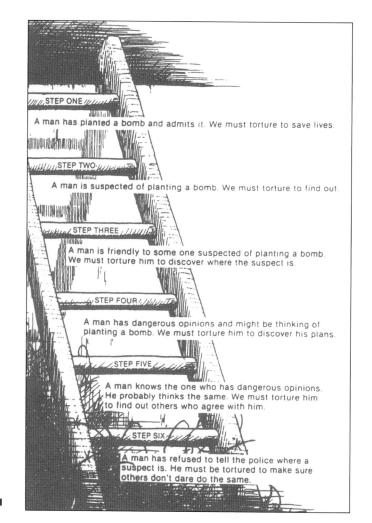

The ladder of torture.
© **Amnesty International**

– Chapter Six: Persecution –

Information: Torture

Sri Lanka is one of nearly 100 countries where torture is used on detainees and prisoners. In 1993 Amnesty International reported that torture had been used in 96 countries in the previous year. Torture - a deliberate way of inflicting pain on another person - forces us to ask questions about ourselves. Read the information about the Milgram experiment and decide what you think.

The Milgram experiment

For many years it was thought that torture was something that was carried out by monstrous people who suffer from personality disorders. Psychologists believed that 'normal' people could never be torturers. But in the early 1960s, the trial of Adolf Eichmann, a Nazi war criminal, caused people to question this notion. People who witnessed Eichmann's trial in Jerusalem noted how ordinary he appeared to be.

The psychologist **Stanley Milgram** started to examine what makes ordinary people commit crimes such as torture. He set up a psychological experiment to examine how far people would go when given orders to hurt other people. He recruited some actors who trained to act as 'learners' in his experiment. He also placed an advertisement in a local newspaper asking for volunteers to help in a study of memory and learning methods. The volunteers were told that they would act as 'teachers'.

The 'teachers' were told that their job was to punish the 'learners' when the latter made a mistake in their memory tests. Every time the 'learner' made a mistake, the 'teacher' was to give the 'learner' an electric shock. The teachers were told by Stanley Milgram that the experiment was to test the theory that people who were punished for their mistakes learnt things more quickly.

Stanley Milgram built a special machine to give the electric shocks. The machine had many levers. Each lever increased the strength of the electric shock. For each mistake the 'learner' made, the teacher had to use an extra lever to give a bigger shock. Some of the levers were also marked with the words 'extremely dangerous'. The machine did not really give the 'learner' electric shocks. The 'learner' who was an actor simulated the pain of a shock and made many protests about his treatment. The 'learner' also made many mistakes. At 150 volts the 'learner' was screaming with pain and asked the experiment to be ended. Stanley Milgram and his colleagues ordered the 'teacher' to carry on. Most of them did. Some 65 per cent of all the 'teachers' administered shocks at 450 volts. The 'teachers', however, were very tense when they did so.

Before the experiment Milgram discussed with fellow psychologists what proportion of 'teachers' would be giving 450 volt electric shocks. They believed that less than 1 per cent of all the 'teachers' would administer electric shocks at 450 volts. Stanley Milgram and his colleagues were very surprised by the results.

There has been further research on torture since the Milgram experiment. In the 1970s research was carried out in Greece on people who had perpetrated torture under the military governments of 1967 to 1974. Psychologists found that there were no personality differences between torturers and the general population. Indeed many of the torturers were young national service conscripts. In their training, however, the torturers had been taught to think that they were defending good values.

Discussion point:

⇨ Read the information about the Milgram experiment above. Discuss what the Milgram experiment and the research in Greece tell us about people who are torturers. What can people who are concerned about human rights learn from this research?

Information: What is torture?

Torture can be used to extract information from prisoners or people in detention. But torture often has another aim: political control and the control of dissent. An individual who has been tortured may flee his or her country after torture or cease to be involved in political opposition. If many people involved in political opposition are tortured, many more people will be fearful of any political involvement.

Torture can include the following:

- The ill-treatment of prisoners and detainees, such as starvation, the use of leg irons and handcuffs in a way that causes pain, beatings and solitary confinement
- Forms of punishment such as electric shocks, beating the feet and hanging a person for a prolonged period
- The misuse of drugs, for example injecting people with drugs that paralyse them for a period of time
- Sexual torture such as the rape of women in prison
- Psychological torture such as making threats against family and friends

British links with torture

Some of the UK's closest allies use torture on prisoners and detainees. For example, Turkey, a close ally and a prospective member of the European Union, has been criticised for torturing prisoners. Some human rights activists believe that the UK government should put more diplomatic pressure on Turkey to stop torture.

The UK is also known to have exported torture equipment to several countries that regularly torture prisoners and detainees. As controls on such exports are inadequate, it is possible that British business could continue to export torture equipment.

The exports include:

1983: The export of leg irons by Hiatts & Co, a company based in the West Midlands. As a result of a campaign by Amnesty International, UK government export licences were refused for future exports.

1991: Hiatts & Co were discovered promoting the sale of leg irons through a US-based associate company.

1991: Electronic Intelligence, a British-based company, was discovered to have installed a torture chamber in Dubai. The torture chamber used sound and high intensity lighting causing the person inside to scream in agony within moments.

Working with people who survive torture

Most people who are tortured do not survive. A small number of refugees who have been tortured do flee to the UK. Here they may need help to enable them to recover from past experiences. A charity called the Medical Foundation for the Care of Victims of Torture provides such help.

The Medical Foundation was founded in 1985 by members of Amnesty International's Medical Group. It has grown to be an organisation that sees over 6,000 people a year from many different countries including survivors of the Nazi Holocaust. At present most of the Medical Foundation's clients come from Iran, Iraq and Turkey.

The Medical Foundation employs about 50 staff, but a large part of its work is done by volunteers. The staff and volunteers include social workers, psychiatrists, psychotherapists, GPs, physiotherapists, art therapists, nurses, a careers adviser and an information officer. The Medical Foundation offers a wide range of services to people who have survived torture and their families. They include:

- Making reports to help asylum seekers who have been tortured apply for asylum in the UK
- Psychotherapy, art therapy and music therapy to help survivors of torture come to terms with their experience and rebuild their lives

  Medical treatment and physiotherapy for people who have physical injuries as a result of their torture
- Advice and support for clients who are having other problems in their lives such as not being able to find housing
- Training for doctors, nurses, teachers, social workers and other workers who may encounter survivors of torture during their work

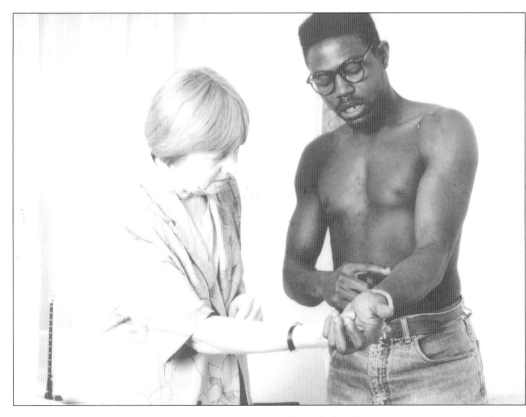

Dr Gill Hinshelwood examines scars on a patient's arm.
© **Helen Stone / Medical Foundation**

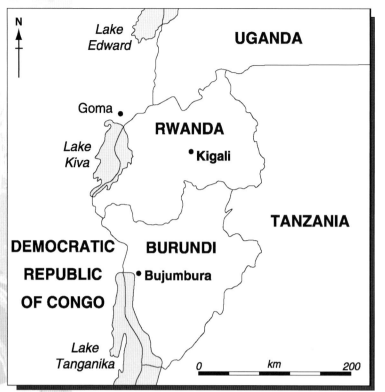

Events:

The **Twa** (Pygmies) were the original inhabitants of Rwanda. Today many Twa still live as hunter-gatherers in the forests. About 1,000 years ago the ancestors of the Hutu migrated to central Africa. They cut some of the forest cover to plant crops. Then in the 17th and 18th centuries, the Tutsi migrated into Central Africa from Sudan and Ethiopia. They were taller and were cattle-herding nomads.

The **Tutsi** soon ruled much of Rwanda, apart from the north. But there was also much intermarriage between Tutsi and Hutu. In the 19th century the Tutsi King Kigeri Rwabugiri set up a unified state with its own army.

About 4,000 Rwandans live in the UK. The number of Burundian refugees in the UK is about 1,000 people.

Rwanda

Population: 8.2 million
Capital: Kigali
Ethnic groups: 90 per cent of the population are Hutu, 9 per cent are Tutsi, and the rest are the Twa.
Languages: The official languages of Rwanda are French, Kinyarwanda and English. Many people also understand Swahili.
Economy: Over 90 per cent of people live in rural areas in this densely populated country. Most people are farmers. Coffee is the main export crop. Rwanda has a large foreign debt caused by a drop in coffee prices. The high population density means that smallholdings are very small and few can make a living as farmers.

1894: Rwanda and Burundi become part of German East Africa. To bring the country under control, the Tutsi are given political power, education and used as colonial administrators. This reinforces the differences between Hutu and Tutsi. Many Hutu resent the power given to the Tutsi.

1911: There is an Hutu uprising in northern Rwanda.

1914-1918: During the First World War Belgian forces occupy Rwanda and Burundi.

1923: The League of Nations gives Belgium the mandate to govern Ruanda-Urundi. The Belgians reinforce differences between Hutu and Tutsi. Hutu people cannot go to university or college. The Belgians also introduce identity cards stating a person's ethnic group. It was these cards that were used to identify Tutsi in the 1994 genocide.

1950s and 1960s: Political parties begin to emerge calling for independence. Hutu political leaders demand more power, but local Tutsi chiefs resist. As the Hutu rebel, there is much tension and violence. Over 10,000 Tutsi are killed and 120,000 Tutsi refugees flee to Uganda, where many of them remain until 1994.

1961: The Belgians leave. Rwanda and Burundi become separate, independent states. In Rwanda, the Tutsi monarchy is abolished. Hutu Gregoire Kayibanda becomes Rwanda's first president.

1963: Tutsi rebels enter Rwanda from Uganda. This causes fear among the Hutu who turn on their Tutsi neighbours, killing over 20,000 people. Another 150,000 Tutsi flee.

1973: President Kayibanda is overthrown in a coup led by Juvenal Habyarimana, a Hutu from northern Rwanda. All political parties are banned. Habyarimana rules Rwanda until his murder in 1994. Quotas are introduced in education and employment to ensure fairer representation of ethnic groups.

1990: The Rwandan Patriotic Front (RPF), a mainly Tutsi rebel group, invades Rwanda from Uganda. After successes in the first weeks of fighting, the rebels are forced back by the Rwandan army, helped by French, Belgian and Congolese troops. Over 100,000 people are killed.

1992: Conflict reignites. By mid-1993 nearly 1 million Rwandans have fled as refugees.

1993: President Habyarimana signs a power-sharing agreement with the RPF. The UN sends a mission to monitor the peace agreement. But many politicians, especially Hutu extremists, resist the idea of sharing power with the Tutsi-led RPF. Politicians, newspapers and radio stations begin to voice anti-Tutsi feelings. The Government also begins to arm and train young Hutu men, forming them into militia know as the interhamwe.

1994: President Habyarimana and President Ntaryamira of Burundi are killed after their plane is shot down over Kigali. The RPF are blamed. The interhamwe begin attacks on the Tutsi and moderate Hutu. The UN withdraw its observers stating that there is no peace to monitor. Between April and June 1994, an estimated 1.5 million Tutsi and moderate Hutu are killed. Rwanda descends into chaos. This allows the RPF to enter the country. After taking the capital city Kigali, the RPF form a new government. The interhamwe flee to neighbouring Congo (then called Zaire). 2 million Hutu refugees now fear for their lives and flee with the interhanwe. The refugees gather in camps around the town of Bukavu and Goma in the Congo. Lacking clean water, thousands of refugees soon die of cholera.

1995: The conflict in Rwanda spills over into the Congo. The interhamwe and the Congolese army attack local Congolese Tutsi. The Congolese army then tries to force all refugees back into Rwanda.

1996: Rwandan troops invade the Democratic Republic of Congo to stop the interhamwe organising themselves as a guerrilla army and attacking Rwanda. The Rwandan army also attacks the refugee camps in order to prevent the refugees from joining the interhamwe and to drive them home. (Most of the refugees do return.)

Today: Trials of people accused of the 1994 genocide begin in Tanzania and also in Rwanda. Elections are held, but in 2004 over 60,000 Rwandans remain as refugees and another 150,000 are internally displaced.

The International Criminal Court

If the Tutsi and Hutu people are to live together in peace, it is important that those who committed acts of genocide in 1994 are brought to justice so that individuals can be punished instead of whole groups of people being associated with guilt. In future, people who have committed acts of genocide, crimes against humanity and war crimes, will be tried by the new International Criminal Court set up in 1998.

Information: Burundi

Refugees from Burundi at Kigembe camp in Rwanda. Plastic sheeting is essential for shelter in winter.
© UNHCR / B. Press

Population: 6.2 million

Capital: Bujumbura

Ethnic groups: 84 per cent of Burundi's population are Hutu, 15 per cent Tutsi and about 1 per cent are Twa.

Languages: Kirundi and French. Swahili is also understood by many people.

Economy: Over 90 per cent of people are farmers. Coffee and tea are the main exports in this poor country.

Events:

Burundi's first inhabitants were Twa. Between 1000 and 1500 AD, the ancestors of the Hutu migrated to central Africa practising settled agriculture and clearing much of the forest to plant crops. Between 1600 and 1800, a new group of cattle herding nomads migrated to central Africa from Sudan and Ethiopia. They were the Tutsi, distinguished by their height and finer features.

Today's Burundi was ruled by Tutsi kings (called the mwami) and a princely class. Ordinary Tutsi and Hutu, however, were in much the same economic position and intermarriage was common.

1894: Burundi and Rwanda become part of German East Africa.

1914-1918: During the First World War, Burundi is occupied by the Belgians who invade from the neighbouring Belgian Congo.

1918: Germany is defeated. The League of Nations gives Belgium the mandate to control Burundi. The country is known as Ruanda-Urundi. As in Rwanda, the Belgians favour a small Tutsi elite, and introduce identity cards stating a person's ethnic identity.

Burundi

1962: Burundi gains full independence with the mwami as head of state. He tries to grant equal political power to Hutu and Tutsi.

1965: The newly-elected prime minister, a Hutu, is murdered. Hutu parties emerge victorious in the new elections but the mwami appoint a Tutsi prime minister. In response, the Hutu-dominated police force rebel. Tutsi extremists respond to the rebellion. Over 3,000 Hutu are murdered in Tutsi revenge attacks and thousands flee as refugees to neighbouring countries.

1966: The continued unrest leads to the removal of the mwami and the establishment of a republic headed by a Tutsi president. Most Hutu politicians and army officers are removed from their jobs.

1972: Extremists in the Tutsi-dominated army murder at least 150,000 Hutus after an unsuccessful Hutu-led rebellion. Some 300,000 Hutus flee to Rwanda, the Congo (then called Zaire) and Tanzania. No one has been tried for the 1972 genocide.

1980s: Human rights abuses worsen. Members of Hutu opposition groups are detained and tortured.

1987: Pierre Buyoya, a Tutsi, becomes president as a result of a coup d'etat. The Tutsi-dominated army kills at least 20,000 unarmed Hutu. International pressure forces Burundi's president to appoint a Hutu prime minister. In the next three years, human rights conditions improve. More Hutu are appointed to senior civil service positions. But the Tutsi-led army resists change.

1993: Elections are held. Melchior Ndadaye becomes Burundi's first Hutu president, but the campaign heightens tensions between Hutu and Tutsi. In October 1993, Tutsi army officers surround the presidential palace. Melchior Ndadaye is killed. In some parts of Burundi, Tutsi are killed in revenge for the coup. In other areas, Hutu are killed by the army. Over 50,000 people die and 700,000 people, mostly Hutu refugees, flee to Rwanda.

1994: A new government is formed. Within two months, its Tutsi president is killed in an air crash with President Habyarimana of Rwanda. Burundi drifts towards civil war.

2000: A peace agreement is signed in Tanzania. But fighting continues between the government forces and rebels.

Today: Fighting continues. Tutsi soldiers and militia kill civilians. Hutu militia kill Tutsi civilians. By 2004, over 300,000 people have been killed in the civil war. About 375,000 Burundis are living as refugees or in refugee-like situations in neighbouring African countries. Another 500,000 people are internally displaced. There are severe human rights violations. Amnesty International lists continued massacres, extrajudicial executions by the security forces, destruction of farmers' properties, looting and the conscription of children into rebel forces.

Burundi

Renovat's story

Renovat is an 18 year old Tutsi from Lugazi, a village near Bujumbura in Burundi. Renovat and his family have spent time living in a refugee camp in Bujumbura.

"After President Ndadaye was killed in October 1994, some of our neighbours started stealing our family's goats, cows and crops. One night people came with machetes and spears, so our family ran away with other neighbours. My grandparents were so old that they could not run and escape. They were killed and the houses were burned by people who were once my friends."

"We arrived at Quartier Four camp after running 13 kilometres through the bush. Conditions in the camp are difficult. There is not enough water to drink or wash with, nor enough soap, clothes, blankets or sleeping mats. We are only able to eat once a day. My father is fortunate. He has been able to get money by helping out in the office of a local vet."

"Despite the risks, my father decided to return to our village to see if it was safe to return with our family. He came back and the news was that it was still too dangerous. But one of our Hutu neighbours had harvested our family's crops and was saving them for us so we have seeds to plant when we return. This kindness shows that not all our Hutu neighbours hate the Tutsi. It is the politicians who are causing the problems."

"We are frightened of members of the FRODEBU Party, which is mainly Hutu. I trust only the people of Burundi. We lived together and we will live together. The people are brothers and sisters. They want peace but everyone is afraid."

Joyce's story

Joyce is Rwandan and a child of a mixed marriage. In 1994 she fled with her family to a refugee camp in the Congo. Later the family was forced to return to Rwanda. Although life was fine at first, Joyce was later threatened by soldiers in the new government. She became a refugee again and fled to the UK.

"I was born in Rwanda. As for my parents, one is a Tutsi and one is a Hutu. When I was young everything was peaceful. But we could not remain in our own country. We fled to the Congo and all we could take with us was some food and clothes. Then everything was stolen from us by Congolese soldiers when we entered the refugee camps north of Goma in the Congo. Here they did not welcome us; they welcomed our belongings."

"When the war started in the Congo, the camps were attacked by soldiers. We had no choice but to leave. We had been forced to leave our country and now we were forced to return."

"We hoped that the new government could rebuild the sunken bridge between Hutu and Tutsi people. But there is no reconciliation to be had because genocide is still going on. In the daylight you are at school and your colleagues are at school, but the following day you realise someone is missing. Many young people are taken at night by the authorities. Because of this people do not sleep in their houses but in the bush. I wonder about people who were members of the new government but have now left Rwanda. I think they did not realise how undemocratic and unjust the new government would be."

Information: Genocide

Genocide is the deliberate extermination of an ethnic, religious, political or national group. The murder of 1 million Rwandan Tutsi and Hutu opposing the government in 1994 was genocide, as was the Nazi murder of Jews, Roma and others during the Second World War.

The Nazi Holocaust and the events in Rwanda in 1994 pose many important political and moral questions to all of us. Three groups of people are involved in genocide. They are:

- The perpetrators
- The victims
- The bystanders

In Rwanda the interhamwe were the perpetrators. They acted on the orders of the Government and army. The interhamwe were also knowingly provided with weapons by the French government.

In Rwanda the victims were Tutsi as well as Hutu who opposed government policies. Ordinary Hutu who tried to stop the killings were also murdered sometimes.

In Rwanda there were many bystanders. There were people who watched their neighbours being killed and did nothing. The UN and politicians in individual governments were also bystanders. Both knew what was happening in Rwanda but chose to do nothing. But the television coverage of the murders in Rwanda meant that a far larger number of people were bystanders. Every person in the world who watched the television news during April to June 1994 was a bystander to the genocide in Rwanda. After watching the news, very few people in the UK took action such as writing to their MP.

Genocide does not happen suddenly. There are many conditions that must arise before a group of people become victims of genocide. These are the stages:

- The victim group is stereotyped and defined as being 'different from the rest of society'. The rest of society readily believes that the victim group is different.
- The victim group may experience racial attacks and discrimination by ordinary people.
- The victim group loses many of its legal rights.
- The victim group is dehumanised by politicians, the media and then by ordinary people. Ordinary people cease to see the victim group as human beings just like themselves.
- There is a catalyst event that starts the genocide. This is an event that gives the perpetrators an excuse to carry out genocide.
- The perpetrators of genocide are led to believe that they are morally right in their actions. They continue to carry out the genocide.

Victims of a massacre during the 1994 genocide.
© Panos Pictures / Martin Adler

Genocide in the 20th century

After the mass murder of Jews and Roma in the Second World War, the United Nations passed an international law to prevent future genocidal murders. This is known as the 1948 *UN Convention on Genocide*. To use this international law a UN member state must challenge an offending country with evidence which shows that the offending country is deliberately inflicting on the group "conditions of life calculated to bring about its destruction in whole or in part." But this international law is rarely used. There are many cases of genocide in the 20th century before and after the *1948 UN Convention on Genocide*. In almost all cases, the UN, individual governments and other bystanders have done little.

It is sometimes difficult to decide when ethnic conflict becomes genocide, but the genocides of the 20th century must include:

The Armenians in Turkey 1915-1920: Over 1.5 million people were murdered or died of starvation and disease.

The Jews of Europe 1933-1945: Some 6 million Jewish people were murdered by the Nazis.

The Roma of Europe 1939-1945: Up to 200,000 Roma (Gypsies) were murdered by the Nazis and their supporters.

Selected groups in the Soviet Union 1935-1953: Groups of people such as small landowners were murdered by the government of Joseph Stalin. It is difficult to estimate how many people were killed, but some people believe that as many as three million people were murdered at the time.

Bangladeshis 1971: Between 1.5 and 2 million Bangladeshi people were murdered by the government of West Pakistan and its supporters during the 1971 War of Independence.

The Hutu of Burundi 1972: Some 150,000 Hutu people were killed in revenge attacks following an unsuccessful Hutu-led coup d'etat.

Cambodians 1975-78: Between 1 and 2 million Cambodian people were murdered by the Khmer Rouge government in Cambodia.

East Timorese 1975-2002: Over 250,000 people were killed or died of starvation in East Timor between 1975 and 2002. The Indonesian army murdered whole villages it suspected of supporting the East Timorese independence movement.

Eritreans and Ethiopians 1980: Over 250,000 people, mostly Eritreans and Tigrayans, were killed by the Ethiopian government during the 'Red Terror.'

The Maya of Guatemala 1980-1994: At least 50,000 people were killed and many more Mayan Indians moved from their land.

The Kurds of Iraq 1980-2003: At least 200,000 Kurdish people were killed by Saddam Hussein's government. Up to 500,000 people were also forced to move from their villages.

The Nuba of Sudan 1990: The Nuba mountains have been sealed off since 1990 and many Nuba people have been deliberately killed by government forces and militia.

Bosnians 1992-1995: At least 200,000 people were killed in the civil war in Bosnia. This was fought between three groups of people: Bosnian Serbs, Croats and the Bosnian army. The latter comprised mostly of Bosnian Muslims.

Rwandans 1994: As many as 1.5 million Tutsi and moderate Hutu were murdered between April and June in 1994.

Burundi 1994 up to present: At least 300,000 people have been murdered by extremist groups. Both Hutu and Tutsi have been targeted.

Kosovars 1997-1999: Some 25,000 Kosovar Albanians were killed by the Yugoslav army and armed Serbian extremists.

Groups in the Democratic Republic of Congo 1997 until present: As many as 4.7 million people have been killed or died of starvation or disease in the Democratic Republic of Congo. Particular ethnic groups have been targeted in the fighting.

Unaccompanied Rwandan children in the care of UNICEF. One of them has been attacked for appearing to be a Tutsi.
© H. J. Davies / Exile Images

Activity 👆

Moral questions about genocide

Learning objectives: To enable students to debate some of the moral questions about genocide.

Time needed: At least 1 hour for students to prepare the questions and then another hour to present the issues they have examined.

Instructions: Students need copies of the background information on Rwanda and Burundi. They also need copies of the information on genocide. If possible, the first part of the activity should be organised in a computer suite to enable students to facilitate internet research on genocide.

The teacher should introduce the activity, providing a definition of genocide as well as that of perpetrator, victim and bystander. Television footage can also be used.

The students should be divided into pairs. Each pair should be given one of the questions below. Each pair should prepare a short presentation (up to five minutes) that aims to answer the question that they have been allocated.

1. What were the causes of the genocides in Rwanda and Burundi?
2. How is it possible for a society to descend into such a level of barbarity?
3. Could genocide happen in the UK?
4. How should we judge the behaviour of people who saw their neighbours being killed and did nothing?
5. How should we judge our own behaviour after we saw the genocide on television and did nothing?
6. What should governments and the UN have done to prevent the genocide?
7. A number of people living in refugee camps in the Democratic Republic of Congo were involved in genocide. Should aid agencies provide food to the refugee camps, knowing that they are also feeding people who have committed crimes against humanity?
8. How can there be forgiveness and reconciliation when such a large number of people on both sides have lost relatives?
9. Do we need an international criminal court to try people who have committed genocide?
10 How can the world ensure that genocide will not happen again either in Rwanda and Burundi or anywhere else?

Kosovar refugees forced to flee. © UNHCR / R. LeMoyne

This chapter examines warfare as a cause of flight of refugees. It looks at the causes of war, the media in times of war, the arms trade, child soldiers, and the links between nationalism and war. Conflicts in the Democratic Republic of Congo, Angola, West Africa and the Caucasus are used as case studies.

James Appe's story

"We arrived home on the evening of the third day of our flight. Everything was changed. Houses that were once beautiful lay in ruins. The orange and mango leaves in the compound were dying, having been severely scorched by the raging fires as they consumed the building. The world was silent. Not a soul was seen. Neither was there any sign of animal life. It had rained during the night, and the footmarks left in the wet sand by the heavy boots of soldiers sent shivers down my spine. They were the footmarks of death."

"At the entrance to our compound we met the rotting carcass of our once much loved dog Bobi, with hundreds of grey flies hovering around the open mouth. There was a bullet hole in the head, and traces of the scattered brain were still visible around the head and ear. Nobody talked. We put our things down and I went into what used to be my house."

"I stood there gazing at the pile of ashes of destroyed furniture. The ugly sight of the burnt iron bed at one side of the wall did not detain me. I moved to the iron box where I had stored all my precious books. The lock had burnt loose. I tried to open it. The lid came off by itself, and I stared with hot tears in my eyes at the destruction within. My 'African Encyclopaedia' had been on top of the pile and the black lump of ashes on top of the ruin must have been the pages of my beloved book. It was not the paper itself that provoked tears in my eyes, it was the message, the words, the information in the book that made me weep."

Taken from "Flight and Other Stories" by James Appe. He was born in Uganda but was forced to become a refugee in Sudan and then in the UK. He has published a number of short stories based on his experiences as a refugee.

Activity ☞

War and children

Learning objectives: The activity aims to develop empathy towards refugee children who have fled warfare. At the end of the activity, students will also have considered the effects that warfare has on children.

Time needed: 30 minutes

Instructions: Students will need copies of James Appe's story. They will also need copies of refugee children's paintings on flight from war, which can be obtained from the UNHCR London office. (There are also paintings reproduced in *One Day We Had to Run* by Sybella Wilkes.)

The teacher should explain that war can affect people physically and psychologically. Autobiographical writing and paintings reflect our emotions. Refugee children's paintings often reflect their feelings about war, flight and exile.

Students should read James Appe's account, then look at the refugee children's paintings and consider the following questions:

- What is being depicted in the paintings?
- What feelings are being portrayed in the paintings and in James' story?
- How do you think war affects refugee children?

Information: Refugees from the Democratic Republic of Congo (formerly Zaire)

About 28,000 refugees from the Democratic Republic of Congo live in the UK.

Population: 53.6 million in 2001
Capital: Kinshasa
Ethnic groups: There are over 200 ethnic groups. The main ethnic groups are the Kikongo, Luba, Mongo, Bwaka, Hutu and Tutsi. Some of the fighting in eastern Congo involves different ethnic groups fighting with each other.
Languages: French is the official language and the language of government. Kiswahili, Tshiluba, Kikongo and Lingala also have official status and are widely used. There are at least another 200 languages and dialects.
Economy: The majority of people are subsistence farmers, although fighting has disrupted farming and caused many people to die of hunger. The Democratic Republic of Congo is the world's largest producer of copper and has considerable resources of other minerals such as zinc and tin. Coltan, a mineral component of mobile phones, is also abundant. The illegal trading of diamonds and coltan gives an income for the guerrilla armies, thus worsening the fighting.

Events:

Before colonisation, the Democratic Republic of Congo was a collection of small states along the River Congo. Information about the country reached Europe between 1840 and 1870, through the newspaper coverage of David Livingstone's and Henry Stanley's expeditions.

1884: The Berlin Conference draws up the borders of the free state of Congo which becomes the personal property of the King of Belgium.

1908: The country becomes a Belgium colony. The Belgians extract the country's timber and mineral resources, but do little to develop roads, schools and hospitals. They also prevent opposition to their rule, sometimes violently.

1955: The Belgian government allows African political parties to operate. Most of these new parties call for independence.

1960: Congo wins its independence. Patrice Lumumba becomes its first prime minister. Within days the army revolts and Colonel Joseph-Desire Mobutu seizes power. Local people in the Shaba region start the fighting as they are angry that the mineral wealth of the region does not really benefit them.

1961: Mobutu returns power to Joseph Kasavubu, who has arrested Patrice Lumumba and delivered him to Belgian mercenary soldiers who kill him.

D R Congo

1965: Mobutu seizes power again in a coup d'etat. Thousands of his opponents are arrested, tortured or killed, and all opposition political parties are banned.

1989: Student demonstrations are held in Kinshasa and Lubumbashi universities. Mobutu's security forces intervene. 50 students are killed.

1990 and 1991: More students are killed in demonstrations.

1993: Shopkeepers refuse to accept the new banknotes given to the army as pay. The army riots. Mobutu sends his security forces to kill political opposition. Over 1,000 people die. Fighting also breaks out in Shaba Province and in eastern Zaire, where people of Rwandan origin are attacked. The Red Cross estimates that over 10,000 ethnic Rwandans are killed.

1994: Over 2 million Rwandan refugees cross the border into Zaire. They and local Rwandans become the targets of harassment from the Zairean military and non-Rwandan groups.

1997: Mobutu leaves Zaire and dies. Country rebel soldiers organise themselves in northeast Zaire and form the Alliance des Forces Democratiques pour la Liberation du Congo-Zaire (AFDL), supported by the Rwandan government and led by Laurent Kabila. Rwandan soldiers and AFDL forces attack Hutu refugees in Rwandan refugee camps. An estimated 600,000 to 700,000 refugees return to Rwanda. Another 200,000 people flee deeper into the Congolese rain forest. Thousands died or are murdered. The rebels enter the capital city Kinshasa and seize power.

1998: A rebellion against the new government starts in eastern Congo. The Rassamblement Congolaise pour la Democratie (RCD) wants to overthrow Laurent Kabila. The Rwandan and Ugandan governments help the rebels. The RCD rebels soon capture a large part of the country. This initial success stops when Angola, Zimbabwe, Namibia, Chad and Sudan provide support for the Congolese government.

2001: Kabila is assassinated and replaced by his son. There are peace talks but the civil war continues.

2002: Congo is effectively divided into three parts. The Mouvement pour la Liberation du Congo (MLC) holds the north, RCD factions hold the east, and Joseph Kabila's government hold the south and west.

2003: Thousands of people are killed in Ituri Province in fighting between different ethnic groups.

Today: The war has killed an estimated 4.7 million people. Nearly 440,000 refugees have fled the Democratic Republic of Congo to neighbouring countries or to Europe. An estimated 3.2 million people are internally displaced. There are violent attacks on people of Rwandan descent, particularly Tutsis, in eastern Rwanda, Kinshasa and urban areas. Extrajudicial execution, murder, torture, arbitrary arrest and forced conscription are common. NGOs, church workers and journalists face harassment.

Dido's story

Dido Natabwe Lusamba is Congolese. He is an art history graduate from the Academy of Fine Arts, Kinshasa, Congo. He came to Denmark in 1984 and now runs Alpha Print in Copenhagen. He also draws cartoons, paints and sculpts.

"I grew up in Lubumbashi, a city in southern Congo. I grew up with ethnic conflict being part of everyday life. In 1984 I had to flee the country after taking part in a student demonstration. I feared I would be arrested. Many people in my country have disappeared after being arrested and were never seen again. And a student friend of mine was shot on the same night that I fled."

"My parents, brothers and sisters still live in the Congo. I have not seen them since 1984. But a recent letter from home informed me that soldiers have evicted my parents from their house without an explanation or compensation. As a postmaster, my father had lived there since 1967."

"My first night in Denmark was spent in a very short child's bed. I was staying in a room at the Goldberg Refugee Reception Centre with seven other refugees. All my new roommates were Iranians and they had never seen anyone from the Congo before or been close to a black man. They gave the child's bed to me. But we soon got to know each other better."

"I spent six months in the refugee reception centre while the Danish government considered my case. We used our spare time in the camp to write a play. With four Iranian actors, Iranian music and Danish everyday sounds we produced a mime. The audience was local people and after the performance everyone celebrated. I have also produced a cartoon book for adults. The book looks at unrest between different ethnic groups in the Democratic Republic of Congo."

"I get inspiration for new projects by being with other people. In my experience, too, different people can get to understand each other by working on artistic or creative activities. One of my next projects will be directing Danish and refugee school students. They will be producing a play about human rights."

© **Dido Natabwe Lusamba**

Information: Why do we fight?

The conflict in the Congo has taken more lives than any other war since 1945. But since then hundreds of other wars have been fought. These wars have been fought for many different reasons. Academics who study warfare have many different theories as to why we fight. A number of anthropologists and psychologists believe that human beings are naturally aggressive. War and violence are unavoidable because of human nature. Recently women have begun to research warfare. Some argue that combatants in war are almost always men. Our traditional view of men and boys as 'tough' results in men growing up to be aggressive and inclined to use force to solve conflict.

Other academics do not focus on the individual characteristics of human beings. Conflicts take place when nation states or groups of people try to increase their share of resources, land or power. There may be

- conflicts between countries over disputed territory;
- wars of independence, between a colonist and the colonised;
- conflicts over who holds political power within a country;
- conflicts over control of economic resources within a country;
- conflicts between different ethnic groups within a country;
- conflicts between different religious groups within a country.

Some conflicts are between countries. Others are civil wars fought within a country. Some conflicts produce large numbers of refugees. Other wars produce fewer refugees.

Patterns of warfare are now changing. Fewer wars are fought between different countries. Most of today's wars are civil wars fought within a country. Today's wars also produce larger numbers of civilian casualties. In the First World War only 10 per cent of casualties were civilians. Today 85 per cent of all people killed in war are civilians.

There are also more countries where a civil war has led to the collapse of all effective government. Such countries are known as failed or collapsed states. The Democratic Republic of Congo, Somalia and Georgia are such collapsed states.

Many children in Congo have become orphaned as a result of the conflict.
© UNHCR / C. Sattlberger

Learning objectives: At the end of the activity students will have an understanding of the numbers of conflicts being fought today. Students will also understand that many of these conflicts receive very little coverage in the media.

Time needed: 30 minutes

Instructions: Prior to the activity the teacher will need to collect press cuttings and internet news cuttings of different conflicts. Photocopied A3 world maps, atlases and small coloured stickers are also needed.

The teacher should introduce the discussion by brainstorming wars that the students know are being fought. These should be listed on the board. The class should then be divided into groups. Students should work in groups of three or four around a table. Each table will need a world map, an atlas, coloured stickers and a selection of photocopied news cuttings.

Students have to mark all the different conflicts they can find on the world map, using the stickers. When they have completed the task, the class should come together for a discussion.

Discussion points:

⇨ How many conflicts are being fought today?

⇨ How many conflicts did your class know about before you did this activity?

Learning objectives: The activity aims to help participants understand the causes of the conflict in the Democratic Republic of Congo. It also aims to improve their communication skills.

Time needed: 1 hour with homework

Instructions: Some big sheets of white paper, coloured paper and felt pens are needed. The information on the Democratic Republic of Congo needs to be photocopied so that everyone has this material. Articles from the internet or newspapers may also be used.

Divide the group up into threes and fours. Each group is going to make a strip cartoon or collage to show the causes of the conflict in the Democratic Republic of Congo.

Discussion points:

⇨ What factors have led to the conflict in the Democratic Republic of Congo?

⇨ What can ordinary people in the Democratic Republic of Congo do to work for peace?

Information: War and the media

In some parts of the world, television radio and newspapers are used to encourage young people to become soldiers. War is portrayed as being manly or glamorous. Viewers are encouraged to take sides. In times of war or crises, almost all governments use the media to get support for their cause. The media can be used to promote support for a war or to get soldiers to join the armed forces.

Such use of the media is known as propaganda. Propaganda is the use of the media to create certain actions or beliefs. Propaganda can include deliberate lies. Propaganda may also be a partial truth - things are concealed to give the impression something else is happening. Propaganda is a type of media bias. Bias is the one-sided coverage of events or issues so that only one set of views is put forward. Newspapers and television may be guilty of media bias. There are many ways in which newspaper articles can be biased. These include:

- Putting forward only one viewpoint
- Quoting or interviewing a limited group of people
- Not telling the whole story, just a small part
- Using emotive language to discredit people who have opposing views
- Using photographs that add to bias or do not tell the whole story

An example of media bias during wartime

All the expressions were used in the British press during one particular week of the 1991 Gulf War.

(Source: The Guardian)

We Have...	*They have...*
Army, Navy and Air Force	A war machine
Reporting guidelines	Censorship
Press briefings	Propaganda

We...	*They...*
Take out	Destroy
Eliminate	Kill
Neutralise	Kill

We launch...	*They launch...*
First strikes	Sneak missile attacks
Pre-emptively	Without provocation

Our boys are...	*Theirs are...*
Professional	Brainwashed
Dare devils	Cannon fodder
Young knights of the skies	Bastards of Baghdad
Loyal	Blindly obedient
Desert rats	Mad dogs

Our boys are motivated by...	*Their boys are motivated by...*
An old-fashioned sense of duty	Fear of Saddam

We...	*They...*
Have precision bombs	Fire wildly at anything in the skies

- Chapter Seven: Fleeing from war -

Learning objectives: At the end of the activity students will have thought critically about the portrayal of warfare on television.

Time needed: This is a homework activity although it will need teacher introduction and explanation during a lesson as well as analysis, feedback and discussion in a subsequent lesson.

Instructions: Students will need multiple copies of the survey. The teacher should also have a TV schedule for the week in question.

At the start of the lesson the teacher should explain that students are going to monitor how warfare is portrayed on television during a three-day period. The teacher should divide up evening TV viewing so that each pupil has a number of TV programmes to monitor.

Students should fill in the forms. At the end of the three-day period the class should collate, analyse and write up their results. Students can use graphs and pie charts to illustrate their results. Alternatively computer programmes can be used to collate and analyse individual and class information.

Discussion points:

⇨ What type of TV programmes included most warfare?

⇨ How did warfare on television affect members of your class?

⇨ Do you think boys react differently to war and violence on television than girls?

Survey of war on television

Name of television programme:

_____

What kind of programme was it?

☐ News

☐ Documentary

☐ Drama/Film

☐ Children's TV

☐ Other (describe)

How was the violence portrayed?

☐ Heroically

☐ As a terrible event

☐ Neutrally

☐ Other (describe)

How did the violence affect you?

☐ I found it entertaining

☐ It excited me

☐ It made me want to be a soldier

☐ It frightened me

☐ I found it interesting and informative

☐ It made me angry

☐ Other (describe)

Information: Refugees from Angola

Economy: 71 per cent of the labour force work as farmers. The main crops are maize, sugar cane, palms, coffee, cotton, sisal and vegetables. Angola was once a major food exporter but the civil war has disrupted farming. It also has many natural resources and is potentially one of the richest countries in Africa. The war has totally disrupted the economy. There is virtually no industry and transport is poor.

Events:

1482: The first Europeans arrive in Angola when the Portuguese explorer Diego Cao reaches the mouth of the River Congo. For over 300 years Portuguese colonisers make lots of money out of the slave trade, offering certain ethnic groups money for the capture of slaves, which precipitates much internal conflict.

Over 14,000 refugees from Angola live in the UK.

Population: 12.3 million in 2003
Capital: Luanda
Ethnic groups: There are 7 main ethnic groups in Angola and many smaller minorities. The conflict in Angola had an ethnic dimension. The Ovimbundu comprise 37 per cent of the population. The Kimbundu (sometimes known as the Mbundu) comprise 26 per cent of the population. They speak Kimbundu as their first language. The Bakongo make up about 15 per cent of the population, living mostly in northern Angola and in Cabinda (as well as Congo-Brazzaville and the Democratic Republic of Congo). They speak Kikongo as their first language.
Languages: The official language of Angola is Portuguese. The most important African languages are Umbundu, Kimbundu and Kikongo.

1450-1850: War and slavery reduce the population from 18 million to about 8 million. The slaves are transported to North America, Brazil, Sao Tome and Portugal, nearly half die during the journey.

1850: The Portuguese control the coast of Angola, and Angolan traders and local lords the interior. Slavery is still legal.

1884: The Berlin Conference grants Angola to the Portuguese.

1895-1921: Military campaigns give Portugal control of the interior. Portuguese settlers are encouraged to come and live in Angola to strengthen the Portuguese presence. By 1950 over 350,000 settlers have arrived. Many of the Portuguese migrants are poor people who cannot read or write and compete with Angolans for jobs. The latter lose out. They want independence.

1956: The Popular Movement for the Liberation of Angola (MPLA) is founded seeking an end to Portuguese rule. Other resistance movements are formed, including the Union for the Total Independence of Angola (UNITA) and the National Front for the Liberation of Angola (FNLA).

1961: The war of independence begins. MPLA guerrillas storm Luanda's prisons while Portuguese targets are also attacked in north west Angola. The Portuguese army responds by bombing villages and using napalm.

1965: The war forces 400,000 Angolan refugees into neighbouring countries. But the MPLA, FNLA and UNITA also fight each other with more Angolans killed than when fighting the Portuguese. The superpowers worsen this conflict by arming different groups. The US and South Africa back UNITA, the Chinese arm the FNLA, and the Soviet Union help the MPLA.

1974: Portugal's military government is overthrown. The three independence movements sign a ceasefire and begin to plan for an interim government. But soon the MPLA, FNLA and UNITA are fighting again. The MPLA sets up a government in Luanda. The FNLA and UNITA form an alternative government in Huambo. The war worsens after South Africa invades Angola. Cuban troops arrive to support the MPLA - they manage to drive back the South Africans.

1976-1980: There is a lull in the fighting and some economic recovery. But fighting between the Angolan government and UNITA starts again in 1980.

1984: Over 600,000 people are internally displaced in Angola. Luanda's population doubles as the displaced flee to the capital city of Luanda. Drought and the war leads to famine in 1984 and 1990.

1991: The UNITA and MPLA sign a peace agreement to be monitored by the UN.

1992: Elections are held. The MPLA wins 57 per cent of the votes and UNITA 32 per cent. UN monitors declare the elections to be generally free and fair. Yet Jonas Savimbi, President of UNITA, refuses to recognise the result. UNITA soon reorganises its army and begins to seize towns and villages. The civil war starts again.

November 1994: Another ceasefire and peace treaty - the Lusaka Protocols - are declared after peace talks are held in Zambia. The UN continues to monitor the peace. But the ceasefire does not last.

1999: Full-scale war begins again. The UN withdraws all its peacekeepers stating that there is no peace to keep.

2001: The Angolan armed forces push UNITA to the south and east. UNITA's president, Jonas Savimbi, is killed. After the death of his successor in March 2002, UNITA and the Angolan government sign a peace accord.

Today: There is still peace but the humanitarian situation has worsened. Much farmland cannot be used because landmines have been laid there. There are also many human rights concerns. It is not safe to travel in many parts of Angola. Government and UNITA soldiers are still terrorising ordinary citizens. There is little central government control outside the big cities. Some 800,000 people are still internally displaced and about 300,000 people are refugees.

Refugees in Angola

Sousa Jamba's story

Sousa Jamba is a writer who fled from Angola in 1976. He now lives in London.

"In 1976, at the height of the first bout of the Angolan civil war, I fled with my sister Noemia to Zambia. My sister was married to an Angolan with Zambian roots and I lived in Zambia until 1985 when I went to join the UNITA guerrillas in the Angolan bush. I then worked as a reporter and translator for the UNITA news agency. My experiences of that part of Angola formed the background to *Patriots*, my first novel."

"In 1986, aged 20, I came to Britain on a scholarship to study journalism. I was the given money by the Scottish Arts Council to work with school students in schools in southwest Scotland. I am now living in London and my second novel, *A Lonely Devil*, was published in 1993."

Here is an extract from 'Patriots'. The book follows the life of Hosi Mbueti. As a boy Hosi fled Angola after the death of his parents. Ten years later Hosi returns from exile to join UNITA. He finds himself fighting against his brother Osvaldo, who many years before chose to fight for the MPLA. In the extract Hosi is still a boy and still living in Angola. The civil war has just started.

Displaced Angolans at a bomb-damaged station at Luena, southern Angola.
© **Clare Crawford**

"Valeriana Mbueti rushed off to the kitchen to get her sister some food. Aunt Laura turned to Hosi at last and said: 'It has come at last Hosi.'

'What, Auntie?'

'The war.'

'What did I hear you say, Laura?' said Nathaniel Mbueti.

'The war. In Huambo people are killing each other. There was a time when we thought it would all end in Luanda. We were mistaken. It is now here.'

Nathaniel Mbueti ordered Hosi to go to bed. Hosi stalled for a while but a few fierce looks convinced him that his father meant business.

That night Hosi wondered what would happen next. There was talk of war everywhere. There were armed men everywhere. Children who had recently been playing mothers and fathers were now playing soldiers. They would divide themselves into three movements - UNITA, the MPLA and the FNLA - and then throw stones at each other. Hosi himself was a bit old for the game, and though the other children had tried to persuade him to play, he hadn't done so.

Hosi was worried, but not very worried. He knew there was nothing he could do to prevent the war, so at some point he began to enjoy the feeling that was spreading among the other children. Everyone wanted to have a uniform and a wooden AK-47. Still, now and then he did wonder whether there would be a time when there would be humans and dogs rotting in the streets."

Information: The arms trade

Landmines are just one military item sold to poor countries of the world. Many people believe that the arms trade worsens poverty and thus conflicts. The arms trade can eventually cause more people to become refugees. These are the arguments that organisations like **Campaign Against Arms Trade** use in their work.

Poor countries spend money on their armed forces, which could otherwise be spent on development projects to help poor people. Poverty causes discontent and can contribute to instability and conflicts. In 1993 the world's poor countries spent over £75 billion on their armed forces. Over £10 billion was spent on importing weapons from rich countries. The money to buy one British Aerospace Hawk fighter jet could be used to provide clean drinking water to 1.5 million people.

The arms trade causes poor countries to go into debt. Throughout the 1970s poor countries borrowed money at low interest rates to be able to purchase arms. In the 1980s interest rates went up and some countries found they could not pay back their debts. If a country goes into debt it cannot use public money to help poor people. Food subsidies, education and health projects may have to be cut in a country facing debts. This can again lead to discontent and conflicts.

Second-hand weapons are making conflicts worse in many poor countries. Since the collapse of the Soviet Union and the end of the Cold War, governments throughout Europe have been reducing the size of their armed forces. Many weapons from European countries have been sold to poor countries. The wars in Afghanistan, Liberia, Sierra Leone, Somalia and Sri Lanka are being fought with second-hand weapons. All these conflicts produce large numbers of refugees.

Arms sales can help governments that abuse human rights hang on to power. Many governments rule countries by force rather than consent. These governments rely on powerful security forces to keep its people in check. Powerful security forces have to be armed. Repressive governments kept in power by arms sales include Iraq, Nigeria, Turkey and the Democratic Republic of Congo. These are all countries from which political opponents have had to flee as refugees.

Arms sales can prolong international conflicts and heighten tensions that lead to war. For example, the Iran-Iraq War of 1980-88 was partly caused by the massive arms buying by both countries during the 1970s. Other regional conflicts made worse by arms buying include North Korea and South Korea, Greece and Turkey, India and Pakistan and the Arab-Israeli conflict.

An anti arms trade demonstration put on by Campaing Against Arms Trade.
© **CAAT**

Suppliers and importers of weapons

Top 20 suppliers of major conventional weapons, 1993-97

1 USA
2 USSR/Russia
3 UK
4 France
5 Germany
6 China
7 Netherlands
8 Italy
9 Canada
10 Spain
11 Israel
12 Ukraine
13 Czech Republic
14 Sweden
15 Moldova
16 North Korea
17 Uzbekistan
18 Belgium
19 Belarus
20 Australia

Top 20 importers of major conventional weapons, 1993-97

1 Saudi Arabia
2 Taiwan
3 Turkey
4 Egypt
5 South Korea
6 China
7 Japan
8 India
9 Greece
10 Kuwait
11 United Arab Emirates
12 Thailand
13 Malaysia
14 Pakistan
15 USA
16 Iran
17 Germany
18 Spain
19 Finland
20 Indonesia

(Source: Stockholm International Peace Research Institute Database)

Learning objectives: At the end of the activity students will understand arguments for and against the sales of arms.

Time needed: 30 minutes

Instructions: The students should be divided into pairs. Each group should be given the student instructions and statements.

Student instructions: Many different countries have supplied weapons and landmines to the Angolan government and the mujahideen. Organisations like Campaign Against Arms Trade believe that this sale of arms has made the war in Angola much worse. Not everyone agrees with their views about the arms trade. In pairs look at the statements below and see if you agree with them. Discuss your views with your partner.

Activity

The arms trade

Statements

The UK should not sell arms to countries that are fighting wars. Arms sales only worsen conflicts, causing deaths, injuries and more refugees. **Agree/Disagree**

The UK does not need to bother about which country or group buys its arms. The decision about using arms lies in the hands of the buyer, not the seller. **Agree/Disagree**

The UK should not sell arms to countries that have bad records of human rights.
Agree/Disagree

The UK should be allowed to give military aid and sell arms to countries that are facing invasion or danger from other nations. **Agree/Disagree**

If the UK stopped making arms, up to 625,000 people could lose their jobs and the country would lose a valuable export. **Agree/Disagree**

If the UK did not sell arms to countries at war or with poor human rights records, other countries would still make the sales. **Agree/Disagree**

The UK government should be finding ways of making the British economy less dependent on the sale of arms. **Agree/Disagree**

Information: Landmines and cluster bombs

Landmines are small explosive devices laid in the soil. They explode when a person treads on them. Most people who step on landmines lose a limb, but children are more likely to be killed. The UN Working Group on Mines estimates that 800 people die every month from mine-related injuries. Many more people lose their arms or legs.

In Cambodia **1 person in 280** has lost limbs as a result of landmines.

In Angola **1 person in 470** has lost limbs as a result of landmines.

There are many different types of landmine. Some landmines are meant to 'self-destruct' after a period of time. But self-destruct landmines do not always work properly and at least 10 per cent remain active.

Landmine injuries cause an enormous economic burden to a poor country. They remain active long after a war has finished. They create no-go areas and prevent refugees returning to their homes. Landmines prevent people from growing food or grazing animals.

A landmine costs about 70p to manufacture and lay. But it is an extremely lengthy process to remove them. It costs at least £200 to remove a landmine. Over 100,000,000 landmines are still in place around the world. The worst affected countries are:

Afghanistan	**Angola**	**Cambodia**	**El Salvador**	**Ethiopia**
Iran	**Iraq**	**Kuwait**	**Laos**	**Mozambique**
Liberia	**Nicaragua**	**Rwanda**	**Somaliland**	**Sri Lanka**
Sudan	**Uganda**	**Vietnam**	**Western Sahara**	
Former Yugoslavia		**Zimbabwe**		

Countries which produce or have recently produced landmines include:

Argentina	**Austria**	**Belgium**	**Chile**	**China**
France	**Israel**	**Italy**	**Portugal**	**Russia**
Spain	**UK**			

The UK has not produced whole landmines for ten years. But it is producing parts for landmines and other explosive devices, which can act like landmines.

The use of landmines is governed by international law. The *1980/81 UN Inhumane Weapons Convention* was intended to stop landmines being used against civilians. But it failed to stop the production of mines. Some countries did stop producing landmines. Belgium, Norway and Sweden, for example, have banned the production and export of landmines.

In the early 1990s many non-governmental organisations working in poor countries or with refugees campaigned against the manufacture and use of landmines. Among those supporting a ban on landmines was the late Princess Diana. As a result of the campaign the UK government announced a ban on the export of landmines in 1994. But this ban did not include the export of self-destruct landmines.

The British and US armies continue to use another deadly weapon called cluster bomb. This is a type of bomb that breaks up into about 200 small 'bomblets' when it hits the ground. The bomblets are scattered over a wide area and each one contains an explosive - enough to kill a person. The case of the bomblet is made of metal, so when the bomblet explodes metal fragments fly everywhere. Like landmines, many of the bomblets do not explode immediately but remain active on the ground. Here curious children may pick them up. Like landmines, the remains of cluster bombs also stop refugees returning.

The British and US armies used cluster bombs in Iraq. Iraq, Afghanistan and Sudan are most badly affected by the remains of cluster bombs. The use of cluster bombs in the 2003 Iraq War prompted non-governmental organisations to get together again to campaign for a ban. In November 2003 a number of US and European charities formed the Cluster Bomb Munitions Coalition.

Activity ☞

Producing a campaign poster

Learning objectives: The activity aims to make students more aware of political advertising.

Time needed: At least 45 minutes

Instructions: Students will need art materials and large sheets of A1 or A2 paper. They should be given copies of the information sheet on landmines and cluster bombs. Access to the internet would also help students carry out research. The teacher should introduce the activity by explaining that larger campaigning organisations use advertising as part of their campaigns. Students can be shown examples of campaign advertising.

The students' task is to produce a poster advertisement for the Cluster Bomb Munitions Coalition. The advertisement should aim to get ordinary people, including teenagers, to write to their MPs to ask the UK government to stop using cluster bombs.

Student Action for Refugees get students to campaign against Government asylum policies.
© **STAR**

Information: War and refugees in West Africa

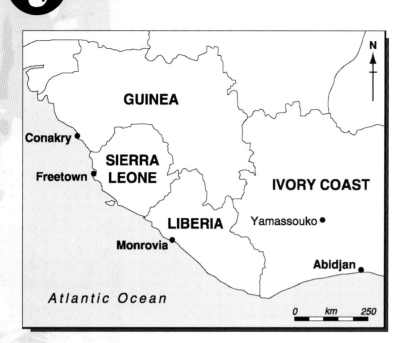

Conflict in Sierra Leone, Liberia, the Ivory Coast and Guinea has caused nearly 2 million people to flee from their homes. About 17,000 Sierra Leonan refugees live in the UK. They have joined a community that dates back to the 19th century.

Sierra Leone

Population: 5.4 million
Capital: Freetown
Ethnic groups: The Temne (30 per cent of the population) and Mende (30 per cent) are the two largest ethnic groups. About 10 per cent of the population identify themselves as Krio and are the descendants of freed African slaves returned by the British in the 19th century. There is also a Lebanese minority group living in Freetown. The Lebanese and the Krio dominate commercial life causing some resentment among other ethnic groups.
Languages: Official language is English. Krio (an English-based Creole), Mende and Temne are the most widely spoken languages.

Economy: Most people survive by farming. Sierra Leone is one of the world's poorest countries despite its many natural resources such as gold, diamonds, iron ore and tropical timber.

Events:

1989: Civil war begins in neighbouring Liberia. Sierra Leone sends troops to Liberia as part of the West African Peace Keeping Force (ECOWAS). The conflict spills over into Sierra Leone. Rebels belonging to the National Patriotic Front of Liberia advance into eastern Sierra Leone, partly to gain revenge for Sierra Leone's support for the ECOWAS. Over 200,000 people flee as refugees.

1991: Another 150,000 people are internally displaced. More and more Sierra Leoneans are dragged into the fighting. A new rebel group begins to emerge: the Revolutionary United Front (RUF) led by Foday Sankoh.

1992: President Momoh is overthrown in a coup led by junior army officers. Captain Valentine Strasser becomes president. He is 25. Although elections are promised, opponents of the new government face detention without trial, torture or extrajudicial execution. Despite promises to end the war, violence soon spreads throughout Sierra Leone. Rebel soldiers and the regular army are accused of murder. The rebels - RUF soldiers, current or ex-Sierra Leonean army soldiers or common criminals - attack villages creating panic. People flee their homes which are looted. Gold and diamonds are smuggled out of the country and used to finance the war.

1994: Fighting worsens. Over 200,000 people flee as refugees, with a further 900,000 internally displaced.

1996: Valentine Strasser is overthrown and replaced by Julius Maada Bio, another army officer. He signs a peace agreement and agrees to hold elections. Ahmed Tejan Kabbah is elected president.

May 1997: The democratically elected government is overthrown in another coup. Fighting and human rights abuses follow. Many civilians have limbs amputated by rebels, girls are raped and children forced to become soldiers. Eventually President Kabbah is restored to power but fighting continues in many parts of the country.

1999: RUF rebel soldiers enter Freetown. Media coverage of the destruction of parts of Freetown results in the UK government intervening.

2000: British troops are invited to train and support the Sierra Leonean army. The power of the RUF begins to decline. By 2001 there is very little fighting.

November 2001: UN peacekeepers (UNAMSIL) arrive in Sierra Leone.

Today: There is peace in Sierra Leone, but over 200,000 people have been killed since 1992. Most of the eastern part of Freetown has been completely destroyed. Some 68,000 people remain as refugees and a further 100,000 are internally displaced.

Refugees from the Ivory Coast

Population: 16.4 million
Capital: Yamassouko
Ethnic groups: 30 per cent of the population are migrants from other African countries. The main ethnic groups are the Akan, Baole, Bete, Dyula and Senufo.
Languages: French is the official language. African languages are spoken in rural areas, mostly Bete, Baule and Mandekan.
Religions: Excluding migrants, some 12 per cent of Ivorians are Christian, mostly Roman Catholic. Another 25 per cent are Muslim, mostly living in the north. Some 63 per cent of the population practice traditional beliefs. The migrant population is largely Muslim.
Economy: The Ivory Coast is the world's largest producer of cocoa and also produces significant amounts of coffee.

Events:

1960: The Ivory Coast gains independence from France. Felix Houphouet-Boigny governs the country until his death in 1993.

1970s-1980s: The Ivory Coast is a stable and fairly prosperous country. But in the 1980s, the world market prices of coffee and cocoa fall. There are economic problems. Its debt grows. The government is forced to make cuts in education and healthcare.

Early 1990s: Students and workers demonstrate against these cuts. The government closes schools and universities. It sends the army onto the streets of Abidjan. As a result of continuing unrest President Houphouet-Boigny is forced to hold the first multi-party elections in 1990. He wins but still experiences considerable opposition, mostly from students.

1993: President Houphouet-Boigny dies and is replaced by Henri Konan Bedie, who introduces the nationalist policy of 'Ivorian-

ness'. Many migrants and some Muslims are deemed to be non-Ivorian. Attacks on Muslims and people of migrant origin increase throughout the 1990s.

1995: Further presidential elections take place following weeks of violence and demonstrations. Most opposition parties boycott the elections and Bedie returns to office.

1999: Alassane Ouattara, a Muslim from the North, returns to the Ivory Coast and announces he intends to re-enter Ivorian politics. Almost immediately, there are moves to deny that he was an Ivorian citizen.

Late 1990s: The Ivorian army increases in size and power. Eventually there is a coup. General Robert Guei, the new President, promises free and fair elections. During the election campaign, there is much unrest and violence. The Ivorian army executes hundreds of political protesters and migrants. Muslims and political activists are also detained and tortured.

2000: General Guei is declared winner of the 2000 elections. There are continued demonstrations against his rule. Eventually he is forced out of office and replaced by Laurent Gbagbo in October.

September 2002: Violence erupts again with soldiers staging an uprising against President Gbagbo. The fighting spreads rapidly throughout the Ivory Coast. Liberia is accused of backing one rebel group.

By August 2004: Some 100,000 people have fled as refugees and 700,000 people are internally displaced. A ceasefire and peace agreement is negotiated. This allows for some of the rebel leaders to enter government. But the potential for further fighting is high. The country is now split: migrants and the population of the mainly Islamic North have given their support to the guerrillas.

Refugees from Liberia

About 3,000 Liberian refugees live in the UK.

Population: 3.2 million
Capital: Monrovia
Ethnic groups: Liberia is a multi-ethnic country. Inter-ethnic conflict was one of the causes of the civil war. Americo-Liberians, the descendants of freed African slaves from America, make up 5 per cent of the population but have dominated politics and control much of the country's wealth. Other large ethnic groups include the Kpelle, Basse and Gio/Mano. There is also a small Lebanese community, mostly living in Monrovia.
Language: English is the official language. Most people speak Krio, also called Liberian English. Krio is derived from the English of American slaves and influenced by the local languages of Liberia.
Economy: Most Liberians work on the land. The country's main exports are rubber, coffee, cocoa, diamonds and iron ore. Liberia's wealth is in the hands of a few people. Inequality is another cause of today's conflict.

Events:

1821: The first Americo-Liberians arrive. Before, local chiefs ruled Liberia.

1847: Libera becomes independent.

1927: The US-owned Firestone Tyre and Rubber Company sets up its first rubber plantation in Liberia. By 1950 Liberia's economy is totally dependent on the company.

1971: President William Tubman dies after ruling for 27 years. William Tolbert Junior, another Americo-Liberian and a member of the True Whig Party, succeeds. But resistance to the True Whig Party and the dominance of Americo-Liberians is growing.

1980: Tolbert's government is overthrown in a military coup led by Samuel Doe. All political parties are banned.

1984: The ban on political parties is lifted and elections are held in 1985. Samuel Doe wins although there are widespread allegations of fraud. Between 1985 and 1989, there is growing opposition to Samuel Doe's rule.

1989: Fighting breaks out in northeastern Liberia. Charles Taylor leads a new opposition group, the National Patriotic Front of Liberia (NPFL). The fighting between the NPFL and the Liberian army quickly turns into an ethnic conflict between the Krahn people, the Gio and Mano.

1990: NPFL guerrillas advance on the capital city Monrovia. The NPFL and Liberian army kill many civilians and are accused of human rights violations. As the NPFL enters Monrovia, it splits into two groups who fight each other. Guerrillas capture and kill President Doe. Amos Sawyer becomes interim president of Liberia, but in reality his government has little control over the country. By the end of 1990 some 300,000 Liberians are refugees and another 500,000 are internally displaced. Other West African nations fear that fighting in Liberia could destabilise the whole region. They call for peace talks but the NPFL refuses to attend. Later ECOWAS, a peacekeeping force made up of soldiers from Nigeria, the Gambia, Ghana, Sierra Leone, Guinea and Togo, arrive in Liberia.

1991: Liberia's conflict spills over into neighbouring Sierra Leone, with NPFL guerrillas invading and arming a Sierra Leonean rebel group.

1993: Peace talks continue and a ceasefire is announced. It does not lead to peace. New rebel groups enter the fighting.

1994: The conflict worsens. Soldiers in the Liberian army and the guerrillas act outside the control of their leaders. As in neighbouring Sierra Leone, the guerrillas use child soldiers, some as young as 10.

1995: Liberian rebels attack the Ivory Coast.

1996: There is further fighting around Monrovia. Later there are further peace talks and a government is formed.

1997: Presidential and legislative elections are held. Charles Taylor becomes president. Liberia experiences two years of relative calm.

1999: Peace ends when a rebel force attacks towns in northern Liberia.

2002: Another rebel group organises guerrillas and starts to march towards Monrovia.

March 2003: The rebels enter Monrovia and demand the removal of President Charles Taylor and the set up of an interim government. Human rights organisations and many governments also demand that Charles Taylor steps down and is tried for crimes against humanity.

August 2003: Nigerian peacekeepers arrive in Liberia. Charles Taylor eventually leaves and a peace agreement is signed with the rebel groups.

Today: A new government is formed and elections are scheduled for 2006. But Liberia faces many challenges. Demobilising guerrillas, many of whom are teenagers, is one of the biggest hurdles. Over 250,000 people have been killed since 1989. Virtually the whole population of Liberia has been displaced at one time or another during the war. Today 200,000 people are still internally displaced and a further 200,000 are refugees.

Guinea

Population: 9 million
Capital: Conakry
Ethnic groups: Peuhl (40 per cent), (Malinke 30 per cent), Soussou (20 per cent).
Languages: Official language is French. Mandekan, Soussou and other African languages are also spoken.
Economy: Most Guineans are farmers. The country also has large reserves of bauxite.

Events:

1906: Guinea becomes part of the French West African Federation. Pro-independence parties began to organise in the 1950s.

1958: Guinea wins its independence, with Ahmed Sekou Toure as its first president.

1984: Toure dies and is succeeded by General Lansana Conte, who takes power in a military coup. Despite opposition to his rule, President Conte holds power by winning elections in 1993 and 1998.

Since 1989: Guinea has hosted thousands of refugees from Liberia, Sierra Leone and the Ivory Coast. Rebel soldiers from all three countries have also used Guinea as a base.

2000: Fighting breaks out in southeastern Guinea between rebel soldiers and the Guinean army. Over 80,000 Guineans flee as internally displaced people. Thousands of refugees from Liberia, the Ivory Coast and Sierra Leone are also endangered in this fighting.

Emile's story

"I, Emile Delano Cooper am dedicating this essay to the loving memory of all the innocent boys and girls who have died as a result of the senseless Liberian civil war."

"By African standards my family is not a large one. It is composed of six persons: my father, my mother, a brother, two sisters and myself. I am the third child of the family. Presently we are refugees in Ghana. Refugee is a word I never dreamed I would be called by! This proves that no one knows what the future has in store. Since the war began we have had many hard times. We have gone through sleeping in a decent home with warm beds and drinking cold water from the ice-box, to sleeping on the ground in the open air with mosquitoes feasting on our blood and drinking unsafe water that makes us ill often. Living as a refugee is a painful pleasure. Painful because we have to work very hard sometimes. We depend on food rations from the UN and contributions from relatives and friends to keep us alive. A pleasure because we have learned the dignity of working with our hands. I could never have imagined myself working in a garden as a means of getting additional food. Now I am proudly doing it."

Liberian and Sierra Leonean displaced persons in Upper Lofa.
© UNHCR / L. Taylor

Information: Child soldiers

Child soldiers are young people under 18 who fight in wars. During the last 20 years at least 300,000 young people have been involved in wars in different parts of the world. It is believed that recently there has been an increased use of children and young people in wars. It is mostly boys who fight as child soldiers, but in some parts of the world girls are recruited too. Some child soldiers are as young as 9 or 10.

Sometimes children are forced to become soldiers. They might be taken out of their schools or away from their villages. But frequently children join voluntarily. When a young person's school is destroyed, or when family and friends are involved in the conflict, fighting can seem attractive. It may seem better to become a soldier than to sit at home being frightened and helpless. Some children become soldiers so that they can receive food, clothing and shelter.

Most organisations working with children believe that it is damaging and wrong for children to fight in wars. Fighting has major effects on children. They can be wounded and permanently disabled. Witnessing violence is also very traumatic. Some child soldiers suffer permanent psychological damage and are unable to lead a normal life after the conflict ends.

Children who are soldiers miss out on their education. This may prevent them from finding work afterwards. Child soldiers may also be rejected by their families and communities after a war and be forced to live alone.

Child soldiers have fought in the conflicts in Sierra Leone, Liberia, the Ivory Coast and Guinea. In Liberia many child soldiers were given drugs before they were sent to fight. One former Liberian child soldier said that children, often drugged were "the bravest and most reckless of soldiers".

In Liberia and Sierra Leone, children's organisations such as UNICEF are helping child soldiers. They work with the governments of these countries to stop children being recruited into the army. They also support former child soldiers in rehabilitation centres. Here the young people receive food and shelter, education and training for employment. The former child soldiers also receive counselling to help them overcome traumatic experiences. UNICEF also tries to reunite child soldiers with their families.

Countries where children are recruited into armies or guerrilla forces

- Burma
- Congo-Brazzaville
- Democratic Republic of Congo
- Ivory Coast
- Liberia
- Sierra Leone
- Somalia
- Sri Lanka
- Sudan

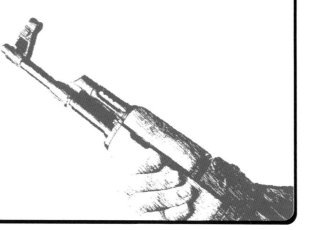

Information: Child soldiers and human rights law

There are a number of international human rights laws that are meant to ensure that combatants and victims of armed conflict are treated humanely. But it is only recently that human rights activists have begun to campaign against the recruitment of child soldiers.

The most important international human rights laws that govern the treatment of combatants and victims of armed conflict are the *1949 Geneva Conventions.* The Geneva Conventions grew out of the early work of the International Committee of the Red Cross. The Swiss businessman, Jean Henri Dunant, founded this organisation in 1863. He was very shocked by the treatment of soldiers at the Battle of Solferino in 1849, where over 40,00 men died in one day. Dunant's experiences led him to believe that injured soldiers needed protection and humane treatment.

One of the first successes of the International Committee of the Red Cross was the signing of the *First Geneva Convention* in 1864. This international law protects sick and wounded soldiers on land. Later, in 1949 more countries signed the *Geneva Conventions of 1949.* The Conventions are:

- Geneva Convention I: This protects sick and wounded soldiers on land.
- Geneva Convention II: This protects sick, wounded or shipwrecked combatants at sea.
- Geneva Convention III: This protects prisoners of war.
- Geneva Convention IV: This protects civilians who are in the hands of the enemy, for example civilians living in occupied territories. This Convention has been used to try and protect internally displaced people.

In 1977, many of the world's nations met again and signed the *1977 Additional Protocols to the Geneva Conventions.* The *1977 Additional Protocols* recognised that children were now fighting as child soldiers. The Protocols states that no child under 15 should be allowed to join an army. In 1989, the *UN Convention on the Rights of the Child* was signed. Article 38 of this Convention states that no child under 15 should be allowed to join an army.

However, the UN defines a child as a person under 18. All the other parts of the *UN Convention on the Rights of the Child* protect children under 18 except Article 38.

Article 38 of the Convention on the Rights of the Child in simple language

1. Countries who have signed the Convention must make sure that children in armed conflict benefit from the humanitarian laws that exist.
2. Countries who have signed the Convention must do everything they can that no children under 15 are being asked to fight in conflict.
3. Countries who have signed the Convention must not recruit any children under 15 into the army.
4. Countries who have signed the Convention must make sure that children who are affected by armed conflict are taken care of and protected.

Most children's charities believe that 15 is still too young to fight in battle. They campaigned to change the *1989 UN Convention on the Rights of the Child*. As a result of the campaign, a number of countries signed the *2000 Optional Protocol to the Convention on the Rights of the Child on the Involvement of Children in Armed Conflict*. This states that no child under 18 should join armed forces. By 2003, 109 countries had signed. However, many countries have not done so, including the UK, the US, Germany, Denmark and Ireland.

Discussion point:

⇨ Do you think that young people should be allowed to join the British army at 16? Or should the minimum age by 18?

Learning objectives: The activity aims to develop participants' campaigning and lobbying skills. The group is going to be asked to run a campaign to get the UK government to sign the *2000 Optional Protocol to the Convention on the Rights of the Child on the Involvement of Children in Armed Conflict*.

Time needed: 2 lessons or 2 hours

Instructions: The information about child soldiers and lobbying should be photocopied in advance. Pens, paper, word processing or desktop publishing software are also needed.

Divide the students into groups of fours or fives. Explain the purpose of the activity. Give them the information about child soldiers and campaigning. Tell them to design a campaign to get the UK government to sign the *2000 Optional Protocol to the Convention on the Rights of the Child on the Involvement of Children in Armed Conflict*.

Get the groups to design a campaign leaflet and a strategy for campaigning. When the groups have finished displaying their leaflets, get them to present their campaign strategies.

Activity ☞

Lobbying and campaigning

A young boy enlisted by the Sudan People's Liberation Army (SPLA). © **Panos Pictures / Martin Adler**

Information: Lobbying

Lobbying means approaching people who hold power to get them to change laws or practices. Pressure groups will lobby people in power. Lobbying has to be planned carefully.

You should first think about what you want to achieve. What laws or practices do you want to change? Who are you going to approach? Obviously, your aims determine who you will approach. If you want to change things that are happening abroad you could write to the ambassador of that country. If you wish to change things in the UK you may want to lobby your MP or other people in power.

What methods are you going to use? If you want to approach your local MP it is probably best to write to him or her. You could also invite your MP to your group.

Submitting a petition to the Prime Minister at 10 Downing Street is one way of lobbying.
© **Refugee Council**

Campaigning

Campaigning is about getting a group of ordinary people to carry out a particular action. People organising a campaign plan it very carefully. They consider many of the following questions:

- What do you aim to achieve in your campaign?
- Who is the target audience?
- What methods are you going to use? You must use methods that are appropriate to your audience.
- What are you going to ask people to do?

Producing a leaflet

What do you wish to achieve?

Who is the target audience? The audience will determine the look and feel of your leaflet, and you should use appropriate language for your target audience.

What message do you wish to communicate? You should decide on the message you want to get over.

What kind of images and pictures will you use to put across your message? Are they negative or positive images? Do they reinforce stereotypes?

Information: Refugees in the Caucasus

find themselves living in the Russian Empire.

1908: There is a revolution in Turkey led by the Young Turks who are extremely nationalistic. The Sultan is removed and replaced by a more democratic government. There is increased repression of Turkey's minority groups, while the Armenians are suspected of sympathising with enemy powers.

The Caucasus is a multi-ethnic region. Since the break-up of the Soviet Union in 1989, increasing nationalism has led to ethnic conflict and the movement of large number of refugees. Today there are over 1.4 million internally displaced people in the Caucasus.

Armenia

Population: 3.1 million
Capital: Yerevan
Ethnic groups: Armenians make up 95 per cent of the population, but there are small numbers of Azeris, Russians and Kurds. Armenians also live in Cyprus, Turkey, Syria, Lebanon, Iran, Georgia, Russia, the US and France.

Events:

15th century: Much of Armenia becomes part of the Ottoman Empire.

1827: With the Russian conquest of the Caucasus, large numbers of Armenians

1915-1917: The most tragic event in Armenian history takes place - the genocide of Armenians. After military setbacks in the First World War, violent attacks on Armenians start, as nationalists use them as scapegoats. 1.5 million Armenians are shot or die of starvation or disease. Thousands are deported from their homelands and die on death marches. One third of all Armenians die in this holocaust. The perpetrators of this crime have never been brought to justice. Even today the Turkish government denies that it ever occurred. Some 500,000 Armenians flee into exile to Russia and Middle Eastern countries during the First World War.

1918: The First World War ends. Armenia becomes an independent state. But independence does not last long.

1920: The Soviet Union and Turkey invade Armenia.

Caucasus

1922: Armenia becomes part of the Soviet Union. Many Armenians find themselves living outside the Soviet Republic of Armenia, including Armenians living in Nagorno-Karabakh. This is a region where most of the population are Armenian but it is located in Azerbaijan.

1988: Encouraged by greater freedom, Armenians in Nagorno-Karabakh demand to be united with Armenia. Some Armenians in this area take up arms to fight for this. Ethnic Azeris living in the area are attacked and thousands of them flee as refugees. The conflict lasts until 1994.

1990: The Soviet Union collapses. Armenia declares itself to be an independent state.

1994: There is a ceasefire in Nagorno-Karabakh. But there is still no peace in this region. Armenian nationalist guerrillas occupy part of Nagorno-Karabakh. All attempts for lasting peace fail.

Azerbaijan

Population: 8.4 million
Capital: Baku
Ethnic groups: Azeris (81 per cent), Armenians (5 per cent), Russians (5 per cent). Most Azeris are Muslims.

Events:

19th century: Azerbaijan is divided between the Russian and Persian Empires. Its extensive oil reserves are first exploited at the end of the 19th century.

1918: At the end of the First World War, Azerbaijan is an independent country for a short period.

1920: The Soviet Union invades Azerbaijan, which becomes a republic within the Soviet Union.

1988: War breaks out in Nagorno-Karabakh, a region in Azerbaijan where the majority of the population are Armenian. Ethnic Azeris are forced to flee Nagorno-Karabakh, where they fear the nationalist Armenian guerrillas. Elsewhere in Azerbaijan, ethnic Armenians flee their homes fearing revenge attacks.

1990 and 1991: Inter-ethnic violence between Azeris and the minority Armenian population cause dozens of deaths in Baku.

Today: Some 760,000 Azeris are still internally displaced and unable to return to their homes in Nagorno-Karabakh. Although there is a ceasefire, there is no peaceful solution to this conflict. Human rights are not respected in Azerbaijan and political opponents of the government risk arrest.

Georgia

Population: 5 million
Capital: Tbilisi
Ethnic groups: Georgian (70 per cent), Armenian (8 per cent), Russian (6 per cent), Azeri (5 per cent), Ossetian (3 per cent), Greek (1.8 per cent), Abhazian (1.8 per cent). There are also Ukrainian, Kurdish, Georgian Jewish and 17 other groups.

Events:

Early 19th century: Most of present day Georgia becomes part of the Russian Empire

1918: After the First World War, Georgia becomes an independent state.

1921: The Red Army invades Georgia, which becomes part of the Soviet Union.

1989: In South Ossetia, very few people speak Georgian. South Ossetians living in Georgia want their region to be reunited with North Ossetia (part of Russia). The Georgian government rejects this proposal. There are violent clashes between Georgians and South Ossetians. Thousands of people fled.

1990: South Ossetia declares itself to be an independent republic within the Russian Federation. In response to this, the Georgian army enters South Ossetia. Fighting follows. 130,000 Ossetian and Russian people flee as refugees to Russia. Georgians are also internally displaced in the fighting.

1991: Georgia declares itself independent of the Soviet Union. Ruled by nationalist politicians, Georgian becomes the official language. Soon after independence, two wars break out in South Ossetia and in Abkhazia.

1992: A ceasefire is signed in 1992. The Georgian army withdraws many of its soldiers from South Ossetia but fighting and human rights abuses still continue. Ossetian people are the target of nationalist Georgian militia. The militia do not appear to be under the control of the Georgian government. The Georgian militia are trying to terrorise the Ossetians into leaving for North Ossetia. Soon after, fighting breaks out in Abkhazia. Here, Abkhaz nationalists proclaim independence. Ethnic Abkhaz militia fight the Georgian army and nationalist Georgian militia.

1994: There is a ceasefire and peace agreement.

2001: There is further fighting in Abkhazia. There is also an inter-ethnic conflict between Armenians and ethnic Georgians in Javakhetia in southern Georgia. Political leaders in Adzaria, another region of Georgia, have also announced they want independence.

Today: The government of President Eduard Shevardnadze is overthrown in November 2003. But like the previous government, the new Georgian government has no control of the countryside. A once prosperous country is one of the poorest states in central Asia. Some 70 per cent of Georgians live without a permanent supply of electricity and running water. Although there are ceasefires, there is still no solution to the conflicts in South Ossetia and Abkhazia. Some 260,000 Georgians are still internally displaced by recent conflicts and 20,000 people have fled as refugees.

Since 1988, ethnic conflict has uprooted several hundred thousand Azeri people.
© UNHCR / A. Hollmann

Information: Russia

Much of the northern Caucasus is part of Russia. It is a very multi-ethnic region. Russians are the largest ethnic group. Other ethnic groups include Tartars, Chechens, Ossetians, Armenians, Cherkassians and Jews. During the last 15 years, there have been two inter-ethnic conflicts in the Russian part of the northern Caucasus.

Chechnya

This is now an autonomous republic within Russia. In 1990 some 57 per cent of the population were Chechens and 23 per cent ethnic Russians. Most Chechens speak Chechen as their home language. Most are Muslims and their culture and traditions are different from their Russian neighbours. Many Chechens still work as herdsmen or farmers.

During the 19th century, when Russia attempted to colonise Chechnya, Russian soldiers met fierce resistance from Chechen fighters. Between 1944 and 1957 Joseph Stalin deported many Chechens to other parts of the Soviet Union. As a result of this experience plus their greater poverty, many Chechens felt they were facing discrimination by the Russian community particularly in employment.

This discrimination led many Chechens to support the idea of independence from Russia. Chechens declared an independent state in 1991. They organised their own army and government. In early 1995 the Russian army marched into Chechnya to put an end to the independence movement. The Russian government believed that allowing the Chechens independence would encourage other minorities to want their own states.

Thousands of people were killed in the fighting. Over 150,000 people from all ethnic groups were internally displaced. In 1996 there was a ceasefire, but no solution to the conflict. In 1999 there were a number of bomb explosions in Moscow. Chechen terrorists were blamed for the explosions, although there was no proof of Chechen involvement. Soon after the Russian army marched back into Chechnya. Grozny was destroyed and thousands more killed. Today, Chechen army has retreated to the mountains. It has been joined by armed Islamic fighters from other countries, most of whom believe they are fighting a holy war. The Russian army and armed Chechen guerrillas are known to have perpetrated terrible human rights abuses. These include extrajudicial executions, arrests, torture and rape.

Some 370,000 people are still internally displaced by the conflict. Most of these displaced people live in very temporary shelters, halls, schools factory buildings and railway carriages.

North Ossetia

This is an autonomous republic within Russia. It borders Ingushetia. Like most of the neighbouring republics, it is a multi-ethnic state. Its population is made up of Ossetians, Russians and Ingush people. Many people in North Ossetia are refugees from South Ossetia. Most of them live in very poor conditions.

During the 1940s Stalin forcibly moved large numbers of Ingush to central Asia and altered the borders of North Ossetia and Ingushetia. After the collapse of the Soviet Union many Ingush who lived in the eastern part of North Ossetia hoped that their land would be transferred to the autonomous republic of Ingushetia. But in 1992 fighting broke out between Ingush and North Ossetia militia. Over 65,000 Ingush refugees fled North Ossetia.

Arseni's story

Caucasus

Arseni is from South Ossetia. She has been forced to flee as a refugee and is now living in North Ossetia.

"Georgians came many times and burnt Ossetian houses in our village. I do not remember how many houses were burned. I heard recently that all the Ossetian houses were burnt. There were five or six houses on my street that were set on fire."

"After this we fled to the forest. Every night we went to sleep in the forest, as we felt that it was safer to be there as the Georgians only came to burn houses when it was dark. We had gone to the forest every night at midnight. But my husband's mother was old and ill. My husband said it would be better to go home. On the way back to our house we passed a group of Ossetian watchmen on the street. They did not have any weapons. Later that night my husband heard many cars near our house. He went outside, although I tried to stop him. When he stepped outside they started to shoot and he was wounded in the leg."

"There was heavy shooting. Everyone in the house got down on to the floor, my neighbour, my husband's mother and myself. Bullets went through all the windows."

"An ambulance came the next day to take people who had been wounded to the hospital. But we were afraid to leave the house because we knew that the Georgian militia were still watching. After the ambulance went, the militia came and arrested us all. There were six men in civilian clothes, all of them armed. They accused me of cooking food for Ossetian fighters. I do not cook because I never have any spare food. But they blamed me all the same. I was very frightened."

"One of the Georgian militia was our neighbour. He questioned me again and let me go. After this we left our village for good. My husband joined us after he had left the hospital."

Refugees in North Ossetia. © **UNHCR / T. Bolstad**

Information: Nationalism

Nationalism is a political or cultural movement where the priority is the future of a particular national group. Many sociologists believe that European countries and the former Soviet Union are experiencing a rise in nationalism. In the Caucasus and former Yugoslavia increased nationalism has led to war between different communities and the movement of refugees.

To understand nationalism we have to examine what we mean by 'nation' and 'nation-state'. A nation is a community of people of mainly common descent, history and language who inhabit a certain area. A nation-state is a nation which governs itself. The nation-state is the dominant form of political organisation today.

Some historians believe that nation-states are a modern political trend. During the Middle Ages, ordinary people had personal allegiances to their locality and region but not to a 'nation'. There was little central government in most countries and ordinary people had no democratic rights. But in the 18th century nation-states and nationalism began to develop. French nationalism grew from the French Revolution in 1789. German nationalism grew after the unification of Germany. Turkish and Arab nationalism developed at the end of the 19th century.

Other historians believe that nationalism and the nation-state evolved slowly and that they are not unique to the modern world. And today, some political scientists believe that the nation-state is becoming less important. Nations are organising themselves into trading blocs like the European Union. Multinational companies have much more power over governments than ever before. In the past nationalism has led to self-determination for colonised people. For example, the growth of Indian nationalism in the 1920s and 1930s eventually led to Indian independence in 1947.

But at times of economic crises nationalism can be very appealing to people. Everybody likes to belong to a group and feel proud of it. Nationalism may grow at times when other political ideas have been discredited. Nationalism can also lead to racism and the exclusion of minority groups. Nationalist politicians may portray minorities and outsiders as hostile or threatening. At its extreme, nationalism can lead to civil war. This is what is happening in the Caucasus. Today, in countries such as Armenia and Georgia, politicians have used nationalism as a way of maintaining their power. In both these countries, politicians and the press have:

- used heroes from folk stories to create a national identity;
- linked the idea of 'nation' with membership of the majority ethnic group thus excluding people who belong to ethnic minority communities;
- linked the idea of nation to membership of a particular religious group;
- linked the idea of nation to the use of a particular language or dialect;
- restricted the civil rights of some minority groups;
- created scapegoats and promoted the idea that minority groups or foreign nations are acting against the interests of their nation;
- used newspaper and television to promote nationalist ideas.

Discussion points:

⇨ What are the links between nationalism and racism?

⇨ Find out what the word 'patriotism' means. How does patriotism differ from nationalism?

⇨ Can patriotism be a good thing?

Learning objectives: At the end of the activity students are more aware of nationalism in modern Britain.

Time needed: 1 hour

Instructions: Old tabloid newspapers are needed for this activity. Students could be asked to collect them. Students will also need a highlighting pen. Introduce the activity and divide the group into pairs. Each pair should have two copies of tabloid newspapers. Students should examine the newspapers and look for stories, which they believe may promote nationalism. Such stories could include:

- Negative references to foreign nations and the European Union
- Negative references to minority groups
- Stories about national heroes or the royal family
- Exaggerated stories about sporting successes

They should mark each story with a highlighting pen. The class should then come together and look at the discussion points.

Discussion points:

⇨ How did the students decide whether a newspaper story promoted nationalism or not?

⇨ How many of such stories did they find in each newspaper?

⇨ From where do the students think these stories came?

⇨ How do newspapers and television influence what we think of as being British?

Learning objectives: This activity aims to explore the many different groups to which students belong. It aims to help students recognise that difference and diversity are positive.

Time needed: 45 minutes

Instructions: Old newspapers and magazines, large sheets of paper and coloured pens are needed. Divide the class into pairs. Each pair should use its own ideas, newspapers and magazines to make a list of as many social groups that people can belong to. Examples of social groups include religions, gender (male or female), type of job, ethnic groups, hobbies and interest groups, political beliefs, home language, sexuality and football team supported.

After 20 minutes come together. Make one big list of all the groups to which people can belong. Pin the list up. The pairs should then examine the discussion points.

Discussion points:

⇨ Students should use the list to think about how many different groups they belong to.

⇨ Can belonging to a tight-knit group be a bad thing?

⇨ Diversity and difference among people is positive. Do you agreed or disagree with this statement? Why?

Insiders and outsiders

Learning objectives: The activity aims to help students think about the formation of groups and the exclusion of outsiders.

Time needed: 1 hour

Instructions: The ideal group size is about 20 people. Stickers, paper, marker pens and chalk are needed. Divide up the group and give about a third of them stickers. Send the students with stickers into another room. They are the 'outsiders'. The rest of the group are 'insiders'. Sit with them and explain that they are going to work out some rules for break time in school. They will be able to make up five rules that will govern the lives of insiders and outsiders. Any rule that gets a majority vote will be passed.

Rules could include:

- Outsiders may not enter chalk circles unless invited.
- Outsiders may only use toilets marked with a sticker.

After five rules have been decided, they should be written on a large sheet of paper. The outsiders should then be invited back into the room. They should be told that it is an ordinary break time, but they must follow the rules decided by the insiders.

After ten minutes of the 'break' stop the simulation. Ask the students to discuss and write down answers to the following points.

Discussion points:

⇨ Do you think that the rules were fair?

⇨ What was the worst thing about having a sticker?

⇨ Were there any disadvantages about being an insider?

⇨ Did any of the outsiders try to do something that was forbidden to them? If so, how did the insiders react?

⇨ How did the insiders feel about the outsiders? Did they feel sorry for them or hostile towards them?

⇨ How do you think this game relates to everyday events in the world?

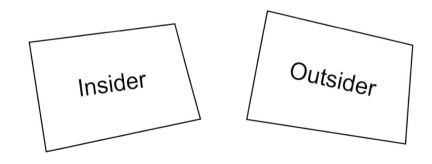

 # Journey to safety

Tajik refugees in Afghanistan. © UNHCR / A. Hollmann

This chapter looks at the difficult and dangerous journeys many asylum seekers are forced to make in order to reach safety. It uses case studies of Somali and Afghan asylum seekers as examples. The chapter also examines the smuggling of asylum seekers.

Arjun's story

"We drove from Jaffna to Colombo by car and then took a plane to Singapore. We arrived in Singapore and stayed there for one week. There were plenty of people. They wanted to go to Germany and all different countries. We stayed in our hotel for one week. The agents arranged all that. My dad gave money to them. And they gave us food and stuff."

"Then we arrived in Bombay. From there I think it was Africa. And we stayed for two years because we had all these problems with passports and everything. The agents were messing us around and they lied to us. We stayed in a big house and we had to cook. We had no money but sometimes my Dad sent money to us."

"Two men died there. They got sick with malaria. Many people get sick there. All sorts of people came to the house, Sri Lankans to go to Germany, to Britain, to France and other places. Mum was angry with the agents because we were going to come to Britain straight away from Colombo, but the agents made us stay in Africa for a long time."

"There were six or seven rooms upstairs and downstairs in the house. Downstairs it was a big place and we could play there. I know some children because I stayed for two years and I got some friends. But I couldn't go to school."

"Then I came to Holland and from Holland I came to Germany, Germany to France and it's a long story! This was all because of the agents as well. We spent a lot of money because of the agents."

"I stayed in Germany for six months. We stayed with Auntie, which was nice. From Germany I went to France in my uncle's car. Then we stayed in my uncle's house in France for about a week. We left France in my uncle's car and went to Dover. I didn't have a passport of my own. I had to dress up as a girl so when they asked for a passport we showed a girl's passport and we came through. I was wearing a hat. My sisters, they were laughing at me."

"My Dad was in Britain, so that's why we came to Britain you see. He was over here before us and had lived in England for about six years."

Arjun is a Tamil from Sri Lanka. He lives in the UK now.

Large numbers of Sri Lankans have been repeatedly displaced by the ongoing conflict.
© UNHCR / M. Kobayashi

How many goodbyes do you know?

There's the 'I hope I will see you again' goodbye

The 'I don't care if I never see your ugly face again' goodbye

The 'can't see my grandpa again' goodbye

The 'praying to the person who is going to Heaven' goodbye

There's the 'waiting to say goodbye' goodbye

The 'butterfly on a cup' goodbye

The 'goodbye, mama, goodbye, I'll never see you again' goodbye

There's the 'nalingiyo mingi' goodbye

The 'je t'aime vrais beaucoup, mais il faut que je parte' goodbye

Note: *Nalingiyo mingi* means 'I love you very much' in Lingala, a language widely spoken in the Democratic Republic of Congo. *Je t'aime vrais beaucoup, mais il faut que je parte* in French means 'I love you very much but I have to go'.

The poem was written by a group of young Congolese refugees who met to support each other at the Medical Foundation for the Care of Victims of Torture.

Discussion points:

⇨ What feelings might Arjun have felt at the different stages of his long journey?

⇨ Trace Arjun's journey using an atlas.

⇨ How do you think the young people were feeling when they wrote their poem about saying goodbye?

⇨ Think of a time in your own life when saying goodbye to someone mattered a lot. How did you feel?

⇨ Working in pairs or in a group make your own list of different ways that you can say goodbye.

⇨ The word origin (etymology) of 'goodbye' is a shortened form of 'God be with ye', a way of saying goodbye used in 16th century England. Can you find the word origins of 'farewell'? Can you find the word origins of other ways we say goodbye?

⇨ Write your own poem about saying goodbye.

Learning objectives: At the end of the activity students will understand some of the decisions refugees make when beginning their journey to safety.

Time needed: 30 minutes

Instructions: Refugees leave their homes in fear and some have to leave very quickly. They have to leave many things behind. Obviously many material possessions are left behind but also family and friends.

Students can work in pairs or individually. Put the class in the position of having 30 minutes to pack their bags. They should make a list of all the things they would take with them. (They would have to carry all these items.) Then the students should make a list of all the things that they value that they would have to leave behind. The class should come together for a plenary where ideas should be shared.

Activity 👆

What would I take and what would I leave?

Information: Refugees from Somalia

Most of the animals are exported to Saudi Arabia to provide food for pilgrims attending the Haj. Payments from Somalis working abroad are also important. Since the beginning of the 20th century Somali sailors have worked in the British merchant navy. Today many Somalis work in Europe or the Gulf States and send money home.

Events:

Archaeologists believe that Somali people have lived in the Horn of Africa for over 4,000 years. Ancient Egyptians knew Somalia as the 'Land of Punt' (land of frankincense). By 900 AD, Somali nomads are living in present-day Somalia and parts of present-day Ethiopia, Djibouti and Kenya. They are converted to Islam.

Over 205,000 Somali refugees live in the UK. Somalia has now split into four different administrations.

Population: An estimated 8 to 10 million
Capital: Mogadishu
Ethnic groups: Most people are ethnic Somalis and speak Somali. Somalis also live in Ethiopia, Djibouti and Kenya. There are also minority groups living in Somalia. They include the Bravanese, who live in the southern coastal towns and speak a dialect of Swahili called Brava. Although most Somalis belong to the same ethnic group, Somali society is very divided. The Somali population belongs to different clan families. Many Somalis give support to different political groups on the basis of the clan to which they belong.
Religion: Somalis are usually Sunni Muslims.
Land and economy: Most of Somalia is semi-desert. In southern Somalia fruit and subsistence crops are grown. About 60 per cent of Somalis live from grazing sheep, cattle and camels.

1884: The Berlin Conference divides up the African continent between the European imperial powers. The northern part of Somalia becomes British Somaliland. The Italians take control of the south.

1897: The Anglo-Abyssinian Treaty allocates the Ogaden region of British Somaliland to the Ethiopians. In the early years of the 20th century Sheikh Mohammed Abdilleh Hassan, called the 'Mad Mullah' by the British, leads rebellions against the Ethiopians, British and Italians. Although unsuccessful, he is credited with founding modern Somali nationalism. Other political leaders soon join him in calling for an independent Somali nation.

1939-45: In the Second World War the UK use British Somaliland as a base to fight the Italians in Eritrea, Abyssinia and Italian Somaliland. Many Somalis join the British armed forces and Italian Somaliland is captured.

1950: Somalia is again divided. The Italians return to the south with UN backing. The British continue to administer British Somaliland. Growing numbers of Somali people begin to demand independence.

1960: British and Italian Somaliland gain independence and unite to form one country. But the country is extremely poor. There are deep clan and political divisions but Somalia is a democracy and human rights are respected.

1969: The Somali government loses public support. President Abdirashid Ali Shermaarke is assassinated and army officers seize power in a military coup. Major General Mohammed Siad Barre becomes president of the newly named Somali Democratic Republic. An unelected body, the Supreme Revolutionary Council, rules the country. Political opposition is banned. The new government promises to improve the lives of ordinary people. The Somali language is written down and there is an educational campaign to help all Somalis learn to read and write.

1970: The Somali goverment gets military aid from the Soviet Union. The country soon has one of the largest armies in Africa.

1977: War breaks out with Ethiopia over the disputed territory of the Ogaden, which President Barre wants to bring into 'Greater Somalia'. But military aid from the Soviet Union stops. The US give military aid to the Somali government. But neither superpower contribute much to the economic development of the country. In the late 1970s, President Barre experiences opposition to his rule. Three political opposition parties start to organise themselves. They include the Somali National Movement (SNM). All soon resort to armed struggle in order to overthrow President Barre. The civil war begins. At first the fighting is worst in northern Somalia.

1988: The SNM attack northern towns. The Somali government responds by bombing Hargeisa and Burao. Over 72,000 people are killed in Hargeisa. 400,000 flee as refugees, some to the UK. Fighting moves to central Somalia.

1991: Somali guerrillas march into Mogadishu. President Siad Barre leaves the country. But the guerrilla groups begin to fight each other. The civil war worsens. Nearly one million people are internally displaced. Somalia is facing severe food shortages as a result of drought and the disruption of farming. UN relief agencies are criticised for their slow response.

May 1991: The SNM declare independence in the north. There is still a fragile peace in the new Republic of Somaliland. But it is an unrecognised state and does not qualify for international aid, desperately needed for rebuilding.

1992: The Red Cross warns that 4 million Somalis are at risk of starvation. Fighting prevents food aid from being distributed. Some 500,000 Somalis die of starvation including half of all children under five. US troops land in Mogadishu in 'Operation Restore Hope'. Food aid is delivered to hungry people, but the US army cannot disarm the guerrilla groups.

1993: A UN peacekeeping force takes over from the US in Mogadishu. Fighting continues.

1995: US troops leave Somalia.

2000: Further peace talks are held. Abdiqassim Salad Hassan is elected President of the Transitional National Government. But there is still much fighting in most towns in the south and east. In early 2004 some 400,000 people are internally displaced within Somalia and up to 1 million people are refugees, mostly in Kenya, the Gulf States, Europe and North America.

Somalia

Somalia

Sado's story

"I came back from Sunday school and I remember seeing that our living room as well as our kitchen had collapsed. Then I saw tanks in front of our house and they began firing. It was terrible."

"We ran as fast as we could, my mother holding my hand. There was also Feriyo, my friend, as well as her granny who was running behind us because she could not catch up with us. She was old. President Siad Barre's picture was everywhere. I used not to look at him, but while we were running I saw a huge picture of him and I was scared."

"Feriyo fell down while we were still running and there was this deafening noise. I let go of my mother's hand and ran back to help Feriyo but she wouldn't stand up. I shook her saying, 'Feriyo, stand up.' I begged her to stand but she wouldn't."

"I have lots of friends here in my new school in London, and they are all nice but I still remember Feriyo. She was so nice."

Sado was eight years old when she fled from Somalia.

Somalian refugees at
Dagahaley Camp in Kenya
© UNHCR / P. Moumtzis

Adil's story

Somalia

"Some neighbours were leaving. My mother agreed and she took me to the family's house. She gave them money to take care of me and take me to Kenya. Then we went to Kismayo. That's where the family told me that they did not have any money. They denied they had money and eventually told me to go, as they did not have anything for me. That's when my nightmare started."

"I eventually got a boat going to Kenya. It was a very long journey. The family did not like the idea of me going for free. I had to sit in the worst place in the boat. They had this big box where they had everything. I had to sit between the boxes. I had a big towel, this big white towel. I covered myself with the white towel. They had some water, they had some food, but I did not ask for it. I just covered myself up. I did not care."

"Sometimes there was screaming because they thought the boat was going down. But I did not care. I thought, 'if I die, I die.' The last day we had run out of everything. We had run out of the biscuit, we had run out of water. It was the worst day, even worse than when we met another boat that had broken down in the sea. I have seen a lot of people sinking, a lot of people crying for help and they were just next to us. Some were trying to catch on to our boat, but the sailors were pushing them away saying 'We can't take you, it's too small and we already have enough people.' It was very sad and I felt guilty for leaving these people to die, but there was nothing I could do. There was nothing anyone could do."

Adil reached Kenya. Later, his brother, who lives in Sweden, sent him some money to enable him to come to Europe.

Learning objectives: The two drama activities can be used to develop greater insight into the journeys that people make when they move to different countries.

Time needed: At least 20 minutes for each activity.

Instructions: You will need a hall to do this activity. Using chalk draw a start line and five or six circles about two metres diameter. Each circle will represent a country. Teachers will need to be sensitive in choosing countries. For example, if there are many refugee children whose origins are in one particular country, it may be better not to use that country.

Suggested countries are:

- UK
- Ireland
- Somalia
- India
- Australia
- Russia

Students should set off from the start and mime their journey from one country to another. The circles should then be rubbed out and the students should form a large circle. The teacher can then introduce the idea that there are many parts to a journey. Students should, one by one, volunteer to go into the middle of the circle and mime parts of a journey to another country. They may wish to mime:

- Packing their bag
- Selecting mementos
- Saying goodbye
- A clandestine escape
- Crossing a border on foot
- Catching a plane, and so on.

These two activities can feed into more work about journeys.

Activity ☝

Journeys

Activity 👆

Making a multi-media representation of a journey

Learning objectives: Students will use a range of materials to make representations of a refugee's journey.

Time needed: At least 3 hours

Instructions: Students will need copies of Adil's and Sado's stories. They will also need access to a range of art materials. The teacher should hand out the testimonies. Students should read them and make a list of how the two refugees might have felt at different stages of their journey. Students should then represent the journey, using paints, collage, prints, papier-mâché, cartoon or in three dimensions. Students should ensure that Adil's and Sado's voices are not lost.

Activity 👆

Goldova to Manchester

Learning objectives: The game simulates the flight of a family of five people from a fictional country to Manchester. At the end of the game the participants will be aware of some of the difficult decisions made by refugees who have to flee.

Time needed: At least 1 hour with extra time for discussion.

Instructions: The game works best with a class of 20 to 30 students.

In order to run the game, the teacher or group leader will need:

- A hall or empty space
- Chalk or sugar paper and a marker
- A stop watch and a whistle
- Coloured stickers - each family of five needs to wear a sticker of the same colour
- Blank sheets of paper and pencils - enough for everyone who is a member of a family
- Cheap envelopes

The teacher or group leader will need to prepare the money and scenario cards in advance. Photocopy the sheets of money on page 338, so that each family group has $3,300. Photocopy the scenario cards - you will need one set of them for each family group (if you have four family groups, you will need four sets of the scenario cards). Put each scenario card into an envelope and mark the cover of the envelope with the number that is on each scenario card.

Mark out the hall, using the chalk or signs made on the sugar paper. The signs should read:

Golum - a village in Goldova
Molensk - a village near Golum
Deep in the Goldovan Forest
The border between Goldova and Russia
A Polish country lane
Warsaw
A small town in the UK
Manchester

Divide the participants up into groups of five. These are the family groups. Give each family member stickers of the same colour to identify themselves. Each person in the family group should also be given a pencil and a blank piece of paper. Any extra student can take the role of helper. Helpers might give out the scenario cards and keep time.

The teacher or group leader should then set the scene and explain that the game simulates the flight of a family of five people from a fictional country. The leader should explain the aim of the game, namely to

- stay alive;
- reach safety;
- stay together as a family if possible.

Give each family group a copy of *scenario card 1*. Hold on to the rest of the scenario cards (or give them to a helper). Explain that everyone in the family will have to take a role.

After ten minutes blow the whistle and say that the situation has changed. Give each family a copy of *scenario card 2*, then set the stop watch. Each family has five minutes to decide what to take with them on their journey.

After five minutes blow the whistle. Any group who has not finished deciding what to take with them stops and leaves unallocated items behind.

Give each family a copy of *scenario card 3*. They have four minutes to decide what to do. After four minutes blow the whistle and move the families on to the next scenario. Give out the numbered scenario cards when they are requested.

Blow the whistle at intervals of three minutes to move on to the next scenario.

At the end of the game bring the families back together again. It is now time to debrief the participants. Explain that for them, this was a game, but everyday refugees have such experiences and have to make similar decisions. The following discussion points can be used. Students may wish to use them to produce written work about refugees' journeys.

Discussion points:

⇨ Was everyone in your family still alive at the end of the game?

⇨ Did your family manage to stay together?

⇨ How did you feel at the start of the game when you were deciding to leave your village?

⇨ Did anyone reach Warsaw? How did they feel?

⇨ Did anyone reach Manchester? If so, how did that person feel?

⇨ What have the students learned about refugees' journeys from playing this game?

Scenario card 1

Goldova is a small country with a population of 10 million. Of its people only 4 million are ethnic Goldovans. Another 6 million belong to various ethnic minority groups.

You are all members of the same Goldovan family. You live in a large village called Golum which is about three hours by road from the capital of Goldova. It is a good place to live and all the different ethnic groups have always got on well. There are five people in your family:

- Mother, aged 42. She is a doctor in the local clinic.
- Father, aged 43. He manages a saw mill.
- Emil aged 15. He studies at school.
- Adam aged 14. He studies at school.
- Grandmother, aged 72. She is the maternal grandmother and has always helped look after the children.

You have a large house and your family is one of the wealthier families in the village. Like many families, your parents are in a mixed marriage: Mother is an ethnic Goldovan although your Father is not. You speak Goldovan at home, although Mother and Father speak Russian. Mother speaks some English, too, because she has a sister who lives in Manchester. Her sister sends her books to improve her English. Father's brother manages a shop in Moscow, Russia.

In your family team decide who is going to be Mother, Father, Emil, Adam and Grandmother. These are the roles you will have during the game.

Until recently life has been good in Golum. But about two years ago, a new government was elected in Goldova. The new government believed that only ethnic Goldovan people should be allowed to vote. Schools should only teach in the Goldovan language.

Many people opposed the new government. One opposition group decided to arm itself and fight the Goldovan government. In the last month the fighting has come nearer to your village.

Your family is discussing whether to leave Golum or stay.

You think that it is best to leave Golum, but you do not know where you should go. All you want is a calm place where the family can be together. Discuss this.

You are sad about leaving your home. Talk about it.

You are worried about the journey. Talk about your worries with the family.

Grandmother is worried that she will not survive a difficult journey. Discuss this with the rest of the family.

You cannot imagine what it will be like in a new country.

Scenario card 2

One evening your neighbour rushes into your house. She says that the Goldovan army is close to your village. She has heard that it is arresting all non-Goldovans, as well as its political opponents. She says she has heard that some non-Goldovans have been beaten and killed in prison. She says she is scared.

Mother and Father decide that the family must flee.

You have four minutes to decide what to take with you. Each person can carry five items. What do you choose to take?

1. Money - a maximum of $3,300. Who is going to carry it? Each of you can carry some money, or you might entrust it to one person.
2. Mother's medical bag. It contains some basic medicines and items such as her stethescope.
3. A blanket
4. A sleeping bag
5. Mother's passport
6. Father's passport
7. Adam's passport
8. Emil's passport
9. Grandmother's passport
10. Plastic sheeting
11. A gold necklace
12. Bread
13. Biscuits
14. Matches
15. A plastic water carrier
16. Address book
17. A photograph album
18. Torch
19. English dictionary
20. Emil's coat
21. Adam's coat
22. Grandmother's coat
23. Mother's coat
24. Father's coat
25. Grandmother's walking stick
26. A compass
27. A folding travel map of Europe
28. A cup
29. A saucepan
30. Another sleeping bag
31. A radio
32. A sharp knife

Scenario card 3

After packing, the family walks to the next village. Grandmother is struggling. Father meets an old friend who says he knows someone who can take them to the border - for a sum of money.

- The family has a choice. They can pay $1,000 to go by lorry to the border.
- Or the family can carry on walking, but leave grandmother behind.
- What do you decide to do? Discuss this with your family.
- If you decide to go by lorry to the border, give $1,000 to your teacher and ask for scenario card 4.
- If you decide to keep walking, grandmother leaves the game. Ask for scenario card 5.

Scenario card 4

You are at the border. It is chaotic. There are thousands of refugees waiting to cross. The border is only open for two hours every day. You have heard a rumour that the border is going to be closed soon, because the refugees are not wanted by neighbouring countries.

Then Mother meets someone who says that they know how to get to Europe. It will mean crossing the border illegally late at night. On the other side someone will meet them and take them by lorry into Europe, probably to Germany. It will cost $1,000 for each person

Do you take up this offer?

You only have $3,300 - enough for three people to flee. Who should go to Germany? If you decide to take a chance and go to Germany, give the teacher the money. Those who decide to make the journey should pick up *scenario card 6*.

Or do you remain hiding in the woods near the border? Those who decide to stay should pick up *scenario card 7*.

Scenario card 5

You have walked for days and are close to the border. Everyone is tired, cold and exhausted. During the journey you have used up all the food you brought. Father's blisters have become badly infected and Mother thinks he needs urgent treatment with antibiotics.

Did mother bring her medical bag? If not, Father will die. He is out of the game. Everyone else should then take *scenario card 4*.

If the family brought the medical bag, Father will live. Take *scenario card 4*.

Scenario card 6

The lorry you are hiding in is stopped by a Polish policeman on a remote country road. The lorry driver panics and tells the policeman that there are refugees hiding in the back. The policeman makes everyone get out of the lorry. All the refugees are told to line up by the side of the lorry while the Polish policeman waits for backup to arrive.

You wait in a line. If someone distracts the policeman you could run into the woods.

Do you decide to take a chance and escape? If so pick up *scenario card 8*.

Or do you play safe? You know you will be sent back to the Goldovan border. But at least you might be reunited with the rest of your family. If you decide to play safe, pick up *scenario card 9*.

Scenario card 7

You move back and hide in the woods. Did you bring matches, blankets, sleeping bags, warm coats and plastic sheeting with you?

If you did, remain together and wait. How do you feel while waiting?

If not, Grandmother dies of hypothermia. She is out of the game. The rest of the family should remain together and wait. How do you feel while waiting?

(Students should wait at the side until the end of the simulation.)

Scenario card 8

You are now hiding in a forest in Poland. You don't know where you are. You are hungry.

You decide to follow the road out of the forest and after about three hours you reach a small town. There is a railway station in the town. You decide to try and get to Warsaw and see if you can find any Goldovans. You have two choices. You can change some money and buy a railway ticket to Warsaw. This costs $30 for each person. Or you can hitchhike to Warsaw.

Do you have enough money? If you decide to take the train to Warsaw, pick up *scenario card 11*.

If you decide to hitchhike to Warsaw, pick up *scenario card 12*.

Scenario card 9

You are deported from Poland and are sent back to Goldova. You are sent by plane to the capital city, but know you have to leave the capital as quickly as you can. You need to hide, some place that the Goldovan army will not find you. It is best to travel to the border. You need money to make the journey. You also need food, a coat and a sleeping bag. Everyone needs at least $200 to be able to survive near the border.

If you have money, make the journey. Pick up *scenario card 10*.

If you don't have the money for the journey, you will be arrested and are out of the game.

Scenario card 10

Hide in the forest and wait. Your money is running low. How do you feel while you are waiting?

(Students should wait at the side until the end of the simulation.)

Scenario card 11

Take the overnight train to Warsaw. You arrive at 7am in the morning. You have a wash at the station then walk the streets, listening for your language. After 10 hours you hear someone speaking Goldovan. You are so happy. You stop this man and explain your situation.

He tells you that he is working in the market selling fruit. He is saving up to pay a people smuggler to take him to London. He asks you to join him. He says it is hard work and will take nearly a year to save the money. You will have to share a room with five other Goldovan refugees. The man also says that it is illegal for Goldovans to work in Poland and that you have to be careful of the police. If they catch you, they will send you back to Goldova.

You have to decide what to do.

Do you stay in Warsaw and work in the market to earn enough to go to London? If so pick up *scenario card 13*.

Or do you work in the market for a month, then use your money to go to Moscow. You have an uncle in Moscow and you know he will help you. He might have heard from the rest of your family. If you decide to go to Moscow pick up *scenario card 14*.

Scenario card 12

It takes you two days to get lifts to Warsaw. You have to sleep in the woods. There is no opportunity to buy food and you do not have anything to eat.

Your lift sets you down somewhere in Warsaw. You wander around for two hours, then suddenly you faint from hunger. When you wake up you are in a police cell. Before very long you are handcuffed and put on a plane to Goldova.

How do you feel about being sent home?

(Students should then wait at the side until the simulation is finished.)

Scenario card 13

You work in the market for a year. It is a cold, miserable job in the winter. You are always hungry and you miss your family a lot. But now you have enough money to pay the smuggler.

You are told to go to a house late at night. You are told that you will then be taken by lorry to London. You are told that you can only take a small bag with you.

What would you put in your bag? Make a list of five items that you would take with you on your journey. Then pick up *scenario card 15*.

Scenario card 14

You reach Moscow safely after a month working in the market. Your uncle says that you can stay with him and help in the shop until things get better in Goldova. How do you feel about staying with your uncle?

(Students should then wait at the side until the end of the game.)

Scenario card 15

You have been in the lorry for about 48 hours. You don't know where you are. The man next to you did not bring enough water. He is in a bad way and you are worried that he will die.

Did you bring a water bottle? If not, you are out of the game.

If you did, pick up *scenario card 16*.

Scenario card 16

The lorry stops and the driver opens the back. The driver says 'England, England'. It is early in the morning. You are hungry and thirsty, almost collapsing.

You walk for about ten minutes then have to rest. You see a police station. You could go in and ask for help. You could tell the police that you are a Goldovan asylum seeker. But the police might be like the Goldovan police. They might beat you. They might send you back to Goldova.

If you decide to enter the police station pick up *scenario card 17*.

Or you could keep walking and see if you can find someone speaking Goldovan.

If you decide to stay on the streets pick up *scenario card 18*.

Scenario card 17

You decide to enter the police station. You say the words 'asylum seeker'. The policeman can see that you are in a bad way. You are given food and drinks then taken down to a police cell. You can't understand what the policeman is saying.

You wait in the police cell. How do you feel? Pick up *scenario card 19*.

Scenario card 18

You walk and walk and walk for two whole days but you don't hear anyone speaking Goldovan. You have had little to eat and have slept on a park bench.

You sit down and rest, then stand up to start walking again. All of a sudden you feel faint and collapse with hunger. You then wake up in hospital. The doctors and nurses treat you kindly and you are warm and well fed.

A Goldovan interpreter says that he will take you to a refugee advice centre and they will help you apply for asylum. You will be allowed to live in a hostel until the UK government decides if you can stay here or not. The hostel could be anywhere in England, Scotland or Wales. You tell the Goldovan interpreter that you have an aunt living in Manchester. The interpreter asks you where she lives. Did you bring your address book?

It's the end of the game. You have reached safety, but how do you feel? Are you together as a family? Can you contact your aunt? Will you be allowed to stay in the UK? What will happen to you? Will you be able to find a job?

Scenario card 19

A Goldovan interpreter arrives. He says that he will take you to a refugee advice centre and they will help you claim political asylum. You will be allowed to live in a hostel until the UK government decides if you can stay here or not. The hostel could be anywhere in England, Scotland or Wales. You tell the Goldovan interpreter that you have an aunt living in Manchester. The interpreter asks you where she lives. Did you bring your address book?

It's the end of the game. You have reached safety, But how do you feel? Are you together as a family? Can you contact your aunt? Will you be allowed to stay in the UK. What will happen to you? Will you be able to find a job?

Information: Refugees from Afghanistan

Nearly 55,000 Afghan refugees live in the UK.

Population: 27 million in 2002
Capital: Kabul
Ethnic groups: Pushtuns, Tadzhiks, Uzbeks, Turkomen, Hazara and Aimaq. The Pushtuns are the largest ethnic group and live in eastern Afghanistan as well as Pakistan.
Languages: Pushtu and Dari (Persian)
Religion: Almost all Afghans are Muslims. The majority are Sunni Muslims. 15 per cent are Shi'a Muslims and another two per cent are Ismaeli Muslims. Shi'a Muslims face persecution in Afghanistan by the Taliban. Most Shi'a are Hazara people from central Afghanistan. Until 20 years ago there were also small populations of Sikhs, Hindus and Jews, although many of them have fled abroad in recent years.
Land and economy: Afghanistan is a mountainous country. Most people work as farmers, keeping animals or growing wheat, fruit and vegetables. Some farmers also grow opium poppies to be processed into heroin. Since 1979 fighting has disrupted the economy and today Afghanistan is one of the world's poorest countries.

Events:

1767 to 1973: Afghanistan is ruled as one country by a succession of tribal leaders and kings. Although governments rule from the capital city Kabul, they never have much control over the countryside. Afghan people owe their loyalty first to their families and then to their tribal leaders. In the countryside little has changed in the last 500 years.

1933: King Zaher Shah comes to the throne. He introduces a new constitution and political parties are made legal. He also passed laws that change land ownership and help poor farmers.

1973: King Zaher Shah is deposed. His cousin and former prime minister, Mohammed Daud, makes himself president of a new republic. To start with, the new government includes members of all political parties. As time goes by, the Government becomes less tolerant of opposition parties. Many leaders of opposition parties flee as refugees.

Afghan child at a camp in Pakistan.
© UNHCR / P. Benatar

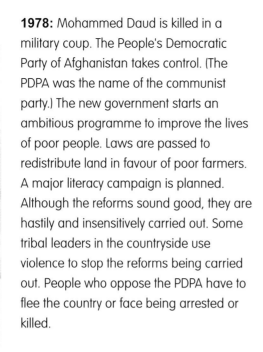

Afghanistan

1978: Mohammed Daud is killed in a military coup. The People's Democratic Party of Afghanistan takes control. (The PDPA was the name of the communist party.) The new government starts an ambitious programme to improve the lives of poor people. Laws are passed to redistribute land in favour of poor farmers. A major literacy campaign is planned. Although the reforms sound good, they are hastily and insensitively carried out. Some tribal leaders in the countryside use violence to stop the reforms being carried out. People who oppose the PDPA have to flee the country or face being arrested or killed.

1979: Armed resistance to the PDPA grows stronger. These fighters are known as mujahideen. The PDPA start to lose control. On 27 December, Soviet troops enter Afghanistan. Now the mujahideen grow more organised. The US, Saudi Arabia, France and the UK supply them with arms. The fighting gets worse. Many more people flee as refugees. By 1982 over 3.3 million refugees have fled to Pakistan and 2.8 million to Iran. Nearly 3,000,000 people are internally displaced. In Pakistan most of the refugees live in camps on the Afghanistan/Pakistan border. The United Nations High Commissioner for Refugees (UNHCR) and other aid organisations provided food, schools, clinics and employment training centres. But despite these efforts life is very hard for the refugees. The welcome from Pakistan is under increasing strain. Both refugees and local people cook with firewood. With nearly 3 million extra people in North West Pakistan, forests are quickly cut down. Afghan refugees also compete with local people for jobs and are often prepared to work for lower wages.

1989: Soviet troops withdraw from Afghanistan. Everyone expects the Afghan government to fall within weeks of their departure. But President Najibullah's government survives partly because the mujahideen are not united in their opposition. Fighting continues, especially around Kabul, Kandahar, Jalalabad and in parts of western Afghanistan.

1992: The mujahideen enter Kabul and President Najibullah is overthrown. But the mujahideen are unable to form a government and soon start to fight each other. The fighting is intense and Kabul is almost destroyed. Its population drops from 2 million to 500,000. There are no services in the city and most poor people cannot afford sufficient food.

1995: A new political group, the Taliban, emerge. They are young Pusht speaking men, many of them educated in fundamentalist religious schools in Pakistan. They are joined by small numbers of fundamentalist Muslims from other nations, including Osama Bin Laden, a Saudi millionaire. The Taliban soon control much of Afghanistan.

1996: The Taliban capture Kabul. The city soon sees an end to the fighting. While not supporting the Taliban, many ordinary people welcome this relief. But the severe interpretation of Islamic law causes hardships for some groups, particularly girls and women. They are excluded from education and work, and obliged to wear the burqa, a garment that covers the entire body. The Taliban also ban certain recreational activities such as videos, music, kiteflying and chess. Afghanistan is divided. The Taliban control the Pushtun areas of the country, plus the major cities of Kabul and Herat. Opposition forces control most of the non-Pushtun areas in the north.

September 2001: Ahmed Shah Massoud, leader of the northern opposition to the Taliban, is killed allegedly on orders by Osama Bin Laden. Two days later, 3,000 people are killed in the September 11 terrorist attacks in New York, Washington and Pennsylvania. Osama Bin Laden is blamed and the Taliban are pressured into handing him over to Western authorities. Within weeks US forces attack Afghanistan, with the aim of destroying the Taliban administration and Osama bin Laden's fighters. In November the Taliban abandon Kabul.

December 2001: The Bonn Agreement is signed, which sets up an interim Afghan administration, headed by Hamid Karzai, a Pushtun.

Today: The International Security Assistance Force, with soldiers from many different countries, now patrols Kabul, providing protection to government buildings. But there is still fighting between US troops and remnants of the Taliban in parts of the country. Lawlessness is rife and most of the country outside Kabul is not under the control of central government, but of warlords whose loyalty cannot be guaranteed. Refugees have started to return, with some 1.5 million returning to Afghanistan by March 2003. But nearly 2 million Afghans still live outside their country, as refugees in Iran, Pakistan, Russia, Europe and North America.

Afghan women and children at Shamsabad Refugee Settlement in Iran.
© **UNHCR / A. Hollmann**

Afghanistan

Burhaan's story

"I am from Kabul. The fighting has been going on in my country for many years. My father, my mother and my little sister were killed by a bomb three years ago when I was 15. It is very difficult for me to talk about this."

"My father used to have a tobacco shop. At one o'clock he came back from the shop to have a meal with my mother and sister. I was at school. At two o'clock I came home and saw what had happened. My whole street had been destroyed. There was nothing left. No father, no mother. My home was finished. When I saw this I fell to the ground. I was in hospital for one month. I couldn't speak at all - I couldn't even make a sound."

"After my parents were killed I stayed in Afghanistan for two years with my mother's sister. Then I went to Pakistan to live with my older brother and sister. I stayed there for a month. My brother and sister then paid a man five thousand dollars to get me to England."

"I came here in a lorry and a boat. For two months I didn't speak to anyone or see anyone. I slept and ate on the lorry. I was sick every day on the lorry. I only had enough food and water for one month. After this time all my food and water was finished. Five or six times I had to get out and steal food. I had never stolen before. My mother and father taught me not to steal."

"When the lorry got to England I hid outside, underneath the lorry. I stayed in this space for a long time. It was raining very heavily and the driver was going very fast. It was terrible and I was frightened. I was holding on very tight and my arms were very painful."

"I thought, 'why have I come here? I don't like England'. The wheels were spraying water all over me and I was very wet and dirty. Then after about six hours I fell."

Afghan refugees at Kot Chandna refugee village in Pakistan.
© UNHCR / A. Hollmann

"One or two days later I woke up in hospital. I didn't know where I was. A woman brought me to social services and they gave me money and somewhere to stay. I go to school now. I am learning to speak English. I would like to work in fashion making clothes. I am very good at cutting and working with material. I can't go back to Afghanistan - peace, no - there is fighting, fighting all the time. I want to go back to my brother and sister in Pakistan. I send them letters and sometimes we speak on the telephone. I want to join them again but I can't because I haven't got any money."

- Chapter Eight: Journey to safety -

Information: Smuggling

In recent years more and more refugees have been forced to pay smugglers, in order to reach safety. People smuggling also receives much more media coverage and is the subject of a great deal of political debate.

People smuggling means helping a person cross a border illegally. Those who may be smuggled across borders may be endangered people fleeing for their lives. Or they may be migrants who simply want to work and earn money in a richer country.

In the UK people smugglers are always portrayed as bad people in the press. Individuals convicted of people smuggling may receive a long prison sentence. But smuggling is not such a simple good versus evil issue. People smugglers do enable refugees to reach safety. Perhaps we need to examine people smuggling in different ways. People who argue that people smugglers should be punished, use a range of arguments to back their cause:

- People smugglers place refugees and migrants in unacceptably dangerous situations. In October 2003, the Italian government charged Turab Ahmed Sheik, a Pakistani people smuggler with the murder of 283 people who drowned when his overloaded boat sunk in the Mediterranean Sea. Hundreds of people lose their lives every year while trying to enter Europe, Australia or North America.

- Smugglers make a profit from the plight of vulnerable people. They charge people huge sums of money for a journey. People may have their belongings stolen or be left on their own en route. Some migrants are forced to work for smugglers once have reached Europe. Any money they earn goes to the smuggling agent to pay off the cost of the journey.

- Smugglers bring in illegal immigrants. Illegal immigrants usually work in low-paid jobs, undercutting legal workers. They do not pay taxes so do not contribute to the society in which they live.

People who believe that people smuggling is a more complex issue have other arguments:

- Refugees only pay smugglers because they cannot enter Europe, North America or Australia legally. Demanding visas from endangered people fleeing human rights abuses or war zones stops them fleeing. To obtain a visa, a person needs a valid passport. But it is governments which issue passports, often the very authority from which the person fears persecution. Even if an endangered person has a valid passport, obtaining a visa can be problematic. The journey to the embassy may be perilous, and the visit may be interpreted as evidence of dissent. The wait for the issue of a visa may be dangerous in itself. A visa may also be refused. The UK has repeatedly imposed visa requirements when refugee claims from a particular country have increased, for example on Sri Lankans in 1985, on Turkish nationals in 1989, on Ugandans in 1991, on Colombians in 1997, and on Zimbabweans in 2002. Consequently an endangered person must either try and board an aircraft without a passport and visa, pay for forged travel documents, or pay a smuggler to bring them illegally.

- Not everyone who helps smuggle people is associated with criminal activity. Some smugglers do so for humanitarian reasons. In 1998, two German priests were imprisoned for smuggling a Kurdish refugee into Denmark.

- We don't know a lot about smuggling and illegal immigration. We don't know if the numbers of illegal immigrants who have used smugglers to enter Europe have increased or decreased.

Afghanistan

Hanif's story

Hanif has paid a smuggling agent to help him reach safety. He was born in a village north of Kabul. Until 1997 he was a civil servant. The Taliban came to arrest him. Fortunately he was not at home.

"I went into hiding after they came to arrest me. I was lucky I could contact my brother-in-law. He arranged the sale of some land and also my car. Together with my savings I used this money to pay a smuggler to take me to Australia."

"First I went to Pakistan. In Peshawar I kept asking people how to find the smugglers. Eventually we found some people who said they could take me. I paid them about 10 years' salary. They gave me a fake passport and a plane ticket to Indonesia. In Jakarta I went straight to this house. We stayed for over a month in the house and we could not go out. We were told that if we left the house the police would arrest us and send us back to Pakistan. Then one night some men collected me in a car and took me to a boat. The boat took us to Australia."

Discussion points:

⇨ Use the internet to find out who were Nicolas Winton, Raoul Wallenberg and Chiune Sugihara. What did they do for which they have been remembered?

⇨ Have we judged them as good people or bad people?

United Arab Emirates officials continue to deny that they use trafficked young children from other countries as camel jockeys.
© **Eric Jones / Anti-Slavery International**

Trafficking

Traffickers pose as people who help a desperate and poor person to find a job in a rich country and to help them get there, usually for a big fee, but then, on arrival, the person is forced to work against their will and for the profits of the trafficker(s). Victims of trafficking are usually exploited sexually or for their labour. They are often locked up and have their passports taken away so that they are unable to leave. Victims of traffickers are extremely fearful of trying to contact the authorities as they have no documentation and are likely to be deported back, but also because the traffickers may beat them or exploit them even more. Traffickers are often involved in prostitution. There is some evidence that Eastern European criminals may be involved in trafficking refugees and migrants, as well as controlling prostitutes.

Learning objectives: The activity develops participants' debating skills and enables them to consider arguments about smuggling.

Time needed: About 1 hour to prepare the arguments and 1 hour to present the debate.

Instructions: The group will need the information sheets about smuggling and to have examined some of the issues about the smuggling of asylum seekers. The teacher should then introduce the idea of debate to groups who are not familiar with debating skills. The motion for debate is:

'This House believes that those who help endangered people enter the UK should not be punished'.

Preparing for the debate

A good debate is not a series of public speeches. It is an argument, the object of which is to persuade people - the audience or judges - either that a certain state of affairs exists or a certain course should be taken or rejected. In persuading people, a debater must build up his or her own individual case while, at the same time, presenting a consistent and complementary line of argument with their team colleague that rebuts the case of their opposition.

The class should be divided into two equal groups. One group should prepare a speech in favour of the motion. The other group should prepare a speech against the motion.

When you are making a speech, you are delivering a great deal of information very quickly to the audience. Sadly, most humans don't have a very long attention span and it is unlikely they will take in all the information unless you make it easy for them. This means structuring the speech. You should not have more than three or perhaps four different arguments in your speech.

Divide your speech into sections and signpost each section. Make sure each section has an introduction and a summary all of its own. In other words, keep drumming your points home by repeating them constantly.

You will find it easier to make notes, rather than writing out the speech word for word. For example:

- Visa requirements mean that endangered people can no longer enter Europe legally. Therefore they have no option but to use the services of smugglers.
- Raoul Wallenberg, a Swedish diplomat was a smuggler of endangered people. We regard him as a hero.

Make sure you summarise all your arguments at the end of the speech. Timing is very important in the context of structure. If you have two points of roughly equal importance, make sure you spend equal time on them.

Finally, although you may have lots of different points, don't forget that they all tie into one guiding principle - you are trying to argue for or against the motion.

The Debate

You will need to lay out the room. You will need three tables, each of which should be able to accommodate two people. Debating follows a set format. The class needs to decide on:

- A chair
- A first proposer
- A first opposer
- Members of the audience

- A time keeper
- A second proposer
- A second opposer

The proposers argue for the motion - they argue that the trafficking of asylum seekers is morally wrong. The opposition argues against this. The order of speaking is:

1. Chair's introduction - to introduce the debate and to introduce each speaker
2. First proposition speaker - for no more than five minutes
3. First opposition speaker - for no more than five minutes
4. Second proposition speaker - for no more than four minutes
5. Second opposition speaker - for no more than four minutes
6. Floor debate - for 10-15 minutes
7. Opposition summary speech - for no more than four minutes
8. Proposition summary speech - for no more than four minutes
9. Voting

It is important that good timing is kept. The time keeper should indicate with a bell or knock, the beginning of the final minute of each speech.

The floor debate allows members of the audience to react to the debate so far. Points must be addressed to the Chair and begin with the speaker's name. The main speakers do not speak during the floor debate. But in their summary speeches they must deal with the points made during the floor debate.

After the summary speeches have ended, the audience votes. The Chair should ask those who support to raise their hands. If they have a majority, the motion has been passed.

Speakers address the audience at a Refugee Council event in the House of Commons.
© **Refugee Council**

9 Refugees and displaced people in poor countries

Ntamba refugee camp in Burundi. © UNHCR / A. Hollmann

This chapter examines the needs of refugees in poor countries and looks at refugees in camps, refugees' nutritional needs, family tracing, internal displacement, and fundraising for refugees in poor countries. There are case studies of Burmese, Bhutanese, Sudanese and Eritrean refugees as well as internally displaced people from Colombia.

Burma

Mi Mee Ong's story

Mi Mee Ong is from a village in Mon State, Burma. She belongs to the minority Mon ethnic group. She is 57 years old and is married with seven children.

"I left my village 15 years ago. We spent four years in Loh Loe Camp in Thailand. Five months ago we moved back into Burma to Plat Hon Pai. The camp was about an hour's walk from the Thai border."

"One July day I was in the refugee camp. I saw the Burmese troops when they arrived at my house. They came inside, they cooked inside and they ate. They then arrested my son. Two of my sons were there, one ran away and they arrested the other. They wanted to arrest my husband but he was sick with a fever and he couldn't go. One soldier was going to beat him but another soldier said, 'He's sick, don't beat him, don't take him.' One of our neighbours was eating in our house and he was arrested too."

"The soldiers fired a gun and ordered everyone to come out of their houses. Then they grabbed them by the hands, took them to the road and made them walk in front of them. The soldiers fired their guns. They arrested many people and then they left for another part of the camp."

"There was still a soldier in my house who stayed to cook and eat. He told me to stay in the house and not to go outside. I stayed in front of the house but I couldn't see much. I saw army porters with soldiers around them. The soldiers cooked food and gave the porters only a little rice to eat while the soldiers ate together. The soldier stayed in my house for more than two hours. When he left I saw people running from another part of the refugee camp. I went and hid in another house."

"Soon more soldiers came. They ordered us all to leave and then they burnt our houses. They took my son and I had lost everything I had. I had gathered things for my house for years and then I lost it all. I couldn't sleep that night, only sit there."

"I was afraid the soldiers would come back. The next morning my daughter came and we decided to go back into Thailand. My husband walked very slowly with his stick and our youngest son came with us too. When we got here we stayed in a shelter with four other families. It is very hard to build another shelter because my husband is always sick. My son managed to escape. The Burmese army took him as a porter. They did not feed him properly and they threatened him with a knife."

Testimony collected by the Karen Human Rights Group, Thailand.

Harka's story

Harka is a Bhutanese refugee who now lives in Nepal.

"My father was a farmer. He worked at home. Our house was made of stone and mud. It had a thatched roof. There was a flower garden in the front of the house. There was a paddy field and just above the paddy was our land where we grew mustard and wheat."

"The armies of Bhutan forced us to leave the country. We brought some rice, clothes, pots and plates with us. On the way we stayed in India for three days. There we heard about all the Bhutanese people who were forced to leave their country and going to Nepal, so we went with them. Now we are in Nepal."

"We came directly to the camp. At first there were not many refugees there, but day by day the numbers increased and now there are too many."

"The first night we arrived in the camp we slept in the open. The next day my father bought some bamboo and he made a small hut from the bamboo. We put the plastic roof on which we carried from Bhutan."

"In Bhutan there were seven members of my family, but now there are only five. My father and brother died in the camp. In the camp some people are dying due to lack of medicines. Some die due to lack of nutrition. I'd like to go back to my country quickly, but if I go now the army will beat me and put me in jail. I will go back when all the refugees go back."

Bhutan

Discussion points:

⇨ Make a list of the things that Mi Mee Ong and Harka need to be able to live safely and in dignity.

⇨ Log on to the internet and find out why refugees have fled from Burma and Bhutan. What organisations are helping these refugees?

Bhutanese refugee with her passport at a camp in Nepal.
© H. J. Davies / Exile Images

Information: Refugees in poor countries

Most of the world's refugees live in poor countries. Here, many of them live in camps - in tents or other types of temporary shelter. Other refugees may live in urban areas where they face different challenges.

Basic needs in refugee camps

Refugee camps are meant to provide for refugees who have just arrived in a new country. The camps are meant to be temporary, to meet needs for a short period of time, but many refugees end up living in camps for years.

Many refugee camps are located in border areas, near to where refugees entered their new country. They are not always safe places, as they are often near to fighting. Security is a basic need in a refugee camp.

Everyone not just refugees needs clean water, food and shelter. Water is the most immediate need, as no one can live for very long without something to drink. Water is also needed for cooking and washing. There are several different ways of providing clean water. If there are water-bearing rocks under a refugee camp, a well can be drilled. Alternatively water can be collected from a lake or river, purified, then brought by pipe or tanker to the camp. The job of ensuring that there is enough clean water in refugee camps is the responsibility of water engineers. They also organise sanitation and the digging of latrines. This is an important task and stops disease from spreading.

Getting food to refugees in camps is another problem. Food is bulky and refugee camps are often in isolated areas without good transport. The food provided should not need too much cooking otherwise much local firewood will be used. Often the trees around refugee camps are very quickly destroyed causing environmental damage. Food should also be appropriate to local tastes and must provide enough energy, protein, vitamins and minerals.

Bhutanese mother and child visit a clinic at Goldhap Camp in Nepal.
© UNHCR / A. Hollmann

Refugees also need shelter. If there is no local building material, like wood or palm leaves, the refugees will need tents and plastic sheeting brought to them.

Health care

Clinics are another important part of a refugee camp. Infectious diseases may also spread quickly in refugee camps, where people may live close together and lack clean water and sanitation. Many new refugees are not in good health. They may have war injuries from their home countries. Often refugees have walked many miles before getting to the safety of a camp. They may not have eaten well for many weeks. One of the urgent jobs of the doctors and nurses who work in refugee camps is to treat newly arrived refugees. Hungry children may need special meals so that they can regain the weight that they have lost.

Becoming self-sufficient

Refugee camps are meant to be temporary. But sadly, many refugees end up living in camps for many years. For such refugees, the chance of training and work is important. In Kenya, Somali and Sudanese refugees are now growing vegetables in gardens around their homes. In other parts of the world, refugees have been given training in leatherwork, crafts, tailoring and mending cars.

Finding lost family

When refugees flee war and other dangers, it is easy to be parted from members of their families. Social workers from organisations like UNHCR and the Red Cross help families find those they have lost.

Organisations helping refugees

UNHCR staff at Mugano Camp in Burundi, registering new arrivals.
© **UNHCR / A. Hollmann**

Many different organisations may work in a single refugee camp. They might include local health and education departments, as well as other people working for the host government. Staff from UNHCR and non-governmental organisations such as Medicins Sans Frontieres, Oxfam and Save the Children may also work in refugee camps. Local people and small local organisations may also help the refugees, even in the poorest countries. For example Tanzanian Boy Scouts have been very generous in helping Burundian and Rwandan refugees in eastern Tanzania.

It is important that all the work to assist refugees is well coordinated to ensure that all the needs of refugees are met. The UNHCR is usually responsible for coordinating emergency aid to refugees.

Impact of camps

Organisations such as UNHCR work to ensure that refugee camps do not have a negative impact on the local area.

- There may be deforestation and soil erosion, as refugees cut firewood for cooking.
- Food prices may rise near refugee camps. While this is good for farmers who are selling food, any local person who is not a food producer may suffer.
- There can be tension between refugees and local people who may be very poor themselves and may resent the aid which refugees are receiving. In such circumstances, aid organisations also help the host population.
- Refugees may compete with local people for work. Sometimes refugees are willing to work for lower wages than local people. Again this can cause tensions.

Refugees in cities

Although most refugees in poor countries live in camps, a small number live in towns and cities. They may live in shanty homes at the edge of a city, often in great poverty. There are particular problems in helping refugees who live in cities because they are living in different places. More positively, it can be easier to find work in a city.

Information: Education for refugees in poor countries

For both adults and children, education is essential to help rebuilding lives in a new country. But many refugee children in poor countries do not go to school. Poor countries such as Pakistan, Kenya and Tanzania, are barely able to provide for their own children's education let alone for refugees. Only 12 per cent of the world's refugee children are currently in school. Very few refugees get the chance to attend secondary school, college or university. Today organisations like the UNHCR and Save the Children are trying to get more refugee children into schools.

Refugee children need education as soon as possible after leaving their home country - even if this means a school under a tree in a refugee camp. For children who have fled fighting, a school can give a sense of stability and security, and the chance to make new friends.

For teenagers, particularly boys, the opportunity to go to school can take the pressure away from being a child soldier. In countries such as Afghanistan, Angola, Liberia, Mali, Sierra Leone, Somali, Sri Lanka and Sudan, children as young as 10 may be encouraged to fight. Education can offer an alternative future to that of being a child soldier.

Education can deliver messages important to the survival of newly arrived refugees. In refugee camps, schools have been used to deliver messages about health care, family tracing and landmine awareness. For example, schools in Rwandan refugee camps in Tanzania were used to deliver messages about the prevention of diseases.

Schools can free mothers of childcare responsibilities enabling them to work. This may be important in refugee camps where there are large numbers of single mothers.

In the long-term, schools can be used to try and solve the conflicts that cause people to become refugees. Dance, drama, music, sport and discussion can be used to bring young people of different ethnic groups together, and to break down the hatred that causes wars. In the former Yugoslavia there are a number of small organisations working with young Bosnian, Serbian and Croatian refugees to try and build peace.

Ethiopian children having lessons
at a refugee camp in Sudan.
© **UNHCR / V. Spärre-Ulrich**

Learning objective: To make students aware of the needs of refugees in poor countries.

Time needed: 30 minutes or more

Instructions: The cards below need to be prepared in advance. The teacher should introduce the activity by explaining that the majority of the world's refugees have fled to neighbouring countries, which are themselves poor. News footage can also be used to introduce the activity. The students should be divided into pairs. Each pair should receive a role card and the needs card. Each pair should then rank the needs cards in order of priority.

Needs cards

You have arrived in a refugee camp in a new country. You are tired, hungry and frightened after escaping a massacre in your hometown. You had three children: a son aged 13, a daughter aged 11 and a baby of five months. You became separated from your partner and the two oldest children when you were fleeing from your home.

The refugee camp is home to 40,000 people. It is located in a country where a different language is spoken. Although warm in the day, the nights can be very cold in this country. There are lots of different things you need. Some of them you need immediately. Rank the needs cards in order of importance.

Food	A tent	Cooking pots
A warm jumper	A radio	A cow
Firewood	Doctors and a clinic	A knife
A job to earn money	A language class	Toilets
A bucket	Blankets	Money
Clean water	Wood and bricks for a permanent home	£100
Social workers to trace the missing children	Ground rice and other baby food	A passport

Discussion point:

⇨ Are there any other things that you need for your survival that were not listed?

Information: The Sahrawis

In the area around Tindouf, Algeria, 200,000 Sahrawi refugees wait for a settlement to the conflict between Polisario and Morocco.

SAHRAWIS

© Chris Madden

IN 1976 MOROCCO INVADED WESTERN SAHARA USING NAPALM AND CLUSTER BOMBS. FIGHTING DROVE ABOUT 40,000 SAHRAWIS FROM THEIR HOMES. SOME WENT TO ALGERIA, OTHERS HID IN REMOTE DESERT AREAS.

THE REFUGEES SETTLED IN CAMPS IN THE TINDOUF REGION OF ALGERIA. IN THE EARLY DAYS CONDITIONS IN THE CAMPS WERE GRIM. THERE WAS NOT ENOUGH FOOD AND WATER.

ON WINTER NIGHTS THE DESERT TEMPERATURE DROPS BELOW FREEZING. IN THE FIRST WINTER IN ALGERIA THE REFUGEES DID NOT HAVE ENOUGH CLOTHES, BLANKETS OR TENTS.

The Sahrawis (continued)

© Chris Madden

TODAY CONDITIONS IN THE CAMPS ARE VERY DIFFERENT. THE SAHRAWI REFUGEES RUN THE CAMPS THEMSELVES. MOST OF THE REFUGEES BELONG TO ONE OF FIVE COMMITTEES.

THE HEALTH COMMITTEE IS RESPONSIBLE FOR WATER SUPPLY SANITATION AND HEALTH EDUCATION.

THERE ARE CLINICS, HOSPITALS AND NUTRITION CENTRES IN THE CAMPS. ALL THE REFUGEES ARE GIVEN TRAINING ABOUT HOW TO PREVENT DISEASES.

THE EDUCATION COMMITTEE RUNS CAMP NURSERIES AND ORGANISES THE ANNUAL LITERACY CAMPAIGN

© Chris Madden

Hafsa Houd's story

Hafsa Houd lives in a camp in Tindouf, Algeria.

Hafsa Houd
© **Mark Luetchford**

"I fled my home in Ouserd when the Moroccans invaded in 1975. We walked all the way to the camp, and when we arrived there was nothing. We started to work together so we could survive in this hostile environment."

"My family followed me into exile a year later, and since then we have lived here. Life is very hard. In the winter it is cold and in the summer it is very hot. We have to constantly repair and replace our tents that only last three or four years. Sometimes there are not enough tents and families have to share their living space. This is how we are: we share everything, it is part of our culture."

"We grow what food we can, and I help out in the garden when planting and harvesting is needed. There is still a problem with food supplies. Many of our children are ill due to the inadequate diet. My first grandchild goes to the clinic for regular check ups, but there is still a shortage of medicines if he is ill."

"I have benefited from education. Like most women I could not read or write before I came to Tindouf. I attended classes. My children have also received a good education in the camps. This is important, as education will help us when we return."

"We are refugees. We are dependent on help from humanitarian organisations because we have been forced to live in the desert where no one can survive without outside help. All I want is to be able to return home; that would be the best present from the international community."

You can read some Sahrawi children's stories on the Spanish Voices website at: www.oneworld.net.

Rwandan refugees at Katale camp in former Zaire. Essential food items have been airlifted because road transport is too slow.
© **UNHCR / H. J. Davies**

Information: Ensuring refugees get enough food

Securing supplies of clean water and food to refugee camps are priority tasks for those working with refugees. Everyone needs good food to remain healthy. Those who do not have enough food, or enough of the right food will suffer from malnutrition. Malnutrition stops children from growing. It makes people more susceptible to diseases because their bodies are weakened.

Every year malnutrition contributes to the deaths of 6 million children. There are many more malnourished people in the world, not just refugees. Even in the UK there are people who are malnourished because they do not eat the right types of food. But refugees in poor countries are a group who are at particular risk of malnutrition because they have fled from their land and livelihoods.

There are two types of severe malnutrition. Kwashiorkor is severe malnutrition caused by a lack of protein in the diet. This type of malnutrition causes fluids in the blood to escape. Children with kwashiorkor usually have swollen bellies as well as swollen faces, legs, arms hands and feet. The other type of malnutrition is called marasmus. This is caused by a lack of energy-giving foods in the diet. Children with marasmus are very thin. Their faces may be wrinkled from extreme weight loss.

A Rwandan child at a camp in former Zaire, receiving aid from a French military hospital.
© UNHCR / L. Taylor

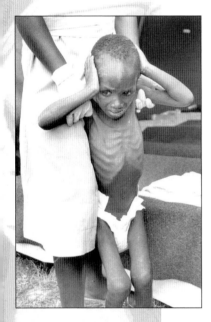

Refugees in poor countries are particularly vulnerable to malnutrition. Usually they have little money, so they cannot buy food in local markets. They may have had to flee at very short notice and could not bring much food with them. Sometimes refugees have travelled for weeks with little or no access to food. Some refugees are more vulnerable than others to malnutrition. Very young children are at risk because they are growing very rapidly. Pregnant and nursing mothers are also vulnerable to malnutrition because they need more energy than other adults. Some elderly refugees are also at risk because they may be isolated and have a harder time accessing food.

Organisations working in refugee camps first secure food supplies. At the same time, doctors, nurses and health workers will set up malnutrition screening programmes. Parents are encouraged to bring their children to clinics. Here the children are weighed as underweight children may be suffering from marasmus. Their upper arms are also measured with a simple tool called a Mid Upper Arm Circumference bracelet. This shows children who may have kwashiorkor.

Children who have severe malnutrition are then sent to therapeutic feeding centres. These are like hospitals. The children remain there and are fed 6 to 12 meals of high-energy food every day. As the children's health improves they may move on to a supplementary feeding centre. Supplementary feeding centres are for children with less severe malnutrition. In such a centre children's health is checked regularly. Parents are then given supplementary food to take back for the family. The family will usually be given three types of food:

- A cereal
- A high protein food
- A high energy food

The supplementary food is prepared in the families' home or shelter. Families may be able to buy vegetables and spices in local markets to make the supplementary food tastier.

Information:
The nutritional value of foods used in supplementary feeding centres

Food	Energy in calories per 100g	Protein in grams per 100g	Fat in grams per 100g
Cereals			
Maize	350	10	4
Wheat	330	12.3	1.5
Rice	360	7	0.5
Rolled oats	380	13	7
Proteins			
Dried beans	335	22	1.5
Groundnuts	580	27	45
Dried milk	500	26	27
Cheese	355	22.5	28
Dried eggs	575	45.5	43.
Canned meat	220	21	15
Canned fish in oil	305	22	24
Oils and fats			
Vegetable oil	885	0	100
Margarine	735	0	82
Miscellaneous			
High protein biscuits	482	16.7	15.5
Jam	265	0	0
Sugar	400	0	0
Salt	0	0	0
Dried fruit	270	4	0.5
Soya fortified flour	370	20	6

(Source: Medicins Sans Frontieres)

Rwandan children at a camp in Tanzania, picking up every grain that falls to the ground during food distribution.
© **UNHCR / B. Press**

Creating a menu for a supplementary feeding centre

Learning objectives: Students are to create a menu for a supplementary feeding programme in a refugee camp. The activity develops students' numeracy. It also makes them aware of the nutritional value of different types of food. The activity should also be used to create empathy for refugees living in camps.

Time needed: About 45 minutes

Instructions: All students will need a copy of the information sheets on food in refugee camps and the nutritional value of different foods. The teacher should then explain about the risk of malnutrition in refugee camps and how this is treated. Students then use the information about foods of different nutritional values to design a supplementary feeding menu for young children.

The menu should have:

- Some cereals
- High protein sources of food
- High energy sources of food

Each day's food should provide about 1,200 calories of energy. The child should also receive foods that contain 35-45 grams of protein and 35-45 grams of fat per day.

Burundian refugees at Kigembe Camp in Rwanda. Basic rations of maize and pulses are provided by World Food Programme and the Tanzanian government.
© **UNHCR / B. Press**

Discussion point:

⇨ What factors influenced your choice of foods?

Information: Refugees from Sudan

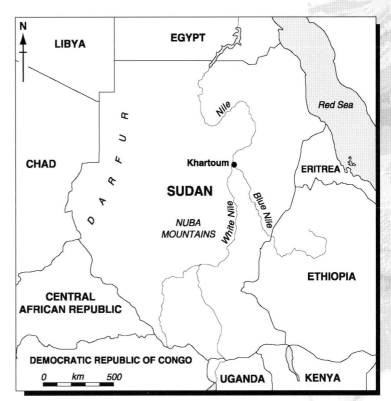

There are about 7,000 Sudanese refugees living in the UK.

Population: 31.8 million

Capital: Khartoum

Ethnic groups: About 40 per cent are Arabs and mostly live in northern Sudan. In the North another large ethnic group are the Nile Nubians, who consider themselves the descendants of the ancient Kingdom of Nubia. Ethnic groups living in central and southern Sudan include the Nuba, Dinka, Nuer, Shilluk and Azande.

Languages: Arabic, Dinka, Nuer, Shilluk, Zande and Bari.

Religions: About 70 per cent of the population are Sunni Muslims, 18 per cent Animists, 9 per cent Christian. Most Christians and animists live in southern Sudan.

Economy: Some 62 per cent of all Sudanese work on the land. The main export crops are cattle, cotton, sesame and gum arabic. Southern Sudan has reserves of oil. High levels of military expenditure have prevented economic investment.

Events:

Sudan was called Kush by the ancient Egyptians and Nubia by the Greeks. Over many centuries the region came under the influence of different cultures. In the 7th century Arab peoples moved south and conquered northern Sudan. At the same time there were small Nubian Christian kingdoms along the River Nile. By the 19th century Sudan began to attract the attention of European powers.

1889: An Anglo-Egyptian army defeats the Sudanese army of Mohamed Ahmad al Mahadi at the Battle of Omdurman. The UK and Egypt establish joint rule over Sudan.

1920s: The British move to separate the Arab and Muslim North from the African South. The two parts of Sudan are ruled separately.

1956: Sudan becomes independent. Even before independence there is fighting between the Sudanese army and rebel soldiers in the South, who fear they will be dominated by the North. Their rebellion develops into Sudan's first civil war, which lasts until 1972. At the same time, the Sudanese government spends a lot of money on weapons but little on infrastructure. Thousands of people are killed and many more flee as refugees to Ethiopia, the Democratic Republic of Congo and Uganda.

1970s: The price of cotton - a major Sudanese export - drops. Oil prices rise. Sudan is in debt. The International Monetary Fund (IMF) recommends harsh measures such as abolishing food subsidies and cutting public spending. In the late 1970s food prices rise.

Sudan

Many Sudanese join protests against the IMF programme. Others turn to Islamic fundamentalism. President Nimeiri is eventually forced into coalition with the fundamentalist Muslim Brothers. Nimeiri imposed shari'a (Islamic law) on Sudan. This is opposed by Christian southerners. A group of southern soldiers found the Sudanese People's Liberation Army (SPLA) to fight for an independent southern Sudan.

1983: The civil war starts again.

1988: The war intensifies. Over 250,000 people starve to death in southern towns because the Sudanese government and the SPLA prevent food aid from reaching the hungry. Refugees flee to Ethiopia and Uganda. Over 1 million people flee to Khartoum to escape fighting and famine. They live in slums on the city's outskirts. In the South, thousands of boys are seen walking towards Ethiopia having fled villages in the Bahr el Gazal region to escape attacks by government soldiers. They want peace and a chance to go to school.

1989: Another coup installs Brigadier Omar al Bashir as president. Human rights violations worsen. The Sudanese people experience mass detentions, extrajudicial executions, the banning of political parties and trade unions, media censorship and the abolition of an independent, secular judiciary. Government forces also seal off the Nuba mountains. At the same time the southern Sudanese fight among themselves. More than 5,000 people are murdered in and around the town of Bor in a feud between two factions of the SPLA.

1993: Famine in southern Sudan worsens. Over 400,000 people flee as refugees, mostly to Ethiopia, Kenya and Uganda.

1996: Fighting breaks out again between two southern guerrilla factions.

2004: The two southern guerrilla factions sign a peace agreement. But fighting breaks out in the Darfur region on the border with Chad. Arab militia and the Sudanese armed forces attack the villages of African Muslims causing them to flee. By mid-2004 over 700,000 Sudanese are refugees, mostly in neighbouring countries. Another 4.8 million people are internally displaced.

Sudanese refugees at Itang camp in Ethiopia. Their immediate needs are food, shelter and clothing.
© UNHCR / A. Hollmann

– Chapter Nine: Refugees and displaced people in poor countries

Chol Paul Guet's story

Chol was among a group of Sudanese boys who fled after Sudanese soldiers attacked his village. He and thousands of other boys walked hundreds of kilometres towards Ethiopia. His story was collected by Sybella Wilks who worked for the United Nations High Commissioner for refugees in Kenya.

"It was something like an accident when I ran away from my village. We were playing at about five o'clock when the soldiers came. We didn't know where we were going to; we just ran. The soldiers divided into two groups, one for the village and one for our herds of cattle. My brother helped me to run. We didn't know where my mother and father were; we didn't say goodbye. When there is shooting, when you hear 'bang, bang, bang', you don't think about your friend or your mother, you just run to save your life."

"I didn't see the soldiers, I just heard the shooting, the screaming and the bombing that went 'dum, dum, dum, dum,' like this and killed many people. It all just happened, like an accident and we ran without anything - nothing, no food, no clothes, nothing. In the day the sun was hot and your feet burn. So we walked at night when it is cold, because then you don't say all the time 'I want water, I want water,' People died of hunger. I saw many dying. Even my friend died. There was no water, no food. When I saw my friend dying I carried on walking. You see sometimes you can help, and then sometimes you can't."

"After two months we came to the Anyak tribe who knew the way to Ethiopia. They helped us get fish and make dried fish. Not bad! To go to Ethiopia to the Panyido refugee camp, there was a big river we had to swim across. Many people drowned on the way. In Panyido we did not have much food for two months, but at least there was peace."

"I spent three years in Ethiopia and felt well. I went to school and lived with five other boys. Then the United Nations left and we had to run. You see the new president of Ethiopia did not want refugees. We couldn't do anything, what could we do? It was not our country. So we had to swim and then swim again. Some trucks took us from the border to Kapoeta town (in Sudan); it took two weeks. They gave us food, one hand like this, only one handful to last one week."

"At Kapoeta, after three days the United Nations said 'Take them to Narus.' What was happening we didn't know. When we asked people, they said there was fighting and bombing and the soldiers might get us. In Narus (Sudan) we started building our schools and getting books, but we had to leave after only two months because of more fighting. So we went to Kenya where we would be safe."

"Now I live with the other boys in Kakuma (Kenya). We cook for ourselves and build our own homes. I like playing basketball, but there is also football and school. I say, let us stay here where it is safe. In England, you are safe, now let us stay here safely. Now we want to learn. One day I will be an engineer to build Sudan like other countries in Africa. I don't know whether my mother and father are dead or alive. I was young when I left Sudan I am an old man now. My mother will not know me."

Chol's story and others like his are published in "One Day We Had to Run" by Evans Brothers with UNHCR and Save the Children.

Comparing your life with Chol's

Learning objectives: At the end of the activity students will have considered the similarities and differences between their lives and that of Chol.

Time needed: 45 minutes

Instructions: Each student will need a copy of Chol's story, his daily timetable and two 24-hour clocks. They will also need coloured crayons to complete the 24-hour clocks. The students can work individually or in pairs. Using the information given, the students first make a key to show the different activities in a typical weekday: sleeping, getting washed and dressed, school, homework, housework and so on. The students then transfer this information to one of the 24-hour clocks.

Using the information about Chol's day, the students make a key and shade in the 24-hour clock for Chol. The students should then read Chol's story. They should think about the similarities between Chol's life and their own. They should consider all aspects of his life: his family, home, his day, migration, education and his aspirations.

See page 339 for a larger 24-hour clock diagram.

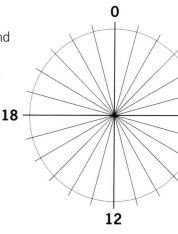

Discussion points:

⇨ What similarities are there between Chol's life and yours?

⇨ What differences are there between Chol's life and yours?

Chol's day

Chol lives in Kakuma refugee camp in Kenya. This is a special refugee camp. Many of its inhabitants are Sudanese boys and young men who have fled Sudan without parents. The boys and young men live together in groups of five or six. They take it in turns to cook and collect water. Here is what happens on a typical school day.

6.00 Sunrise. Wake up!

6.15–6.45 Wash and dress.

6.45–7.15 Collect water and some firewood.

7.15 Eat some breakfast.

7.30 Collect my things and walk to school.

8.00–13.00 School. We study maths, English, science and geography today. We also play football.

13.00 Come home. Cooking. We also cook maize and beans for lunch. We eat together and then rest because it is hot.

15.00 Homework.

16.00 Queue to collect more water. Housework. I have to wash some clothes and tidy up.

17.00 We all work together to prepare food for later. I make some bread. We cook vegetables and more maize too. We cook on firewood.

18.00 Cooking done, one person looks after the food. Now we can relax. We play football for a while.

18.30 It gets dark. There is no electricity where we live.

19.00 Supper and talking.

21.00 Sleep.

Information: The Sudanese boys' march

In 1988 thousands of Sudanese boys were seen walking towards Ethiopia. They were mostly between 8 and 16 years old. Most of the boys had come from villages in the Bahr el Gazal region of Sudan. Here they had fled attacks by Sudanese government soldiers. But as well as looking for peace and safety, the boys wanted the chance to go to school. (Most schools in southern Sudan had been closed because of the fighting.)

The boys walked nearly 450 kilometres to Panyido refugee camp in Ethiopia. It was a dangerous journey. Some of the boys were killed by wild animals on the way. Others had died of hunger and disease. To get into Ethiopia the boys had to cross a river and some of them drowned. When the Sudanese boys arrived in Ethiopia they were tired and very hungry. But at Panyido camp they received the care that they needed: food, clean water and the education that they so wanted. Nearly 5,000 boys lived in dormitories at night and went to school in the day.

The refugee boys' peaceful life ended in 1991 when there was a change of government in Ethiopia. The Sudanese refugee children were no longer welcome in Ethiopia. They were told to leave and go back to Sudan. For nearly a week the boys had to run from Panyido refugee camp. Many of them drowned crossing the river to go back to Sudan. Others were attacked by the Sudanese army and air force that dropped bombs on the returning refugees.

The boys settled for a while in Pochala and Nasir, two towns in southern Sudan. But they had to flee again when fighting came near these towns. They travelled to Narus, another town in southern Sudan. But there was not much food here and many of the boys fell sick. The United Nations, who were responsible for looking after the boys, decided that they would be safer in Kenya. They crossed the Kenyan border in trucks. After three months in a temporary camp, the boys were moved to Kakuma camp in Kenya. Many have lived there since then. The younger children are now grown up, although other unaccompanied Sudanese children have continued to arrive in Kenya since 1995.

Most of the older boys and men live in group houses. Five boys and men live and cook together. All the housework is shared. There are schools and training projects for the refugees. But life in the camp is not easy. There are many problems facing the young people and those who look after them. Many of the boys have seen terrible fighting and as a result still have nightmares and find it difficult to cope. Some of the boys in Kakuma camp have also been child soldiers in Sudan. Children as young as ten have been forced to fight in southern Sudan. Child soldiers find it particularly hard to adapt to a more peaceful life. A few of the child soldiers have returned to fight in Sudan.

Most of the boys and young men are also without their parents and family. They have lost people who can give them advice and support. As a result a number of the boys have turned to crime. In the late 1990s social workers helped some of the refugee boys and men return to their home villages. In 2000 and 2001 the US agreed to take 3,800 of the Sudanese refugees from Kakuma. They flew to the US to begin a new life: to find work and complete their education.

More information about the settlement of the Sudanese boys in the US can be found on the website of the US Committee for Refugees at: www.refugees.org

Information: Family tracing

When war breaks out in a country it is easy to be parted from family members. Parents are often separated from their children or a husband may lose his wife. In such situations family tracing is very important. Organisations like the Red Cross and Save the Children are involved in family tracing. If family tracing is successful, divided families can be reunited.

Tracing is divided into three different stages. The first stage is identification and documentation. This involves listing the lost family members, interviewing the family about themselves and the way that they became separated. Tracing is the second stage. This is the process of looking for someone. Reunification happens if tracing is successful. The family is brought together.

Different methods are used to trace a person. In some situations office-based tracing methods can be used. An advertisement can be placed in a newspaper, on a poster or on the radio. The advertisement will give details about the missing person. This type of tracing was used to trace Kosovar refugees in 1999. Lists and pictures of missing people were posted in refugee camps. Red Cross tracing volunteers also look for people by travelling to different areas. The volunteer may have to make a difficult and uncomfortable journey to a remote area.

A good tracer has many different skills. He or she will have a detailed knowledge about a particular area. A good tracer is also imaginative and uses lateral thinking. The tracer may use deduction and hunches to try and find out where people might be: "… that displaced persons' camp in the capital has a lot of people from the same area, so let's ask there."

The Red Cross has the largest family tracing service. It helps bring together close relatives who have been separated by armed conflict, political upheavals or disasters. The Red Cross Tracing Service may also trace people on compassionate grounds, for example people who were very close friends.

It is a free service and in great demand. At present the Red Cross Tracing Service receives an average of 800 enquiries every day. It can take up to two years for a case to be examined.

Someone living in the UK who wishes to trace a lost relative contacts the headquarters of the British Red Cross. The enquirer has to fill in a tracing form giving information about the person being sought. The inquiry is then recorded on a computer. The British Red Cross then decides whether to accept the tracing request. Sometimes, if there is severe fighting in a particular country, the Red Cross tracing service is suspended.

The details about the lost person are then sent to the central Tracing Agency of the International Committee of the Red Cross (ICRC) in Geneva. From there the information about the lost person goes to one of the Red Cross national societies. Then volunteers start to search.

The Red Cross also runs a family message service. This is often the only way for family members to keep in contact if they have been separated in wars. In severe fighting normal communications like post and telephones may break down.

In the UK a person wanting to send a family message contacts their local Red Cross office and collects a family message form. They write the message and post the form to the British Red Cross headquarters in London. Only family news may be sent; no political news is allowed. The form is then sent to the Red Cross society in the relevant country and is delivered. The message service allows for a return message. Sometimes the family message service brings very bad news. If this is the case, the Red Cross will deliver such messages in person.

Both the tracing service and the family message service have been very important in southern Sudan.

Activity

Tracing a relative

Learning objectives: For students to experience part of the process of family tracing.

Time needed: 40 minutes

Instructions: Copies of the tracing form and information on family tracing are needed. Students can work in pairs or small groups.

Atak Deng is a 30 year old man from southern Sudan. In 1997 he became separated from Achan, his sister. They both fled from their home in a small town in southern Sudan after fighting destroyed their neighbourhood.

In 1998 Atak's aunt received a letter from Achan. It said that she was a refugee in London. But since then the family has heard nothing from her. Letters sent to London have not been answered. Atak now wants to trace his sister. He fills in a Red Cross tracing form.

The students should imagine that they are Red Cross volunteers in the London office. In groups they should work out a strategy to trace Achan.

> ✚ Red Cross National Headquarters
>
> **TRACING FORM**
>
> TO: RED CROSS DATE: 25 August 1994
> REF: 000001
>
> **SOUGHT PERSON**
>
> 1 Full Name (as used locally) - underline surname — Jacinta Paulo
> 2 Name at Birth — Jacinta Paulo
> 3 Father's Full Name (or head of family group) — Alphons Paulo
> 4 Mother's Full Name — Francisca Paulo
> 5 Date of Birth — 26.5.71 Sex: F Marital Status **N/K**
> 6 Place of Birth — Huambo, Angola Nationality Angolan
> 7 Country of origin — Angola
> 8 Profession/Occupation — Student
> 9 Name and Ages of Others with Sought Person — none
> 10 a) Last Known Address: 33 Acacia Road London SE15
> b) Telephone No.
> 11 Place and Date of Last News — address above 1993
> 12 Circumstances leading to the loss of contact — fighting in Huambo
>
> **ENQUIRER**
>
> 13 Full Name (Indicate Mr/Mrs/Miss) — Joaquim Paulo
> 14 Nationality — Angolan
> 15 Address — PO BOX 45231 Huambo Angola
> 16 Telephone No.
> 17 Date and Place of Birth or Age — 02.12.73
> 18 The Person to be traced is my — Sister
> 19 The media may be used if necessary for search — Yes

An example of a completed tracing form.

Information: Refugees from Colombia

About 40,000 Colombians live in the UK.

Population: 43 million
Capital: Bogota
Economy: Colombia is a middle-income country, but economic inequality is one of the main causes of the current conflict. Some 70 per cent of arable land is controlled by just three per cent of the population. Colombia's main exports are oil and petroleum products, textiles, processed food and drink, coffee, bananas, cut flowers, sugar cane, cotton and vegetables. A major illegal export is cocaine - often sent for processing in laboratories in other Latin American countries.

Events:

17th and 18th century: Spanish control gradually extends into the interior of Colombia.

19th century: There is growing opposition to Spanish rule.

1819: Colombia (then called New Granada) gains full independence as part of Gran Colombia, comprising modern Panama, Venezuela, Colombia and Ecuador. Political tensions cause Gran Colombia to split up in 1831. New Granada becomes an independent state, made up of modern-day Colombia and Panama.

1850: The Liberal Party and Conservative Party are formally established. Conflict between these two parties continues to dominate Colombian politics to the present day. In the 19th century the Liberals draw most of their support from urban traders, artisans and industrialists. They are anti-colonial and wish to transform New Granada into a modern nation, separating church and state, promoting a more democratic form of government and investing in education. The Conservatives wish to preserve colonial structures and institutions, and maintain strong links between church and state, as well as a more authoritarian government. They are supported by large landlords and the Roman Catholic Church. Landless labour and peasant farmers often give their support to the party of the local landowner. Conflict between supporters of the two parties leads to political instability and periods of armed rebellion in the later years of the 19th century.

1899: Supporters of the Liberal Party attempt a revolution, known as the War of a Thousand Days. It costs more than 100,000 lives and leaves the country devastated.

1930s and 1940s: Colombia grows richer. The ruling Liberal Party grants more rights to workers in Colombia's new industries.

1946: Liberal Party rule ends with the election of President Mariano Ospina Perez, a Conservative. This ignites local tensions between the two political parties, resulting in violent political conflict, particularly in rural areas.

1958: Violence worsens with the assassination of a popular Liberal politician. Some 2,000 people are killed and much of Bogota is destroyed. Although order is restored in Bogota, civil war engulfs the countryside. Conservative and Liberal leaders organise their own guerrilla armies but some guerrilla groups begin to operate independently of political leaders. Communists, too, begin to organise their own guerrilla units. In the period 1948-1958 - La Violencia - some 250,000 people are killed and over 2 million internally displaced. Eventually there is a peace agreement between the Conservative and Liberal Parties. The Presidency is to be alternated between the two parties and posts in the cabinet, judiciary and civil service divided between the two parties. Although the pact overcomes some of the traditional political rivalries, it means that no third party can challenge the Liberals or Conservatives. It also causes a great deal of voter apathy.

1960s: Growing poverty and a sense of political powerlessness leads some rural people to support left-wing guerrilla organisations, mainly the Revolutionary Armed Forces of Colombia (FARC) and the National Liberation Army (ELN). The Colombian army, often supported by large landowners, sets up right-wing guerrilla groups and death squads to counter the left-wing guerrillas.

1985: Nearly 300,000 people are internally displaced. The complex conflict has continued to the present day. In some areas, a triple alliance of drugs barons, the army and right-wing paramilitary groups target people they suspect of sympathising with left-wing groups. In other areas, the drugs barons give support to left-wing groups. All political opposition, human rights activities, trade unionists and community workers are also at risk. Fear of being murdered by the Colombian army and death squads has forced thousands of people to flee. Others have fled in fear of left-wing guerrillas.

1998: Andres Pastrana is elected president on promises of peace. In 1999 over 5 million Colombians march for peace. To create space for peace talks, President Pastrana allows a 'demilitarised zone' in southern Colombia, in part of the country largely controlled by FARC. Here the guerrillas run their own government and have effectively formed a state within a state. FARC obtains money from its own taxation, the drugs trade, extortion and kidnapping.

2000: Peace talks break down in 2000 and President Pastrama loses much of his support. He is replaced in 2002. By 2004 some 2.8 million Colombians are internally displaced and 230,000 are refugees in neighbouring countries. Many others have fled to North America and Western Europe. Human rights activists, journalists, teachers, community leaders, candidates for government office, socialists, trade unionists and others who challenge the power of the rich, the army, or guerrillas are at risk.

Colombia

Claudia's story

Claudia is 10 years old. She was born in a village in Colombia, but attacks by armed men caused Claudia and her family to flee from their home. They are now among the 2.1 million internally displaced people in Colombia.

"Before we fled, we worked in the fields. My family sold things like maize, cocoa and rice. Then in 1997 we were threatened by armed men. Many people in the village were killed by them, they came looking for certain people and read out a list of names."

"We had to run to save ourselves. You go with what you are wearing, we had to leave our animals behind. It was very scary, because on the same day we left, planes flew overhead dropping bombs."

Maria's story

Maria is a mother of five children and is internally displaced. She is living in a makeshift camp in a town in northern Colombia.

"Before we were displaced we worked in the fields. A women's group, made up of about 15 of us, used to sell produce in the community shop. We sold things like maize, cocoa and rice. We would also take out goods to Turbo, a nearby town, to sell."

"Then in February, we were threatened by the paramilitary, although they had been in the area for some time. When they arrived in our village, they accused us of collaborating with the guerillas. They came to the village and gathered us together, they told us they were looking for certain people and read out a list of names. Then they told us that we had three days to leave. They took one man aside and cut off his arms and legs. Then they cut off his head as well. They killed him because they said he was not worth anything. Then the paramilitaries started shooting into the air and the children began crying and screaming."

"Some people fled to Panama and others to Turbo. Many families got split up. People want to return, but they are afraid of the paramilitaries. We went to Turbo. Some people left with nothing, others managed to take some stuff with them."

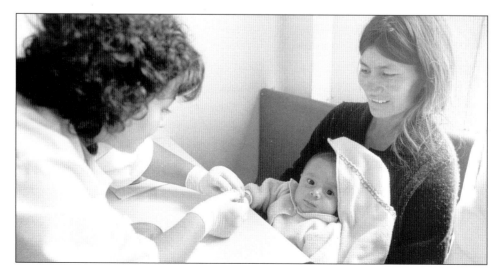

© **UNHCR / P. Smith**

Information: Internally displaced people

Internally displaced woman from Pavarando in Mutata Municipality in Uraba.
© **UNHCR / P. Smith**

Most Colombians who have fled from their homes are not refugees. They are internally displaced people - people who have fled from their homes in fear but have not crossed an international border. Today, there are more internally displaced people than refugees. Their numbers can be hard to estimate, but it is likely that in 2003 there were over 25 million internally displaced people in the world. Some 2.1 million Colombian people were internally displaced. There are also larger numbers of internally displaced people in Sudan, the Democratic Republic of Congo and Afghanistan. Almost all internally displaced people live in the world's poor countries. The majority of the world's internally displaced people are women and children.

There are many similarities between internally displaced people and refugees. Both groups have fled from their homes in fear. Both are seeking safety. But internally displaced people are usually more vulnerable than refugees.

Firstly, while fleeing from their homes many internally displaced people get stranded in the middle of fighting. Here organisations like the Red Cross or other non-governmental organisations cannot reach them. Internally displaced people may be stranded without much food in the middle of a war zone.

There are international human rights laws to protect refugees. The *1951 UN Convention Relating to the Status of Refugees* protects refugees from being sent back to their home countries and to situations where they would face danger. The United Nations High Commissioner for Refugees is an organisation that ensures that this international law is respected. Internally displaced people do not have this legal protection.

Internally displaced people may live in camps. More often, they build their own shelter on the outskirts of towns and cities. Most of Colombia's internally displaced people are living in city slums.

Research activity

⇨ Visit the website of the Internal Displacement Project at: www.idpproject.org.uk. Make a list of the main groups of internally displaced people in today's world.

⇨ Which continent hosts the largest numbers of internally displaced people?

Preparing a school assembly on internally displaced people

Learning objectives: Students will develop their collaborative and planning skills. The activity will also consolidate their knowledge about internal displacement. The assembly itself aims to create empathy with displaced children. One class could prepare the assembly and present it to the school.

Time needed: At least 1 hour

Instructions: Students will need copies of the information about internally displaced people, as well as the Colombian children's stories. Students may also wish to collect other material from the internet or television.

Students should work as a class to prepare the assembly:

- It could open with the children's stories and with news footage.
- Another group of students could present information about internally displaced people.
- Other students could present information about an organisation that works with internally displaced people.
- The assembly could end with prayers or poems.

"We are birds of the same nest
We may wear different skins,
We may speak in different tongues,
We may believe in different religions,
We may belong to different cultures,
Yet we all share the same home –
Our Earth."

From the Athava Veda

Information: Refugees from Eritrea

Over 15,000 Eritrean refugees have fled to the UK since the mid-1960s.

Population: 4.3 million plus an exile population of about 350,000.
Capital: Asmara.
Ethnic and language groups: Most people identify themselves as Eritrean, although there are 9 different ethno-linguistic groups. About half of the population speak Tigrinya, and another 30 per cent Tigre. Arabic, Saho, Beja, Afar, Baza, Barya and Bilen are also spoken.
Religion: About half of the population are Christian and half are Muslim. Most Christians belong to the Eritrean Orthodox Church.

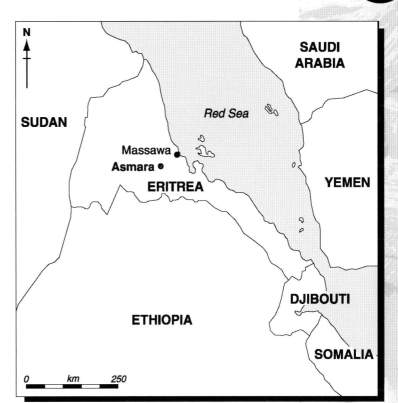

Events:

Until the late 19th century Eritrea was a collection of small kingdoms ruled by local nobles and influenced by many of the great powers in the region, including the Turks, Greeks, Arabs, Egyptians and Persians.

1871: Yohannes IV, an Ethiopian, unites Ethiopia and Eritrea as one country. Colonial powers begin to take an interest in the Horn of Africa. The Italians want to colonise the country and send an army to conquer Ethiopia and Eritrea.

1889: The Italians are defeated in battle and leave Ethiopia, but remain in Eritrea. In the next 30 years over 60,000 Italian settlers arrive. Eritrean national identity begins to grow under Italian occupation.

1914-1918: During the Second World War, the British army forces the Italians out of the Horn of Africa. Somali, Eritrean and Ethiopian soldiers fight alongside the British. At the end of the war, Eritrea becomes a British Protectorate.

1950: The British call on the UN to decide Eritrea's future. There are three options: incorporation within Ethiopia, federation with Ethiopia or independence. The UN decide that Eritrea should be federated with Ethiopia, but have its own regional government.

1951: The UN agreement comes into force, but Ethiopia ignores large parts of the UN plan. Eritrean factories are closed and moved to Ethiopia. There is no investment in the economy. Tigrinya and Arabic are no longer taught in Eritrean schools. Eritrean political parties and trade unions are banned. By 1960 there are about 3,000 Eritrean political prisoners in Ethiopian jails.

1961: The Eritrean Liberation Front (EPLA) is founded to fight for independence. Later, in 1962 the Ethiopian government manages to get a majority of its supporters elected to the Eritrean assembly, the latter then vote for complete unity with Ethiopia.

Eritrea

1974: Famine hits large parts of Ethiopia and Eritrea. Emperor Haile Selassie's government collapses. A new military government takes power under Colonel Mengistu. The Eritrean people hope that the new Ethiopian government will restore autonomy but it draws its support from the same people who backed Haile Selassie. Colonel Mengistu's government - called the Derg - increases military spending, and receives military aid from the Soviet Union. The policy of neglect in Eritrea, Tigray and other provinces continues.

1970s: The war worsens in Eritrea. Over 30 per cent of the population flee from their homes. The EPLF, now the main group fighting for independence, control much of Eritrea, where it sets up democratic local government, schools and clinics. The Ethiopian government continues to launch attacks in Eritrea. Its army also executes civilians in the 'Red Terror', during which an estimated 250,000 people are murdered in Ethiopia and Eritrea.

1983 and 1985: Two disastrous famines hit Eritrea and Ethiopia. Soil erosion and the continued lack of agricultural investment reduce farmers to subsistence level. They have no savings and nothing to fall back on. Up to 300,000 people die of hunger. Millions of Eritreans and Ethiopians walk to refugee camps. Further famine hits Eritrea in 1987.

1990: Over 750,000 Eritrean refugees are living in Sudan, some in appalling conditions in refugee camps. But in 1991 EPLF and opposition forces in Ethiopia make military gains and the government of Colonel Mengistu collapses. The EPLF forms a provisional government in Eritrea in order to rule the country until a referendum on independence.

1993: The referendum is held and most of Eritrea's population vote for independence. Eritrea becomes Africa's newest country. The EPLF then renames itself the People's Front for Democracy and Justice (PFDJ). In the years after independence about half of all Eritrean refugees return home. In the period after independence, Eritrea has good relations with Ethiopia.

1998: The Eritrean and Ethiopian air forces bomb each other's towns over disputed land. Fighting on land follows. The fighting worsens in early 1999, and continues on and off throughout the year. Over 30,000 soldiers are killed. Thousands of people are internally displaced, including those expelled from Ethiopia.

2000: Fighting between Eritrea and Ethiopia ends in 2000, but nearly 50,000 Eritreans are still displaced as a result. Over 300,000 Eritrean refugees still live in Sudan. Some live in camps and others live in cities. Recently small numbers of Eritreans have fled human rights abuses. The country is now a one-party state tolerating no political opposition. Journalists and government opponents have been jailed.

© UNHCR / P. Moumtzis

- **Chapter Nine: Refugees and displaced people in poor countries -**

Betiel's story

Betiel is now in her 20s. Here she tells of her flight to Sudan in 1989.

"Living in a village in Eritrea was like living in heaven. I know it sounds too good to be true, but I could tell you those were the happiest days of my life. However, the fairy tale did not continue. On 29 September, my grandmother announced that we were leaving the village for good. She told us that we were going to Sudan to live with my parents. I had not seen them since they had left the country. Long before I came to my grandmother's village, we used to own a chemist's shop in Asmara, the capital city of Eritrea. However when the war between my country and Ethiopia got worse, my parents decided to help our soldiers by providing them with medicine. When the Ethiopian government found out that my parents were supplying medicine to the enemy, they burnt the chemist's shop down and tried to kill them."

"Even though I missed my parents very much, I did not want to leave the village and friends who I loved. I cried and a little voice inside me screamed silently. But who would listen to a child and who would understand how I felt?"

"On 30 September we were ready to leave. My grandmother had arranged everything we needed - the luggage and dried food. The time had come when I had to say goodbye to those people I loved and admired, and believe me it was the hardest thing I ever did. That night we had dinner with my uncle's family. While we were having dinner, they were discussing where they were going to hire a camel and how we were going to get out of the village without the soldiers noticing us. I was quiet. I felt that my life was ruined and I blamed my parents. I blamed them for leaving me first, then taking me away from my friends. I was too selfish to notice that they were saving my life and giving me a better future."

Learning objectives: The activity helps students develop their organisational and communication skills.

Instructions: The children will need paper to design sponsorship forms and some buckets for the activity. Prior to carrying out the activity, the teacher should have contacted an organisation that works with refugees in poor countries. It might provide a speaker or promotional literature on its work. The students might want to look at the promotional literature and the messages it carries.

The activity should be introduced by explaining that Eritrean girls and women living in the refugee camps in Sudan walk an average of 4.5 kilometres every day to collect water for their families. This task is time-consuming and prevents many girls from attending schools. The group is going to walk 4.5 kilometres carrying a bucket of water, to raise money for work with refugees in poor countries.

The students will need to set a day for the walk and to plan the route that participants will take. They could walk around a football pitch or the playground, for example. The route must be safe and away from roads. Students may have to get permission for the walk if they are going to use a football pitch.

Sponsorship forms should be designed. They must have a contact name and address on them, and explain how the money collected is going to be used.

Activity ☝

The water activity for fundraising

Students may like to publicise their fundraising activity in the local paper or on local radio. They can draw attention to the problems faced by many refugees in poor countries, and also the way that organisations are working to support them.

The students should collect sponsorship from family and friends. On the day of the walk they will need buckets and access to a tap.

Students can be given responsibility for different tasks.

Job description - Liaison
- Securing permission to run the fundraising activity
- Liaising with teachers and the head teacher
- Ensuring that parents/carers give permission for under 16s to be involved in out of school fundraising activities

Job description - Logistics
- Organising the venue and route
- Ensuring that there are enough taps and buckets for the activity
- Coordinating arrangements and schedules for the day

Job description - Health and safety
- Researching what needs to be done to ensure that the activity complies with health and safety requirements
- Conducting a risk assessment for the activity
- Ensuring that the activity is conducted in a safe manner on the day

Job description - Publicity
- Conceiving key messages about the event - these include the value of the fundraising activity, as well as information about the charity for which the money is being raised
- Publicising the event in the local media

Job description - Art and design
- Designing publicity and the sponsorship forms

Job description - Financial management
- Assessing what costs may be involved in running the fundraising activity - if there are small costs involved, the financial manger will need to budget for them
- Managing a system for donations to be received and banked safely
- Setting up arrangements to keep any large amounts of money secure
- Ensuring that the charity receives the money you have collected

After the walk, it is important for students to discuss how they felt, and what they learned from the activity. All reputable non-governmental organisations will acknowledge the receipt of money raised in such events. An acknowledgment letter should also be shared with the class.

10 Refugees in Europe

Asylum seekers at Sangatte Red Cross Shelter in Calais, France. © H. J. Davies

This chapter gives a background to refugees who arrive in the UK and Europe, and examines how they apply for asylum and how their basic needs are met.

On exiles and defeats

No. It was not the bad time in Chena,
nor the sudden grim prosecutions
in improvised war councils.
No. The blind gun that hits me on the shoulder
didn't defeat me,
nor the investigators' black hood of horror
nor the grey hell of the stadiums
with their roars of terror.

No. Neither was it the iron bars at the window
cutting us in pieces from life,
nor the watch kept on our house
nor the stealthy tread,
nor the slide into the deep maw of hunger.

No. What defeated me was the street that was not mine,
the borrowed language learned in hastily set up courses.
What defeated me was the lonely, uncertain figure
in longitudes that did not belong to us.
It was Greenwich
longitude zero
close to nothing.
What defeated me was the alien rain,
forgetting words
the groping memory,
friends far away
and the atrocious ocean between us,
wetting the letters I waited for
which did not come.

What defeated me was yearning day after day
at Jerningham Road
agonising under the fog
at Elephant and Castle
sobbing on London Bridge.

And I was defeated step by step
by the harsh calendar
and between Lunes-Monday and Martes-Tuesday
I had shrivelled into a stranger.

What defeated me was the absence of your tenderness, my country.

by Maria Eugenia Bravo Calderara

Translated by Cicely Herbert and taken from Prayers in the National Stadium published by Katabarsif Press in 1992. Maria Bravo is Chilean and has worked for the Refugee Council. She was imprisoned and tortured in Chile in 1973. Afterwards she was released and came to the UK as a refugee.

Refugee

So I have a new name, refugee
Strange that a name should take away from me
My past, my personality and hope
Strange refuge this.
So many seem to share this name, refugee
Yet we share so many differences.

I find no comfort in my new name
I long to share my past, restore my pride,
To show, I too, in time, will offer more
Than I have borrowed
For now the comfort that I seek
Resides in the old, yet new name
I would choose - friend.

Poem by Zimbabwean student Ruvimbo Bungwe at Villiers High School, Southall.

Discussion point:

⇨ What did each poet feel about their new life in the UK?

Information: Statistics about refugees

Refugee communities in the UK from 1970 to the present

Country of origin	Date of arrival	Estimated size of community 2004
Uganda	1972–	44,000
Chile	1973–79	3,000
Ethiopia and Eritrea	1973–	30,500
Cyprus	1974–	24,000
Vietnam	1975–1992	25,000
Iran	1978–	50,000
Afghanistan	1979–	55,000
Iraq	1980–	55,000
Sri Lanka (Tamils)	1983–	71,000
Somalia	1988–	195,000
Turkey	1989–	60,000
Democratic Republic of Congo	1989–	18,000
Sudan	1990–	9,000
Colombia	1990–	10,000
Angola	1990–	16,000
Bosnia	1992–96	6,000
Eastern European Roma	1992–	14,000
Algeria	1994–	14,000
Sierra Leone	1994–	17,000
Kosovo	1995–	28,000
Zimbabwe	1999–	6,000

Sources: Kushner and Knox.

UK asylum applications and categories of decisions as a percentage 1989–2003

Year	Asylum applications	Refugee status	Leave to remain	Refusal
1989	11,640	32	55	13
1990	26,205	23	60	17
1991	44,840	10	44	46
1992	24,605	6	80	14
1993	22,370	9	64	27
1994	32,830	5	21	74
1995	43,965	5	19	76
1996	29,640	6	14	80
1997	32,500	13	11	76
1998	46,015	17	12	71
1999	71,160	42	12	46
2000	80,315	10	12	78
2001	71,700	9	17	74
2002	85,865	10	24	66
2003	49,370	6	11	83

Source: Home Office. Figures exclude dependants.

Discussion points:

⇨ Look at the two tables of statistics. What are the main trends shown in the statistics?

⇨ What might be the reason for these changes?

Information: Applying for asylum in the UK – what happens to asylum seekers

When endangered people flee from their homes and come to the UK, they have to apply to the Government to be given refugee status and be allowed to stay in the UK. The process of applying for refugee status is also known as 'applying for asylum'. People who have applied for asylum, but have not yet been given a decision allowing them to stay are known as asylum seekers.

The Home Office is the government department that decides if asylum seekers can stay or not. Decisions about asylum seekers are made in a section of the Home Office called the Immigration and Nationality Directorate. The flow diagram on page 216 shows how people apply for asylum in the UK. Most European countries have a similar process.

People queuing outside the Immigration and Nationality Directorate's offices in Croydon.
© **Refugee Council / David Levene**

You arrive in the UK.

Go though immigration control at the airport or port. You apply for asylum later. However, people who do not apply for asylum on arrival in the UK may find it difficult to get money and housing.

Go to immigration control at the airport or port and ask for asylum. You will be given a short interview. At this interview immigration officers will ask you questions about your journey to the UK. You may be fingerprinted.

You can be told that your application for asylum is 'clearly unfounded' if you come from a country that the UK government thinks is safe. If this happens you are likely to be held in an immigration detention centre. You are then likely to be sent back to your home country.

You are told that you can apply for asylum. Usually you are given an appointment for an interview with an immigration officer. You have to tell the immigration officer about the persecution you suffered in your country. After the interview you have another five days to collect extra written evidence to back up your application for asylum.

If immigration officers think that you have fled from your home country because you have a "well-founded fear of being persecuted for reasons of race, religion, nationality, membership of a particular social group or political opinion", you will be given refugee status. You get a UN refugee passport. You can stay in the UK as long as you need. You can work and bring your immediate family to the UK.

Some asylum seekers are given a form to complete. This form is called a statement of evidence form. You fill this in, explaining how you and your family were persecuted in your home country.

Immigration officers at the Home Office make a decision about your case. This can be quick or take many months.

You might be given a temporary status called humanitarian leave to remain in the UK or discretionary leave to remain in the UK. This allows you to stay in the UK for a limited period of time. This kind of permission to stay in the UK is given to people who are not judged to be refugees but have other humanitarian reasons why they cannot go back to their country.

You can be refused refugee status or leave to remain in the UK.

You can be removed from the UK. Usually a person who is removed is taken to a detention centre and held there until there is a place on a flight going to their home country. In 2003 about 10,000 refused asylum seekers were removed from the UK.

You can appeal against your refusal. About a quarter of people who appeal actually win and are allowed to stay in the UK.

You might decide to leave the UK.

Information: Detention

An increasing number of asylum seekers are being held in detention centres when they arrive in the UK. Refugee and human rights organisations are concerned that the UK government detains asylum seekers to give a message that the UK does not welcome asylum seekers. Refugee organisations are also concerned that vulnerable asylum seekers are being detained, including families with children, young people on their own, and asylum seekers who are severely traumatised or even mentally ill.

Detaining asylum seekers and refugees has a long history in the UK. During the Second World War over 27,000 refugees were detained in army camps. At that time 56,000 refugees had escaped from Nazi-occupied Europe between 1933 and 1939. Newspapers and some politicians feared that the refugees would not be loyal to their new country. It would also be easy for spies to live among the refugee community. After Germany invaded the Netherlands, the British government decided to detain German refugees in camps where conditions were very harsh.

Asylum seekers continued to be detained after the Second World War. In 1987, a ship called the Earl William was used to detain asylum seekers. It was moored off the port of Harwich. There were many complaints about conditions on the ship. Eventually, the Earl William drifted from its moorings after a storm. After this the Government decided not to use this ship as a detention centre.

Since 1992 about 8,000 asylum seekers have been detained every year in detention centres like Harmondsworth, Middlesex and Campsfield House near Oxford. Asylum seekers can also be detained in prisons and in police cells. Some asylum seekers are detained when they first arrive. Others are detained prior to being removed from the UK.

Asylum seekers may be detained because the immigration officer thinks they might disappear or go into hiding. They can also be detained because they have no address to go to, they have forged documents or they have no documents at all.

For asylum seekers kept in detention, normal rules of justice do not apply. Unlike criminals, no court is required to give permission for the detention of an asylum seeker. Most people in detention centres do not know when they will be released. They have little or no contact at all with lawyers.

Recently, refugee and human rights organisations have become aware that asylum-seeking children are being held in detention centres. Some of the children are unaccompanied and have come to the UK by themselves. Other children are being held with their families, either when they first arrive or just before they are removed from the UK.

The Refugee Council is an organisation which believes that the detention of children is always wrong and that detention of children violates their human rights as children. Detention can also damage children's development and psychological well-being.

Newroz Ay was one child who was held in detention for 13 months. Her story is featured on page 218.

Newroz Ay's story

Newroz Ay is a 13 year old Kurdish girl. Her parents are from Turkey, but Newroz, her two sisters and brother were born in Germany. In 1999 the German government tried to send the Ay family back to Turkey. They fled to the UK, but in 2002 they were detained. Between July 2002 and August 2003 the four Ay children and their mother were held in Dungavel detention centre in Scotland. In August 2003 the family was flown back to Germany. Here Newroz Ay tells her story.

"We came to England in 1999 because the Germans wanted us to go back to Turkey and we were scared that we wouldn't be safe there. All our relatives have escaped to other countries. Kurdish people cannot live freely in Turkey. We aren't even allowed to keep our Kurdish names but are forced to change them into Turkish ones."

"We paid a lot of money to hide in the back of a lorry and come to England. We spent a day and a night in the lorry and it was very hard. In the night it was freezing and in the day it was very hot. We didn't have enough air to breathe and my little sister and brother nearly died because they couldn't breathe properly. We didn't have any space to move around. The driver did not know we were inside, so we had to be totally quiet. We could drink almost nothing because there was nowhere to go to the toilet. Suddenly I felt the lorry being lifted into the air and was terrified. I was so relieved when it was put down in the boat. When they opened the lorry in England we were caught and taken to the police station. We claimed asylum and were given a house in Gravesend, Kent. My brother had his own room and me and my two sisters shared a room. We did things that other families did like watching TV and going shopping. The house had a garden which we all played in and in the summer we had barbecues and invited our friends from school. I think the time we lived in that house was the happiest in my life."

"When my dad went to sign on at the police station last May they arrested him and deported him first to Germany and then to Turkey. We have not heard anything from him since then. We cry when we think about him. Then immigration people came to our house and told us we had to go with them. We didn't want to go because we wanted to go to school. We were crying and scared. First they took us to a detention centre at Gatwick Airport and then two weeks later to Dungavel in Scotland. My hair started falling out when they put us in detention and I was diagnosed with depression. I didn't realise that a detention centre was like a prison with barbed wire and everyone locked in. I hate only seeing metal fences and no trees."

Discussion points:

⇨ What do you think about the detention of children like the Ay family? Do you think that it is wrong, or can the detention of children be justified in some circumstances?

⇨ Very few rich countries detain asylum-seeking children. One country that does so is Australia. Use the internet to find out about the experiences of asylum-seeking children in detention in Australia.

"Our room in Dungavel is very small. If my little sister is playing on the floor then there is no room for anyone else to walk around. Sometimes the guards come into our room without knocking to do roll call and we get scared. My little sister wakes in the night crying out, 'Why are we here? When are we going home?' There is not much to do here. The school lessons are aimed at primary school children and we are only allowed outside from 4 to 5 pm."

"If we could go back to our country we would do it, but our lives won't be safe there. My mum is very upset because she came to two democratic countries, England and Germany, and they treated us like this. I hope that one day we will get freedom."

Learning objectives: The activity develops students' skills in constructing arguments. It also enables students to consider the human rights of detaining asylum-seeking children.

Time needed: 2 hours plus homework

Instructions: The class should be divided into groups of six or seven. Each group should have access to a tape recorder with a microphone and blank tape. Each student should also have a copy of the typed information.

The students are going to make a 10 to 15 minute radio documentary which will explore issues surrounding the detention of asylum-seeking children. The theme of the documentary will be the exploration of whether detention is a violation of the human rights of children.

Students will take on different roles during the production of the documentary. The roles are:

- **Journalist.** The journalist asks the questions and provides the commentary on the tape, and works with the editor to write the journalist's script.
- **Editor.** The editor works with the journalist to write the script and makes the final decision about the content of the documentary.
- **Producer.** The producer takes charge of technical matters, such as finding a quiet place to record, and operating the tape recorder.
- **Detainee 'Abdul'.** He is an unaccompanied young person aged 16. Abdul has recently been detained and tells the radio journalist about his experience.
- **Detainee 'Mary'.** She is 14 years old and arrived in the UK with her mother. After seven months Mary and her mother were detained. She tells the radio journalist about her experience.
- **Director, Refugee Council.** The director represents a refugee organisation which believes that detention is always wrong. In particular the director of the Refugee Council believes that detaining children damages them. The director gives the radio journalist the Refugee Council's opinions and tries to answer some of the points made by the Home Office minister.
- **Minister, Home Office.** The minister supports the detention of some asylum seekers, particularly those who might go into hiding.

Illustration: **Newroz Ay**
Source: **The Guardian**

Activity

Writing to your MP about the detention of children

Learning objectives: Students learn to write letters to an MP expressing an opinion about a particular issue.

Time needed: 20 minutes

Instructions: Students should have completed the earlier work about the detention of children. They should have access to the information sheet about detention and Newroz Ay's story. The teacher should introduce this activity by explaining that one way that ordinary citizens can work to change things that they consider to be wrong is by writing to their MP.

Students are going to write to their MP about the detention of asylum-seeking children in the UK. The teacher should explain how to construct the letter. Students should then compose their letters.

Forest Gate Community Sch
Forest Street
London E7

Dear Home Secretary,

We are writing to tell you about my friend, Natasha, who you want to deport back to Angola.

We have known Natasha for several years and she is a really nice person. She has never hurt anyone. She is used to living in Forest Gate.

We can't understand why you want to send Natasha who is only 12 years old, back to a place which is so full of blood. It is a place of bad memories. When she was seven, she saw soldiers kill her two year old brother. Her dad was taken to prison. Her family lived in fear. She remembers seeing dead bodies on the streets and walking over them. As we are writing this letter, we are also upset and so is Natasha. How would you like to be forced back to a place where they killed your family? Natasha is our friend. We have played, studied and grown up together. Please, please, please don't send Natasha away, you will be breaking too many hearts and destroying our friends life.

It is all up to you. Can you please help us? We will do anything to help our friend. We are spending all our time on helping Natasha, that's how important she is to us. Angola is not Natasha's home, England is. After all she and her family have been through, how can you even of think of sending her back?

from
Jasvinder Rekhi, Monira Khatun, Shamima Patel, Jusna Begum and Ms Thakor.
(students and teachers at Forest Gate.)

The letter can be sent if the students feel very strongly that the detention of asylum-seeking children is wrong. The MP's response should be fed back to the class for student comment.

Learning objectives: The activity helps students reflect on the needs of those newly arrived in the UK.

Time needed: 15 to 20 minutes for the initial part of the activity, then about 30 minutes for the diary.

Instructions: Divide the students up into pairs and give them the scenario below. When the students have produced their list of needs the group can come together for a short discussion.

Needs in a new country

Applying for asylum is not the only difficulty that faces asylum seekers when they arrive in the UK. Housing, a job and schools for children have to be found. Many newly arrived refugees also have to learn a new language and find out about their rights in a new country. As a result the first few months in the UK for refugees are often very difficult.

Try putting yourself in the shoes of a newly-arrived refugee. Imagine that civil war has broken out where you live. You arrive home and find your house has been destroyed. Most people have left your home town and you have been told that your friends and family have fled.

You walk to a port town. By chance there is a cargo ship in the port. You manage to persuade a sailor on the ship to take you on board (after you have paid him £50). The boat sails to a new country. Here the journey ends and you are made to get off the boat. You are taken to see the immigration officials. What will happen to you?

In your pairs make a list of the things that you will need in the new country

* immediately;
* during the next six months.

The pairs should then divide into three groups. One third of the pairs should then imagine that they are an elderly refugee. Another third should imagine that they are a young mother with a small child. The third group of pairs should imagine that they are an unaccompanied refugee child aged 12. The pairs should list the particular needs of these three refugees.

Discussion points:

⇨ What did you learn about the life of a newly-arrived refugee from this activity?

⇨ Do some refugees need special help and support?

Information: Shelter and sustenance in a new country

Asylum seekers are no longer allowed to work in the UK. But they still need support and housing. Very few people can get along without the peace and security of a home. For many refugees who have experienced war, torture or the death of close relatives, good housing is needed to recover from such experiences.

Until the late 1990s asylum seekers were allowed to work after they had lived in the UK for six months. If an asylum seeker could not find work, he or she could claim benefits. But successive governments said that allowing asylum seekers to work acted as a 'pull factor' causing people to migrate to the UK.

At the same time almost all of the UK's asylum seekers and refugees lived in Greater London, where the housing shortage is worst. While some of them were lucky and found housing quickly, other asylum seekers and refugees found themselves living in poor housing in London.

Between 1995 and 2000 asylum seekers lost their rights to work in the UK and to claim benefits. Since then the National Asylum Support Service, a new Home Office department, has provided housing and financial support for asylum seekers who come to the UK.

After asylum seekers have applied for asylum, they then apply to the National Asylum Support Service for a cash allowance and housing. About 30 per cent of people choose to live with friends or relatives and will get a cash allowance from the National Asylum Support Service. The money they receive is about 70 per cent of the amount that a British person would receive as benefits.

Asylum seekers without anywhere to live are allocated housing by the National Asylum Support Service. Almost all of the housing is outside London as the Government has decided that too many asylum seekers are settling in the capital. The Government has decided to 'disperse' asylum seekers around the UK. They have no choice about where they will live. If they refuse an offer of a house in a certain town or city, they lose all right to housing and benefits.

While some of the housing offered to asylum seekers is good, dispersal has caused problems. Some asylum seekers are being sent to areas that have no existing refugee communities, and report loneliness and isolation in their new homes. In some areas asylum seekers have also been victims of racial harassment or racial attacks. Some asylum seekers, who gain refugee status and are allowed to stay and work in the UK, also move back to London and other big cities.

In 2002 the Government changed asylum law by passing the Nationality, Immigration and Asylum Act through Parliament. This allows the National Asylum Support Service to deny all benefits and housing to asylum seekers who do not apply for asylum immediately on arrival in the UK. Some asylum seekers have been forced to sleep on the streets as a result of this legal change. Others have gone to court and won the right to housing and subsistence support.

The Government is planning more changes to the way asylum seekers are housed and supported. In future, some asylum seekers will be housed in accommodation centres. These will be settlements housing about 800 asylum seekers. Most of them would be located in rural areas, far from cities. Here they would be fed and receive healthcare, schooling, adult education and legal advice. They would remain in the accommodation centre until their application to remain in the UK was decided upon. Those allowed to stay would then move into their own homes. Those who were not given permission to stay in the UK would then be removed from the UK.

Despite being very expensive to build, the Government says that accommodation centres make it easier to remove asylum seekers who have been refused permission to stay in the UK. Construction of the first accommodation centre has started.

Discussion points:

⇨ Why might asylum seekers and refugees wish to settle in London?

⇨ Do you think that asylum seekers should be allowed to live where they want to? Or do you think that they should be dispersed throughout the UK?

Learning objectives: To help students empathise with students who are new to their school.

Time needed: 45 minutes

Instructions: This activity can be used as a follow on from the activity on page 221. The students should be divided into threes and fours. In their groups the students should discuss how it would feel to arrive in the UK from another country. They can decide from which country they have come. The groups should talk about arriving in the UK, their new home, food, their first day at school and other new experiences.

They should then write a letter to an imaginary friend they left in their home country, to tell them about their new home.

Activity ☞

How does it feel to be new?

Many asylum seekers have no support at all and are left to fend for themselves.
© **Refugee Council**

Information: Finding a job

Most refugees want to work after they arrive in the UK. However, if you are new to the country, finding a job is not always easy. Since July 2002, newly arrived asylum seekers are not allowed to work. A person can only work legally if they have refugee status or leave to remain in the UK.

Even if you can work legally, there are lots of barriers that make it difficult for refugees to find work:

- You might not speak much English.
- The skills that you gained in your home country may not be useful in the UK.
- You might not know what kinds of jobs are on offer in your new town or city.
- You might not know where jobs are advertised in the UK.
- You might be sent to live in a place where unemployment is high for everyone.
- Employers might have prejudices about refugees. They might think that refugees are unskilled and uneducated.
- Employers are often confused about a person's immigration status. Some employers make mistakes and tell refugees they are not allowed to work when in fact they are.
- Employers might be worried about employing refugees thinking that they might go back to their home country.

Organisations like the Refugee Council help refugees find employment. They give advice about career and learning opportunities. The Refugee Council also runs English language classes and training schemes, so that refugees can update their qualifications or gain new skills. Refugees from poorer countries may have had little opportunity to use information technology. The Refugee Council offers many training courses in information technology.

A lot of refugees do find work. Some are lucky and obtain a job which is as good as the one they left behind. But many refugees find that they cannot get good jobs. Some find they are trapped in low paid work.

© Refugee Council / David Levene

The Refugee Council and the Government have both carried out research on refugees' work experiences. Here are some of the results.

Economic activity of refugees

	Men	Women
Employed	2%	23 %
Unemployed	42 %	21 %
Student	13 %	11 %
On training scheme	4 %	0 %
Looking after family	4 %	39 %
Retired	3 %	3 %
Sick or disabled	6 %	3 %

Source: Home Office, 1995.

English language ability at time of arrival

I could speak no English	35.5 %
I could speak a few words	18.3 %
I could speak enough English to get by	15.9 %
I could speak conversational English	12.6 %
My English was fluent	17.2 %

Source: Refugee Council, 1989.

Discussion points:

⇨ Do you think that asylum seekers should be allowed to work when they first arrive in the UK?

⇨ What do the statistics show you?

⇨ The unemployment rate for adult men in Britain is about 14 per cent. Why do you think that refugees are more likely to be unemployed than the 'average' person?

⇨ How might refugees be helped to get work?

Information: Iraq

Population: 24 million

Capital: Baghdad

Ethnic groups: About 70 per cent of the population are Arabs. Another 23 per cent are Kurdish, mostly living in the Kurdish Autonomous Area in the north. Other groups include the Turkmen, Assyrians and Armenians.

Languages: Arabic is the official language of Iraq. Iraqi Kurds speak Kurdish as their first language. Assyrian, Turkmen and Armenian are spoken by the respective minority groups.

Religion: Shi'a Muslims make up 55 to 60 per cent of the total Iraqi population. The majority of Shi'a Muslims live in southern Iraq and in the poorer suburbs of Baghdad. Despite being in the majority the Shi'a Muslims of Iraq are usually poor. Shi'a Muslims believe that Ali and his descendants are the leaders and successors to the Prophet Mohammed. The most important Shi'a shrine is at Kerbala in Iraq - this is where Ali was killed. Sunni Muslims make up 20 per cent of the Iraqi population, and mostly live in northern Iraq. The Assyrian and Armenian communities are Christian.

Economy: The north of Iraq is mountainous and the south is desert. Iraq's main export is oil. Iraq is also the world's largest producer of dates. Until 1990, Iraq was a middle-income country whose major source of income came from the export of oil. Iraqi oil sales are now restricted by UN resolutions, as is other trade with Iraq. Economic life was severely affected by the embargo. Although food and medicine were exempt from sanctions, the UN embargo hurt the poorest most of all. Hundreds of thousands of Iraqi children have died as a result of malnutrition and lack of basic medicines.

Events:

Iraq has been the seat of many ancient civilisations. The Sumerians, Akkadians, Babylonians and Assyrians lived there. The Greeks called the region 'Mesopotamia'. Archaeological evidence also shows that Kurdish people have lived in northern Iraq for over 2,000 years. From the 16th century the territory that is now Iraq was ruled by the Ottoman Empire.

1914-1930: During the First World War Iraq's Arab population rises up against their Turkish rulers. The British, knowing that Iraq has rich reserves of oil, occupy the country. After the First World War Iraq is placed under a League of Nations mandate and administered by the British.

1920: As the Treaty of Sevres is signed, the Kurds of northern Iraq have hopes of independence, as it promises autonomy for both the Armenian and Kurdish people. But the Treaty of Sevres is never honoured.

1923: The Treaty of Lausanne divides the Kurdish population between Turkey, Iran, Iraq, Syria and the Soviet Union.

1931: Iraq gains full independence.

1940s and 1950s: There is a rise in Arab and Kurdish nationalism. Many Iraqi Arabs support the Ba'ath Party which promotes the idea of a single Arab nation which will redistribute wealth and help ordinary people.

1958: The King is overthrown and a new government installed. A group of Kurds, led by Mullah Mustafa Barzani founds the Kurdish Democratic Party (KDP). It calls for Kurdish autonomy within Iraq, which the Iraqi government rejects. Mustafa Barzani returns to the Kurdish areas of northern Iraq and starts a guerrilla war.

1968: The Iraqi government is overthrown again. The Ba'ath party comes to power.

1979: Saddam Hussain, a senior member of the Ba'ath Party, becomes president. He crushes all political opposition. Between 1979 and 2003, Amnesty International regularly document extra-judicial executions, detentions, torture and large-scale disappearances. Up to 150,000 Kurdish people are murdered. Over 300,000 people, mostly Shi'a Muslims, are deported to Iran.

From 1980: The Iraqi government starts a war with Iran. Iraqi troops cross into Iran to reclaim the Shatt-al-Arab Canal. The war lasts eight years and costs thousands of lives. Throughout the war, the Iraqi government receives aid from Saudi Arabia and Kuwait. The UK and the US sell weapons to Iraq - they do not seem to notice its human rights violations. The Iranian government supports Kurdish guerrillas who are fighting in the mountains of northern Iraq. The Kurds soon control much of northern Iraq.

The Iraqi Government tries different methods of crushing Kurdish opposition. Kurdish villages are destroyed and 500,000 Kurds removed from their homes and forced to settle in southern Iraq. At least 100,000 Kurds are murdered.

From 1987: The Iraqi government uses chemical weapons against the Kurds. In March 1988 6,000 Kurdish people are killed when chemical weapons are dropped on the town of Halabja.

1988: The Iran-Iraq war comes to an end on 20th August. During the next two weeks the Iraqi army drive Kurdish fighters out of northern Iraq. Over 450 Kurdish villages are destroyed and 80,000 Kurdish refugees flee to Iran and Turkey.

1990s: In August 1990 Iraq marches into oil-rich Kuwait. To protect western interests the UN launches a military campaign against the Iraqi regime. Kuwait is liberated, but the campaign stops short of toppling Saddam Hussain. Many Kurds and Iraqi Arabs see it as the time to act.

March-April 1991: There are uprisings in Kurdistan and southern Iraq, but they are met with brutal repression by the army and security services. In southern Iraq an estimated 150,000 people are arrested as a result of the uprising. Up to 20,000 people may have been killed. Fearing what might happen next, over 1.5 million Kurds flee to Turkey and Iran. Thousands of Kurds die in the cold mountains during their flight. Kurdish refugees begin returning home after the US and British governments prevent Iraqi aeroplanes from flying over northern Iraq. In October, the Iraqi government withdraws all troops, funds and services from most of Kurdistan. The Kurds set up their own administration and a Kurdish parliament in northern Iraq. The Kurdish administration is able to raise taxes but it lacks funds and international recognition.

Iraq

1998-2003: In December 1998, the US and UK launch their bombing campaign 'Operation Desert Fox', to destroy Iraq's nuclear, chemical and biological weapons programmes. In 1999, the UN Resolution 1284 creates the UN Monitoring, Verification and Inspection Commission (Unmovic) with Hans Blix as chairman. Unmovic is responsible for inspecting for weapons of mass destruction and destroying them. Despite Unmovic finding no evidence of weapons, the US and the UK continue to state that Iraq is a threat to world peace.

2003: On 20th March, British and US troops enter Iraq from Kuwait. Baghdad falls to US troops on 9th April 2003.

Today: There is great uncertainty about future peace in Iraq.

A street in Baghdad, Iraq's capital city.
© **Refugee Council**

Iraqi refugees in the UK

There are about 55,000 refugees from Iraq currently living in the UK. About half of them are Kurds. They started arriving in the UK after 1988. Many of them are young single men aged between 15 and 25 years. The community mostly lives in Greater London, but the dispersal of asylum seekers throughout the UK means that Iraqi Kurdish communities have grown in places like Hull and Manchester.

The Kurdish Cultural Centre is one of several community organisations working with Iraqi Kurdish refugees. It provides an advice service for refugees who have just arrived in the UK. It helps them find a solicitor who can assist them in applying for asylum. The Kurdish Cultural Centre also helps asylum seekers find housing and healthcare. As many Iraqi Kurdish refugees arrive without English, the Kurdish Cultural Centre also provides English classes. It organises many cultural events, notably the Nawroz festival - Kurdish New Year, celebrated in the Spring. Members of the Kurdish Cultural centre run a Saturday school for Iraqi Kurdish children. Here they can learn the Kurdish language.

There are also many Iraqi Arab refugees in the UK. The community dates back to the 1950s and mostly lives in cities such as London and Manchester. Many Iraqi Arab refugees are well educated: a survey carried out in 1998 indicated that 60 per cent of men had first or higher degrees from a university. Some of the refugees have been active in opposition politics.

The UK also has a small Assyrian refugee community of about 6,000 people. Many Assyrians live in west London.

Information: Refugee community groups

There are over 700 refugee community organisations in the UK. These self-help groups work with specific communities. They may offer long-term support and help refugees to gain control over their own lives.

Some refugee community organisations represent specific ethnic, political or religious groups from particular countries. Among the services that refugee community groups offer are:

- Advice on immigration law, welfare rights and housing
- Café facilities, food parcels and second hand clothing
- English language classes, employment training and careers advice
- Saturday schools for refugee children
- Youth clubs
- Senior citizens' clubs
- Women's groups
- Cultural events and outings
- The production of newsletters and information
- Campaigning on issues affecting refugees from that community

Learning objectives: The activity helps develop students' interviewing and questioning skills.

Time needed: Preparation time in a previous lesson, plus the lesson with the visiting speaker.

Instructions: Students will be interviewing a speaker from a refugee community organisation. There are over 700 such organisations in the UK. The Refugee Council or a refugee support teacher from your local authority will be able to supply teachers with the addresses of local organisations with good speakers.

In the lesson prior to the visit of the speaker, the teacher should brief the students about the country from which the speaker has come. Students should then work in pairs to make a list of questions to ask the speaker. These should be saved for the subsequent lesson. Students should choose one member of the class to meet the speaker, one person to introduce the speaker and another student to thank the speaker.

Students should ask their questions and record the answers. At the end they should write down the three most important things they have learned from the visit of the speaker.

Activity ☝

Interviewing a speaker from a refugee community organisation

Kurdish Iraq

Choman's story

Choman is 18 years old. She is Kurdish and was born in Iraqi Kurdistan. Here she describes how it felt to arrive as a young refugee.

"It was war again, running away from your land, marching through the mountains to reach a peaceful place and getting separated from your parents. Two years ago, on a misty evening in September I arrived at Heathrow airport, alone and scared, but full of hope. I was happy as I was going to be with my parents again after being away from them for over a year."

"So I arrived in England. Before I came I thought of England as a country where all doors are open to you, where you are safe and free, where you can get anything you want. I thought of England as a green land, full of rain. English people, respectful and friendly. This is what I was thinking about during my journey. I was thinking about starting again, being happy, seeking knowledge so that maybe someday I can help my country. England to me was a mysterious land where I was going to fulfil my dreams. England was also the place where my parents lived. The minute that my mother hugged me crying, I thought that all my sorrows had ended and life was going to be sweet and happy again."

"I was so enthusiastic about starting school and learning English. I had been away from school for two years because we were travelling and did not have a permanent place to live. I promised myself not to miss school again and not to waste more time. I had to be serious and work hard, there was no time for being lazy. So, ten days after my arrival I started going to a school close to my house, called Hampstead School."

"The problem was that at my age I should have been doing A-levels, but because I didn't speak any English they put me in year ten with students who were three years younger than me. The teachers didn't believe that I would be able to do GCSEs with so little English. I was told that the best thing for me was to stay in year ten until my English was better and maybe in two years I could attempt GCSEs."

"Being with younger people is not a problem if they are mature. But when you are a teenager a three-year difference is quite a big gap, especially if you don't speak the language and you are new to the culture. It is at this time that you need friends the most. But I was shocked to find out that in the lunch queue they used to laugh at me and say that I never had decent food in my country. They said I had always been hungry that's why I ran away from my home. Some people treated me like a fool because I couldn't speak English well. Some just ignored me as if I didn't exist."

"Nobody wanted to sit next to me in lessons and no one wanted to have me as their partner in PE. I was all alone in the corner and did not understand the jokes during the lessons. I couldn't understand the subjects we studied because of my English and could never express myself during any simple discussion. I was too scared to talk because I knew that if I made a mistake some of them would laugh at me. Once I even got beaten up by a group of students who used to bully everyone. They beat me one evening when I was walking home alone. They said they couldn't stand me because I was a refugee who lived on the Government's money (which they considered to be their own money). After this I lost all my confidence and began to think that I was the most unwanted person on earth. I used to cry on my own and thought about leaving school. I started to believe that what other people thought about me was true."

> *I was thinking about starting again, being happy, seeking knowledge so that maybe someday I can help my country. England to me was a mysterious land where I was going to fulfil my dreams.*

"I almost gave up. The reason that I didn't was because of my mother's help, the support I got from my teachers and the school charity called 'the Children of the Storm' which helped me to learn English. The charity helped me to socialise with others. Miss Demitriades who runs the charity was someone who always listened, gave us advice and had time to give us a hug on the depressing days. So there was still hope. There were people who cared and helped, so I carried on. I had to anyway because I believe life is a fight. I managed to do three GCSEs eight months after my arrival which I counted as a big success. Now I am doing three A-levels in maths, physics and art. I speak English quite well and sometimes I write poetry in English, other times I translate my poems from my language. I have some published work and I have made a few nice friends who can accept me as I am."

"I am planning to study philosophy at university. The love of my life is poetry and writing and I always dream of the day when I can go home."

"Now I take care of my parents who don't speak English. I hate the letters which tell me about changes in income support, paying council tax, decrease in housing benefit, surgery appointments and so on. There is always a form to fill in, a letter to reply to ... proof of being a student, proof of receiving income support, of not being entitled to some things and being entitled to others. Sometimes I miss a few lessons to get these things straight."

"The other side of the story is living in two completely different cultures. There is the British culture which I live in from morning until evening, and my Kurdish culture as I get home. The British culture which breaks all the rules, uncovers all the secrets and has a great sense of adventure. The Kurdish culture where every little thing is forbidden, all the feeling repressed and is really hard for a girl like me to say or do what she wants. I am divided between the two cultures and sometimes I think I don't belong to any of them. There are strong and weak points about both cultures, and I can't totally accept or refuse either, so now I don't fit in any of them perfectly. Sometimes I feel I need to change my character or lie to avoid serious clashes."

"At other times I feel so depressed because I can't get in touch with my family back home. I only get to hear about my brothers and sisters when someone travels back home. Often I feel I can't fulfil the expectations of my parents, my brothers and sisters back home, Kurdish society and myself. I always feel left behind, and I want to read and read to conquer my depression. I will carry on as long as there is someone I can share my sorrows with. I shall not stop. If I feel lonely and depressed I sing, and I try and remember that only one's words can stay."

Since writing this, Choman has gained her degree and is now a published writer.

A Kurdish family, resettled in the UK.
© **Refugee Council**

Refugees in Europe: Gezim's story

"My name is Gezim and I am 11 years old. I have two brothers. Qendrim is eight and Gentrim is six. We used to live in Prishtina, where we had a house with a small garden. The house wasn't that big, but we grew our own fruit and vegetables in the garden. Musli, my father, had a job as a chef."

"Gezim and I are both disabled. We have an illness that causes our muscles to lose strength. Both of us find it difficult to walk. In Prishtina, before the war, we went to a special centre for disabled children which was run by Oxfam. There we had physiotherapy and also parties."

"When the war started, we wanted to stay in Kosova, but the Yugoslav police came and told us to move out of our house. We packed what we could carry and went with our neighbours to the hills. I was in a wheelchair and Gentrim was put in a pram. It was hard for my parents to move us."

"When we got to the hills my parents helped make a shelter in the forest out of branches and plastic sheets. We stayed there for three weeks. There were about 90 of us there. No one had much to eat, all we had was the food we took with us and milk that we brought from a farm. Everyone was scared, although all the parents tried to make us children think it was a big adventure."

"Then soldiers came closer and you could hear guns. We decided it would be safer to go back to our home in Prishtina. We were there for another six weeks until the police came again and told us to leave Kosova. So we went to the railway station to catch a train. We left my grandparents behind. My grandfather is very old and he could not have made the journey."

"There were thousands of people at the railway station. They were all trying to leave. My dad put me on his back and Qendim held on to our mother. My aunt carried Gentrim. My dad pushed on to the train with me, but the others could not follow us. I was really scared as I thought we would lose each other, but my dad managed to pull everyone else through the train window. We had to leave my wheelchair at the station. When we got to the border, I was very scared. There were policeman shouting and screaming. My mother said they were Macedonian policemen, not Serbs, but I was still afraid. At first they said we would have to go back. My mother started crying and someone from the Red Cross saw her. They helped us cross the border."

"We were taken to a refugee camp called Stenkovic. We lived in a tent and each day we were brought food to eat. After a while, Oxfam brought us mattresses, blankets, soap and a bucket. They found wheelchairs for me and Gentrim. Oxfam put up a tent for disabled refugees to use. They picked up my brothers and took them to the special tent by car. But life in the camp was hard. There was not much to do, although there were some small playgrounds."

"We all wanted to leave the camp. Some refugees were given the chance to go to other countries like Germany. But we came to Ireland. The decision to come here was not really ours. We were told we could be on a flight to Ireland the next day, so we just decided we would have to go."

"When we first came to Ireland we stayed in a hotel. Then we were given a flat in a city called Cork. I saw doctors at a hospital. I have been able to move my arms and legs much more since we came to Ireland. We are able to go to school again and I like playing with the other Kosovan children. My father has found work in a chocolate factory and this helps with the money. Although I am happy here, I wish we could go home to Prishtina. My grandparents are still there. I miss them and I would like to see them again."

Refugees in Europe: Quang Bui's story

Quang Bui's brother escaped from Vietnam by boat and was allowed to settle in Sweden as a refugee. Quang Bui and his parents were later allowed to join him.

"My parents are not as strict as other Vietnamese parents. I don't know what they think. I think they like living here. I've been here a long time - eight years in fact. I know almost everyone, and indeed enjoy living here. Sometimes I ask friends to come fishing with me. We make a barbecue, we play cards and we fish."

"When I first came there were some Swedish blokes, a bit older. They called us 'yellow necks', but we, the Vietnamese, helped each other. We stood up against them. We stuck together, because there were not so many of us in Sweden. Nowadays in the high school there is no problem. We all mix together. They are a great crowd and I'm good friends with everyone."

"At the leisure centre you can see your friends, play cards, pool or table tennis. There should be more places for the young people - for instance leisure centres open till late at night, and Macdonalds which everyone likes and a night cafe and a disco."

"Where I am living there is a place where you can play pool. You can sing karaoke in Vietnamese. You can talk with friends and eat Vietnamese food. But when I am there I don't usually sing. I don't dare!"

In times of crisis, refugees tend to become scapegoats for a situation they can neither comprehend nor control. The long wait for a legal status adds to their plight.
© UNHCR / H. Gloaguen

Information: Statistics about refugees in Europe

Austria

Population	8,000,000
Asylum applications 2002	37,000
Asylum applications per 1,000 population	

Asylum seekers and refugees in Austria: The largest communities of refugees in Austria are Afghans, Iranians and Iraqis. Very few newly arrived asylum seekers are able to get benefits and housing and as a result there are many asylum seekers living in very poor conditions.

Belgium

Population	10,000,000
Asylum applications 2002	21,400
Asylum applications per 1,000 population	

Denmark

Population	5,500,000
Asylum applications 2002	5,900
Asylum applications per 1,000 population	

Finland

Population	5,000,000
Asylum applications per 2002	3,100
Asylum applications per 1,000 population	

France

Population	60,000,000
Asylum applications 2002	58,100
Asylum applications per 1,000 population	

Germany

Population	83,000,000
Asylum applications 2002	71,100
Asylum applications per 1,000 population	

Greece

Population	11,000,000
Asylum applications 2002	5,700
Asylum applications per 1,000 population	

Ireland

Population	4,000,000
Asylum applications 2002	11,600
Asylum applications per 1,000 population	

Italy

Population	58,000,000
Asylum applications 2002	14,800
Asylum applications per 1,000 population	

Luxembourg

Population	500,000
Asylum applications 2002	2,000
Asylum applications per 1,000 population	

Netherlands

Population	16,000,000
Asylum applications 2002	18,700
Asylum applications per 1,000 population	

Portugal

Population	10,000,000
Asylum applications 2002	200
Asylum applications per 1,000 population	

Spain

Population	41,500,000
Asylum applications 2002	6,200
Asylum applications per 1,000 population	

Sweden

Population	9,000,000
Asylum applications 2002	33,000
Asylum applications per 1,000 population	

UK

Population	60,000,000
Asylum applications 2002	110,700
Asylum applications per 1,000 population	

New members of the EU

Cyprus

Population	705,000 in the south, 200,000 in the north
Asylum applications 2002	1,000
Asylum applications per 1,000 population	

Czech Republic

Population	10,000,000
Asylum applications 2002	8,500
Asylum applications per 1,000 population	

Estonia

Population	1,500,000
Asylum applications 2002	10
Asylum applications per 1,000 population	

Hungary

Population	10,000,000
Asylum applications 2002	6,400
Asylum applications per 1,000 population	

Latvia

Population	2,500,000
Asylum applications	50
Asylum applications per 1,000 population	

Lithuania

Population	3,500,000
Asylum applications 2002	300
Asylum applications per 1,000 population	

Malta

Population	500,000
Asylum applications	500
Asylum applications per 1,000 population	

Poland

Population	39,000,000
Asylum applications 2002	5,200
Asylum applications per 1,000 population	

Slovak Republic

Population	5,500,000
Asylum applications 2002	9,700
Asylum applications per 1,000 population	

Slovenia

Population	2,000,000
Asylum applications 2002	700
Asylum applications per 1,000 population	

Total populations are for 2002 and are to the nearest 500,000. The asylum statistics are from the European Council for Refugees and Exiles at: www.ecre.org.

Total asylum applications in the EU 1992-2002:

1992	1993	1994	1995	1996	1997	1998	1999	2000	2001	2002
675,500	516,400	310,700	275,000	233,500	252,800	311,400	396,700	391,300	388,400	381,600

Extension activities

- Calculate asylum applications per 1,000 population for each EU country.
- Which country received the most asylum applications in 2002?
- What might be the reasons that this country received most asylum applications?
- Which country received the most asylum applications per 1,000 population in 2002?
- Why might asylum applications per 1,000 of population be a better measure than total asylum applications?
- Use the internet to find out about asylum seekers and refugees in each EU country. Write down two or three sentences of key facts about each EU country (Austria has been completed as an example).
- Using flags make a display about asylum seekers and refugees in the European Union.

European statistics

Activity: Making an information leaflet about refugees in Europe.

Learning objectives: The activity helps students develop their research and writing skills.

Time needed: 1 hour

Instructions: Students will need access to the internet, desktop publishing packages, pens and paper. The teacher should point out key design features of an information leaflet.

Students are going to make an information leaflet about refugees in Europe. The leaflet should be about 500 words long and its target audience are teenagers and young adults. The leaflet's aim is to provide information about refugees in the EU. The leaflet can provide basic facts. Alternatively students may wish to design a question and answer leaflet. Students can devise their own questions or use some of the suggestions below.

- Who are asylum seekers and refugees?
- What causes people to become asylum seekers?
- How many asylum seekers arrive in the EU?
- Do EU countries accept their fair share of the world's asylum seekers and refugees?
- Do refugees benefit European countries?

Activity ☞

Making a difference

Writing leaflets

Writing information material for the general public is a skilled job. Here are some points that you need to consider when preparing an information leaflet:

⇨ What is the purpose of your leaflet? What do you want to achieve with it?

⇨ Who is your target audience? The target audience will influence your writing style and design of your leaflet.

⇨ What key messages do you want to communicate?

Hands around Europe

Learning objectives: At the end of the activity students will have generated positive messages that reflect a Europe that treats its minorities better. The activity is a good way of concluding work about refugees in Europe.

Time needed: 30 minutes

Instructions: The class will need coloured paper, pens, scissors, glue and pictures of the flags of the 25 member states of the EU.

The teacher should introduce the activity by reflecting on previous work about refugees in Europe. Students should then be encouraged to share some of the things they have learned about refugees in the UK and in other European countries.

The teacher should acknowledge that life for refugees can sometimes be difficult, but there is potential for change and improvement. Young people, as individuals can all contribute towards making the world a better place for refugees. The teacher should ask students for some ideas of how they, as young Europeans, can make the world a better place for refugees. Students should share their thoughts beginning the sentence with:

"I want to ...."

Some of the students' ideas should be written up on the board. Student should then draw carefully around one of their hands. They should then write on their hand their message about how they, as young Europeans, can make the world a better place for refugees. Each hand should be decorated with a European flag. The hands with their messages can be mounted and arranged around a map of Europe for display.

Messages from Refugee Council supporters to welcome refugees. © **Refugee Council**

11 New to school

© Refugee Council / David Levene

This chapter examines educational issues that affect young refugees living in the UK at school. It then discusses how all school pupils can work together to support their newly arrived peers.

Metin's story

"When we came to England we stayed with our friends, all our family stayed in one room. We didn't go out that much and the room was very small. We were there for about a month, I think. I knew my mum didn't have any money for the things I wanted, so I didn't ask for anything. But I wanted some toys and games and other things."

"I wanted to go to school, but on my first day at school, I cried, as I didn't want to be there. I didn't understand anything and I didn't have any friends. I thought I would understand the teacher, but I didn't. My face was red, I think. After some time because I didn't understand any English, they took me to a special class."

Metin is a Kurdish boy living in the UK.

Serpil's story

"When I started school everybody kept staring at me. I was embarrassed and shy. Even at dinnertime I was scared to have my dinner. They were talking about me. I know they were talking about me because they were calling my name. I was really upset then."

"I told my Mum and Dad and they told me when I get to learn English they wouldn't say anything to me. I kept crying and said to my Dad, 'I don't want to go to school, I don't want to see them laughing at me and see them talking about me'."

"I had two Turkish friends at school, but not that close. Sometimes they helped me, but most of the time they didn't. When they translated anything they were embarrassed. They were embarrassed that the other kids would say, 'Don't talk to that girl, she doesn't speak English'."

"Teachers were always helping me with my work. There was a separate teacher who came to help me. I really like that teacher. I was happiest with her and not with the children in the class."

Serpil is an 11 year old girl from Turkish Kurdistan.

Parviz's story

"Here I like learning English because I need to use English for speaking to people. I like TV because it helps me learn English. I like my new friends and they help me in school and outside school. I also like being away from fighting because I don't like fighting. I don't like the racism in the UK because I think all people are equal. I also don't like not understanding people. Often I don't understand the words people say so I just have to look them in the face."

Parviz is a 14 year old Kurdish boy from Iran.

Mahmut's story

Kurdish

"I am Kurdish. I speak Turkish and I understand Kurdish but I can't read or write them. I came to London from Turkey when I was eight. In Turkey we start school when we are seven so I didn't know much about school when I came to London."

"I've been in six schools in four years and lived in five different houses. Each time I changed schools I had to make new friends which was very hard. My little brother used to cry because it was so hard for him to get used to a new school. I used to get really hurt when other children teased me and made me look stupid because I didn't know English. When you're new you get picked on a lot. It sometimes happens even now."

"We came to London because of the political situation in Turkey. People were always harassing and terrorising Kurdish people. I wish people understood more about refugees and had more respect for people's different backgrounds."

"I interpret a lot at the doctor's, solicitors and job centres. I don't take as much time off school as I used to. My mother is learning English and my brother can help now too."

"I'd like to be an interpreter, a teacher in a junior school or a computer operator. I also want to travel to visit my relatives in Cyprus, France and Germany."

Discussion points:

⇨ How did Metin, Serpil, Parviz and Mahmut feel in their new schools? Do you think refugee students or other children who have just arrived in your school might feel like this?

⇨ Do you think Metin and Serpil felt left out in their new schools? Have you ever felt left out at school? What did you do about it?

Learning objectives: To get students to reflect on how they felt when they started a new school.

Time needed: 25 minutes

Instructions: Students will need large sheets of paper and felt pens. The class should then be divided into threes or pairs. The teacher should introduce the activity by talking about welcoming new pupils into school. For them, whether they are refugees or not, the first days in a new school can be difficult.

Students should be asked to think back to their first day at secondary school. Using the paper, students should make a list of words that describe their feelings on that day.

After students have completed their word lists, some of the words should be shared with the class. The class should then consider the following discussion point.

Discussion point:

⇨ What would have made your first week in secondary school easier?

Activity ☞

New to school

Activity

New pupil

Learning objectives: This is a drama activity that helps students reflect on how new pupils are treated in their school.

Time needed: 30 minutes

Instructions: The class should be divided into groups of four. Each group is going to produce a three-minute role play or drama about the arrival of a new pupil in their class. The aim of the drama is to show how new pupils are treated in their school.

After students have planned their drama performances, these should be shared with the whole class.

Information: Refugee children at school

There are over 90,000 refugee children attending schools in the UK. They have come from many different countries including Afghanistan, the Democratic Republic of Congo, Iran, Iraq, Somalia, Sri Lanka and Turkey. In one London school there are refugee children from 51 different countries.

The biggest populations of refugees live in Greater London where over 7 per cent of all school students are asylum seekers or refugees. Schools in cities such as Glasgow, Liverpool, Manchester and Sheffield have also received many refugee children. Refugee populations are smaller in other parts of the UK, but today refugees do live in almost every town and city.

Activity

Find *Starting Again* on the website of Save the Children Scotland at:
www.savethechildrenscot.org.uk.

- Summarise and write down the main points in the report.
- Do you think that refugee children in your own school have similar experiences to those in Glasgow?

Refugee children have the same rights to go to school as any other child in the UK. Their educational needs are just like other children. However, many refugee children do need extra help at school when they first arrive in the UK. They need a warm welcome in a new school. Refugee children may also need help to learn English. An English language teacher or teaching assistant may sit in class with a refugee child, helping them learn English, or sometimes a refugee child may go to special classes.

Most refugee children settle well into their new schools. But some refugee children report that they are bullied when they first arrive. Bullies may pick on refugees because they are new and because they do not speak English. Save the Children Scotland, a non-governmental organisation working with children, recently did some research about the experiences of refugee children in Glasgow. The researchers interviewed 700 refugee children before publishing *Starting Again*, their research report. Many of the children had mixed experiences of life in Glasgow. They had made new friends and were enjoying school. But they also experienced bullying and often felt unsafe where they lived. The publication of *Starting Again* helped some children think about how they might welcome refugee pupils in their schools. A number of children, both refugee and non-refugee, then worked together to produce a video and teaching materials about refugee children. In doing this, the children hoped for greater awareness of refugees and a greater welcome to newcomers.

In other parts of the UK children have worked together to make their school more welcoming to children newly-arrived from other countries. Some school students have set up befriending projects. Other students have prepared welcome leaflets, or started clubs for children who are new to their schools. These are all examples of young people working together to make a difference.

Learning objectives: The activity helps develop students' planning skills.

Time needed: At least 1 hour

Instructions: The teacher or group leader will need to copy the table below so that every group has a copy. The activity should then be introduced to the class. They are going to work together to plan how they can better welcome new arrivals. Students should then be divided into fours.

Students should first discuss how new arrivals are presently welcomed in their school. They should spend about five minutes doing this and then summarise their ideas on the sheet. The groups should then move on to discuss how they would like new arrivals to be welcomed. They should spend about 10 minutes doing this, then summarise their ideas on the sheet. Finally the groups should move on to discuss how they are going to implement their ideas for a better welcome.

The class should come together and each group should present their ideas from the last column - ideas for achieving a better welcome. The teacher or group leader should list all the ideas on the board.

The whole class should then move on to think about how practical the ideas are. The students should vote to decide if each idea for a better welcome is achievable and realistic given constraints of money, time or people.

Any ideas that are not achievable or realistic should be dropped. The class will then be left with a list of ideas to make their school more welcoming. One idea can be taken as a class project after a vote. Alternatively students can work in small groups to further research, plan and implement their ideas.

Planning a better welcome for new arrivals

How are new arrivals treated in our school today?	How would we like to make our school more welcoming?	What action are we going to take?

Activity 👆
Class friends

Learning objectives: This activity is used to help students plan a peer befriending system.

Time needed: 1 hour

Instructions: The activity requires large sheets of paper, marker pens and class copies of the *Guide for Official Class Friends* opposite. The teacher should start this work by explaining that the school has several pupils who come to the school during the school year. Many of these are moving into the area for the first time. These pupils do not get introduced to the school in the same way as those who arrive at the start of Year Seven.

To welcome and help these pupils properly, they will have class friends or buddies when they first arrive. Then explain that welcoming a new pupil is still everyone's responsibility. The whole class is expected to be helpful and supportive to the new pupil.

The class should then be divided into groups of three or four. Using the large sheets of paper, each group should then list what help a new pupil needs when they first arrive in our class. Students should record their answers on a spider diagram. These lists can then be collected and displayed around the room.

The teacher should then bring the class together for discussion. The teacher can add scenarios not considered, for example, the new pupil does not speak English. The booklet will then be given to the nominated friends.

Activity 👆
Making a welcome poster

Learning objectives: By making a welcome poster, students develop their skills of cooperation.

Time needed: 1 hour plus time to collect the translation in different languages of the word 'welcome'.

Instructions: Students will need access to art materials and paper. They also need a copy of the Refugee Council's Welcome poster from which they can copy the translations of the word 'welcome'. Students may also find new languages they can translate 'welcome' into.

Students should work in pairs, and design a poster or artwork that gives a welcome in refugee languages. The work can be displayed in a school foyer or for an event such as Refugee Week.

Guide for official class friends

Thank you for agreeing to welcome and support new pupils to your class. It's a very important job you are doing. Can you remember your first day at this school? Many pupils have found it quite frightening. Some of you may have come in the middle of a term and will know it can be even harder to find out where to go and what to do. Imagine if you can't speak any English or come from a country where schools are different!

You can see how important it is to make new pupils feel welcome and happy. This is everybody's job, but it's yours in particular for the first three weeks of a new pupil's time here. Because your job is so important, you will get recognition for it. We will mention your work as a 'class friend' in your Record of Achievement, so that when you are looking for a job people can see that you can be given important responsibilities. We will also reward your good work in other ways.

Must I do all the things you list in this booklet?
These have been some suggestions, but you will find out what each new pupil needs most. The most important thing is that you do what you think is best, as you become experienced in welcoming new pupils.

What if the new pupil and I don't get on?
As long as you have tried to assist the pupil, and made sure she/he understands school routines and where to go for help, then there is no reason why you should be together if you don't get on.

What if the new pupil doesn't need much help?
Sometimes the new pupil will not need help and will make friends quickly. Then you will be stepping back quite early on and leaving them to get on with it.

When do I finish being the pupil's class friend?
Within three weeks. Sometimes your teacher will debrief you afterwards to find out how it went and learn from your experience. Don't forget to ask other 'official class friends' in your form or your teachers for help whenever you need it.

Your job on the first day:

* Go to reception and collect the new pupil. Make sure you introduce yourself and learn her/his name. Explain you will be looking after her/him.

* Introduce the new pupil to your class and teachers. Make sure the teachers can say the pupil's name correctly. If he/she is new to English, introduce him/her to pupils who speak the same language.

* Show the new pupil where toilets, refreshment facilities, the dining room and other important places are located.

* Help her/him fill in his/her personal timetable and planner. Explain any referral systems.

* Show him/her where to go for each lesson. Introduce her/him to the teachers. Sit with her/him at first in lessons, or if you are in a different learning group ask someone who is in the same one to make sure he/she knows where to go.

* Make sure she/he is not lonely during breaks and lunchtime. If she/he doesn't want to join you, make sure she/he knows about places to go, including the resource centre or club activities.

Important community languages

Albanian
Arabic
Amharic
Armenian
Bosnian
Chinese
English
French
Kikongo
Kurdish Kurmanji
Kurdish Sorani
Lingala
Persian
Polish
Portuguese
Punjabi
Pushto
Romanian
Russian
Somali
Spanish
Tamil
Tigrinya
Turkish
Urdu
Vietnamese
Welsh

THANK YOU AND GOOD LUCK!

Reflecting on what we have done to welcome new arrivals

Learning objectives: This activity develops students' skills of self-evaluation.

Time needed: About 30 minutes

Instructions: The activity can be carried out to help students evaluate any action they have taken to make their school more welcoming. Students will need copies of the questions, as well as large sheets of paper and pens on which to record their answers. The teacher should introduce the activity by stressing the importance of self-evaluation.

The students should work in groups to consider the questions. After about 30 minutes the class should come together for a plenary.

Questions

⇨ Have we changed the ways that we, as individuals, act towards children who are new to our school?

⇨ Have we made our school more welcoming for new arrivals?

⇨ What were the greatest successes of our work?

⇨ What were the greatest challenges?

⇨ What would we do differently next time?

The Refugee Council's welcome board at its day centre in South London.
© **Refugee Council / David Levene**

Information: Lunchtime Link

Lunchtime Link is a scheme that has been operated by community service volunteers in London. Groups of sixth form students receive some appropriate training, then help a small group of students who speak little English. They commit one lunchtime a week to the scheme.

The training consists of four lunchtime sessions held once a week at the beginning of term. After that, the lunchtime sessions are held once a week. Students who have helped on the scheme said that volunteering did not interfere with their school work.

The volunteers do not give formal English lessons. Instead, through the use of specially chosen games, the volunteers provide assistance with spoken or written English. For example, volunteers play scrabble with younger students during a lunchtime session. Scrabble helps students improve their vocabulary, spelling and conversational skills.

Teachers are present for a few trial sessions, but after this the scheme is led by older students, without the presence of members of staff. But there are members of staff involved in the project. They arrange the training and also some of the feedback sessions where volunteers discuss how they are getting on.

When planning a Lunchtime Link scheme you need to consider practical issues such as:

Keys - Who has the keys to the door of the room you are using? Have you made arrangements to collect keys? Do you have a back-up procedure in case you or the teacher is away on a particular day? All these details need to be sorted out.

Register - Teachers should be able to provide you with a list of names and tutor groups of the younger students who will attend the scheme. A register should be taken at each session but this does not need to be called formally. If a student is absent for a few sessions, the teacher should try and find out if he or she still wants to come to Lunchtime Link. If a student is not attending it may be that things are going wrong with the scheme, so getting feedback from the younger students will enable problems to be corrected.

Storage - You will need a safe, locked place to store the register, games and dictionaries.

Notebooks - Each of the younger students should be given a notebook by the school. They should bring them to each Lunchtime Link club. Writing down new words reinforces the learning that takes place through the games.

Lunch passes - If these are needed, the link teacher will need to arrange for these to be collected.

Information: Saturday schools

Every Saturday about 10,000 refugee children can be found learning their first language in living rooms, church halls and schools throughout the UK. They are students in Saturday schools run by refugee communities. Here students learn their home language. They also participate in other activities such as music, drama and sport. Some Saturday schools also help children with their English and maths.

One Saturday school is the Iranian Community Centre's school in London.

There are over 55,000 Iranian refugees in the UK. Most of them arrived after 1979 following a revolution in Iran. Farsi is the language spoken by most people in Iran. Farsi lessons are the main activity of the Iranian Community Centre's Saturday school.

Over 70 children attend the school. They meet in a school building which is empty on Saturdays. There are three different Farsi classes and also Iranian music, dance and drama classes, and an English class.

The teachers at the school are all volunteers. Parents help run the school, helping in class and in the library.

Discussion point:

⇨ Going to school on a Saturday may sound like a bad idea, but can you think of some reasons why refugee children may want to attend Saturday schools?

Tamil refugee children attending Tamil classes at their local Tamil community group.
© Exile Images / H.J. Davies

Information: Separate education?

Today, newly arrived asylum-seeking children go to ordinary schools when they arrive in the UK. But in future, a small number of asylum-seeking children will not be able to go to an ordinary school. Instead they will be sent to live in large reception centres called accommodation centres. Here they will receive their education in a separate unit. These asylum-seeking children will have little contact with other children.

Setting up accommodation centres for asylum seekers required changes to the UK's refugee law. These changes to the law were made in 2002 when Parliament voted to pass the Nationality, Immigration and Asylum Act 2002.

Accommodation centres will be very expensive to build and maintain. But the UK government argued that it needs them. They are meant to prevent asylum seekers working illegally and to stop asylum seekers who have been refused the right to stay in the UK from disappearing.

But the proposal to provide separate education for asylum-seeking children attracted a lot of criticism. When the Nationality, Immigration and Asylum Act 2002 was being debated in Parliament, MPs of all political parties argued against the separate education of children in these centres. MPs, teachers, children, children's charities and refugee organisations **campaigned** against separate education in accommodation centres, arguing that it is undesirable. They argued that

- attending normal school may be therapeutic for an asylum-seeking child whose recent life experiences might include war;
- children in accommodation centres are likely to be slower in their learning of English as they will not be mixing with other children who are native speakers of English;
- education units in accommodation centres will be expensive to build and maintain. It is cheaper to educate children in ordinary schools;
- asylum-seeking children are often successful ambassadors for their communities and often help build links between their community and the rest of British society.

Asylum City is a report that outlines some of the objections to accommodation centres and is available at: www.asylumsupport.info/asylumcity.pdf. The website of the Immigration and Nationality Directorate of the Home Office lists some of the reasons why the Government wants to build accommodation centres.

Discussion points:

⇨ What do you feel about separate education for asylum-seeking children?

⇨ What kind of activities could a refugee support organisation do in order to campaign and lobby against the separate education of asylum-seeking children?

⇨ Make a list of all the different types of activities, for example, organising a demonstration.

> **NOTE**
>
> To **campaign** means to work to change laws or practices in a way that benefits a target group or person.
>
> To lobby means to work to change the opinion of people who hold power. Campaigners will usually lobby people who hold power. They might meet with or write to MPs or to government ministers.

Hoan Nghênh
Vietnam

Karibu
SWAHILI

Jamé Zamangas Tumen ilestyr
POLISH ROMANY

مرحبا بكم
ARABIC

بە خێر بێن
KURDISH (SORANI)

Mirë seerdhët
ALBANIAN

Dobro došli
BOSNIAN

Xêr hatin
KURDISH (KURMANJI)

Bienvenus
FRENCH

Welcome
ENGLISH

እንኳን ደህና መጣችሁ
AMHARIC

Ilǒ Lā
IBO

Bienvenidos
SPANISH

- Chapter Eleven: New to school -

12 Immigration law and refugees

UK Parliament. © Refugee Council / Iris Teichmann

This chapter examines how laws are made in the UK. It explains recent immigration and asylum laws and the effects they have on ordinary people. It also outlines European community laws and policy changes that affect asylum seekers and refugees.

Gerard's story

"I am a member of the Movement for Democratic Change (MDC) in Zimbabwe. My whole family are members. We had a rally to demonstrate against the farm invasions in my home town of Bulawayo. This was the first time I knew that I was in trouble. I was taken to the police station and shown into a room where they said, 'you want to sell our country to the white man'. They also said we were trying to assassinate the President. They started hitting me, beating me up and torturing me. They made me stand with my feet in a bucket of ice. They wanted names of the people I knew who were also MDC members. But they couldn't get anything out of me. They put me back into a cell and later released me."

"My parents told me to move to a holiday home away from the city. I then heard that - around the end of 2000 - some government supporters had come to the family home and were asking for me. They stoned our family home. Soon afterwards, they came for my friend Godwin. They beat him very badly. He was in hospital for weeks and then died from his injuries. Around this time, my brother left for Canada and my cousins left too. My mum, my stepfather and my youngest brother also left. I don't exactly know where they are. Maybe they are in Canada too. In the end it became too much for me and I decided to leave for the UK."

"I arrived in the UK last January. I claimed asylum straightaway. I would really like to go to Canada to join my family but I hoped that I would be safe here. I lived for a time in Wolverhampton. It was ok until November, when I was told to report to an office at Gatwick Airport. I asked if I was being returned to Zimbabwe, and I was told it was just a routine interview. But when I got there, I was told, 'Our job is to return you. I am detaining you'. I got into an argument and said that I didn't have any family in Zimbabwe any more because they had all gone to Canada. I was taken to Harmondsworth detention centre. I had with me only the clothes I was standing in."

"They tried to send me back on several occasions. I said I would not get onto the plane to Zimbabwe and so they tried to force me to go. One time, my trousers and clothes were torn and the cabin crew appealed to the captain, who said he couldn't carry me. But finally, on the 17th December, the British guards managed to get me into the plane before the passengers arrived. They handcuffed me, dragged me into the place, put me in a choke-hold and pinned me to the seat. When we arrived in Harare, they dragged me off to the Zimbabwe authorities and left me there."

"The CIO [the Zimbabwean intelligence service] people said, 'We've been looking for you. You have sold out your country and you are going to prison for a long time. What have you been saying in the UK?' I had to get out of there. I just knew that I had to take my chance. I asked to go to the toilet and snuck out of the window, and ran away to the airfield, where somebody gave me a lift into Harare."

Discussion points:

⇨ Do you think Gerald was treated fairly in the UK?

⇨ Should he have been allowed to stay?

Gerald later escaped from Zimbabwe and spoke to the Observer newspaper from a secret location in South Africa.

It is immigration laws that decide the fate of asylum seekers like Gerald. The implementation of immigration laws determines if an asylum seeker can remain in the UK or not. This is why organisations supporting asylum seekers and refugees spend a great deal of time examining asylum and immigration laws, and campaigning against laws that they think are unfair to asylum seekers and refugees.

Information: How laws are made

Each country has its own laws. In the UK there are three types of law:

- **Case law** - These are laws that have developed over hundreds of years from judgements made in courts. If a judge decides on a case in court, then other judges will normally follow this judge's lead and give the same decision when similar cases come before them. The judge who made the first decision has made a kind of law because his ruling will normally be followed. This is called case law.
- **Statute law** - These are laws made by Parliament or the Scottish Parliament. They are known as Acts of Parliament.
- **European community law**

Statute law

Parliament passes about 100 new acts of Parliament every year. Most of these originate with the Government and are sponsored by the Government.

Government ministers and their civil servants discuss key issues as part of their job. The Government proposes new laws as a result of the key issues they have identified. Sometimes the Government might want to consult with the public about proposed changes to the law. A government department might publish a **Green Paper**. This allows the Government to consult with the general public, experts and pressure groups by asking their opinions on a number of key options.

After a Green Paper is published, a government department might release another type of document called a **White Paper**. This outlines the Government's proposals to change law. The general public, experts and pressure groups can also respond to the proposals in a White Paper.

A new law in the making is called a **bill**. Its contents are written down by Parliamentary draftsmen. These are civil servants who have also trained as lawyers. Each bill will be made up of different parts known as clauses. After a bill has been written, it can be presented to Parliament.

The Parliamentary year begins with the **Queen's Speech**. This is a ceremony that takes place every year, usually in early November. The Queen reads out a list of bills for debate during the next year.

Every bill must then complete certain stages in the House of Commons and House of Lords before it can become an **Act of Parliament**. Many bills start this process in the House of Commons, although some bills do start in the House of Lords. Usually a bill about something that is technical starts in the House of Lords.

For a bill starting in the House of Commons, the first stage is known as the **First Reading**. Here a government minister lets MPs know that a new bill is going to be debated.

> **Chamber of House of Lords or House of Commons**

> **First Reading**

Second Reading	The bill then proceeds to the **Second Reading.** Here a government minister explains the purpose of the bill. There is usually a lengthy debate about the bill. The House of Commons then votes to decide whether the bill should continue its passage through Parliament. Pressure groups often send briefings to MPs before the Second Reading of a bill, in order to try and influence the debate.
Committee Stage	The bill then goes into the **Committee Stage**. Here a Standing Committee of MPs – a group of 15-50 MPs from different parties – discuss the details of the bill. The MPs in the Standing Committee make the changes to the bill, known as amendments. As in the House of Commons, MPs will vote whether to support amendments or not.
Report Stage	After the discussion in the Standing Committee is completed, the whole House of Commons will be told about what has happened and what has been changed in the committee meetings. This is known as the **Report Stage**.
Third Reading	The House of Commons then debates the bill again in the **Third Reading**. The bill cannot be changed at this stage. MPs vote to accept it or reject it.
First Reading	The bill then goes to the **House of Lords**. It is given its **First Reading**, as in the House of Commons.
Second Reading	The bill then proceeds to the **Second Reading** in the House of Lords. Here a member of the House of Lords who represents the Government explains the purpose of the bill. There is then a debate about the bill. The House of Lords then votes to decide whether the bill should continue its passage through Parliament, although it is rare that the House of Lords rejects bills that are sponsored by the Government. Pressure groups, too, may send briefings to members of the House of Lords before the Second Reading of a bill in order to try and influence the debate.
Committee Stage	The bill then goes into the **Committee Stage**. Here a Standing Committee of Lords discuss the details of the bill and make changes.
Report Stage	After the discussion in the Standing Committee is completed, the whole House of Lords will be told about what has happened in the **Report Stage**.
Third Reading	The House of Lords then debates the bill again in the **Third Reading**. Unlike in a Third Reading in the House of Commons, further changes can be made to a bill in its Third Reading in the House of Lords. The Lords then vote to accept the bill or reject it.
Consideration of Amendments	Any changes made to a bill in the House of Lords do have to be considered by the House of Commons. The House of Commons usually accept most of the Lords' amendments. If MPs in the House of Commons do not, they can send a note to the House of Lords explaining the reasons. A bill can go from the House of Commons to the House of Lords for a while until an agreement can be reached in a process known as 'ping-pong'. If the House of Lords and House of Commons cannot agree, the House of Commons can re-introduce the bill in the next Parliamentary year. The House of Lords is not allowed to reject a bill that has been passed by the House of Commons in two successive years.

Parliamentary debates and Standing Committee debates are published every day in a report called Hansard.

When both Houses of Parliament have voted to pass a bill, it then goes to the Queen to be given **Royal Assent**. The Queen is the Head of State in the UK. Usually the Queen signs the bill to announce that she has given her agreement. Queen Anne was the last monarch to reject a bill and refuse to give it Royal Assent.

When Royal Assent is given, the bill becomes an Act of Parliament. New statute law has been made. But even after Royal Assent, laws may not change immediately. Those affected by new laws may need time to adapt to changing situations. A Government minister sometimes announces a Commencement Order to Parliament, giving the dates when new laws take effect.

Royal Assent

Learning objectives: The activity helps students become familiar with the definitions of political terms.

Time needed: 30 minutes

Instructions: Students will need access to the internet. They should log on to the Explore Parliament site at www.explore.parliament.uk, and use it to find the definitions of the words listed below:

Parliament
Government
Prime minister
Cabinet
Government departments
Civil servants
House of Commons
Member of Parliament
House of Lords

Activity ☞

Understanding politics

The Refugee Council regularly meets with MPs in the House of Commons to discuss the impact of government law on asylum seekers and refugees.
© **Refugee Council**

Information: Immigration law and refugees

Immigration law determines what groups of people should be allowed to enter the UK and what social rights they should have when they are here. During the last 100 years many immigration laws have been passed. In the UK the first major restrictions placed on post-war immigrants came with the passage of the 1962 Commonwealth Immigrants Act. Until 1985 asylum seekers faced few restrictions. But since then they have been viewed as a group of people that the UK government believes should be kept out.

News laws have been introduced since 1985 to try and prevent the entry of asylum seekers. Pressure groups representing refugees argue that these legal changes have sought to do three things:

- To build barriers that stop asylum seekers from entering the UK
- To make life difficult for those asylum seekers who do enter UK in the hope of deterring others
- Cut down on the proportions of asylum seekers who are given refugee status or leave to remain, and increasing the proportions of asylum seekers who are refused permission to remain in the UK

Barriers

Refugee Council image:

BAA Heathrow

Refugees seeking asylum must apply now to avoid future problems.

Further information can be obtained from the Immigration Officer in the Arrivals Hall.

Les réfugiés cherchent asile politique doivent faire leur demande dès à présent afin d'éviter des problèmes dans le futur. N'hésitez pas à vous demander aux agents du service de l'immigration situés au terminal d'arrivées, afin d'obtenir de plus amples informations.

Los refugiados que busquen asilo politico deben solicitarlo eneste momento para evitar futuros problemas. Pueden obtener más información de los officales de l'inmigración en el terminal de llegadas.

This notice is published by Heathrow Airport Limited 234 Bath Road Harlington Middlesex UB3 5AP

© Refugee Council

Did you know!
The nationals of most refugee-producing countries need visas to come to the UK. This makes such a journey very difficult for people fleeing persecution. To obtain a visa, a person needs a valid passport, which many endangered people do not have. To obtain a visa to come to the UK, a person needs to travel to a British embassy to collect the visa. If there is war in a refugee-producing country, or if the British embassy is being watched by security forces, it can be too dangerous to travel to obtain a visa.

Did you know!
The UK government fines airlines and shipping companies £2,000 for every person they carry who lacks the correct travel documents. Many asylum seekers do not have the required passports and visas. An airline company such as British Airways has two options when an asylum seeker tries to board a plane without the correct documents. That person can be stopped from boarding the plane. Or the airline can let the asylum seeker on to the plane, but pay the fine. What do you think airlines do?

Did you know!
Asylum seekers can be stopped when they arrive in the UK, and told that they do not have a strong claim to asylum. This might be because they have come from a certain country which the UK government does not believe persecutes its citizens. Asylum seekers who are stopped are not usually allowed to fill in forms which allow them to claim asylum and can be removed from the UK within a few days.

Deterrents

Did you know!

About 8 per cent of all asylum seekers are held in detention when they arrive in the UK.

Did you know!

Asylum seekers are not allowed to work in the UK.

Did you know!

Asylum seekers are not allowed to collect income support and other social security benefits. Instead they receive an allowance which amounts to 70 per cent of income support.

Did you know!

Most new asylum seekers cannot be given local authority (council) housing.

Cutting down on the proportions of people allowed to stay in the UK

Did you know!

In 1990 some 89 per cent of all asylum seekers were given refugee status or leave to remain in the UK. Only 11 per cent were refused. In 2002 32 per cent of asylum seekers were given refugee status or leave to remain and 68 per cent were refused.

> **NOTE**
>
> A **visa** is a stamp put into a person's passport. It allows them to enter a certain country.

An example of a visa to the UK.
© **Refugee Council**

Information: Immigration and asylum laws 1905-2004

Immigration and asylum laws are the responsibility of the Home Office and the Home Secretary in the UK.

1905 Aliens Act
This stopped immigrants and refugees entering the UK without the permission of an immigration officer at the port. Sick or 'undesirable' people were prevented from entering, but those escaping persecution were meant to be allowed to enter. Some Jewish refugees were sent back to Russia and Poland. This law was passed as a result of pressure from anti-immigration groups such as the British Brothers League.

1914 Aliens Restriction Act
This gave the Home Secretary the power to refuse entry to or deport any non-British citizen. Refugees were meant to be allowed entry to the UK.

1919 Aliens Restriction Act
This gave the Home Secretary power to refuse entry to or deport non-British citizens. It made no allowance for the entry of refugees, unlike the 1905 and 1914 Acts. Many Jewish refugees fleeing persecution in Eastern Europe were prevented from entering the UK by this law.

1935 Visa and work permit requirements
German refugees escaping the Nazis were told that they needed visas to come to the UK. Visas were often conditional on having a job in Britain.

1948 British Nationality Act
This gave all citizens of Commonwealth countries full rights as British subjects, including the right to settle in the UK and to vote. This Act was passed when the UK was short of workers and needed people for vital industries and services. Men and women from the Caribbean, India, Pakistan, Bangladesh and other former British colonies settled in the UK.

1951 UN Convention Relating to the Status of Refugees
The UK signed this international law which is meant to govern how governments treat asylum seekers and refugees.

1962 Commonwealth Immigrants Act
This restricted the entry of Commonwealth citizens. Only those who had work vouchers could come to the UK. This Act was passed as a result of racist campaigns against black workers already in the UK.

1971 Immigration Act
The 1971 Immigration Act is the most important recent piece of immigration law. This law gave the Home Secretary the right to make and change 'immigration rules' without needing to change British law. The Immigration Rules decide, in practice, whether and how a person can enter or stay in the UK. Changes to the Immigration Rules are simply presented to Parliament, which may or may not debate them. Parliament cannot amend the Immigration Rules but can only accept or reject them. The 1971 Immigration Act also gave the Home Secretary the right to detain immigrants and asylum seekers in prisons, police cells and immigration detention centres.

1981 British Nationality Act
This changed the rights of some people to British citizenship. Children born in the UK who do not have British parents, no longer have the right to British citizenship. Hong Kong Chinese and East African Asians who held British passports were prevented from settling in the UK.

1985-1995 Visas

The nationals of more countries were required to obtain visas to come to the UK. Visas were introduced specifically to keep asylum seekers out. Visas were introduced for Sri Lankans in 1985 after Tamil asylum seekers came to Britain, for Ghanaians in 1986, for Turkish citizens in 1989, for Ugandans in 1990, for Bosnians in 1992 and for Sierra Leoneans in 1994.

1987 Immigration (Carriers Liability) Act

This law fined airlines and other carriers £2,000 for every person brought to the UK without the correct passport and visa.

1988 Changes in social security regulations

Asylum seekers were only allowed 90 per cent income support after 1988.

1990 Dublin Convention

Britain and 11 other European Union countries signed an agreement which only allows asylum seekers to apply for refugee status in 1 EU country.

1993 Asylum and Immigration (Appeals) Act

All asylum seekers, including children, had to be fingerprinted when they applied for asylum. A new system was introduced as the ports of entry where some asylum seekers were not allowed to make a claim for asylum because their cases were judged to be unfounded. Asylum seekers also have restricted rights to council housing. They could only be given temporary housing by a council if they were judged to be homeless.

1993 Immigration Rules changes

This made it more difficult to be given refugee status. After the change to the Immigration Rules more asylum seekers were refused the right to stay in the UK, in particular those who make a stop in another country before arriving in Britain.

1996 The Asylum and Immigration Act

This Act denied two groups of asylum seekers all access to benefits, even though most of them had no money. The two groups that lost access to benefits were asylum seekers who applied for asylum after they entered the UK, and those who were refused asylum in the UK (even though they might wish to appeal). Refugee organisations estimated that 46,000 asylum seekers were at risk of being left destitute and homeless.

The Act also introduced a system where the Home Office listed some countries as 'safe'. If asylum seekers came from one of these countries they may be denied the opportunity to have their asylum application considered.

1999 Immigration and Asylum Act

All asylum seekers lost their right to benefits and local authority (council) housing. Instead they were supported by the National Asylum Support Service, a new Home Office department. It gave asylum seekers vouchers which they could exchange for food in certain supermarkets. It also provided housing and dispersed asylum seekers anywhere in the UK.

2001 End of support voucher

After a campaign led by refugee organisations, faith groups and trade unions, the National Asylum Support Service withdrew the use of vouchers and allowed asylum seekers to get cash support on a weekly basis.

2002 End of right to work

Asylum seekers lost their right to work in the UK. Previously they had been allowed to apply for permission to work after they had been in the UK for six months.

(continued over page)

2002 The Nationality, Immigration and Asylum Act

This introduced the following:

- English language and citizenship tests for people applying for British nationality

- The legislation needed to set up accommodation centres (reception centres) for some groups of asylum seekers

- The law needed to give the Home Secretary power to remove support and housing from asylum seekers who did not apply for asylum immediately on arrival in the UK

2004 Asylum and Immigration (Treatment of Claimants, etc.) Act

This Act introduced the following:

- Removal of cash support and housing for asylum-seeking families who have been rejected and have not left the UK

- Restriction of asylum seekers' rights to appeal against a negative decision

- The laws needed to tag asylum seekers electronically

Unregistered Afghan refugees queue to request aid at UNHCR's offices in Peshawar.
© UNHCR / A. Banta

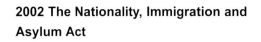

Learning objectives: The activity gets students to think about the effects of changes in asylum legislation on real people. The activity also examines the dilemmas facing workers who have to deal with endangered people.

Time needed: 30 minutes

Instructions: The teacher needs to give an input and explain that airlines and other carriers are fined for transporting people without the correct travel documents. This requirement was introduced in 1987 with the passage of the Immigration (Carriers Liability) Act 1987. This can put ordinary workers in a difficult position. Students should be put in pairs and given the scenario below. They should write down their thoughts and what they decide to do. After the students have finished writing, the class should come together and discuss thoughts and actions. They should finish by looking at the discussion point.

Scenario

You work for British Airways at Nairobi Airport in Kenya. This is an airport that is often used by Somali refugees who are trying to escape to Europe. You know that 5,000 people have been killed in fighting in the towns of southern Somalia during the last year. There is also widespread food shortage in southern Somalia. You have also read in the newspapers of Somali refugees being arrested and mistreated by the Kenyan police.

You have been told by your airline to check all customers' travel documents very carefully and not allow anyone to fly without the correct papers. You have heard of other airline workers losing their jobs for not checking documents.

A young man comes to check in his luggage. He presents a passport and visa that are obviously forged. You look at him and decide that he looks like a young Somali, perhaps no more than 16 years old.

Write down what is going through your mind when you see this young man. Then write down what you decide to do.

> **Discussion point:**
>
> ⇨ Do you think that visas and the system of fining airlines should be used to keep people out of the UK?

There is increased UK immigration control at airports and train stations abroad.
© Ladislav Pflimpfl

Activity 👆

Making a board game

Learning objectives: The activity aims to get participants to think about the hurdles that refugees face when they try to flee to the UK.

Time needed: At least 2 hours, depending on the creative skills of the group.

Instructions: The teacher will need to collect some board games, snakes and ladders, and monopoly are ideal. The class will need counters, felt-tip pens, dice, card, scissors, scrap paper and some large sheets of paper. You will also need to photocopy the flow chart to give to each group.

Divide the class into fours and explain the purpose of the task. After each group has made their board games, they should swap them around so that everyone gets the chance to play the game of other groups. Then participants can come together for a discussion.

Discussion points:

⇨ What kind of hurdles do people face if they want to flee to another country?

⇨ Do you think these hurdles discriminate against refugees?

Activity 👆

The Asylum and Immigration Act 2004 - arguments for and against

Learning objectives: The activity develops students' debating skills.

Time needed: 45 minutes

Instructions: Students will need copies of the details of the main parts of the *Asylum and Immigration (Treatment of Claimants etc) Act 2004* on page 264, as well as smiling and sad face stickers.

The teacher should introduce the activity by explaining that the Government was very concerned about the arrival of increasing numbers of asylum seekers in 2003. Government ministers believed that asylum seekers were unpopular with ordinary people and that it would lose votes if it was not seen to stop the arrival of asylum seekers. In November 2002 the Asylum and Immigration (Treatment of Claimants, etc.) Bill 2003 received its first reading in the House of Commons. This Government argued that the Bill would stop the arrival of asylum seekers who did not have a good case for asylum.

Pressure groups such as the Refugee Council were very active in lobbying against many parts of the Bill. They believed that many aspects of it would harm asylum seekers.

Students are going to examine the different parts of the Asylum and Immigration (Treatment of Claimants etc) Act 2004 to find out the arguments for and against each different clause. They will then simulate a parliamentary debate about the Act, as if it was still going through Parliament as a bill.

Students should work in pairs or in fours. They should first be given the information about the Act. Students should examine the four proposed changes and fill in the empty part of the table. Then using the smiling or sad stickers, students should stick

- smiling faces on the parts of the Asylum and Immigration (Treatment of Claimants, etc.) Act 2004 that they think will benefit asylum seekers;
- sad faces on the parts of the Asylum and Immigration (Treatment of Claimants, etc.) Act 2004 that they think will disadvantage asylum seekers.

Students are then going to simulate the Second Reading of the Asylum and Immigration (Treatment of Claimants etc) Bill 2003 at the time of it going through Parliament. (The Bill became an Act in July 2004)

The classroom can be re-arranged to simulate the chamber of the House of Commons, with government and opposition front benches and back benches, the Speaker's chair and the dispatch box (a diagram of the Common's camber is given on the Explore Parliament website at: www.explore.parliament.uk).

The teacher will need to allocate the following roles:

Home Secretary - This role involves explaining the main sections of the Bill and arguing why they are needed.

Junior Minister in the Home Office - This role involves supporting the Home Secretary and arguing for the Bill.

The Speaker - This MP acts like a Chair and decides who will be called to speak. He keeps the House of Commons in order and will call 'order, order' if a debate gets too noisy. The Speaker has put aside his loyalties to his own political party.

Shadow Home Secretary - This MP represents the official opposition and may argue against part or all of the Bill.

Liberal Democrat Spokesman on Home Affairs - This MP takes the lead on speaking about asylum policy and may argue against all or part of the Bill.

Backbench MPs who support the Bill - They will argue for the Bill.

Backbench MPs who oppose the Bill - They will argue against the Bill.

The Asylum and Immigration (Treatment of Claimants, etc.) Act 2004 – What it means

Changes

⇨ It becomes a criminal offence to enter the UK without a passport.

The Government argues that these changes will ...

Refugee pressure groups argue that these changes will mean that asylum seekers with a good asylum case will be jailed. People fleeing persecution and war often find it difficult to collect passports and visas.

Changes

⇨ Unsuccessful asylum seekers and their children will lose all their rights to support if they fail to obey instructions to leave the UK.

The Government argues that these changes will ...

Refugee pressure groups argue that these changes are inhumane. They punish children for decisions that their parents have taken.

Changes

⇨ Unsuccessful asylum applicants who are not allowed to stay in the UK will only be allowed one chance to appeal against a wrong decision. Unsuccessful asylum applicants who are not allowed to stay in the UK will no longer be allowed to appeal to a judge in a court. (At present unsuccessful asylum seekers can appeal to two different bodies, and if necessary to a court of law. About 25 per cent of asylum seekers who appeal do win their case and are allowed to stay.)

The Government argues that these changes will save money.

Refugee pressure groups argue that these changes ...

Changes

⇨ Asylum seekers aged 18 years or over can be electronically tagged in a manner similar to criminals.

The Government argues that these changes will mean that it does not have to detain asylum seekers who might disappear.

Refugee pressure groups argue that these changes ...

Information: How pressure groups try to influence government

Pressure groups are an important part of a democratic society. A pressure group is an organisation that campaigns to defend the interests of its members or it can campaign for a certain cause. Most pressure groups concentrate on one issue. Pressure groups campaign - they try and change laws or practices. They do this by

- building support with the public;
- organising protest demonstrations and public meetings;
- getting their interests covered in the media;
- lobbying government and others in power - lobbying means working to change the opinion of people who hold power.

Some pressure groups concentrate on lobbying government, parliamentarians and other people who hold power. These groups are sometimes called 'insider pressure groups' because they try influence government from inside. Other pressure groups may organise demonstrations or be involved in other types of protest. These pressure groups are called 'outsider pressure groups' because they try and build support for their cause from outside.

The Refugee Council is an example of an insider pressure group. It employs parliamentary lobbyists and press officers. Some of its recent activities include:

- Attending the annual party conferences of the Labour, Conservative and Liberal Democrat parties, to raise concerns about refugees with MPs, Lords and other party members
- Meeting with government ministers to express concerns about the treatment of asylum seekers and refugees
- Sending press releases and letters to newspapers about asylum seekers and refugees

A Refugee Council lobbyist talks to David Blunkett about refugee issues at the annual Labour party conference.
© **Refugee Council**

During the passage of the Asylum and Immigration (Treatment of Claimants, etc.) Bill 2003 through Parliament, the Refugee Council worked very hard to influence MPs and to try and make the Bill fairer. The parliamentary lobbyists at the Refugee Council

- sent a briefing paper to all MPs before the Second Reading the Asylum and Immigration (Treatment of Claimants, etc.) Bill 2003. The paper outlined the concerns of the Refugee Council;
- met MPs and members of the House of Lords who had concerns about the Bill;
- wrote to the supporters of the Refugee Council and asked them to write to their own MPs. Campaigners used the internet to keep in touch with what was happening.

Learning objectives: At the end of the activity students will have considered the advantages and disadvantages of different campaigning methods.

Time needed: 30 minutes

Instructions: Students will need large sheets of paper and pens. The class should be divided and students should work in groups of three. The teacher should introduce the activity and explain that every person, young or old can, influence the Government in a democratic society.

Students should be set an imaginary scenario: The Government has decided to introduce a Bill to Parliament that will forbid people under 25 from voting in general elections.

Students should be asked to list what they might do about this to prevent this becoming law. Their ideas should be put down on paper. The ideas might include:

- Writing to their MP
- Asking to meet your MP to give your opinion
- Organising a demonstration
- Writing a petition to Parliament
- Joining a pressure group
- Writing a letter to a newspaper about your views
- Keeping up-to-date on the issue
- Raising awareness and support among your friends
- Complaining a lot but doing nothing

The class should come together and form a class list of actions. Then students should go back into groups and discuss the following questions.

Discussion points:

⇨ What are the most effective ways that ordinary people can influence the Government?

⇨ What are the least effective ways that ordinary people can influence the Government?

The Refugee Council produces information about the impact changes in asylum law have on asylum seekers and refugees.
© **Refugee Council**

Information: The European Union

The European Union (EU) had 15 member states in January 2004. In May 2004 a further ten countries joined the EU.

Creation of the EU

The EU had its origins in the European Coal and Steel Community Treaty. On 9 May 1952 six countries signed this agreement: France, West Germany, Italy, Belgium, the Netherlands and Luxembourg. In 1957 these six countries signed the Treaty of Rome. This created the European Economic Community. The six member countries agreed to cooperate between themselves in areas such as foreign trade and agriculture. In 1973 Denmark, Ireland and the UK joined the European Union. Other nations have joined since then.

The Maastricht Treaty was another important agreement signed in 1992. This created the European Union and the idea of citizenship of the European Union (EU). Citizens of the EU still have their national citizenship - like British citizenship or German citizenship. But alongside national citizenship lies EU citizenship. All EU citizens have the right to travel, live, work and study throughout the EU. All EU citizens can vote and stand for election in European and local elections wherever they live. Asylum seekers and refugees do not have the same rights to travel, live, work, study and vote as EU citizens.

Institutions of the EU

The three main institutions of the EU are the European Parliament, the Council of the European Union and the European Commission.

The Council of the European Union is very powerful. It is made up of government ministers from the EU member states. The ministers are helped by civil servants from each EU member state. Which minister attends meetings depends on what is being discussed. For example, if refugee policy is being discussed, the UK government will send a Home Office minister to a Council of the EU meeting.

The Council of the European Union is headed by a Presidency. The Presidency of the Council of Europe rotates between EU member states every six months. For example, in 2005 Luxembourg will hold the Presidency from January to June and the UK will hold the presidency from June until December.

The Council of the European Union takes decisions and makes agreements. In the past it has made many decisions about asylum seekers and refugees. An example of such an agreement is the European Council Directive on Temporary Protection. This came into operation in 2001. It is meant to help EU states deal with emergencies where many thousands of refugees suddenly arrive in Europe. The Directive means that all EU countries

- allow the refugees to stay for a set period of time;
- help the very vulnerable among the refugees, for example the disabled.

The European Commission is based in Brussels and acts like government ministries. It is headed by 20 European commissioners. Each is responsible for a particular area of concern.

The European Commission has a president and two vice presidents. The work of the European Commission is to carry out policies agreed by the Council of the European Union.

The European Parliament is elected by citizens of the EU. Each member of the European Parliament (MEP) is elected for a period of five years. When the European Parliament was first set up, its MEPs had very little power. They could only comment on laws and policies decided by the Council of the European Union. Today, MEPs have more powers and in some areas they can pass European laws jointly with the Council of the European Union. In the last five years MEPs have been given more power to change European refugee policy and to decide who can enter and live in the EU. Despite this, it is the Council of the European Union that makes most decisions about refugees in Europe.

The future

What we want the EU to do is a subject of debate in national parliaments, in the press and among ordinary people. At times the EU may seem to take on too much and get involved in matters that would best be left to individual countries. All EU citizens need to think about the following things:

- How can ordinary people be helped to understand about the EU and the agreements and laws that it passes?
- In what policies should the EU be involved? What policies and areas should best be left to individual nations?

EU Parliament building in Brussels. © **University of Liverpool**

Information: Fortress Europe?

There have been changes in the refugee and immigration laws in all European Union (EU) countries since 1985. As well as legal changes made by individual governments, there have been changes made at European level.

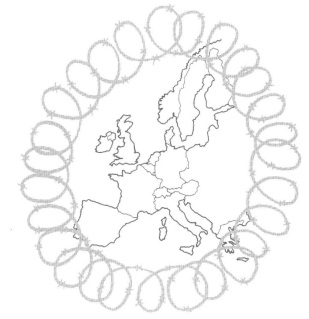

The UK has been a member of the EU since 1972. In 1987 the UK government passed an Act of Parliament called the *Single European Act*. Similar acts were passed in the parliaments of the other member countries of the EU. The *Single European Act* stated that all EU countries should have borders that allow for the free movement of goods, people and investment. There would be fewer customs checks at borders between EU countries.

The governments of some EU countries became worried that terrorists and drug smugglers would be able to travel between EU countries more easily. They also believed that asylum seekers would find it easier to enter the EU. During the last 18 years ministers and civil servants have been meeting to try and find ways of strengthening the borders around the outside of EU countries. In their meetings they have discussed border security, terrorism, drug smuggling, immigration, asylum seekers and refugees.

Ministers and civil servants have formed a special group to discuss immigration and asylum seekers. It meets in secret and does not give reports about the meetings to national parliaments.

The Refugee Council and other organisations that work with refugees are very concerned about the effects of trying to strengthen the borders around EU countries. The Refugee Council believes European governments are not respecting the human rights of endangered people. Asylum seekers with a good asylum case are being prevented from reaching safety. Europe hosts just 7 per cent of the world's refugees and displaced people. If affluent nations cannot share responsibility for victims of conflict and human rights abuse, the Refugee Council argues that one cannot expect the world's poorest nations to continue to provide sanctuary to refugees.

Other pressure groups have advanced different arguments. They argue that EU countries should allow more immigrants to enter, including asylum seekers. EU countries have an ageing population and need more workers to enter to pay for the pensions bill. European countries also need more people to work in certain jobs.

⇨ What do you think?

Information: Key European agreements about asylum seekers and refugees

The *1990 Schengen Agreement* was signed between a number of EU countries (but not the UK and Ireland). It means that

- there is increased policing of external borders of the countries that have signed the Schengen Agreement;
- there are open borders between Schengen states.

The *1990 Dublin Convention* was signed soon after the Schengen Agreement. This is an agreement that decides which EU state is responsible for looking at an asylum seeker's application. It means that an asylum seeker can only have his or her case heard in one EU member state.

The *1997 Treaty of Amsterdam* gave members of the European Parliament (MEPs) the right to debate European asylum and immigration agreements. It also stated that European countries should work towards treating asylum seekers in the same manner - having a common EU asylum system. However, the UK and Ireland were also granted permission to keep their own asylum laws.

The 2003 European Council Directive laying down minimum standards for the reception of asylum seekers is part of the policy to develop the common EU asylum system. The Directive, which has to be carried out by individual governments, outlines minimum rights to education, healthcare, and work for asylum seekers.

The future

European asylum legislation and policy will continue to change at European level. The Council of Ministers of the European Parliament will continue to

- develop a common EU asylum system;
- develop ways to share the financial responsibility for supporting refugees across the EU;
- work for the better integration of those with refugee status within their new countries;
- strengthen security at the external borders of the EU;
- develop better ways of combating illegal immigration and the smuggling of people.

Learning objectives: On completion of the activity students will have learned to present an argument in writing.

Time needed: 45 minutes

Students will need the information sheet on Fortress Europe and a copy of a sample newspaper editorial. The teacher should explain to the class that the editorial column of a newspaper is a place for the editor to give his or her opinion about an event or an issue.

Using the information about Fortress Europe, students should write their own newspaper editorial about changes in the treatment of asylum seekers in Europe.

Activity ☞

Writing a newspaper editorial about Fortress Europe

A sample editorial.
Source: The Sunday Times, 5/9/2004.

THE TIMES

LANGUAGE BARRIER

The positive case for immigration must be made

Sensible politicians are often reluctant to discuss questions of race and immigration because the terms of debate have become so circumscribed that anyone who tries to advance new thinking runs the same danger as a mountaineer leading his companions up a sheer rockface. One misplaced step in difficult territory and he risks doing injury to himself, and damaging the chance for his party's progress. The criticism visited on David Blunkett for talking about "swamping" in a radio interview yesterday demonstrates once again how attempts by politicians to engage with racially sensitive issues almost inevitably result in charges of pandering to prejudice.

The Home Secretary's choice of language may not have been the most felicitous but a man who abolished asylum vouchers and has made strenuous efforts to expose the danger from the far-right British National Party is plainly no merchant of hate. Democrats create a dangerous vacuum if they shy away from discussion of the concerns engendered by immigration and the challenges of building a cohesive multiracial society. A refusal to engage will only weaken popular democratic participation, feeding cynicism and extremism.

It is also a failure of liberal nerve to believe that one cannot talk about these questions without automatically legitimising extreme solutions. Democrats should have the confidence to argue that their policies can promote the common good more effectively than the poisonous snake oil of extremists. The feeling of many communities that immigration is altering their environment at a pace and in a way they find disorientating is real. Ignoring those fears will only help extremists to prey on them. Politicians must therefore demonstrate that Government can take action to control the nation's borders and explain how all citizens do benefit from controlled immigration.

In their anxiety to remind fellow citizens that immigration contibutes to society some politicians simply to assert the case as if it were some sort of holy truth rather than argue it in detail. This is a patronising error, especially when the arguments for controlled immigration are so powerful. Those nations, and regions, which most welcome immigration such as the United States and Pacific Canada enjoy the highest levels of economic growth.

It has been proven, generation after generation, that those most motivated to uproot themselves are likely to be innately enterprising and innovative. The creative new businesses of tomorrow naturally gravitate to areas of cultural richness and diversity. Wealth is increasingly likely to be generated in the cappuccino gulches of Notting Hill and Manchester's city centre where new experiences, and people, promote innovation.

The case for managed immigration also needs to be accompanied by measures to maintain agreement on civil, legal and cultural norms. Mr Blunkett's proposals that new immigrants learn English and appreciate the responsibilities of their citizenship are judicious responses to the challenge.

The Home Secretary's bravery deserves to be matched by innovative new debate. There are merits, for example, in exploring new market-based approaches to immigration such as allowing employers who need foreign labour to bid for the visas which would permit overseas recruitment. Proposals such as this deserve to be debated rationally without a restless search for a race card up every sleeve. The only beneficiaries of a circumscribed debate on race are those extremists who benefit from ignorance, cowardice and fear. The content and tone of the debate on the Nationality, Immigration and Asylum Bill in the House of Commons yesterday was encouraging. Politicians can make progress despite all the sensitivities.

Learning objectives: The activity develops participants' debating skills and enables them to consider arguments about migration.

Time needed: About 1 hour to prepare the arguments and 1 hour to present the debate.

Instructions: The group will need the information sheets about Fortress Europe. The teacher can introduce some of the debate about open borders. The teacher should then introduce the idea of debate to groups who are unfamiliar with debating skills - following the instructions given in Chapter Eight. The motion for debate is:

'This House believes that the EU should have borders that are open to everyone'.

The teacher can assist students in the preparation of speeches and questions by using some of the statements below.

Statements

"Europe is a crowded place. Our cities are densely populated and having open borders will only make our cities more crowded."

"Europe's indigenous population is falling because people are having fewer children. We need more immigrants to work here."

"Allowing people to enter the EU freely would stop would-be immigrants using smugglers."

"Having open borders will allow criminals and terrorists to enter more easily."

"If we have open borders, the best workers from poorer countries will come here and their home countries will lose their skills."

"Immigrants have skills we need in Europe."

"Immigrants help create cultural diversity."

"We should retrain our own workers and not rely on those from outside Europe."

"Europe has an ageing population. We need young workers from outside Europe to come here and to pay our pensions bill."

13 Refugees and the media

Press cameras covering the Refugee Council's annual general meeting. © Refugee Council

The way in which refugee issues are covered in the media influences what we think about refugees. It can also influence how we treat refugees in schools and in the community. This chapter examines how the print media reports on refugees.

Roma

Halina's story

Halina is a Polish Roma girl. She is 14 years old and now lives in the UK.

"My name is Halina and I was born in Krakow in Poland. All of my family lived there until 2000. My dad is called Marek and everyone calls my mum Mimi. In Poland my dad used to be a mechanic. We lived in a block of flats with many other Roma people. It was not a good place to live and very overcrowded. Six of us lived in one room: my mum, dad, grandmother and my brothers. The heating did not work in our flats and it was very cold in winter."

"I did not like school in Poland. I did not have many friends. People said bad things to me because of the colour of my skin. But it was worse for my brother. When he was 15 he was beaten up by a group of older boys. As they were doing it they called him a dirty gypsy and told him they would kill him."

"Soon after this we came to London. For the first time in my life people did not notice the colour of my skin. I started a new school. It was hard at first and I got bullied. Other children called me 'refugee' like it was an insult. The teacher said that they had got this idea from the newspapers. The newspapers here write bad things about refugees. But now I can speak and write good English and I can stand up for myself."

"We have just had some bad news. We cannot stay in England and have to go back to Poland. The British government says we are not refugees. I am scared, especially for my brother."

> **Discussion point:**
> ⇨ What did Halina think about newspapers?

Activity ☞

Who influences our opinions?

Learning objectives: At the end of the activity participants will have a better understanding of who influences their opinions. The activity is useful in introducing work about refugees and the media.

Time needed: 45 minutes

Instructions: Some large sheets of paper, thick pens, ball point pens and 'post-its' are needed.

Explain to the group that many different things influence our political opinions, whether these opinions are about refugees, the environment or any other issue. The group is going to examine who influences their opinions.

> **Discussion points:**
> ⇨ Who influences your opinions?
> ⇨ What are the most important influences on your opinions?
> ⇨ How important are newspapers in influencing your opinion about refugees?
> ⇨ Who do you think influences your opinions about other people such as refugees?

Divide the students up into groups of three or four. Give each group a large sheet of paper, pens and 'post-its'. Everyone should draw a circle in the middle of each sheet of paper and write 'me' in the circle. Using the 'post-its' each group should make a list of who influences their opinions. (The list can include things like parents, teachers and television.) They should write each factor on an individual 'post-it' and stick them on the sheets of paper.

Using the 'post-its' on the other side of the paper the groups should rank the factors starting with the most important. The groups should then come together for a discussion.

Learning objectives: The activity aims to help students understand the different types of media that they encounter in their everyday lives.

Time needed: About 25 minutes

Instructions: Students will need copies of the sheets below. Explain to students that 'media' is a much broader term than television and newspapers. The activity is going to examine the relative importance of different types of media in forming our opinions about refugees.

Students should each receive the table below. They should fill it in. They can work collaboratively in groups. When students have completed the table, the class should be brought together. They should decide what type of media is most important for forming their opinions about refugees.

Refugees and the media

Type of media	Do you watch, listen to, read, use it?	Name	Does it cover stories about refugees?
National radio			
Local radio			
Terrestrial television			
Cable and satellite TV			
Broadsheet newspapers			
Tabloid newspapers			
Local newspapers			
Local free newspapers			
Magazines			
Internet			
Television advertising			
Newspaper advertising			
Internet advertising			

Activity ☞

Conducting an opinion poll about refugees

Learning objectives: The activity aims to help participants assess and understand prejudices about refugees.

Time needed: Preparation time, time in a lesson and homework periods are needed for this.

Instructions: Copies of the opinion polls need to be made so that each participant has ten of them. You will also need some large sheets of paper, graph paper, pens, pencils and rulers.

Explain the aims of the activity, and that the group is carrying out an opinion poll in your school to find out about young people's attitudes to refugees. Give each participant ten copies of the opinion poll. They should interview students from other classes. Everyone should try and make sure that they get an even balance of boys and girls in their interviews as well as people from different ethnic groups.

After the opinion polls are filled in, the group should come together to analyse them. The participants can draw graphs to illustrate some of the results. The graphs should be used as a basis for discussion.

Discussion points:

⇨ What proportion of people interviewed gave a good definition of who refugees are?

⇨ How many people thought that the UK accepted too many refugees?

⇨ Did any of the results of the opinion polls surprise you?

⇨ If you worked for an organisation such as the Refugee Council would you be happy about the results of such an opinion poll? How would it influence your work?

⇨ How many people who were interviewed recognised the wealth of skills refugees bring to the UK?

Opinion poll

1. Give a definition of who you think are refugees.

2. Do you know how many people fled to the UK as refugees in 1994? Is it

☐ about 5,000   ☐ about 25,000   ☐ about 40,000   ☐ about 80,000   ☐ about 250,000

3. Would you say that the numbers of refugees presently accepted by the UK every year is too high, too low or about right?

☐ too high   ☐ too low   ☐ about right   ☐ don't know

4. Do you think that people who flee to the UK should have the same rights to housing, health care, social security and education as British citizens?

☐ strongly agree   ☐ agree   ☐ disagree   ☐ strongly disagree   ☐ don't know

5. What benefits do you think refugees bring to the UK?

Learning objectives: The activity aims to help students look at the way newspapers cover stories about refugees.

Time needed: 2 hours

Instructions: A week's supply of broadsheet and tabloid newspapers is needed and also rulers. The instruction sheets need to be copied so that every student has one.

Divide the students into groups and give each group an instruction sheet, two tabloid newspapers and two broadsheet newspapers.

Students instructions

Newspapers are very important in helping us form opinions on many issues, including refugees. Just as two people will tell a story differently, two newspapers will describe events in a different way.

Some newspapers may have a lot of coverage of overseas stories. Others rarely cover overseas stories.

Front page news stories are more important. One newspaper may put a refugee story on the front page, another will put a similar story inside the newspaper.

You are going to survey how different newspapers cover refugee stories. You will need a ruler and a week's supply of four newspapers.

Read each newspaper for **stories about refugees** then fill in a table for each story like the one below.

8 cm

5 cm

Refugee children flourish

OUT of 700 pupils at Star Primary School in Canning Town, East London, 130 are the children of asylum-seekers. The head teacher, Marion Rosen, said that her staff were doubling as solicitors and health advisers (Glen Owen writes).

"I don't think the children should lose the right to attend local schools, they benefit from being surrounded by people who speak English. Many are among the most improving pupils," she said.

Every year around 20 per cent of pupils leave, as their families are moved elsewhere. "That is when we become a support team, gaining legal advice on their behalf," she said.

Despite the turmoil, exam results for 11-year-olds last year were strong enough to place the school in the top half of the Borough of Newham.

How to measure the size of a newspaper story:

5 cm x 8 cm = 40 cm²

Name of newspaper	The Times
Date	24th April 2002
Refugee story on	Refugee children flourish
Is this an overseas or home story?	Home
Position in newspaper	Page 14
Size of story	40 cm²

Discussion points:

⇨ Which newspaper gave most coverage to refugee stories?

⇨ What differences did you notice between the newspapers?

⇨ Were overseas news stories given as much coverage as home stories?

Information: How newspapers are constructed

Newspapers are very important in helping us form opinions on many issues, including refugees. Where a story about refugees is covered is important.

We may read different types of newspaper in our homes:

- Broadsheet newspapers are printed on large sheets of paper. They have more news coverage than tabloid newspapers, with more stories about political events.

- Tabloid newspapers are printed on smaller paper than broadsheets. They have less news coverage than broadsheets and more articles about celebrities and sport.

- Local and regional newspapers are on sale in particular areas. Most of their news coverage is about local issues.

- Local free newspapers are usually delivered to our homes without cost. They rely on advertisements to make a profit.

Almost all newspaper titles are owned by commercial companies. The job of a newspaper editor, therefore, is to make a profit for the shareholders. There are two ways to make a profit: selling lots of copies of the newspaper and selling the space to put advertisements.

Airport crackdown grounds migrants

Mail Foreign Service

BRITISH immigration officials yesterday defended their crackdown on passengers flying from Prague to London.

The officers, deployed at Prague airport to weed out bogus asylum seekers, have been accused of hounding gipsies.

Since the officers arrived on Wednesday under an agreement with the government of the Czech Republic, about 20 would-be passengers have been denied entry to Britain.

But leaders of the country's gipsy – or Roma – community accused the officers of racism.

'The racist content of this measure is obvious,' they claimed in a statement. 'It focuses solely on

'Systematic and continued abuse'

those Czech citizens who have dark skin and are of Roma origin.'

The president of the International Roma Union, Emil Scuka, said: 'IRU considers the activities of British officials discriminatory against the Roma minority.'

But Giles Portman, spokesman for the British embassy in Prague said: 'The colour of the skin is not relevant.'

He confirmed that about 20 Czechs have been denied entry into the UK since Wednesday. He would not say how many were of Roma origin. David Broucher, British

ambassador to Prague, said: 'Unfortunately, the systematic and continued abuse of the UK immigration and asylum system by some Czech citizens has made this unavoidable.'

All passengers on flights from Prague to London are subject to the checks. Czech Prime Minister Milos Zeman called the measure 'practical'.

British immigration officers were granted special powers two months ago to target a number of ethnic groups notorious for trying to enter Britain illegally.

They included Roma gypsies from the Czech Republic, Slovakia and Poland.

Announcing the measure, Home Office Minister Barbare Roche said officers at ports and airports would be allowed to subject them to tough questioning without falling foul of race equality law.

Since the fall of communism in 1989, apparent discrimination against gipsies has forced many to leave Eastern Europe.

They then head for the West,

mostly to Britain, Belgium and Canada, in search of a better life.

Earlier this year the Daily Mail revealed how Czech gipsies were arriving at Stansted airport in Essex on £80 flights from Prague. Once in Britain, they can make a claim for asylum and can stay for months, if not years.

Some were even returning home for medical treatment, claiming the hospitals in the

Czech Republic are better than those in Britain, before returning under a new name and making a new application for asylum.

In March a Go flight arrived from the Czech capital carrying more than 30 passengers who lodged claims for asylum.

They were smartly dressed and their tickets and passports were in order, so there had been no reason to stop them boarding

the plane. The 11 families, from the same gipsy group, claimed they were being persecuted.

Last year the Home Office received 1,230 asylum applications from the Czech Republic.

Many of those were from individuals but some were from heads of families. At the same time Britain processed 970 asylum applications from the country and rejected all but ten.

To sell copies of newspapers, an editor has to target the market and then produce stories that will interest the target readers. Broadsheet newspapers, like *The Guardian*, target people who are interested in politics and world affairs. The editor determines the content of a newspaper. Journalists write news stories and features. Other staff employed by newspapers include picture editors and sub-editors. The latter improve and correct news stories and features, and write headlines.

A newspaper starts with a front page. Front page news stories are those that the newspaper editor has decided are most important. Following the front page are a number of pages of home news stories. After this there are several pages of overseas news stories. Broadsheet newspapers usually have more overseas news stories than tabloid newspapers. While most home news stories are written by the newspaper's journalists, this is not the case for overseas news stories. Many newspapers rely on news agencies to supply them with information about overseas news events. News agencies are commercial companies that gather news across the world. The main news agencies for overseas news stories are Reuters and Associated Press. Consequently, overseas news stories in different newspapers are often quite similar.

Each news story has a headline. Newspapers use headlines to grab readers' attention. The headline also gives key information about the news story. Since headlines have to be short, the words used have a greater significance and more impact than if they were embedded in text. News stories also use photographs. A photograph, like a headline, will grab the reader's attention, as well as conveying images to the reader. All newspaper photographs have captions. These help us interpret images.

Feature articles usually follow news stories. Feature articles may be written by journalists, or by politicians or academics. Feature articles provide comment and analysis of stories that are in the news. All newspapers in the UK also have an editorial column. This is a place for the newspaper editor to give his or her personal opinion about an event or an issue.
Newspapers have space for readers' letters. This is where a reader can respond to a news story and give their own opinion.
There are other sections of newspapers: business pages, sports pages, life style pages and television listings. Many national newspapers also contain colour magazines. Magazines usually contain feature articles, as well as lifestyle articles on topics such as cookery, gardening and fashion.

MPs attack removal of Roma asylum seekers

Tania Branigan

Attempts to prevent Roma asylum seekers from entering the country are pointless and wasteful, members of the new all-party parliamentary group on Roma affairs said yesterday.

Lord Avebury, launching a report which details human rights abuses against Gypsy populations in Hungary, Poland and the Czech and Slovak republics, pointed out they would be able to enter Britain anyway when their states join the European Union next year.

"After May 1 2004 all these people will be coming here legally. Why spend all this money turning Romany asylum seekers back?" he asked. He suggested that EU member states should help attack the root causes of asylum claims.

"People should connect the influx of Romany asylum seekers with the failure of the states concerned to eliminate inequality. If countries eliminated violence and discrimination, people wouldn't be asking for asylum."

Under recent legislation, asylum seekers from accession countries — those which are soon to join the EU — can be deported without appeal, as such states are judged safe.

But those wanting to flee may not immediately be helped when their countries join the union, as free movement could still be withheld for between two and seven years, depending on national rules.

States are supposed to prove they respect minority rights before they join the EU, but Lord Avebury said member countries were failing to press accession states on the matter.

Reports by the EU's enlargement commission, he said, "do not give an adequate picture of the nature and scale of the problem".

He warned the EU against "encouraging states to sit back and relax on the commitments they have made, knowing that it's almost unthinkable the party will be spoiled by risking the timetable"

Peter Mercer, the chairman of the Roma Rights and Access to Justice in Europe organisation, said: "Roma are consistently bottom of the pile. Unless their situation improves, these states should not be accepted into the EU. The human rights record of the EU is at stake."

The parliamentary group's report says Roma have faced increased persecution since 1989 as enforced assimilation under communist regimes "gave way to increased marginalisation and social exclusion, culminating in the present situation of exclusion from mainstream education, inadequate housing within segregated ghettos, disproportionately high unemployment and racist violence".

In Hungary life expectancy for Roma is 15 years below that of the non-Roma population, and in the Czech Republic Roma children are 15 times more likely to be sent to poor-quality special schools for children with learning difficulties.

It warns that even where anti-discrimination legislation has been introduced, it can amount to little more than "window dressing".

"People say that countries have signed up to the human rights convention, as if that's enough," said Paul Stinchcombe, the Labour backbencher who founded the group. "It isn't, because these abuses are still going on."

This week a report by the New York-based Centre for Reproductive Rights revealed that many Roma women in Slovakia were being coerced into sterilisation.

Information: Stereotyping and bias in the media

Refugee organisations and some academics who research refugee issues believe that there is bias and stereotyping in the way that the newspaper media covers refugee issues. This bias may affect the way we view refugees in the UK. It may also contribute to the racial harassment of refugees.

Stereotypes

A stereotype is an oversimplified and inaccurate idea about a particular group, race or sex. Stereotypes are not based on fact, and are often insulting. Stereotypes are dangerous because they can lead to people developing fixed ideas about a particular minority group. Poor quality newspaper and television coverage can lead to some groups being stereotyped.

Bias

Bias is the one-sided coverage of events or issues, so that only one set of views are put forward. Newspapers and television may be guilty of media bias. There are many ways in which a newspaper article can be biased. These include:

- Putting forward only one viewpoint
- Quoting or interviewing a limited group of people
- Not telling the whole story, just a small part
- Using emotive language to discredit people who have opposing views
- Using photographs that add to bias or do not tell the whole story

Discussion point:

⇨ Can you find examples of media bias in the news stories on pages 278 and 279?

Activity ☝

Comparing two different accounts of the same event

Learning objectives: The activity helps students understand media bias.

Time needed: 1 hour

Instructions: A selection of newspapers is needed. They can be purchased in advance, preferably at time when there is a major event that receives coverage in a large number of newspapers. Students will also need copies of the information on how newspapers are constructed on page 278.

The teacher should introduce the task by going through the information sheet and stress that newspaper editors target their market. The class should then be divided into small groups. Give each different group two different newspapers, for example, a tabloid and a broadsheet, or two politically different newspapers.

The class should be told which story to select. Each group should cut out the report of the same event. They should then write a comparison of the two articles, examining factual content.

Discussion point:

⇨ Why were there differences in the accounts of the same event or issue?

Learning objectives: At the end of the activity students will understand that some news coverage is not factual but emotive.

Time needed: 40 minutes

Instructions: Some newspaper cuttings of a refugee issue or conflict situation are needed; the cuttings in this section could be photocopied. The students will also need two highlighting pens of a different colour (two pens will be needed per pair of students).

The class should be divided into pairs. Each pair should be given highlighting pens and copies of the press cuttings. Each pair should mark in one colour all the facts they can find in the articles. All students should use the same colour. The ask the students to mark in another colour all the emotive or biased words that are used.

Pin the sheets on the wall. This will give graphic representation of the relation between fact and emotion in each article.

Activity

Emotion and fact in newspaper reports

Learning objectives: At the end of the activity students have greater awareness of the images that newspaper headlines convey.

Time needed: 20 minutes

Instructions: Students will need a selection of newspaper headlines. The teacher should introduce the activity by explaining the significance of newspaper headlines - that they aim to grab readers' attention. For each headline, students should write down the images that it conveys. They should note that there are no right or wrong answers. The class should then consider the discussion points.

Activity

Headlines!

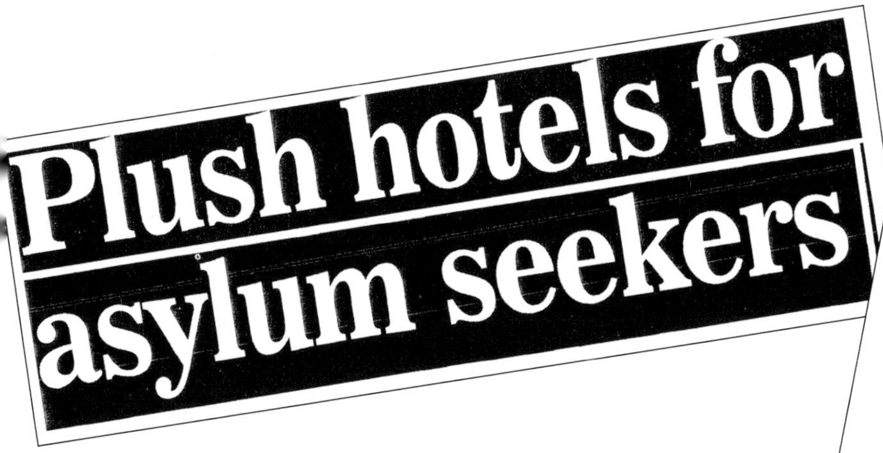

Plush hotels for asylum seekers

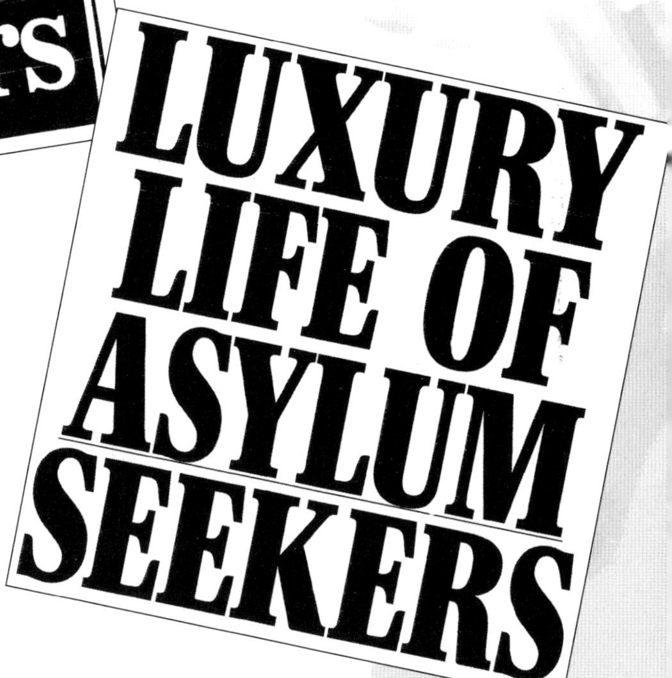

LUXURY LIFE OF ASYLUM SEEKERS

Discussion points:

- ⇨ What images did the headlines convey?
- ⇨ Is there any difference between tabloid and broadsheet headlines?

Learning objectives: The activity helps students understand how the choice of a newspaper photograph can manipulate a reader.

Time needed: 25 minutes

Instructions: The teacher or group leader will need to collect newspaper photographs about refugees. Ideally these should be scanned into a computer and screened to the class using a projector and computer. Students will need paper and pens.

The teacher should introduce the activity by explaining that a photograph, like a headline, will grab the reader's attention, as well as conveying images to the reader. All newspaper photographs have captions. These help us interpret images.

The teacher should show a newspaper photograph on the screen. Students should brainstorm and write down the image that the photograph conveys. The students should then write down a caption for the photograph. The class should then consider the discussion points.

Discussion points:

⇨ What images did the photograph convey?

⇨ How did you feel after looking at the photograph?

⇨ Did your caption differ from the real photograph caption?

Source: **The Sunday Times, 5/9/2004**

EU sights new asylum class, the eco-refugee

Nicola Smith
Brussels

THE European Union's incoming justice commissioner has raised the possibility that asylum status may be granted to a new category of migrant — the "environmental" refugee.

Rocco Buttiglione, who takes up his post in November, says that European asylum rules are unclear about how to deal with immigrants whose environment has been destroyed by natural catastrophes such as drought and famine in Africa.

The commissioner believes there are three possible solutions. "The first is to bring water back to the Sahara and this is better than to bring people to Europe," he said in an interview. "Second, we can help neighbouring countries to absorb refugees. The third option is to bring them to Europe."

Buttiglione, a conservative ally of Silvio Berlusconi, the Italian prime minister, has urged the European parliament to launch a public debate. "I am not saying anyone from a poor country has the inborn right to emigrate to a rich country," he said. "But I think there is an intermediate category. I wish to start a discussion because we need to have an answer."

His comments wer coolly received. Hans-Ge Poettering, leader of the Euro pean parliament's centre right group, said it was no up to Europe to solve all th world's problems.

Timothy Kirkhope, th British Conservative spokes man on asylum in the par liament, was just as dismiss ive, saying: "It is morally sus pect to invite or encourag people to move thousands o miles to places where there i little cultural compatibility when issues should be dea with in their countries."

Buttiglione has already caused controversy by call ing for asylum camps i North African countries suc as Libya to weed out bogu asylum seekers before the reach Europe.

The suggestion may have been prompted by growing anxiety over immigration t Italy, the first port of call fo many illegal immigrants crossing the Mediterranean.

His ideas could land him i trouble when he is grilled i October by MEPs deciding whether to approve his EU appointment.

"Refugee processing cen tres were previously rejected by the parliament," said Gra ham Watson, leader of the parliament's Liberal faction. He promised Buttiglione a "rocky ride" if he chose to argue about immigration.

Elio Desiderio

Migration to Italy may have prompted Buttiglione's idea

Information: Eastern European Roma refugees

Since 1994 over 15,000 eastern European Roma have sought asylum in the UK, mostly from Poland, the Czech Republic, the Slovak Republic and Romania.

Roma/Gypsy/Traveller populations in European countries

Albania	95,000
Austria	22,500
Bosnia-Herzegovina	45,000
Bulgaria	750,000
Croatia	35,000
Czech Republic	275,000
France	310,000
Germany	120,000
Greece	180,000
Hungary	575,000
Ireland	23,000 (includes travellers)
Italy	100,000
Kosovo	43,000
Macedonia	240,000
Netherlands	37,500
Poland	55,000
Portugal	45,000
Romania	2,100,000
Russia	230,000
Serbia and Montenegro	382,000
Slovak Republic	500,000
Spain	725,000
Turkey	400,000
Ukraine	55,000
UK	105,000

Source: D. Kenrick

In the late 1990s, many Roma sought asylum in the UK. The Refugee Council published a report outlining why Roma were fleeing from their country.
© **Refugee Council**

Roma

Who are the Roma?

The Roma are an ethnic minority group in many European countries. About 9 million people in Europe identify themselves as Roma. Other Roma communities live in the Middle East, the US, Australia and South Africa. In the UK, Roma sometimes call themselves gypsies or gypsy travellers.

In the past many Roma were nomadic or semi-nomadic, living in tents or caravans. They spoke their own language called Romani or Romanes. Today many European Roma live in houses. In many parts of Europe the Roma no longer speak Romani.

Linguistic and anthropological evidence suggest that the Roma had their origins in North West India. Today certain Indian minority groups such as the Lambadi or Banjara appear to have linguistic and cultural similarities with European Roma.

During the 11th century some Roma migrated from India to South West Asia, then through the Caucasus and Turkey. In the 14th century, some Roma migrated again, moving to South East Europe. Historical records document a Roma presence in Crete in 1322 and in Prizren, Kosovo, in 1348. During the next 400 years Roma migrated across Europe, often fleeing persecution and forced expulsion. Roma were first recorded in Scotland in 1510. In 1530, Henry VII passed the first anti-gypsy law in England. Ships' captains were fined £40 for transporting Roma to England. To be a 'foreign gypsy' in England at this time became a crime punishable by death.

A third migratory movement of Roma occurred in the 19th and early 20th century. After being freed from slavery in parts of Eastern Europe, many Roma migrated to North America.

Language

About 40 per cent of Eastern European Roma have maintained Romani as their first language. It is an Indo-European language with numerous dialects. Some linguists argue that it is not a single language. Romani appears to be most closely related to Indian languages such as Gujarati and Hindi. In recent years, Roma have begun to publish much of their poetry and stories. But despite this, Romani is a threatened language. Throughout Eastern Europe many Roma families now speak other languages at home.

Numbers in Hindi and Romanian Romani

	Romanian Romani	Hindi
1	ek	ek
2	dui	do
3	trin	tin
4	char	char
5	pansh	panch

- Chapter Thirteen: Refugees and the media -

Polish Roma

Most Roma refugees living in the UK are from Poland. Today there are about 55,000 people who identify themselves as Roma living in Poland.

During the Nazi Holocaust, thousands of Polish Roma were deported to concentration and extermination camps such as Auschwitz and Treblinka. Today, Polish Roma still face deep-seated prejudice. They are often denied entry to public places such as bars and restaurants. Since the end of communism, there has been increased racial violence towards them. As in the Czech Republic and the Slovak Republic, some of it has been perpetrated by far-right 'skinhead' gangs but much is carried out by ordinary Poles on fellow citizens. The houses of Roma have been burnt. According to the European laws in other Eastern European countries, Roma have little redress to police protection in the event of racist violence.

Unemployment among Polish Roma is much higher than among ethnic Poles. Roma, too, are much more likely to be living in overcrowded or sub-standard housing. School attendance among children is poor. Although most Roma children enrol in primary school, their attendance may be sporadic and some drop out. The high level of bullying of Roma pupils by fellow students and teachers contributes to poor attendance.

There were about 6,000 Polish Roma living in the UK in 2003. Very few have been granted refugee status and allowed to stay. UK government policy is that Polish Roma asylum seekers face discrimination but not persecution in Poland so do not qualify for refugee status.

Roma gypsy children. © **Panos Pictures / Mark Hakansson**

Roma

Romanian Roma

The Roma are the largest minority group in Romania, comprising about 2.1 million people - about 10 per cent of the total population. Romanian Roma are a diverse minority group. Some are assimilated into mainstream Romanian society while others form an identifiable minority group living separate lives.

Romanian Roma speak a range of different home languages. Some Roma speak Romanian as their home language, particularly those from towns. Others speak Hungarian or one of the many different Romani dialects.

The first historical evidence of Romanian Roma dates back to 1387, in a document signed by Mircea the Great, a king of Wallachia. From the time of their earliest arrival in Romania, the Roma were targets of persecution. From the late 14th century, many Roma were enslaved. Slaves were kept in shackles and slavery was not abolished in many parts of Romania until 1856. It was the abolition of Roma enslavement that prompted the flight of many Romanian Roma to North America.

The 20th century saw the continued persecution of Romanian Roma. In 1939, Marshall Antonescu, a fascist dictator, came to power in Romania. He allied himself with Nazi Germany. During the Second World War over 26,000 Roma were deported to labour camps in the Ukraine where many died of cold, hunger and disease. Others were murdered. An estimated 30,000 Roma were murdered between 1939 and 1945.

The post-war communist government refused to recognise Roma as a minority group and adopted a policy of forced settlement. In 1989, the communist government collapsed. Although Romania is now a democracy, the situation for the Roma has worsened. Since 1989 Roma have been subject to worsening racial violence. Helsinki Watch, an international human rights organisation, estimates that over 300 Roma have been killed in racist violence since 1989.

Romanian Roma are not able to count on police protection. Between 1990 and 1995 some 30 Roma communities were completely destroyed in mob violence and there was evidence of police involvement. Roma sometimes face other abuse from the police including arbitrary arrest, beating while in detention, and raids on settlements in which armed policemen arrive in Roma settlements early in the morning, often firing shots and forcibly entering homes.

Roma are the poorest ethnic group in Romania. Most live in overcrowded housing in villages or in urban housing estates. Some Roma live in shanty dwellings without water, sanitation or electricity. In 1992 a study at Bucharest University estimated that the unemployment rate among Romanian Roma was 50 per cent, as against 10.5 per cent overall. Roma children find it difficult to enrol at school. Roma children who do go to school face racism and harassment:

"They call me 'Gypsy' and treat my children poorly. The teachers don't pay any attention to the children. They say, 'You are a Gypsy and have no business sending your children here'. You can see the school there, at the edge of the settlement ... it's closed, though it should be open right now ... the teachers just never turn up, or if they do, it's only for a few hours."

About 5,000 Romanian Roma have fled to the UK as asylum seekers. Very few have been granted refugee status and allowed to stay.

Czech Roma

Roma

Czech Roma have also fled to the UK. Like Polish and Romanian Roma, very few have been granted refugee status and allowed to stay.

About 275,000 Roma live in the Czech Republic. Records of their presence go back to 1399. Then they were the targets of violence and population expulsions. At the end of the 19th century, Czech and Slovak Roma were forced to give up their nomadic way of life and settle down.

Czechoslovakia became an independent nation in 1918 but Roma continued to face extreme prejudice. After the Nazi invasion in 1938, Czechoslovakia was again divided. Bohemia and Moravia (today's Czech Republic) were annexed by Nazi Germany and a fascist puppet regime came to power in Slovakia. In Bohemia and Moravia, many Roma were imprisoned in concentration camps or transported to Auschwitz. An estimated 5,500 Roma men, women and children were murdered by the Nazis - some 93 per cent of the pre-war Roma population of Bohemia and Moravia.

Czechoslovakia became one country again in 1945. The post-war communist government followed a policy of forced settlement. The Government moved 200,000 Slovak Roma from their homes in Slovakia and forced them to settle in Western Czechoslovakia, many in homes left by the expelled Sudeten Germans. The ancestors of almost all of today's Czech Roma lived in Slovakia before 1945.

The communist government collapsed in 1989. The Czech Republic and Slovakia split in 1993. Since 1989 there has been an increase in racist violence against Czech Roma. Between 1990 and 1997, a Czech human rights organisation recorded 1,205 serious racist attacks on Roma, 15 of them fatal. In 1998 Helena Bihariova, a 26 year old Roma woman and mother of 4 young children, was assaulted and thrown into the River Labe by a group of men. She drowned, despite the efforts of a witness who risked his own life trying to save her. No one was convicted for her killing.

Roma are much more likely to live in overcrowded housing, some without running water or electricity. Some 70 to 80 per cent are unemployed. Many Roma children have been forced to attend special schools for children with learning difficulties - even though almost all of the Roma children do not have learning difficulties. Such schools offer no possibility of studying for public examinations.

In 1997 Czech and Slovak Roma started fleeing to the UK. Many travelled by coach and arrived at Dover after crossing the English Channel. Once in the UK they asked for asylum. Laws on housing asylum seekers meant that they had to stay in Kent. But very few Czech Roma have been granted refugee status and allowed to stay in the UK.

Roma

Slovak Roma

About 10 per cent of the population of the Slovak Republic are Roma. Most Roma live in eastern and southern Slovakia, often in isolated villages or run-down urban housing developments. Many Slovak Roma still speak Romani.

Slovakia split from the Czech Republic in 1993 to become the Slovak Republic. For five years its Prime Minister was the authoritarian and racist Vladimir Meciar. He was very hostile towards Roma and other minority groups. Meciar's partner in government was the Slovak National Party, a party whose members frequently express anti-Roma views. As in the Czech Republic, there is almost universal prejudice towards Roma and much racist violence. In March 1998, for example, three young Roma children in Presov were badly beaten by six skinheads. Human rights organisations record police harassment, including beatings in detention and the use of electric cattle prods, knives and guns during raids on Roma settlements. Not surprisingly, Roma are often reluctant to report racial attacks to the police.

In 1997 and 1998 about 1,500 Slovak Roma fled to the UK. Many of them settled in London and Kent. Few Slovak Roma are allowed to remain in the UK as refugees.

The European Roma Rights Centre website has lots of useful information about the Roma at: www.errc.org

Roma arrive in the UK as asylum seekers. An asylum seeker is someone who has fled from his or her home country and is seeking refugee status. To be given refugee status, the government of the new country has to decide that the person has left their own country, or cannot return to it "owing to a well-founded fear of being persecuted for reasons of race, religion, nationality, membership of a particular social group or political opinion". *(Definition taken from the 1951 UN Convention Relating to the Status of Refugees.)*

Once a person has refugee status in the UK that person can stay here for as long as needed. But very few Roma asylum seekers are given refugee status and allowed to stay in the UK. This is because the UK government says their experiences in Eastern Europe are of discrimination, not persecution.

Young Roma gypsy people in the market.
© **Panos Pictures / Mikkel Ostergaard**

- Chapter Thirteen: Refugees and the media -

Joseph's story

Joseph is a Roma refugee from the Slovak Republic. He and his family fled to the UK in 1997 and lived first in Kent. But life has not been easy for them in their new home. The Roma were not welcomed when they first came to Dover, Kent.

"We had homes, cars and money but we had to flee from our country. Things are getting worse for us in Slovakia. The main problem is that we are being attacked by gangs of skinheads. In the last three years or so it has been getting worse and worse. Before 1989 the police helped us, now they are helping the skinheads."

"In Slovakia the skinheads wear boots with black laces. If they have beaten up lots of Roma they wear white laces, like a medal. There are also cases of stealing where the Roma are blamed. It's not fair, we have not done it but they blame us."

"I was beaten up one afternoon by a group of skinheads. I remember one behaving like the leader. He beat me very hard. A week later I saw the same man in police uniform. I went to the police station and told them it was one of their officers. They did not investigate. I wrote a letter to them asking why not. Then the next that happened was that the police called me into the police station and questioned me about different crimes."

"I was beaten at the police station and I fell against a window and cut myself. Then they hit me with a chair. They told me that if I kept quiet about what I had done, they would let me off."

"The situation for Roma is getting worse. We want action to change it."

Information: Roma and the media

Many refugee organisations have expressed concern about how some newspapers portray Roma in the UK. Those arriving in Kent in late 1997 and early 1998 were subjected to very hostile media coverage. National tabloid newspapers and local newspapers had hostile and often untrue stories about Roma refugees. One local newspaper, the *Dover Express*, had a headline about Roma refugees that read "We want to wash the human dross down the drain". The newspaper articles in the *Dover Express* were followed by many hostile letters from local people. The newspaper coverage was so extreme that the Kent police warned the editor of the *Dover Express* that he faced being charged with incitement to racial hatred. Indeed, there have been numerous racial attacks on Roma asylum seekers in Kent. For example, a few weeks after the negative media coverage in the *Dover Express* an elderly refugee couple had their house burnt in a suspected racist attack.

Newspapers can also start a process of passing on information about refugees in a way that is similar to Chinese whispers. Some refugees are going to be moving into the town - a simple piece of information - can be embellished each time it is passed on from person to person. The final story can be far removed from the original and have no basis in fact.

But gradually, more sympathetic and welcoming voices are being heard in Kent. Not all local newspapers have been hostile to the Roma refugees. There are many people in Dover who understand why Roma have fled from their home countries and have come to the UK. Local residents have written sympathetic letters to newspapers to explain this. A number of organisations have been set up to welcome and support refugees.

Roma

The Kent Refugee Action Network is one such organisation. It is a pressure group and campaigns to defend the interests of asylum seekers and refugees in Kent. This organisation has used the media to get more sympathetic and accurate information about the Roma into the newspapers. The organisation has

- written letters to local and national newspapers;
- met and talked to local journalists to give them information about refugees in Kent;
- produced information leaflets that responded to some of the negative newspaper articles about refugees.

Another refugee organisation in Margate, Kent, produced a website that contains the stories of refugees who live in Kent. The website also has a question and answer page where ordinary people can find out about refugees.

Both Kent Refugee Action Network and bigger refugee organisations like the Refugee Council collect news stories about refugees. Every day a Refugee Council press officer collects and reads all news stories about refugees. Sometimes the Refugee Council responds to news stories by writing to the editor of a newspaper. Occasionally, the Refugee Council will complain about a news story. For example, in 2000 a newspaper photographer took photographs of refugees entering the Refugee Council offices. The Refugee Council felt that the photographs might put lives in danger and complained. Complaints about newspaper stories are sent to the Press Complaints Commission. Complaints about radio and television stories are sent to OFCOM, the Office of Communications.

> **Discussion points:**
>
> ⇨ How do pressure groups use the media?
> ⇨ What do the Press Complaints Commission and OFCOM do to protect ordinary people?

Activity ☞

Writing to a newspaper editor

Learning objectives: Students will develop their formal letter-writing skills by composing letters to the editor of newspapers that have covered the arrival of Roma refugees in a hostile manner. The activity develops students' powers of media redress.

Time needed: 45 minutes

Instructions: Students will need copies of the information about the Roma, as well as the negative media stories about this group of refugees. The teacher should introduce the activity by explaining that newspapers do not always cover stories in the way that a person or group might like to see the story told. Writing to a newspaper editor is a way of putting across a different opinion.

Divide the class into pairs. Each pair should work together to write a letter to editor to present a different opinion about Roma refugees.

Information: Using the media to campaign for refugees

Almost all pressure groups try to use the media to get publicity for their campaigns. They try to get stories about their campaign on radio, television or in newspapers. Getting a story in the media draws attention to the campaign and enables a pressure group to put across their message. Getting a story in the media may generate more support from members of the public.

Many pressure groups employ press officers in order to get their message into newspapers. The Refugee Council, for example, employs three press officers. A press officer's job is varied. Press officers employed by pressure groups may

- write press releases to respond to a story or to publicise an event;
- organise press conferences to put across a message;
- write letters to newspaper editors;
- stage events or protests that get news coverage;
- respond to the enquiries of journalists.

A press conference is where a person or a group of people want to tell newspapers, television and the radio an important story. Journalists are invited to the press conference. They listen to the information given and then have the chance to ask questions. Press conferences are publicised using a press release. A press release is a one-page sheet that gives key information to journalists. It has to grab their attention.

PRESS RELEASE   PRESS RELEASE

Roma refugees denied rights

2.12.04

Rights for Refugees will be holding a press conference to launch their campaign for Roma refugees. The press conference will be held at 11am on Tuesday, 5th December 2004, at St Andrew's Hall, Mill Lane. Speakers include Natasha Sestak, a Roma refugee and Lord Rees-Martin.

Rights for Refugees campaigns for all refugees. Recently it has been working with Roma refugees from Eastern Europe. It is concerned that very few of them are given refugee status and allowed to stay in the UK. Rights for Refugees believes that the UK government does not recognise how badly Roma refugees are treated in their home countries.

For further information contact William Henry at Rights for Refugees on 0397 26104.

ENDS

The date

This is the 'Who, What, Where, When, Why' paragraph. It gives all the key information to the press.

This paragraph gives additional background information.

Contact details - very important!

Activity

Press conference

Learning objectives: At the end of the activity students will be able to write a press release. Students will also understand how a press conference operates and how pressure groups use the media.

Time needed: 2 hours. The activity can be run in two separate lessons.

Instructions: Students will need copies of the information sheet about Roma refugees, copies of the information sheet about using the press, paper and pens, tape recorders and a blank tape.

The teacher should introduce the activity by giving its aim. Rights for Refugees is an organisation that campaigns to protect the human rights of refugees. The organisation is a pressure group. It is presently concerned about the treatment of Roma refugees in the UK, believing that they are wrongly being refused refugee status and permission to stay in the UK. Rights for Refugees is organising a press conference to present their concerns to journalists.

Students should be divided into pairs. Their first task is to write a press release to publicise the press conference. They should spend about 20 minutes writing the press release.

Students should then be given roles. Three students are needed to play Natasha Sestak, Lord Rees-Martin and William Henry. These three students will need the role cards. The rest of the class will be journalists. They will need paper, pens and the cassette recorders. Everyone should have the background information about Roma refugees and using the press.

The teacher should explain to the class how a press conference works. Panel members and the journalists need about 25 minutes to prepare their presentations and questions. The role play should then start. The three panel members should make short presentations (about three minutes) explaining their concerns. The journalists should then ask questions for about 15 minutes.

After the role play has finished, the class should write newspaper articles or produce radio news stories about Roma refugees in the UK. Newspaper articles can be written in a variety of styles.

Neil Gerrard Mp and the Refugee Council's Chair, Naaz Coker, take questions from journalists, MPs and refugee group representatives on issues affecting refugees.
© **Refugee Council**

Role cards

Lord Rees-Martin, aged 59.

Lord Rees-Martin sits in the House of Lords. He has always been interested in human rights. Recently he has travelled to Romania and the Slovak Republic to find out about the treatment of Roma people. He is concerned that the UK government is not putting pressure on governments in Eastern Europe to improve conditions for Roma in their home countries. Lord Rees-Martin also believes that more Roma deserve to be given refugee status in the UK.

Natasha Sestak, aged 29.

Natasha is a young Roma woman from the Slovak Republic. Until recently she ran a training centre for Roma refugees in her home town. She is also a talented musician. But last year she was returning home from work when she was attacked by a group of young men. She was badly injured. Natasha decided that she must report the attack to the Slovak police. But when she did this they arrested her and charged her with a robbery. In the next two months Natasha was arrested by the police twice more.

Natasha decided that she had had enough. She left the Slovak Republic and travelled to the UK. She is now an asylum seeker. Natasha is now doing voluntary work at Rights for Refugees. She feels that a civilised society is one that welcomes asylum seekers and refugees, and treats them as human beings. She feels that all refugees have much to contribute to their new homeland. Like all who work at Rights for Refugees, Natasha is concerned about the treatment of Roma in the UK. At the press conference, Natasha will talk about her own experiences as a Roma woman.

William Henry, aged 43.

William Henry is the press officer at Rights for Refugees. He believes that the UK government is acting wrongly in not giving the Roma refugee status and allowing them to stay in the UK. William believes that most Roma face persecution and real dangers in their home country.

Roma

Lubomir's story

"Attacks against the Roma got worse after Czechoslovakia split in 1993. In one incident, following a skinhead attack, one Roma died. Many of our people were attacked in Brno, in Usti nad Labem and Prague. People no longer felt safe on the streets. In shops, if a Roma comes in, other people walk out. Roma children are sent to special schools for retarded children, because parents of Czech children make complaints to the school if Roma children are in the same class with their children."

"My daughter went to a normal secondary school, but almost every day skinheads would call her bad names on the bus to school. It became more and more difficult for her to get to school, but we did not want to give up. We were very worried about her. My brother's son, who was 13 at the time, was kicked and beaten when he was alone on the street. In the end, when she was 16, my daughter was expelled, even though she was a good pupil."

"We don't have domestic identity cards. Without them it's impossible to get a medical card. Without a medical card it is very hard to get hospital treatment."

"I decided to speak up in the media about how we were being treated and contacted a TV station. At first, they told me they weren't interested. So I contacted the Human Rights Commissioner in Prague. I went on TV with him and I gave a talk about the situation of Roma. This was broadcast across the country."

"The death threat came in early 1998. It was from a skinhead group called 'White Hammer'. They said that they would kill me, my wife, my children. I wrote to the Ministry of the Interior and asked them to give some protection to me and my family. I got a reply but nothing else. They said my case was nothing exceptional - that all Roma faced such dangers. A representative from the local police said in the newspapers and on TV that I was inciting and provoking problems and that I was organising a rebellion of Roma against the Czech people."

"Skinheads would come into the streets and shout threats. The police did nothing. My family and I felt we had to leave our house and go into hiding. At first, we stayed with my brother but this was not going to be safe for long. Eventually, we ended up living outdoors and slept rough. I contacted the Roma Civic Initiative, which is a NGO, to see if they could help me - but they did not know how. We couldn't go on living without a roof over our heads. I decided to sell everything we had and leave the country."

Lubomir's family applied for asylum in the UK in 1998.

(Source: The Refugee Council. 1999. 'Unwanted Journey: Why Central European Roma are Fleeing to the UK'.)

14 Welcome or unwelcome

Iraqi Kurds returning home. © UNHCR / A. Roulet

This chapter examines the welcome that refugees receive in the UK. Students learn how public hostility towards refugees impacts on their lives. They then consider how they can take action to work for a more welcoming climate. The action focuses on campaigning.

Refugee children's reflections on the welcome they received

These comments were collected by the Children's Society at a conference organised by a group of young refugees living in East London.

"When people think of refugees they don't realise that we are humans, and we have been through terrible things."

"Newspapers and politicians say we should go home. Do you think that if our home was safe we would want to come here? No. We would be in our own home. One day I hope to go home."

"We need to enable wider society to see young refugees as young people - and as talented, resourceful, charming people."

"What have I done to get this abuse from people? You don't want to show your feelings because you worry they might get to you more. Lots of people don't tell they are refugees because they get attacked."

"What helps? Having people to talk to and making new friends who understand you and don't judge you."

"We need to find a way to let people know who you really are. People judge from the outside when they don't know what's inside."

Refugees write down their hopes and aspirations for their new life in the UK.
© **Refugee Week**

Discussion point:

⇨ What kind of welcome did these young refugees have in their new communities?

Information: Research the welcome of refugee children in the UK

While many refugees eventually settle and rebuild their lives in the UK, all too often their early experiences in the UK are miserable. As well as facing stress while trying to cope in a new country, many refugees report that they experience racial harassment. A lot of refugee children state that they did not feel welcome when they first arrived in the UK.

Let's Spell It Out - Save the Children's peer-led research - found that over half the refugee children they interviewed reported bullying in their schools and over 25 per cent reported the existence of racism, although fewer freely admitted to experiencing bullying themselves (15 per cent) or racism (30 per cent). The children in the research were targets of racism from both white and black UK-born students. Less than half the refugee children surveyed knew that their schools had anti-bullying policies.

In another study in the London Borough of Hackney in 1995, some 32 refugee children from a range of national groups, including Bosnians, Turkish Kurds, Somalis and Vietnamese were interviewed. All the children were judged by their parents and teachers to be coping well in school. But 19 of them reported that they had suffered racial harassment. 9 children had to move school as a result of not feeling safe. *Starting Again*, a research report written by Save the Children Scotland in 2002, analysed the experiences of asylum-seeking children settled in Glasgow. Concerns about racism and safety were the worst things experienced by the children.

Isolation is another common experience among refugee children. The Refugee Council's Education Adviser interviewed 32 refugee children studying in London schools. Only one child reported that he had ever visited the home of another student. Refugee pupils' experiences of racism in schools mirror what is happening in the wider community. All studies on the experiences of refugee pupils reveal that many experience racial harassment in their schools and neighbourhoods. At least 44 people have been murdered by racists during the last fifteen years. All of them were people who had come to the UK seeking refuge from persecution.

Ruhollah Aramesh was a 24-year old Afghan refugee. In June 1992 he was murdered by a gang of racists in south London while defending his sister from racial abuse. Ruhollah Aramesh was a much-liked volunteer interpreter at the South London Refugee Project and at the Refugee Council. He had intended to study medicine at university. Another victim was Ahmed Abokar from Somalia, murdered in 1989 by ten white youths, who repeatedly punched and stabbed him in the head. Ahmed had been working with the Scottish Refugee Council in Edinburgh. His attackers made racist remarks in court. Only one of the ten was prosecuted and jailed for 21 months.

For every murder there are hundreds of thousands of incidents of racist abuse, racial attacks, spitting and other abuse, much of which is not reported to the police. Police statistics do highlight two important issues:

- Racial attacks on refugees are increasing in many parts of the UK.
- The majority of perpetrators of racial harassment are young.

Studies show that racist violence is perpetrated by a small number of individuals, but for this to happen there is almost always tolerance of racism within the larger community and widespread negative feelings towards ethnic minority groups.

Information: Racism and refugees

Refugee organisations believe that hostile media coverage of refugees in the UK and the negative remarks of some politicians have led to an increase in public hostility to refugees. In a hostile climate refugees are more likely to become victims of racial discrimination and racial attacks.

But if we are to challenge racism facing refugees (and other groups), it is important to understand how our opinions of different ethnic groups are formed. The word 'race' is often misused. Sociologists tend to use the words ethnic group or ethnic minority to distinguish people from each other. An ethnic group is a group of people who share a distinctive culture. Where such a group forms a minority of the population in a certain country, they are know as an ethnic minority group. Racial prejudice is negative and unfavourable feelings about a particular ethnic group are not based on knowledge or fact.

Racism is where people are treated differently because they belong to a particular ethnic group. Racism can take many forms. People can be victims of violent attacks. They can also be treated differently by employers and by other institutions of society. Institutional racism happens when ethnic groups are treated differently by the institutions in society. Schools, colleges, work places and local and central government have great power on people's lives. Sometimes such institutions can discriminate against ethnic groups, intentionally or unintentionally.

Psychologists and sociologists have come up with four explanations for racism:

The Individual Explanation: Some people are unable to express their feelings and frustrations with life. They find an outlet for their frustrations by being hostile to easily identifiable groups such as people with black skin.

The Group Explanation: All people like to identify with a group or a number of groups. The group can be something innocent such as people who support a certain football club. Or it can be all people who belong to a certain ethnic group. All groups are exclusive and must exclude certain people. People who are excluded from membership of a 'group' may face isolation, discrimination or worse.

The Cultural Explanation: Prejudice about certain ethnic groups is part of the culture of most countries. People are taught to think in racial terms, in their families, at school and through newspapers and books. In the UK, our history as a coloniser of people in Africa and Asia has led us to think about black people in certain ways. As a result ethnic minority communities are **stereotyped**. This means that people have fixed ideas about ethnic groups. These ideas have usually developed without a basis of fact.

The Economic Explanation: When societies are experiencing poverty or unemployment, it is easy to blame an outsider or **scapegoat** for taking jobs or housing. Scapegoating goes hand in hand with racism. Blaming other ethnic groups for taking jobs or housing is a simple explanation for things like unemployment and poverty, but it ignores the real causes. Jews were economic scapegoats in Nazi Germany in the 1930s. Today racist parties in many European countries are blaming immigrants and refugees for unemployment, poverty and homelessness. Refugees may suffer as a result of individual people's hostility. Many refugee and human rights organisations also argue that much recent refugee legislation is racist.

Definitions

A **scapegoat** is a person or group of people who are blamed for a problem that they have not directly caused.

A **stereotype** is an oversimplified and inaccurate idea about a particular group. Stereotypes are not based on fact and are often insulting.

Laws to protect people against racial discrimination

The *Race Relations Act 1976* and the *Race Relations (Amendment) Act 2000* are two laws that are there to protect ordinary people, black and white, against discrimination on the grounds of their ethnic origin.

The *Race Relations Act 1976* enabled ordinary people to go to court, if they believed that they had suffered discrimination due to their ethnic origin. The *Race Relations Act 1976* also set up an organisation called the Commission for Racial Equality. This is a government organisation that tries to stop race discrimination. The Commission for Racial Equality helps ordinary people get help if they believe that they have suffered discrimination due to their ethnic origin. The Commission for Racial Equality can also investigate reports of racial discrimination. For example, it has researched cases of racial harassment in schools.

The *Race Relations (Amendment) Act 2000* was passed as a result of the findings of the Stephen Lawrence Inquiry. This Act of Parliament has extended the powers of the *Race Relations Act 1976*. The *Race Relations (Amendment) Act 2000* requires that public authorities eliminate unlawful discrimination, promote equal opportunities and promote good race relations. The *Race Relations (Amendment) Act 2000* requires all schools to have race equality policies.

Discussion point:

⇨ Discuss what you think "eliminate unlawful discrimination, promote equal opportunities and promote good race relations" means.

The Commission for Racial Equality's website is at: www.cre.gov.uk

---

Learning objectives: The activity aims to get participants thinking about the meaning of the word 'racism'. This activity should only be carried out by a group that knows each other well.

Time needed: 45 minutes

Instructions: Large sheets of paper and marker pens are needed. The information on racism is also needed.

Divide the students up into groups of three or four. Give each group a large sheet of paper and ask them to write down what they mean by the word 'racism'. They should spend about 15 minutes doing this, then come together. Pin up the sheets of paper and discuss the participants' definitions. Then introduce the information sheet and continue the discussion.

Discussion points:

⇨ What do you think racism means?

⇨ How did your definitions differ from those on the information sheet?

⇨ Do you know the names of ethnic groups who have had to become refugees because of racism in their home countries?

⇨ Do you think that racism is a problem in the UK?

Activity ☝

What do we mean by racism?

Activity 👆

Difficulties at the youth club

Learning objective: At the end of the activity students will have considered how they might deal with a racist incident.

Time needed: 45 minutes

Instructions: Students will need copies of the scenario card. Divide the class into fours. Read the scenario to the class. Students should spend 25 minutes talking about the discussion points on the scenario card.

Scenario card

Sarah belongs to Oak Wood Youth Club. She is 16 years old. Her friend Hamid is staying with her and she decides to take him to her youth club.

Hamid is 16 years old. He lives in London. He was born in Sudan. Sarah's parents worked in Sudan in the 1960s and were close friends with Hamid's parents. Hamid's father was a university lecturer but the family had to flee from Sudan in 1990. They came to the UK. Hamid has been to stay with Sarah many times.

Sarah and Hamid enter the building where the youth club is meeting. They are early and only three other people have arrived. Roland, Jane and Maryam are the three people already at the youth club.

Roland asks other members who Hamid is. The youth club members then help themselves to drinks and biscuits. Roland greets Sarah but ignores Hamid. He is heard to mutter, "When did we start letting blacks in then?" The remark is obviously targeted at Hamid. Sarah starts to argue with Roland. Roland then walks out of the door, leaving Sarah, Hamid, Jane and Maryam. The four sit down and discuss what has happened.

Discussion points:

⇨ How do you think Hamid felt when he was told he was not welcome?

⇨ How should Hamid, Sarah and her friends resolve the argument? What should they say to Roland?

⇨ Do you think that anything like this could happen in your youth club or school?

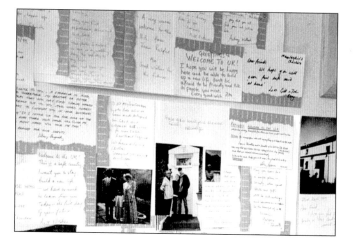

A simple message of welcome can make a difference
© Refugee Council

Information: Racism and refugees - the experience of Newtown

Newtown is a small industrial town in the UK. In the 1950s and 1960s small numbers of Pakistani immigrants arrived in Newtown and found jobs in the local textile factories. They settled in the town centre and their children grew up and attended the two local schools. But apart from British Pakistanis, Newtown was largely white until very recently. Unemployment is higher than the national average, since two local factories closed down in the early 1990s. Newtown's population is also decreasing, as families have moved away in search of jobs elsewhere. Consequently there are a number of empty council homes in Newtown.

The first refugees arrived in Newtown in 1999 when London councils placed 20 homeless refugee families there. Later that year 30 Kosovar families arrived in Newtown. They were part of a group of 2,500 Kosovar refugees who had been airlifted to the UK from refugee camps in Macedonia. The Kosovars were housed in the empty council homes. National and local newspapers ran stories that welcomed the arrival of the Kosovar refugees. Most people in Newtown were happy that their community had agreed to receive 30 Kosovar families. Some local people collected toys and clothes for the Kosovar children.

In 2000 the Home Office asked Newtown Council to find homes for 300 asylum seekers whom it planned to send to live there. Newtown Council found a disused old people's home and thought that it would make an excellent hostel for the asylum seekers. The home was in a village five miles from Newtown town centre.

Newtown Council did not tell local residents about the plans. But news of the plans were leaked to the local paper. Many people in the village were very angry with Newtown Council. As a result there were considerable local objections to it. Some of the villagers organised a sleep-out protest on the site of the planned hostel. This protest was covered by the local newspaper with asylum seekers described in very negative terms. The local newspaper described villagers saying that the asylum seekers would be beggars or members of armed gangs.

The objections of the local people to the hostel for asylum seekers were quite varied. Some villagers were resentful that Newtown Council had closed an old people's home and then re-opened it for asylum seekers. They believed that asylum seekers were getting housing and help that was being denied to British people. Many villagers believed that the arrival of asylum seekers would result in an increase in crime. But no one in the village had ever met any asylum seekers.

The protests were then followed by racial attacks on asylum seekers and refugees already living in the area. At least three refugee children were attacked on their way to school in Newtown. A 20-year old asylum seeker was stabbed outside a supermarket. At the same time at least 16 asylum-seeking children were refused school places, with head teachers conceding to the pressure of other parents.

Some residents of Newtown supported the arrival of the asylum seekers and were concerned about the tense situation. A number of them wrote letters to the local newspaper to express their support for refugees. An organisation called Rights for Refugees decided to organise a meeting to talk to concerned villagers. They explained why asylum seekers were being moved to the local authority and sought to dispel myths. The meeting was successful in that many local residents and members of tenants' associations were brought on the side of asylum seekers. Rights for Refugees also organised a youth project in Newtown.

Young asylum seekers and refugees worked with other school students on Saturdays and made kites. Working together to make and paint the kites brought the two groups of young people together. New friendships were formed.

In another school, Munira, a young British Asian woman, worked with some of her friends and organised a school conference to look at how young people in her school could challenge racism. They used drama to help get people talking to each other. As a result of the conference, the school started a peer mediation scheme to stop bullying including racist bullying.

Asylum seekers did eventually arrive in the village outside Newtown, as well as in the town centre. The youth project has grown into a larger friendship project. Young asylum seekers and refugees work on arts projects and play sports together on a regular basis.

Events similar to Newtown have taken place across the UK.

Discussion points:

⇨ Are refugees made to feel welcome in your local community? Or do you think the situation in your local community is like Newtown?

⇨ In a democracy, should we be allowed to say what we like about refugees?

Newtown

The case study of Newtown shows that school students can do a great deal to challenge racism and to make asylum seekers and refugees feel welcome. Such work can start from small beginnings. Such work might involve:

Direct support - Students can take action in their schools and start projects such as befriending schemes for new arrivals, or peer mediation schemes to stop bullying.

Awareness raising - Students can inform their friends about refugees and challenge some of the current misconceptions and prejudices about refugees. Students might want to make posters and displays.

Campaigning - Students can work with others to change the way people think about refugees.

Learning objectives: At the end of the activity students understand some of the reasons that contributed to the racial harassment of asylum seekers and refugees in Newtown.

Time needed: 20 minutes

Instructions: Students should work in pairs. Each pair will need two copies of a blank A4 sheet and the information on racism and refugees - the experience of Newtown. They are going to examine the causes of an issue: why asylum seekers and refugees are being made to feel unwelcome.

Students should write 'asylum seekers made to feel unwelcome in Newtown' in a column marked issue. They should then work backwards and think about why this is happening, and think of reasons for each occurrence.

Students can also tackle the issue of asylum seekers and refugees not being welcomed in the immediate surroundings of the students' school.

Activity ☞

Why an issue is occurring

Learning objectives: The activity helps students plan to challenge racism in their school and to make new students feel more welcome.

Time needed: 1 hour to introduce the activity, then more time to carry this through.

Instructions: This activity should only be used if a number of students feel and acknowledge that refugees are not being afforded a welcome in their local community.

Students will need individual copies of the Newtown case study. The activity also requires pens and large sheets of paper.

Students should read the Newtown case study. The class should discuss what local people did to challenge some of the racism and hostility to the asylum seekers and refugees.

The class should then be asked if they think refugees are welcome in their own school and community. This discussion works best if it is run as a circle time - students should sit in a circle. Only one student should speak at a time, with an object being given to the student who is to speak.

If the consensus is that refugees are not being made to feel welcome, students should then be divided into groups of four. Using the paper each group should list five things they could do to make their school and community more welcoming for asylum seekers and refugees.

The class should come together and each group should present their ideas. The teacher or group leader should list all the ideas on the board. The ideas should be listed under three headings:

Activity ☞

How can we make asylum seekers and refugees feel welcome?

Direct support   **Awareness raising**   **Campaigning**

Students can then examine how achievable and realistic each idea is, and choose one of these actions to carry through.

Information: Campaigning

To campaign means to work to change law and practice in a way that benefits the aim or people in general. For example, the League against Cruel Sports campaigns to end blood sports. Anti-Slavery International campaigns to end slavery and exploitation.

Campaigning involves building lots of support with the public. In this way it differs from lobbying, as lobbying means working to change the views of people who hold power. Campaigns can be carried out by individuals or small groups of people. More usually, however, a pressure group organises a campaign. You can use many different methods to campaign. These include:

Building support with the public. Campaigning organisations want ordinary people to support their cause and take action. Often they ask members of the public to write to their MPs or to join demonstrations.

Organising protests, publicity stunts and public events. These give publicity to the campaign.

Printing leaflets. These give information about the campaign and ask people to take action to support it. Campaigning organisations often print manifestos. A manifesto is a statement of aims or beliefs.

Researching the issue and publishing the results of the research. Campaigners need evidence to back up their demands. Many campaigning organisations conduct research, then publish this in a form that ordinary people can understand.

Getting the interest of the media. Newspapers, radio and television influence the opinion of members of the public. For this reason many campaigns employ press officers. They work to get the campaign positive media coverage.

Joining with other organisations that might support the campaign. The resources of two or more organisations are better than one. Campaigning organisations often work together. Organisations campaigning to protect the rights of refugees often work with human rights and anti-poverty campaigns.

Lobbying. This is about working with MPs and other people who hold power. Changing something may require someone in power making a decision - perhaps to change a law. Campaigners usually spend a lot of time lobbying, to change the opinion of those who hold power.

Successful campaigns are almost always well planned. They need the following:

- A clear aim - what exactly does the campaign want to achieve? Is it a realistic goal? Can ordinary people understand the aim of the campaign?
- Money - to print leaflets and organise demonstrations and events
- Expert advice - those arguing for change need evidence of why change is needed
- Support from the whole community - this shows that many different people believe the issue is important, not just a minority
- Lots of publicity
- Hard work

REFUGEE COUNCIL

The Refugee Council

The Refugee Council has organised many campaigns to support asylum seekers and refugees. In 2002 the Refugee Council worked with trade unions, faith groups and human rights organisations and lots of ordinary people to campaign to end asylum vouchers. From the end of the 1990s many asylum seekers had been denied cash benefits when they came to the UK. Instead asylum seekers were given vouchers which they could exchange for food, clothes and other necessities in certain designated shops. But what resulted was a chaotic and inhumane system.

Some asylum seekers had to walk for many miles before they could find shops that would accept their vouchers. Asylum seekers were unable to buy cheap fruit and vegetables from markets because market stalls did not accept vouchers. They could not buy bus tickets, second hand clothing and even the cheapest forms of entertainment such as a cup of coffee. Many ordinary people who came into contact with asylum seekers were shocked by the stress that vouchers caused asylum-seeking families.

The Refugee Council's campaign against vouchers had a clear message - end voucher support! This was a message that ordinary people could understand. The Refugee Council then conducted research about vouchers and the impact that they had on vulnerable asylum seekers. The research findings were used when the Refugee Council wrote to the Home Secretary calling on him to end voucher support. This research was also used to write a campaign leaflet targeted at ordinary members of the public. The leaflet asked them to write to their MPs, asking for an end to voucher support.

The Refugee Council also has an urgent action network. Its supporters receive emails, asking them take action - perhaps by writing to a newspaper or their MP. The urgent action network was used in the campaign to end vouchers.

The Refugee Council then met with other organisations. These included Oxfam, trade unions and faith groups. These organisations also met with the Home Secretary. They also got their supporters to take action and write to their MP.

Throughout the campaign the Refugee Council's press officers worked hard to get media coverage about the voucher campaign. Stories about the hardship that vouchers caused appeared on television and in newspapers.

In 2001 the Home Secretary announced that voucher support for asylum seekers would end. Instead they would receive a cash allowance.

Discussion point:

⇨ What factors made the campaign to end vouchers successful?

Activity ☞

Campaigning methods

Learning objectives: At the end of the activity students have a fuller understanding of campaigning methods.

Time needed: 45 minutes

Instructions: Students need access to the internet and copies of the information sheet about campaigning. The teacher should introduce the activity and outline the different campaigning methods that organisations use. This should be listed on the board.

Using ideas from the class the teacher then needs to make a list of five organisations that carry out campaigns - on any issue. Students should then search the internet to answer the following:

- Name of organisation
- What issues does it campaign about?
- What campaign methods are used?

Activity ☞

Writing a manifesto

Aims: The activity aims to enable students to summarise their own ideas about the just treatment of asylum seekers and refugees.

Time needed: 1 hour

Instructions: The teacher needs to explain to the class that they are going to write a ten-point manifesto to demand the fair treatment of asylum seekers and refugees in UK. A manifesto is a statement of aims or beliefs. Many political campaigning organisations publish manifestos that state the things they would like to happen. A refugee manifesto might include statements such as 'no asylum seeker or refugee should be held in detention.'

The class should be divided into groups of three or four. Each group is going to produce their own manifesto. Students can illustrate their manifestos, or use desktop publishing programmes to design them.

After each group has written a manifesto, the class should come together. The manifestos can be pinned up and used as a basis for discussion.

Discussion point:

⇨ What items were common to most manifestos?

George Mitchell School

Students at George Mitchell School in London wrote a manifesto to support refugees' rights. Their manifesto said:

- Refugees should be treated normally and equally. They are no different from anyone else.
- Racism against refugees must stop.
- Everyone has an equal right to education. Because of language and what they have been through refugees have a right to special help to give them an equal chance. This help should not divide refugees from other students.
- All support for refugees should aim to make them feel a normal part of a class.
- Refugees are welcome here.

The manifesto was produced as part of work that the students did in their humanities class. Students produced a drama and video to raise awareness about the needs of refugees. The students were divided into two groups. One group worked with a drama teacher to write and produce a play. The play traced the journey of a group of refugees from Turkish Kurdistan to the UK. The other group of students filmed a video called 'Why?' The video examined the treatment of refugees in the UK, and asked if it was fair. The video shows interviews with refugees. The students also question two MPs and film a demonstration outside a detention centre. The drama and video were shown to other pupils in the school, as well as members of the public. The class also took the drama and video to other schools.

George Mitchell School is not unique in organising such a project. Students at many other schools undertake similar campaigns and awareness raising projects. All of them have similar aims - to make asylum seekers and refugees feel more welcome.

Refugee students tell their stories,
George Mitchell School, London.
© **Refugee Council**

Activity

Organising a campaign for refugees' rights

Learning objectives: The activity is a follow on from the manifesto activity. The activity develops students' knowledge of campaigning methods. It also develops their planning skills.

Time needed: 45 minutes

Instructions: Students will need copies of the information sheet on campaigning and copies of their manifestos. They will also need paper and pens.

The teacher should introduce the activity and recap on campaign methods. The aim of the activity is to produce a campaign strategy to launch the students' refugee manifesto.

The students should be divided into groups of three or four. Each group is to devise a campaign strategy to get the points in their manifesto adopted by the UK government. Students may want to think about:

- A publicity event to launch the manifesto
- Getting the support of the public
- Getting media coverage

- Approaching MPs
- Working with other organisations

Students should write up their campaign strategy. The class should come together and share ideas. Students might want to start their campaign, implementing some of the ideas.

Refugee children present their demands to 10 Downing Street in person.
© **Refugee Council**

15 Hopes and solutions

Young Afghan refugee in Pakistan. © Exile Images / H.J. Davies

This chapter examines the hopes of individual refugees and the solutions to refugee movements. The solutions involve conflict resolution, repatriation, reconstruction, and permanent resettlement in another country. The Palestinians, Kosovar refugees and Iranians are used as case studies.

Three stories about hope

"I hope in the future I will go to college. I want to study English and then I will study architecture or graphic design. When I finish I will work for myself. My dream is to design buildings."

"I think I don't want to go back to my country because here I have got more opportunities. Maybe after 10 or 15 years I will go back to Colombia to see people who are very important to me. We will remember the past and share good moments together. But I am not going to stay in Colombia. When I finish my studies I want to get married and have a family."

Mauricio from Colombia

"We have a dream to make our country democratic and for there to be human rights. I hope that the situation will change and we will go back to our home country. I hope I will receive my friends here as friends in my home country. But until then I am here. Now I want to bring my family here. My child - I didn't see him for more than two years. I want to be a normal member of this society, it is important for me to be accepted in this society. Sometimes I feel I am a stranger, in all the meaning of a stranger. A refugee wants to be a normal person, nothing else."

"I have hope, because if I don't have hope, I can't continue, I can't live. I have hope about the future, even if it's difficult."

Rizgar from Iraq

"The world knows we were at war. You have seen only negative pictures of fighting in Bosnia. I don't want you to see me in that way. I would like to relate to others on equal terms. I don't want people to feel sorry for me."

"I know it will take time, but one day I hope I can feel welcomed in Sweden. I also hope that all the children in the world will not have the experience of war and nobody should go through the things that we did. I hope that all of us, we should forgive each other. I hope that one day people will understand each other better."

Indira from Bosnia

© UNHCR / R. LeMoyne

Discussion points:

⇨ What do Mauricio, Rizgar and Indira hope for in the future.

⇨ How are their hopes different?

Learning objectives: The activity aims to get children to examine their own hopes for the future. These can then be compared with the refugee testimonies in this chapter.

Time needed: 1 hour

Instructions: The group will need paper and pens. Everyone will also need copies of the testimonies of Mauricio, Rizgar and Indira.

Children should first work individually. They should spend 20 to 30 minutes writing about their hopes and ambitions for the future. They should examine areas such as:

- My future education
- My career
- Hopes for my family
- Future relationships and children
- Hopes for my country and the world

After the children have completed their own piece of writing, they should then read the testimonies in pairs. Each pair should then consider the discussion points.

Discussion points:

⇨ How were the hopes of the three refugees similar to yours?

⇨ What key differences were there?

© Refugee Council

Information: Solutions - when people stop being refugees

Refugees like any other human beings have hopes and dreams for the future. They include the ambitions common to all people, but also the hope for peace, the restoration of human rights and, for some people, the possibility of returning home. For others, the idea of home always remains a dream.

Before refugees can return home safely, there must be peace and the restoration of respect for human rights. Conflict resolution is needed before refugees can return home. Conflict resolution involves getting the leading groups fighting each other to agree to peace. Conflict resolution also involves getting ordinary people together.

Once there is peace and respect for human rights, refugees can return home safely. Some refugees go back by themselves or in family groups. Other refugees return as part of voluntary repatriation programmes. Repatriation means the return of people to their country of origin. Repatriation should be voluntary, where people return because they want to do so. (Repatriation can sometimes be involuntary, where refuges are forced to go back to their home countries.)

Voluntary repatriation programmes are usually organised by the UN High Commissioner for Refugees (UNHCR) or the International Organization of Migration (IOM). Refugees receive help so they can return. They may get help with transport, small cash grants and items such as seeds and tools. In 1993 and 1994 over 1.6 million Mozambican refugees returned to their homes after the war in that country ended. The UNHCR helped them return. More recently Kosovar refugees have been able to return home.

If the repatriation of refugees after a war is to be successful, aid must be given to help with the reconstruction of the war damaged country. Repatriation should go hand-in-hand with reconstruction.

Some refugees may never return home. It may be unsafe for them to do so. Wars may last for many years. Sometimes refugees' farms and homes may be occupied by newcomers, preventing refugees from returning. Sometimes too, family ties prevent refugees from returning home. For example, many Chilean refugees who fled to the UK in 1973 chose not to return home when Chile returned to democracy in 1989. Some of these Chileans had married British citizens or had children who had lived most of their lives in the UK and saw themselves as British. For these Chileans their families ties and social networks prevented them from returning home.

It is important to help refugees who cannot or do not want to return to their country of origin. Organisations like UNHCR as well as small community organisations offer support to this group of people, helping them integrate and resettle in their new homeland. Such help is called permanent resettlement support. Retraining and careers advice are an important part of many permanent resettlement programmes.

Activity

- Go to the website of the US Committee for Refugees at: www.refugees.org.
- See if you can find out about other groups of refugees who have been able to return home voluntarily.

Information: The Palestinians

After fleeing their homes in 1948-49, 1967 and since 2001, Palestinian refugees live in many different countries. During the last ten years there have been many attempts to bring Palestinians and the Israeli government together to resolve the conflict in the Middle East.

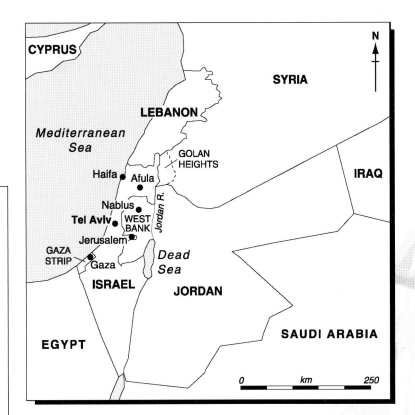

Where the Palestinians live

950,000 in the West Bank
1,100,000 in the Gaza Strip
1,950,000 in Jordan, including over 150,000 new refugees
1,065,000 in Israel, including East Jerusalem
350,000 in Europe, the US and South America
450,000 in Lebanon
470,000 in Syria
135,000 in Saudi Arabia
100,000 in other Gulf states
20,000 in Iraq
130,000 in Egypt

Some 4.1 Palestinians are registered with the United Nations Relief and Works Agency for Palestine Refugees in the Near East (UNRWA). This UN organisation was founded in 1949 and provides education, health and relief services to Palestinian refugees living in the Gaza Strip, West Bank, Jordan, Syria and Lebanon. Not all Palestinians who are living in these countries are registered as refugees with UNRWA.

Events:

200 BC: Different ethnic groups occupy the land that now forms Israel, including Jews and Philistines. The Philistines gave their name to the land of Palestine.

63 BC: The Romans colonise Palestine. In 70 AD the Romans destroy the Temple of Solomon in Jerusalem. Many Jews flee to North Africa, Spain, Turkey, Greece and other parts of the Middle East. During the next 1,500 years descendants of these Jews move to France, Germany, Poland, Russia and other European countries.

1516: The Ottoman Turks capture Palestine. The inhabitants of the country are mostly Arabic-speaking Muslims and Christians.

Late 19th century: Nationalist political movements develop throughout the Arab world. The population of Palestine begins to identify itself as being 'Palestinian Arab'.

1881-1917: There is increased persecution of Jews living in the Russian Empire. Some 4,000,000 Jews flee from Eastern Europe to Western Europe and North America. A small number arrive in Palestine including members of an organisation called Hovevei Zion - the Lovers of Zion.

1897: Hungarian Jewish journalist, Theodor Herzl, sets up the World Zionist Organisation in Switzerland. Herzl believes that Jewish people could only be safe in a Jewish homeland. He meets with political leaders in order to find this homeland; possibilities include Uganda and Palestine.

1917-1919: The Ottoman Turks fight against the British during the First World War. In 1917 the British capture Palestine. At this time the Jewish community comprise 8 per cent of Palestine's population. Soon after, Lord Balfour, the British Foreign Secretary, promises British support for a Jewish homeland in the Middle East. His promise becomes known as the 'Balfour Declaration':

"His Majesty's government view with favour the establishment in Palestine of a National Home for the Jewish People, and will use their best endeavours to facilitate the achievement of this object, it being clearly understood that nothing shall be done to prejudice the civil and religious rights of existing non-Jewish communities in Palestine...". *(Extract from the Balfour Declaration)*

1920-1930: The Jewish Agency buys land titles from absent Palestinian landlords. Palestinian farmers having farmed their land for centuries have no idea that the land titles exist. As a consequence of the sale, they are evicted from their land. The 1920s see growing opposition to Jewish immigration by the Palestinian Arab community. This opposition ends in a violent demonstration in 1929.

1930s: Jewish guerrilla groups such as Irgun and the Stern Gang are formed to fight for independence from the British. Many of those active in these guerrilla groups become future leaders of Israel including Menachim Begin and Itzhak Shamir.

1933-1945: As the Nazis persecute Jews in Europe, many Jews are desperate to leave. But these would-be refugees are usually refused entry to the US, and the UK and her colonies. Consequently some Jewish refugees enter Palestine illegally. But as the Jewish population of Palestine increases, so does Arab opposition to their settlement. In 1936, 1937 and 1938, there are Arab revolts against Jewish settlement and British rule. In 1939 the British try to stop Jewish immigration to Palestine.

1945: At the end of the Second World War, the world sees the horrors of the Nazi Holocaust. Many of the remaining Jewish communities in Eastern Europe feel they have no future there and seek to emigrate to Palestine.

1946: Irgun blow up the King David Hotel in Jerusalem. 98 people are killed including 41 Palestinians and 28 British.

1947: Britain gives notice that it wants to leave Palestine. The UN Partition Plan proposes that Palestine be divided. Most Jews accept the plan but Palestinians reject it because it gives 54 per cent of the land - mostly in fertile areas - to the Jews.

1948: The violence worsens. Many Palestinians flee as refugees, some are driven from their homes by force, including those who live near the village of Deir Yassin. Here Irgun murder 254 men, women and children. By mid-1948 300,000 Palestinians are refugees. On 14 May 1948 the State of Israel is proclaimed with David Ben-Gurion as its first prime minister.

1948-49: The First Arab-Israeli War - Arab armies from Lebanon, Syria, Jordan, Egypt and Iraq invade Israel. Although Israel suffers heavy losses, it wins and captures new territory. During the war, 725,000 Palestinians flee as refugees. They call this time al Naqba (the catastrophe).

Definitions

Arab

A person whose first language is Arabic. Until the growth of Palestinian nationalism in the late 19th century, the Palestinians considered themselves to be Arabs. Now they call themselves Palestinians. Many Jewish Israelis still call the Palestinians 'Arabs'. The reasons for this are complex, but basically it is a rejection of the Palestinian claim to a country called Palestine.

From 1948: Jewish people arrive in Israel from Europe, North and South America, North Africa and the Middle East. Some arrive as refugees, others migrate for economic, religious or political reasons. All Jewish people and their close relatives have the right to live in Israel under the 'Law of Return'. But Palestinian refugees are not allowed back.

1956: The Second Arab-Israeli War - The Egyptians nationalise the Suez Canal, which threatens British and French interests. They give Israel military support and encourage it to attack Egypt. Israel captures the Gaza Strip and Sinai Desert, but is forced to hand back this land after the UN protests.

1964: Founding of the Palestine Liberation Organisation (PLO) - This is an umbrella organisation to which many Palestinian political groups belong. Its member organisations also have military wings that launch attacks on Israeli targets. Palestinian guerrillas have their bases in Jordan at this time.

1967: Growing tension in the Middle East culminates in the Six Day War. Israel invades Egypt, Jordan and Syria, and captures the Gaza Strip, West Bank, the Golan Heights and the Sinai desert. East Jerusalem, including the Old City is annexed and becomes part of Israel. A further 260,000 Palestinian refugees flee to Jordan.

November 1967: The UN passes Resolution 242. This states that the 1949 armistice line should form the borders of Israel and that Israel should withdraw from the territories it captured in the Six Day War. Resolution 242 also calls for settling the refugee problem.

1970-71: Black September - There is fighting between Palestinian guerrillas and Jordanians. Most Palestinian fighters are forced to leave Jordan. They move to Lebanon.

1973: The Yom Kippur War (known in the Arab World as the October War) - Syria and Egypt attack Israel in an attempt to win back land. After initial success the Syrian and Egyptian armies are pushed back and lose more territory.

1974: PLO leader, Yassir Arafat, offers a choice between 'a gun and an olive branch' at the UN. Arab countries recognise the PLO as the sole legitimate representative of the Palestinian people.

1975: PLO guerrillas based in Lebanon launch raids on northern Israel.

1977: A programme to build Jewish settlements in the West Bank starts.

1978: Israel invades southern Lebanon but withdraws after pressure from the UN and the US. Israel and Egypt sign a peace agreement at Camp David in the US. The Sinai desert is to be handed back to Egypt. But other Arab nations denounce President Sadat of Egypt for betraying the Palestinians and making a separate peace with Israel.

1979: A crackdown on the occupied West Bank by the Israeli army is met by strikes and protests. Inside Israel a group of 27 high school students refuse to do their army service in the occupied West Bank and Gaza Strip.

1982: Israel invades Lebanon in 'Operation Peace for Galilee'. The aim is to destroy the Palestinian guerrilla bases. The invasion results in the death of over 19,000 Palestinians and Lebanese. Others are injured or have their homes destroyed. Over 600 Israeli soldiers lose their lives. As a result many Israelis oppose the Lebanese War.

Definitions

Israeli
Someone who is a citizen of the State of Israel. Israeli citizens include Jews, Palestinian Arabs, Bedouin Arabs, Druze and other minorities. But Israeli citizens who are Palestinian Arabs face discrimination in housing, employment and social security. Most Israeli Palestinians do not serve in the army, but many job advertisements call for army service.

Summer 1982: The PLO leave Beirut, supervised by UN peacekeeping soldiers. As soon as they leave, the UN also goes. In September the Israeli army watches as Lebanese Maronite soldiers murder Palestinians living in Sabra and Chatilla refugee camps in Beirut. Over 2,000 Palestinians die. Some 12 per cent of the Israeli population protest about Israel's role in the massacre. The demonstration, plus international pressure, forces the Israeli army to withdraw from Beirut. It remains in southern Lebanon where it arms and trains another force called the South Lebanese Army. The South Lebanese Army fights Palestinians and other guerrilla groups.

1987: There are riots in Gaza after an Israeli settler's truck hits a car containing four Palestinians. This is the start of the first Palestinian uprising or intifada. Palestinian activists demonstrate and throw stones at Israeli soldiers in the West Bank and Gaza Strip. The resistance to Israeli occupation is well organised. Within Israel there is increased tension between Israeli hardliners and 'doves' as to how to respond to the Palestinian intifada. The Israeli Labour Party calls for withdrawal from the West Bank and Gaza Strip negotiated with non-PLO Palestinians. Hardliners call for tough military action to suppress the uprising. A few right-wing extremists believe that Israel should annexe the West Bank and Gaza Strip, and expel the Palestinians to other Arab states.

Palestinian refugee housing damaged near Beirut.
© UNRWA / G. Nehmeh

1989: Violence continues. Over 700 Palestinians are killed and 80,000 injured by the Israeli army in the West Bank and Gaza Strip. Some 8,000 Palestinians are imprisoned without being charged with any crime. Nearly 900 houses are demolished or sealed. Schools and universities are closed for most of the time. In the Gaza Strip and West Bank a greater number of Palestinians give their support to Hamas and other Islamic fundamentalist organisations. Hamas has a military wing which launches terrorist attacks on Jewish targets.

1992: The Israel Labour Party wins a narrow majority in the general election and Yitzhak Rabin becomes prime minister. The US government puts pressure on the Israeli government to negotiate a peace settlement with the Palestinians and other Arab nations. International peace talks start but there is little progress. At the same time as the official peace talks are taking place, Israeli officials are having secret meetings with PLO officials.

1993: The secret meetings between the Israeli government and the PLO continue in Oslo, Norway. In August 1993 the Israeli government and the PLO announce a breakthrough. On 13 September 1993 Yassir Arafat, Shimom Peres and Yitzhak Rabin sign a peace agreement. The peace agreement is made of three parts. The PLO agree to recognise the State of Israel. The Israeli government recognises the PLO as the representative of the Palestinian people. The Palestinians are to be granted self-rule in phases, starting with Gaza and Jericho.

The peace agreement is scheduled to end with final negotiations which would agree the future of Jerusalem, the return of Palestinian refugees and the future of Jewish settlements in the West Bank. The final negotiations are scheduled to start by May 1996.

1994: Palestinian self-rule begins in Gaza and Yassir Arafat returns. But the Palestinians face many social problems, particularly in the impoverished Gaza Strip where unemployment is very high.

1995: Jewish and Arab opposition to the Oslo peace agreement increases. Some 17 Israelis are killed by a suicide bomber who boards a bus in Tel-Aviv. The bomber belongs to the Islamic fundamentalist group Hamas. In November 1995 Prime Minister Yitzhak Rabin is assassinated at a peace rally in Tel-Aviv by a Jewish law student who belongs to an extreme right-wing religious group opposed to the peace process. Shimon Peres becomes acting prime minister. He is determined to carry on with the peace process.

1996-1999: Shimon Peres loses prime ministerial elections to Binyamin Netanyahu, who campaigned against the Oslo peace agreement. Almost immediately the new government allows new settlements to be built in the West Bank. During the next three years, there are attempts to bring the Palestinians and Israelis together. But eventually all peace talks fail.

1999-2000: Ehud Barak wins prime ministerial elections in Israel. He starts peace talks with the Palestinians.

28 September 2000: Ariel Sharon, leader of the right-wing Israeli opposition, pays a visit to the Temple Mount in Jerusalem. This place is know as Haram al-Sharif to Muslims and is holy to both Jews and Muslims. The visit sparks a violent revolt among the Palestinians and the start of the second intifada. By December 2000 over 300 people are killed. Most of the dead are Palestinians who are killed in reprisal attacks by the Israeli army.

2001-2003: Ariel Sharon sweeps to power in prime ministerial elections in Israel. The intifada continues and Sharon vows to crush the Palestinian opposition. His government re-occupies Palestinian territories, which were given back after the Oslo agreement. In the next three years five peace proposals are presented to the Israeli government and the Palestinian authority.

Today: A group of moderate Israelis and Palestinians start their own peace negotiations in Geneva, independent of their political leaders. They reach an agreement. But by the end of 2003 over 3,000 people are killed. Some 2,200 of the dead are Palestinians. Most of them are innocent people killed in reprisal attacks by the Israeli army. Over 800 Israelis also lose their lives, some as a result of suicide bombs placed in markets and restaurants. At least 200,000 Palestinians flee as refugees, mostly to Jordan and Egypt. Thousands of Palestinian homes are destroyed and nearly half of all Palestinian children suffer from malnutrition. This is because curfews prevent their parents from reaching work.

Palestinians

Women refugees, presenting their cases to an UNRWA staff member for badly needed food.
© UNWRA / G. Nehmeh

Afif Safieh's story

At the time he was interviewed Afif Safieh was a diplomat and working in London as the Palestinian Delegate to the UK. He has lived in exile for 35 years. In 1996 the Israeli government blocked his application to return home.

"I was born in 1950 in East Jerusalem but I came from a family who has lived in West Jerusalem before 1948. My family was a Christian family. In May 1948 my family moved from West Jerusalem to East Jerusalem. They spent three months living as refugees in a school classroom. After this they spent some months as refugees in Lebanon and Syria before returning to East Jerusalem at the end of 1949. East Jerusalem and the West Bank of the Jordan were then part of Jordan. My father was a member of the Jordanian Parliament from 1963-66."

"I lived in Jerusalem from my birth until 1966. After I finished High School in 1966 I left Jerusalem to go to Belgium to study at the Catholic University of Louvain. So when the 1967 War took place I was abroad as was my brother. East Jerusalem was occupied during the war and then afterwards annexed by Israel. After the Israelis annexed East Jerusalem they conducted a census. I was not included as a resident of Jerusalem because I was abroad. I ceased to exist from the point of view of the Israeli government, as did a whole generation of Palestinian students. We were not allowed to return to Jerusalem because we were not considered residents. My father used to say, 'In 1967 we lost our country and in 1967 we lost our children'. I have lived in exile since then for nearly 30 years."

"At university in Belgium and then later in France I was President of the General Union of Palestinian Students. In 1976 I started work for the Palestine Liberation Organisation's Observer Mission to the UN. Then from 1978-81 I worked for Chairman Arafat's office in Beirut."

"When the Oslo peace agreement was announced, the BBC interviewed me and asked how I felt about the peace agreement. I said I felt euphoric. I told all my colleagues and friends that I wanted to spend Christmas in Jerusalem. I wanted to take my family with me and to celebrate my daughter's first communion in Jerusalem. The dream became a reality. On 18 December 1993 I returned to Jerusalem. On 19 December 1993 we celebrated my daughter's first communion. The ceremony was officiated by the Patriarch of Jerusalem. The ceremony was meant to be a private affair, but over 800 people ended up coming including all the mayors of West Bank towns and even Shulamit Aloni, then a member of the Israeli government."

"Returning to Jerusalem also meant that I could visit my father's grave. He died in 1983 but I was not allowed to be with him during his last days."

"My feelings during that visit were that the Palestinians were living in a state of limbo, waiting for an end to occupation and waiting for a Palestinian state. Arab East Jerusalem was a sad place, it seemed to be in decline. This was when I thought of returning to Jerusalem to start an English language weekly magazine. I wanted to call the magazine 'The Palestinian'. I was told that I needed to apply for family reunion for this. My mother filled in the forms. These were delivered to the Israeli Ministry of the Interior in November 1994. The people who dealt with me in the Ministry were a Tunisian Jew and an Ethiopian Jew who had only arrived in Israel recently. My family had always lived in Jerusalem yet I had to apply to them to request family reunion."

"The answer was no. I believe there were three reasons for this. Firstly I believe the Israeli Government did not want me to publish my magazine. I also believe that the Israelis do not want Palestinians to return to Jerusalem. There are thousands of Palestinians like me who wish to return to Jerusalem. By giving me family reunion the Israeli government would create a visible precedent and other Palestinians might want to return. Finally I believe that the Israeli government was frightened that opposition parties who do not support the peace process would seize on my case and accuse the Israeli government of smuggling the PLO into Jerusalem."

Palestinians

Activity

Making peace in the Middle East

Learning objectives: At the end of the activity students will understand some of things that might be needed to secure peace in the Middle East.

Time needed: 30 minutes

Instructions: All students need a copy of the student information on page 320. Lots of small pieces of paper or post-its are also needed.

The students should be divided into pairs. Each pair needs to decide what is needed to make peace in the Middle East. The students should then write down all the things they believe will help create peace in the Middle East on the paper or post-its. (These are all the things they have answered with a 'yes'.) One item should be written on each post-it.

Students should then try and rank the items in their list, into the ones most likely to help create peace and the ones least likely to create peace.

A classroom in the new school for boys and girls at Sbeineh refugee camp in the Syrian Arab Republic.
© UNRWA / J. Madvo

Middle East

Student information

Conflicts cause the large-scale movements of refugees, as has been seen in the Middle East. If you think of peace as a state in which the possibility of conflict is reduced, which of these would help to create peace in the Middle East?

To have peace you need:

A strong Israeli army	**Yes/No**
A ban on extremist political parties on both sides	**Yes/No**
Freedom of speech	**Yes/No**
The death sentence for terrorists	**Yes/No**
The fair distribution of wealth between Israelis and Palestinians	**Yes/No**
An end to the Israeli occupation of the West Bank	**Yes/No**
Israeli settlers to give back land in Palestine	**Yes/No**
An Israeli withdrawal from East Jerusalem	**Yes/No**
The Israelis to keep East Jerusalem	**Yes/No**
Israelis and Palestinians to be able to share Jerusalem	**Yes/No**
A strong Palestinian police force	**Yes/No**
A strong Israeli police force	**Yes/No**
Full independence for Palestinian areas	**Yes/No**
Democratic elections in Palestinian areas	**Yes/No**
More jobs in Palestine	**Yes/No**
Somewhere to live for everybody	**Yes/No**
Improved schools, roads and hospitals in the West Bank and Gaza Strip	**Yes/No**
Palestinian refugees in Syria, Lebanon and Jordan to be able to return to their original homes	**Yes/No**
Palestinian refugees to be able to return to the West Bank and Gaza Strip	**Yes/No**
Palestinian refugees to be given compensation for the homes they have lost	**Yes/No**
Ordinary Israelis and Palestinians to be able to talk to each other	**Yes/No**
Palestinians to be forced to leave the West Bank and go and live in Jordan	**Yes/No**

You can add some ideas of your own to the list.

Discussion point:

⇨ Of the items you have answered with a 'yes', what things are most likely to create peace in the Middle East? Why?

Information: Conflict resolution

The Israeli government and the Palestinian authority have many issues to resolve before there can be long lasting peace in the Middle East. Conflicts that must be resolved include:

- **Independence or self rule** - Will an independent Palestinian state be formed or not?
- **Borders** - Where will the final borders of the Palestinian state or autonomous area be?
- **Jerusalem** - The Palestinians want East Jerusalem as their capital. The Israeli government believes that Jerusalem should be the undivided capital of Israel.
- **Refugees** - How many Palestinian refugees will be able to return? Will Israel grant compensation to Palestinian refugees who lost their property in 1948?
- **Settlers** - The Palestinian Self Rule Authority would like to see the dismantling of Jewish settlements in the West Bank and Gaza Strip. Will the settlers be forced to move?
- **Military bases** - There are many Israeli military bases in the West Bank. Will these be dismantled after a final peace agreement?

These issues are to be resolved in negotiations between Israeli and Palestinian officials. But the 50-year conflict in the Middle East has had an enormous impact on the lives of ordinary Israelis and Palestinians. Many people have died. Others have been wounded or lost their homes. There is still a lot of hatred and prejudice on both sides of the conflict. As well as governmental peace talks, there is a need for ordinary Israeli and Palestinian people to come together to resolve conflicts. In a small number of conflict resolution projects in the Middle East, Israelis and Palestinians meet to discuss their differences to try and move forward.

One conflict resolution project is Neve Shalom/Wahat al-Salam. The name means 'oasis of peace' in Hebrew and Arabic. Neve Shalom/Wahat al-Salam is located in the countryside between Jerusalem and Tel-Aviv. It consists of a village and educational centre.

Neve Shalom/Wahat al-Salam is the only village in Israel where Jews and Palestinian Arabs of Israeli citizenship have chosen to live together. There is a bilingual nursery and primary school attended by Jewish and Arab children. This is very unusual in Israel, as most Arab and Jewish children are educated separately.

Within Neve Shalom/Wahat al-Salam is the School for Peace, an educational centre which runs workshops and courses on the Jewish-Palestinian conflict. Both Jews and Palestinians attend the courses. Some of the most important courses are with young people and teachers. Neve Shalom/Wahat al-Salam organises a Youth Encounter Programme. In Israel Jewish and Palestinian young people rarely get the chance to meet each other. To overcome this problem some schools encourage students to attend Neve Shalom/Wahat al-Salam's Youth Encounter Programme. Some 30 Jewish and 30 Palestinian young people meet each other for a four-day workshop. The participants get the chance to talk to people from 'the other side'.

Neve Shalom/Wahat al-Salam trains teachers. By doing this it hopes that school teachers will be better equipped to promote conflict resolution within their schools. Neve Shalom/Wahat al-Salam also offers training to people working in other areas of conflict throughout the world. You can visit the organisation's website at: http://nswas.com

What is conflict resolution?

Conflict resolution is all about creating a peaceful alternative to a situation of despair. It is a process, not a set of easy answers. There are five different stages in conflict resolution:

1. Agreeing that there is a need to get together to resolve a conflict
2. Affirmation - Getting together, and recognising that people on the 'other side' are human beings and have good qualities too
3. Communication - Talking to people on the 'other side' of the conflict about beliefs and needs
4. Cooperation - Working together
5. Problem-solving - Woming up with solutions to the conflict that everyone supports

The workshops that take place at Neve Shalom/Wahat al-Salam help young Jews and Palestinians progress through the five stages and resolve conflicts.

Activity ☞

Conflict resolution

Aim: These are activities to encourage communication, cooperation and problem-solving. Students may like to use them to resolve conflicts within their schools or groups, or to get a feel for what conflict resolution involves.

Time needed: At least 2 hours

Instructions: Big sheets of paper and marker pens are needed. Each participant should write their name in block capitals on the sheet of paper, and tell the group about how he/she got the name, whether he/she likes it and so on. If the person is known by a nickname get them to write it down too and to talk about it.

The group should then be divided into pairs. Each pair should list several controversial issues relevant to their lives that they thought would divide the group. The group should then come together and make a list of the issues. Participants should be asked to state their position on each issue. Those issues that do not divide the group should be struck off the list.

The group should select the two most important issues. The participants then have the opportunity to practise coalition-building skills. Two volunteers should present the case for choosing one or the other of the issues. They should do this in such a way that the whole group does not know what position they took on the issue they were presenting as being important. Participants should then vote on the most important issue to be tackled.

Two members of the group who feel strongly about the issues, but saw it from opposite points of view should then be asked to come to the front. Person A should be asked to state their case. Person B has to listen carefully and then verbally summarise the points made by Person A. Person A then has to say whether Person B has understood and repeated all the main points that he/she made. The process should then be reversed, with Person B stating their case. This part of the exercise encourages people to listen to each other.

Finally, the group should identify areas of common ground between the two different opinions. The group should be broken down into pairs to brainstorm areas of common ground. After this the whole group should come together for a plenary session.

Information: Kosovar refugees

There are about 200,000 Kosovar refugees living outside their country, including 28,000 in the UK. During the last four years many have returned home, some voluntarily and some against their will.

Population: About 2 million

Capital: Prishtina

Ethnic groups: In 1997 some 89 per cent of the population of Kosovo were Albanian and 9 per cent were Serb. Other minority groups include the Roma, Ashkaelia, Turks, the Gorani, Greeks, Serbian speaking Muslims and a small number of people of mixed marriage.

Languages: Albanian, Serbian and Romani are the most widely spoken languages. From the 1960s until 1990, Albanian children received their education in Albanian, while Serbian children received their education in the Serbian language.

Religions: Most Albanians from Kosovo are Muslims, although a small number are Christian. The Serbian population are Serbian Orthodox Christians. Many ancient Serbian churches are located in Kosovo.

Economy: Kosovo's workforce are mostly farmers. Unemployment is very high in Kosovo at present.

Events:

The history of Kosovo is a matter of much argument, with Serbian and Albanian historians disagreeing with each other. But by the 10th century, Albanian and Serbian people lived in the region that is now Kosovo. During the 13th and 14th centuries, the Ottoman Turks moved across South East Europe, conquering and colonising this part of the world. In 1389, the Ottoman Turks fought the Serbian Army and Prince Lazar at the Battle of Kosovo Polje. The Serbs lost, but Serbian folk poems and most versions of Serbian history describe this battle as a heroic defeat. By 1459, all of Kosovo and Serbia were incorporated into the Ottoman

Empire. Serbian people began to migrate north out of Kosovo.

17th century: The Austro-Hungarian army drive the Turks out of Kosovo. But in early 1690, the Austrian army is forced to withdraw from Kosovo, as a mixed Ottoman and Tartar army move north, killing many in its wake. Serbian refugees flee north into modern Serbia. At the same time, there is Albanian migration into Kosovo.

1878: Serbia and Montenegro gain independence from the Ottoman Empire but not Kosovo. Albanian people are forcibly expelled from the newly independent Serbia and Montenegro with at least 200,000 settling in Kosovo and Macedonia. Ottoman Turkish rule finally ends after the First Balkan War of 1912 when the combined forces of Serbia, Montenegro, Greece and Bulgaria drive out the Ottoman army.

NOTE

Kosova is the Albanian way of spelling Kosovo.

Kosovars

1918: Kosovo becomes part of the new country of Yugoslavia.

1939-1945: Albanian and Serbian Kosovars suffer badly during the Second World War. Kosovo is divided in two. Part of it is incorporated into Italian-controlled Albania, the rest occupied by the Nazis. In 1945, at the end of the Second World War, Kosovo becomes part of Serbia, the largest state in the Federal Republic of Yugoslavia.

1945-1960s: Albanian culture is oppressed. Any Albanian who believes that Kosovo should have political independence risks jail. But in 1974 the Kosovo people gain greater rights to control their own police, healthcare and education systems. Slobodan Milosevic removes these rights in 1987.

1990: Thousands of Albanian doctors, teachers and lecturers are sacked. Albanian language schools are closed. Human rights worsen and opponents of the Yugoslav government are arrested or beaten. Many Albanians flee Kosovo. Other people arrive in Kosovo, mostly Serbian refugees who have fled the 1992-1995 war in Bosnia.

Kosovar Albanians organise peaceful resistance to the government of Slobodan Milosevic. They set up a parallel state with their own schools and hospitals. But some Kosovars grow frustrated and form the Kosovo Liberation Army - an armed resistance to the Yugoslav government. They attack Serbian targets. The Yugoslav army and armed Serbian extremists respond by attacking Albanian targets.

March 1998: Violence causes 350,000 people to flee as refugees or internally displaced people. Peace talks are set up between representatives of the Albanian people and the Yugoslav government, led by Slobodan Milosevic. Unarmed peace monitors from the Organisation for Security and Cooperation in Europe (OSCE) are sent to prevent the conflict from spreading.

The peace talks are not successful and the peace monitors are withdrawn. An ultimatum is given to President Milosevic. In April 1999, NATO planes attack targets throughout Serbia and Kosovo. Armed Serbian extremists and regular Yugoslav Army soldiers take revenge on the Albanian population. Fearing further violence, over 750,000 Kosovar refugees flee to Albania, Macedonia, Bosnia and Montenegro. At least 700,000 others hide in remote forests and mountains in Kosovo.

10 June 1999: NATO bombing stops. A peace agreement is signed and the Yugoslav army leaves Kosovo. Troops from NATO enter Kosovo to keep the peace. Within days almost all the Kosovar refugees in Albania, Montenegro and Macedonia return to their homes. But many Serbian people as well as Roma fear for their future and flee to Serbia.

Today: Many Kosovar refugees have returned home from all over Europe. NATO soldiers are still stationed in Kosovo, as part of the K-For force. Kosovo is still legally part of Serbia, but the European Union runs Kosovo's government. Although refugees have returned, Kosovo is far from safe. The country is heavily mined and people are killed or injured every day in landmine and booby trap explosions. There is still violence between Serbs and Albanians in parts of Kosovo.

Fortesa's story

In 2000 Fortesa's parents decided to return to Kosovo.

"My name is Fortesa and I am nine years old. I have a sister called Sara who is six and a baby sister called Gresa who was born in London. My dad's name is Agim and my mum is called Valbona. I was born in Prishtina, the capital of Kosova. We had a flat there."

"We left Kosova in 1995. I was really sad when we had to leave all my friends, but we had to do it. Because I was only five years old when we left, I did not really understand why we had to go."

"We came to London. But I have also got uncles in Germany and Denmark. This is because of the war in Kosova - they left too. It was not nice to be spread around so much, as Albanians like to have their families near them."

"When I started school in London, it was hard for me because I did not know any English. But there were children from lots of different parts of the world in my school and we helped each other."

"When I first came to London, I cried a lot at school, because I remembered the people we had left behind in Kosova. I missed my grandparents a lot. When the fighting started in Kosova, everyone at home was very worried. I started crying again."

"After the war stopped my parents decided to go home. Even though we had a nice flat, they found the life of a refugee very hard. They did not have jobs. My parents decided it would be better to go home to Kosova, even through there are many problems there."

"I was excited, but also nervous when we decided to go home. I remembered quite a lot of what it was like when we lived there before. I remembered my grandparents and I was really excited to be seeing them again. I missed them very much when I was away."

"We packed our bags and met with other refugees in a hotel in Leicester. My Mum and Dad filled in forms. Then a British soldier gave all of us a talk about landmines. These are small explosives that are put in the soil. They go off if a person treads on them. There are lots of landmines in Kosova because of the war."

"The next day we got up early and caught the plane. The plane took a long time to get to Prishtina. Mum and Dad went to sleep, but I was too excited. After we landed, a bus took us from the airport to my grandparents' flat. We lost our own flat - it was destroyed - so we will have to share a flat with my grandparents until we can find somewhere else to live."

"Everyone is busy. They are all helping each other repair their homes. Everyone is cutting wood for the winter. There is no electricity now, so people need the wood for cooking and heating. I know it will be difficult for us now the winter is coming. In England we always had heating."

"Now I am home, I am really happy that we can speak our own language. But it is difficult for me. I have been speaking English so much that I have forgotten a lot of Albanian that I knew. But the main reason that we came home was to be close to our family."

Activity

Repatriation and reconstruction

Learning objectives: Students will understand what is needed for refugees to return home. Kosovo will be taken as a case study.

Time needed: 45 minutes or more

Instructions: Students will need copies of the information on solutions, the information about Kosovo and Fortesa's story. Additionally, the cards below will need to be copied and prepared before the activity. The students should be divided into pairs or threes. Each group should imagine that they are a Kosovar family now living in the UK. The family comprises a father, mother and two children of 7 and 13 years. Another older child is living with cousins in Germany. Before they fled from their village in 1998, the family owned a farm. Their house was badly damaged in the war.

Each group needs a set of cards. The groups will be ranking their cards in order. They need to decide what things are most important to enable the Kosovar family to return. Alternatively, the cards could be sorted into two piles: short-term needs to enable refugees to return and long-term needs for return to Kosovo.

A large bag to carry belongings	News from relatives and friends who have returned that Kosovo is safe
Money - about £500	Four loaves of bread, cheese, eggs and tomatoes
A rebuilt clinic in the village	Assurances from the UN High Commissioner for Refugees that Kosovo is safe
Seeds for planting next years' wheat	A rebuilt school in the village
Training on being aware of the danger of landmines	Blankets
Wood, bricks and cement to help you rebuild the house	Plastic sheeting
Air tickets for the whole family	An air ticket for the child living in Germany
Bus tickets to help you get from the airport to your home	Firewood

Information: Refugees from Iran

Since 1980 over 50,000 Iranian refugees have arrived in the UK.

Population: 66.1 million
Capital: Tehran
Ethnic groups: About 60 per cent of people identify themselves as Persians. 40 per cent of the population belong to minority groups, the largest of which are the Azeris (27 per cent of people), the Kurds (15 per cent of people), Turkmen, Baluchis, Arabs, Armenians, Assyrians and Jews.
Languages: Official language is Persian. Azeri, Kurdish, Turkmen, Armenian and Assyrian are also spoken. Between 1946 and 1979 it was forbidden to speak or write Kurdish, so most Iranian Kurds are not literate in their language.
Religion: Some 80 per cent of Iranians are Shi'a Muslims. Other religious groups include Armenian Christians, Assyrian Christians, the Baha'i, Zoroastrians, Jews and a small number of Catholics and Protestants. Armenians, Jews and the Bahi'a have been persecuted in Iran and many have fled as refugees.

Events:

Iran was known as Persia until 1935. In 1906 the country became a constitutional monarchy ruled by a Shah.

1960s and 1970s: Iran becomes richer as a result of its oil exports. But the country's wealth does not benefit everyone. Poor people in urban areas see little change to their lives. The poor turn to religion and the leadership of Ayatollah Khomeini who inspires many peaceful demonstrations. But these are crushed by the armed forces. Many demonstrators are killed. The Ayatollah Khomeini is forced into exile. In the late 1970s opposition to the rule of the Shah increases.

1979: The Shah is forced to flee Iran. The

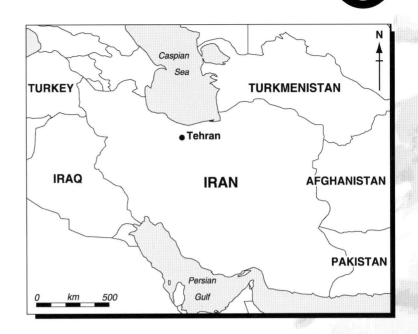

Ayatollah Khomeini leads a new Islamic government. New laws are passed based on shari'a - Islamic law. Women have to wear the hijab (a veil) and are not allowed to study with men. Many women lose their jobs. The Kurdish and Baha'i minorities face persecution. Political opponents of the government face imprisonment, torture and execution. A lot of secular Iranians become very disillusioned with the new Islamic government; many flee as refugees.

September 1980: Iraqi troops cross into Iran to claim territory. The Iran-Iraq War starts and lasts for eight years. Over 500,000 Iranians are killed in this conflict.

Today: Arrests and executions of political activists and independent journalists continue to the present. Women still face arrest or flogging for violating the dress code in parts of Iran. People convicted of adultery risk the death penalty. In the Kurdish areas people suspected of supporting Kurdish political parties are arrested or worse. Human rights workers continue to face severe restrictions on their work and the conditions faced by the Baha'i have not improved. Over 700,000 Iranians live outside their home country. Many of them are refugees.

Activity ☞

See what you can find out about the Baha'i faith. Who was its founder? What are its main beliefs?

Iran

Parveen's story

Parveen is an Iranian refugee who lives in London. Parveen is not her real name, as she is still concerned about the safety of her parents.

"I was born in 1952 in a suburb of Tehran. My father was a university lecturer and the family was big by British standards. I have five brothers and sisters. Four of us have left Iran. My parents and two sisters remain."

"We lived in a big house with an orchard behind it, a place where we played as children. In 1974 I came to London to study. I ended up staying for five years, enjoying life as a student in London and having more freedom than I could have expected in Iran. I got married in 1979 to another Iranian student."

"In 1978 and 1979 there were more protests against the Shah's rule. It looked like there might be a revolution. We decided to return home. If Iran was going to change we wanted to be part of it. We went back but it soon became obvious that life was not going to get better. Khomeini had returned and Iran became an Islamic Republic. Women lost their jobs. I could not work and everywhere we went we had to cover ourselves. Any woman who said 'no, I'm not going to do this', faced beating or prison or worse. I heard that one of my friends from school had been arrested and executed by the religious police."

"In 1981 I had Reza, my oldest son. Later that year my husband got a job in India, for an Iranian company. When Reza was one, I took him to India to visit my husband. He told me he was very glad I had left Iran. He told me he wanted to leave the country and not go back. So we came back to London."

"We were lucky, both of us. We spoke good English and had both lived in London before. Before long my husband found a job. The Iranian refugees who are coming today don't have the advantages that we had."

"After we came back to London I had two more children. When they started school I went back to college and got a teaching qualification. I found work in a college. Many of my first students were refugees. I think I was able to help them because I had been through some of the things that they were going through."

"Reza does not remember anything about Iran. He is now at university. He has a British girlfriend and wants to be a lawyer. The two younger ones are still at school. The children see themselves as British and Iranian. We speak Farsi and English at home. When they were younger the children went to Farsi classes on Saturdays. They didn't like it much at the time, but now I think they appreciate being able to speak and write both languages."

"Of course I see my future here as I have lived more than half my life here. But 'home' will always be Iran, even though I do not think I will ever live there again. I would like the opportunity to travel there more often. I managed to make a visit two years ago, I was very nervous about it and it is not something I am likely to do again in the near future. I miss my parents very much, your parents are always part of what home means."

- Chapter Fifteen: Hopes and solutions -

The Town (Karlsbad/Karlovy Vary)

By Gerda Mayer

Is it an irony that I return
with a heart so trembling,
I who was ever its stepchild?
It begrudged
shelter to my ancestors.
It spat me out.
It welcomes me now
cautiously
as a guest
who comes
and goes again.
It has changed
its language;
it calls itself
by a new name.
It speaks neither my mother
tongue nor the
language of my enemies
(which is the same);
its voice will be
foreign and strangely
neutral and that too
will be difficult
to endure.
It is an irony that I return
like its hailed, like its hallowed,
like its own true love;
I shall fall at its green feet.

Gerda at the age of 11 with her father.
© Gerda Mayer

Gerda Mayer was born in Karlsbad, Czechoslovakia, and came to England in 1939 at the age of 11. Gerda wrote her poem after she had lived in Britain for many years and had been able to return to her home town for a visit. She has published many other poems and writings as well.

Discussion points:

⇨ What is Gerda Mayer saying in her poem about home?

⇨ How does Gerda Mayer's idea of home contrast with that of Parveen?

Information: Home - what does it mean?

The end of a refugee's story is being able to return home in safety and dignity. Some refugees achieve this. Other refugees cannot return home or choose not to do so. For them home often remains a dream.

The idea of home is part of the identity of all human beings. Home can mean many different things:

- Home can be a physical object - the house or flat in which we live.
- Home can be a nation or region.
- Home can be the place where our parents live.
- Home can be a non-material idea - the place where you feel you belong.
- Home can also be a collection of memories.

What does home mean to you?

Activity ☞

What does home mean to me?

A blank version of this diagram can be found on page 339.

Learning objectives: At the end of the activity students will have explored some of the different meanings of home.

Time needed: 30 minutes

Instructions: The students should be divided into threes or fours. Each group should think about words which say something about home to them. For example, they could mention certain people, places, objects, feelings and memories. Each group should write their words on a spider diagram.

The students should then come together. Each group should pin up their diagrams and present them to the rest of the class.

A blank version of this diagram can be found on page 339.

Discussion point:

⇨ What kind of feelings about your home would you have if you had to move to another country?

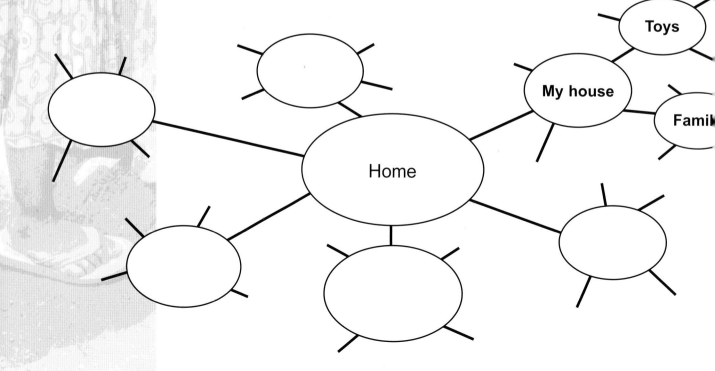

- Chapter Fifteen: Hopes and solutions -

Further resources

Index

Further resources

Background information for teachers

Danish Refugee Council. 2003. *The Legal and Social Conditions for Refugees in Europe*. Copenhagen: Danish Refugee Council.

Kushner, T. and Knox, K. 1999. *Refugees in an Age of Genocide*. London: Frank Cass.

Langer, J. (ed), 1997. *A Bend in the Road; Refugees Writing*. Nottingham: Five Leaves Publications. This anthology comes with a teachers pack. Some of the writing can be used with GCSE and A-Level English classes.

Rutter, J. 2003. *Supporting Refugee Children in 21st Century Britain*. Stoke on Trent: Trentham Books.

Save the Children Scotland and Glasgow City Council. 2002. *Starting Again*. Glasgow: Save the Children Scotland

US Committee for Refugees. 2003. *Refugee Report 2002*. Washington DC: US Committee for Refugees, available at www.refugees.org

Teaching packs about refugees

Every Tree Has Its Roots: Refugees from Vietnam and their Children speak about here and there
Refugee Action, 2003
A CD Rom and booklet featuring selected extracts of the testimonies of 110 Vietnamese refugees. The pack is of particular relevance to history teachers.

I am here: Teaching about Refugees, Identity, Inclusion and the Media
Save the Children, 2004
This is a citizenship resource pack for 11-14 year olds. It contains a video and a 90-page teachers book.

Minority Rights Group booklets

Voices from Angola
Voices from Eritrea
Voices from Kurdistan
Voices from Somalia
Voices from Sudan
Voices from Uganda
Voices from Zaire

These booklets contain the bilingual testimonies of refugee children as well as activities.

Refuge Pack
2002 Aegis Trust
A film resource of the testimonies of refugees with additional teaching material

A Refugee Camp in the Heart of the City
New York: Médicins sans Frontières, 2002
This is a teaching pack in eight units. It aims to make students aware of the conditions faced by refugees living in camps. The pack can be downloaded at from www.refugeecamp.org

To Feel At Home: Refugee Integration in Europe
UNHCR, 1998
This is an action video pack examining the lives of seven refugees in Europe.

Books written for children

Ashley, B. 1999. *Little Soldier*. London: Orchard Books. This is a novel about a former child soldier who flees to the UK.

Filopivic, Z. 1994. *Zlata's Diary*. London: Methuen.

Hicyilmaz, G. 2000. *Girl in Red*. London: Orion Books. This is the novel about a Roma refugee's friendship with an English boy.

Laird, E. 1991. *Kiss the Dust*. London: Heinemann. This is a novel about a Kurdish refugee girl.

Naidoo, B. 2000. *The Other Side of Truth*. London: Penguin. This novel is the story of two Nigerian refugee children living in the UK.

Refugee Council. 1998. *Why Do They Have to Fight: Refugee Children's Stories from Bosnia, Somalia, Sri Lanka and Kurdistan*. London: Refugee Council. The book is based on the testimonies of refugee children.

Serraillier, I. 1956. *The Silver Sword*. London: Puffin. This novel is the story of refugee children's journey across Europe after the Second World War.

Taylor, M. 1999. *Faraway Home*. Dublin: O'Brien Press. This novel is the fictionalised account of children who arrived on the Kindertransporte.

Wilkes, S. 1994. *One Day We Had To Run*. London: Evans Brothers.
The book contains paintings and testimonies of refugee children from Somalia, Ethiopia, Eritrea and the Sudan.

Useful websites

The Internal Displacement Project
www.idpproject.org - Information about internal displacement across the world.

The Refugee Council
www.refugeecouncil.org.uk - General information about asylum issues in the UK.

UNHCR
www.unhcr.ch - The United Nations High Commissioner for Refugees. The website has downloadable teaching resources.

The US Committee for Refugees
www.refugees.org - US specific and global information about refugees.

Organisations

The Refugee Council
3 Bondway
London SW8 1SJ
020 7820 3000
www.refugeecouncil.org.uk
The Refugee Council is the largest charity working with refugees in the UK. It gives practical help to asylum seekers and refugees, and promotes their rights in the UK and abroad. There are offices in London, Leeds, Birmingham and Ipswich. The Refugee Council's work to support young refugees includes

- helping local authorities and schools develop services to support refugee children including those who are unaccompanied;
- providing in-service training about refugees and educational provision for refugee children;
- publishing a wide range of leaflets and books, including advice leaflets for refugees, as well as educational information for teachers, bilingual teaching material for newly-arrived refugees and development education material about refugees;
- answering individual inquiries requesting information and advice
- putting people in contact with refugee community organisations and other refugee agencies in their locality;
- visiting schools and youth groups to speak to young people;
- coordinating teachers' networks on refugee education;
- coordinating the Panel of Advisers for Unaccompanied Refugee Children.

Aegis Trust

PO Box 2002

Newark

Nottinghamshire NG22 0PA

01623 836978

www.aegistrust.org

The Aegis Trust works to prevent genocide. Its Refugee Project has produced teaching material about refugees and conducts workshops.

Amnesty International (UK)

99-119 Rosebery Avenue

London EC1R 4RE

020 7814 6200

www.amnesty.org

Amnesty International is a worldwide human rights organisation. In the UK, Amnesty presents information about the risks that individual refugees may face in their countries of origin, and may provide statements of support for asylum applicants. It also produces a wide range of published material and is engaged in human rights education.

British Red Cross Society

9 Grosvenor Crescent

London SW1X 7EJ

020 7235 5454

www.redcross.org.uk

The British Red Cross operates a tracing and family message service to enable people separated by conflict or disaster to make contact with other members of their family. It also has an education and youth section.

Commission for Racial Equality

St Dunstan's House

200-211 Borough High Street

London SE1 1GZ

www.cre.gov.uk

Development Education Association

33 Corsham Street

London N1 6DR

020 7490 8108

www.dea.org.uk

The DEA has a list of local development education centres.

Greenwich and Lewisham Young People's Theatre

Burrage Road

London SE18 7JZ

020 8854 1316

www.gypt.co.uk

This theatre in education has accumulated much expertise in work examining the settlement of refugees in the UK.

Irish Refugee Council

88 Capel Street

Dublin 1

00 353 8730042

www.irishrefugeecouncil.ie

Jewish Council for Racial Equality

33 Seymour Place

London W1N 5AU

020 8455 0896

www.jcore.org.uk

JCORE produces educational resources on race equality for schools.

INK - Exiled Writers

31 Hallswelle Road

London NW11 0DH

www.exiledwriters.co.uk

This is a group of refugee writers, some of whom do workshops in schools

Minority Rights Group

54 Commercial Street

London E1 6LT

020 7978 9498

www.minorityrights.org

Oxfam

274 Banbury Road

Oxford OX2 7DZ

01865 311311

www.oxfam.org.uk

Refugee Action

3rd Floor
Old Fire Station
150 Waterloo Road
London SE1 8SB
020 7654 7700
www.refugee-action.org.uk
Refugee Action provides advice and support for asylum-seekers and refugees. It has offices in Bristol, Exeter, Derby, Leicester, Liverpool, Manchester, Nottingham, Oxford and Southampton.

Refugee Studies Centre

Queen Elizabeth House
St Giles
Oxford OX1 3LA
01865 270722
The Refugee Studies Centre is an academic research institute. It hosts digitalised library of material about refugee issues available at: www.forcedmigration.org

Refugee Week

c/o Refugee Council
3 Bondway
London SW8 1SJ
020 7820 3055
www.refugeeweek.org.uk

Save the Children

17 Grove Lane
London SE5
020 7703 5400
www.scfuk.org.uk

Scottish Refugee Council

5 Cadogan Square
Glasgow G2 7PH
0141 248 9799
www.scottishrefugeecouncil.org.uk
There are also offices in Edinburgh and advice surgeries in different parts of Glasgow.

STAR - Student Action for Refugees

3 Bondway
London SW8 1SJ
Tel: 020 7820 3006
www.star-network.org.uk

Trentham Books

734 London Road
Stoke on Trent ST4 5NP
01782 745567
www.trentham-books.co.uk
The leading publisher on issues about race equality in education.

Office of the United Nations High

Commissioner for Refugees
Millbank Tower
Millbank
London SW1P 4QP
020 7828 9191
www.unhcr.org.uk
Free resources for schools.

Welsh Refugee Council

Unit 8
Williams Court
Trade Street
Cardiff CF10 5DQ
02920 666250

Index

- Further resources -